# THE BLUE EAGLE FROM EGG TO EARTH

# THE
# BLUE EAGLE
## FROM
# EGG TO EARTH

### By
### HUGH S. JOHNSON

"So the Struck Eagle, stretched upon the plain,
No more through rolling clouds to soar again,
Viewed his own feather on the fatal dart,
And wing'd the fatal shaft that quivered in his heart."

BYRON—*English Bards aad Scotch Reviewers.*

GREENWOOD PRESS, PUBLISHERS
NEW YORK                    1968

Reprinted with the permission of

DOUBLEDAY & COMPANY, INC.

First Greenwood reprinting, 1968

LIBRARY OF CONGRESS catalogue card number: 68-23302

MANUFACTURED IN THE UNITED STATES OF AMERICA

With Love
To Mom

"Everybody in the world's a Rink-Stink
but Hughie Johnson and he's all right."

—THE AUTHOR (1886).

# PREFACE

In any public account of a man's stewardship of so revolutionary an attempt as NRA, readers are entitled to know that man's background and his training for his task. I think mine were singularly appropriate. For this reason, the first fifteen chapters are sketchily autobiographical.

NRA was the greatest social and economic experiment of our age. It was necessarily a process of trial, error, and correction. Mistakes were made. The experiment would be without value if those mistakes were not stated and discussed. This book endeavors to do that. It is a constructive criticism with suggestion for improvement. This effort requires frank and forthright discussion not only of NRA but, in every case where NRA affected, or was affected by, other Departments or Administrations, then of those other government bodies. I wish it were possible to keep out of this book any personalities. I have tried to do it and could not. My final conclusion was that NRA transcends any personal welfare and certainly my own. NRA is a public and not a private matter. I think certain aspects of it are threatened and that it was stopped in its progress by the contrivance of persons—perhaps with the best intent in the world —but, in my opinion, with detriment to the public interest.

If I do not know more about NRA than any person living, I have been remiss. There is a vast public uncertainty and inquiry about NRA. I am writing a book purporting to tell about it. If I know anything which I think the public should have for fair appraisal and protection of NRA and omit it from this book, I shall be guilty of public misrepresentation on a vital matter of national concern. There is an overwhelming reason why I cannot leave undone this thing which I ought to do.

Whatever may properly be criticized about NRA, it created 2,785,000 jobs at a desperate time and added about $3,000,000,-000 to the annual purchasing power of working people. *It did more to create employment than all other emergency agencies put together*, and it did so by creating normal jobs everywhere and without drafts on the Federal Treasury. All other agencies had billions to loan or give away. NRA *gave* nothing. It *took*. It imposed sacrifices. Everybody likes Santa Claus. Nobody favors Simon Legree. Consequently NRA made powerful enemies.

NRA did much more than this. It abolished child labor. It ran out the sweatshops. It established the principle of regulated hours, wages, and working conditions. It went far toward removing wages from the area of predatory competition. It added to the rights and the freedom of human labor.

Now it is simple to say "created nearly 3,000,000 jobs"—"ran out the sweatshops"—"abolished child labor"—et cet., but it is *not* easy to measure, it is impossible to exaggerate, the human value of these things—to temper despair, to restore hope, to awaken the conscience of a country, to help give back to twelve million people the pride and decency of independent living—words cannot define nor even thought appraise the meaning of these benefits. It is for this reason that I regard NRA as a holy thing. Perhaps I am a zealot or even fanatic on this subject, but I feel it so intensely that I will fight for it. I have sacrificed, and will sacrifice, for it and no personal interest, neither my own nor another's, can stand in the way of anything which I think will help it.

For reasons which I shall state in this book, I think that NRA has been put to sleep—that the Codes are being allowed to languish—that the Blue Eagle, without which it cannot live, is dying—that the principles on which the whole plan proceeded are being ignored—and worst of all, that control of its policies is being passed to people who opposed it in the beginning and have fought it through its life.

Now, believing all this earnestly and sincerely, I cannot suffer it in silence if speaking will help. I know that speaking can do much. NRA came into being through an appeal to the public by the President in which he truly said that conscience and opinion were its only supports. Our people rose almost as one man and made *its principal tenets effective in every cranny of this country in four months' time.*

Public conscience and opinion are still all there is to support NRA—but I think they are enough.

I shall make only one complaint in this book and that is that the issues upon which NRA lapsed into its present desuetude were never made with me during my incumbency. I was executing NRA under specific written orders contained in the Appendix. Nobody ever contested those orders. Nobody ever came nobly to the grapple on any cleavage of policy or opinion. On the contrary, although I frequently asked whether my course was wrong, my action too headlong, my voice too vehement, I was never checked nor advised to slow, stop, or divert.

Furthermore, I want to make it very clear that, although I criticize only two persons in this book, I do not impugn their motives. They must have thought they were right. But I do seriously arraign their methods in this—that these issues deserved to be raised, to be debated, to be resolved in plain view and beyond question.

For too little acumen, for too great complacency in not making issues and taking them to the White House, I blame myself —bitterly.

Nowhere in this book will the most diligent reader find any criticism of the President, either expressed or intended to be implied. It will not be found because it is not there, either in this book or tucked away in some obscure corner of my heart or mind. It is necessary for me to say this because I know that there will be attempts to impute it from some of the circumstances related.

I am in such deadly earnest about NRA that if I had such a criticism I would either make it or else not write this book— probably the latter—because NRA is only one part of the greatest social advance of modern times for which the world has the President to thank.

I have no such criticism for it is only plain justice to say of Franklin Roosevelt that I never stood at any crossing of the ways. I never took a firm position, I never raised a major issue, I never even made a mistake or committed one of my many blunders, I never in an emergency took summary action not previously authorized—*that he did not back me to the limit*.

I do not mean that I agreed with all his policies. As shall here be made clear I didn't. I do not even mean that I agreed with all that was done in respect of NRA. It is in just this respect that I must take the greatest blame. *I did not make issues at several critical points where I should have made them*.

For all the harm that flowed from that omission—and sometimes it was great—the fault was mine alone. No principal executive can be expected to *divine* issues that are not presented. Clairvoyance is no proper attribute of a leader.

Some of the things for which I should have fought and did not seemed at the time not worth a quarrel. Others were and I knew they were. I shall call attention to each such incident in this narrative.

On five several occasions I felt that I should resign from NRA and on four I tried to do so. Toward the end my personal affairs were in such state that I had to do so. All this resides in black and white on the face of the record so that my *leaving or not leaving NRA* is no part of this argument. I had to leave.

Nor is the outward *form* of reorganization any part of the argument because that form is almost exactly as I had planned it.

The whole difference of opinion is that I believed that what NRA required was adherence to its principles and reorganization only for the purpose of passing from the phase of Code making to the phase of Code administration and I did want to stay long enough to see that change complete. The idea that prevailed was *not* a change from phase to phase but a paralysis of NRA with an apparent attempt to make a new one.

On this I had no chance to make an issue as shall be related in Chapter XXIX.

I did not realize all this when I laid down my charge. I thought the reorganization was to proceed on developed principles. I was even a little enthusiastic about it. It has only recently become clear that such is not the case. It is for this reason the latter part of this book had to be recast in fighting chapters instead of just remaining a narrative philosophy.

# CONTENTS

# CONTENTS

# THE BLUE EAGLE FROM EGG TO EARTH

# Chapter I

# FAMILY STUFF

"A man's a man for a' that."
*—Robert Burns.*

THE first part of this book is somewhat biographical. I am separated from all records. The family references are largely such memories of fireside narratives as all families treasure. They do not pretend to be accurate and in some cases are no doubt apocryphal.

Some time around 1812, Johnstons and MacAloneys appeared in Astoria, N. Y. (via Halifax), from Aghadowie in Derry, North Ireland. The MacAloneys were rich for those days and started a carpet factory. I never heard of a rich Johnston. Samuel Johnston, who was a building contractor, married Matilda MacAloney and, later, when he was father to eight children—four boys and four girls—he was mustered in as Captain in a New York Irish Infantry Regiment and marched off to the Civil War, leaving his wife and family in the care of the MacAloneys. He was grievously wounded, and, in family mythology, performed such incredible feats of derring-do as capturing a Confederate warship with *a company of infantry.* My boy, Lieut. Pat Johnston, has his great-grandfather's sword, epaulettes and sash, his grandfather's belt and sword, and his father's saber.

Sam Johnston came back from the war in broken health, removed his family to Chillicothe, Illinois, and shortly died. His old house still stands, owned by my aunt. It was one of the first houses built there—about 1830—is entirely of black walnut, and was originally a tavern—removed from the Illinois river bottoms and remodelled by my grandfather.

All those four boys amounted to more or less. Alexander, the eldest, the historian, died, well-loved, as Professor of Political Economy at Princeton—predecessor of Woodrow Wilson. Gilmor was a lawyer and founder of some fraternal society—at one time prominent in Democratic National Politics and temporary Chairman of the Democratic National Committee. Ben was a newspaper man and died as City Editor (or something like that) of the old Chicago *Inter-Ocean*. Sam, my father—a congenital pioneer—was, in my opinion, the greatest man I ever knew.

It was pretty thin picking for that family without a father, but Uncle John MacAloney served them well. He educated Alexander at Rutgers and abroad and kept an eye on the rest. He lived to such a ripe old age that at West Point in 1900 I knew him as an immaculate, delicate, peppery old gentleman who sometimes came up to West Point from New York to see me on Saturdays and wrote me letters full of admonitions backed by Old Testament texts of the harsher kind. He had a house on 84th Street and one at Saratoga.

His family name had become (more euphoniously) MacAlan many years before, but I own my grandmother's prayerbook dated about 1820 and on the fly-leaf is inscribed in her characteristic hand "Matilda MacAloney, Pew 27."

Uncle John's pleasure in his visits to West Point was obscured by the annoyance of encountering a rather fine old soldier, a pre-war graduate of West Point and ex-confederate colonel, who lived near by. They had been David and Jonathan before the Civil War and had married Florida girls who were sisters or cousins. The old Colonel, a federal army officer—according to Uncle John—not only was persuaded by his wife into the Confederacy but, before disclosing this to the Federal Government, permitted himself to be detailed by it to a European mission, resigned abroad, and then participated in negotiations for the commerce raiders, the *Alabama* and the *Florida*, or some other Confederate mission. At least that was Uncle John's story. To him it was nefarious treason and his carefully scissored white beard used to quiver at so much as the mention of his old friend's name. Once they encountered on a West Point road and circled like two venerable game-cocks to keep the whole width of the highway between them—their trouble had happened forty years before!

Uncle John had no direct heirs and I think I might have been better off if I hadn't squandered my furlough money in New York and had to telegraph him at Saratoga—twice—for carfare to Oklahoma. There were no more texts from the major prophets, no more visits after Saturday inspections at West Point and the whole estate went to Uncle Ben's widow who wasn't even a Johnston—much less a MacAlan or a MacAloney.

About one hundred fifty years before the arrival at Astoria the Meads appeared from England at Litchfield, Connecticut. In successive surges they reached western New York and then Chillicothe, Ohio, and about 1835 a colony from the latter place founded Chillicothe, Illinois. They were a thrifty, prudent, God-fearing tribe. My great-grandmother's name was Sargent. She was a Quaker and tried to bring her son Hiram up in that faith but he ran away to New Mexico in the ante-bellum days, started a horse ranch there and experienced sundry adventures that used to thrill my very spinal column as a boy. Once Mexican bandits stampeded his herds across the border and he had to trek back to Illinois for new capital, but on the return trip he found that the Comanches had burned the whole of the Llano Estacado and he had to turn back when hardly half way to his destination. But his fringed buckskin shirt made shoestrings for his grandchildren for a good many years, and his old six-gun which "fanned" from the hammer made the *pièce de résistance* for many a boys' Wild West show. He used to tell me about a terrible drunken old fifer he used to know in Chillicothe, Ohio, who had fought through the Revolution. Grandfather wound up prosaically enough running a drug-store in Chillicothe, Illinois, where my father Samuel and my mother Elizabeth met as children, went through high school together, and never had any other sweethearts.

Matilda Johnston with her eight fatherless offspring was poor but proud, and Hiram Mead (whose children were early motherless) was thrifty, practical and highly skeptical of the ragamuffin urchins at the other end of town. Once a school teacher, under the Mead influence, staged at Commencement a pathetic Horatio Alger sort of dialogue between a poor ragged orphan boy and the banker's little crinolined daughter. She cast my father for the male lead and my mother for the heroine. She thought no props or costumes would be necessary for Sam. But when Matilda heard of these arrangements, she snorted, scraped the bottom of the cracked teapot, and on the climactic day little Samuel appeared, to the consternation of the management and the howling joy of the audience, with his brown locks curled and plastered, a ruffled shirt, new round-abouts, silk stockings *and patent leather shoes.*

That sort of small town social sniping seems to have persisted. But my mother, who at the age of fourteen was running a rather large motherless household, rebelled after about ten years of it, married Samuel who had been reading law and went away with him to Pontiac where, having passed the bar, he tried to practice.

Pontiac did not prove lucrative. It has genealogical importance only because it was here that my father used the double expedient of dropping the T out of his spelling of his surname and inserting a perfectly meaningless L between that and his Christian name to rid himself of the repeated annoyance of having his mail and practice confused with that of another barrister, *colored,* and rejoicing in exactly the same address— "Samuel Johnston, Esq., Attorney at Law, Pontiac, Illinois."

In view of the nature of that practice, I have always wondered what tenor of great affairs had been so sorely turned awry as to warrant this drastic and confusing change. I have a son, a brother, four cousins and two nephews, named Johnston and an equally imposing array of agnation named Johnson. Perhaps it is some humor of the blood and goes back to the MacAlan–MacAloney affair for precedent.

A practice of presumed value was said to be vacant in Fort Scott, Kansas, which in 1881 and for years thereafter was on the edge of one of the toughest areas in the country—the old Indian Territory. There my father took his young wife and there in the following year (1882) I was born.

Fort Scott, in spite of lawlessness across the border, didn't afford much practice either. But homesteads were opening up in Western Kansas and, with his savings so far gone that he had to *walk,* leading two horses, one bearing a pack and the other my mother holding me in her arms, my father trekked more than half-way across Kansas to "take up a claim" at Greenburg. He was a tall, powerful man "handy with his hands" though he wasn't by training a farmer. But everybody in those days knew how at least to live off the soil—where and how to dig wells, to plow, sow, and reap; to grow, slaughter, skin, and cure hogs, sheep, and cattle; to preserve meat and vegetables; to make all garments if not always to spin and

# PHOTOGRAPHS

GREAT-GRANDFATHER FOSDICK

GREAT-GRANDMOTHER FOSDICK

GREAT-GRANDFATHER MEAD

GREAT-GRANDMOTHER MEAD

GREAT-GRANDFATHER GILMOR

GREAT-GRANDMOTHER GILMOR

GRANDFATHER MEAD

GRANDMOTHER MEAD

GRANDFATHER JOHNSTON

GRANDMOTHER JOHNSTON

MOTHER AT FOUR

MOTHER AT FIFTY

FATHER

SELF—AT EIGHT

AT SEVENTEEN

AT THIRTY-FOUR

WIFE
HELEN KILBOURNE JOHNSON

SON "PAT"
KILBOURNE JOHNSTON

weave; to build houses out of sod or logs, and to make butter, soap, and candles. I have seen most of these things done by homesteaders myself.

The almost universal loss of these homely arts is a pity and the fact that they are gone forever from our popular equipment has necessitated and will continue to necessitate, in this country, economic and sociological changes of the most profound import.

We lived out on that howling prairie in a sod-house sixteen miles from a neighbor through a bitter winter, and, while it could well be imagination fed by family stories, I firmly believe that my first recollection is the howling of gray wolves in the wind around the outdoor "meat safe." There *was* a meat safe. There *were* wolves and they howled. But I was less than three years old.

Playing while my mother sewed, I fell and cut my upper lip clear through from nostril to mouth on a sharp table-edge. There was no doctor and it was twenty miles to a "horse doctor." My mother rode there carrying me screaming. When the fussy old vet asked his blowsy wife where his needles were and was told that he had left them in the shed after sewing up "that hawss yestiddy," my mother, over protests that it would "give him a hare-lip," indignantly rode twenty miles back and pulled and held the swollen edges together with "court plaster"—no hare-lip but a slightly twisted face—and a myth among admirers, that this is a saber-cut. It was only a sewing machine.

Farming at Greensburg was too slow. Even before the claim was "proved-up" my father had begun buying carloads of cattle or vegetables in places where they were and shipping them to where they weren't. He began to make a little money. He moved to Emporia and then to Greenwich—both in Kansas —and finally to Wichita where my clear recollections begin.

They had the Tulip Craze in Holland; the Mississippi Bubble in France; the South Sea Delusion in England—and, in America, we had booms. One was in gestation in Kansas and the whole Southwest in these days of the early 1880's. The railroads were building fast. A new inland empire was opening up. New England and New York mortgage money began to flow like water. My father had already seen the possibilities of the railroad junction at Wichita which had long been a principal stage station on the western route. When the agitation began he owned considerable farm property next to the village. Then the lightning struck. Values doubled and trebled over night. He cleaned up once. He built himself a real home on half a city acre, then plunged and cleaned up twice. He was going to be very rich. I remember these things clearly and my canny-minded mother telling him it was exactly time to stop. There was an old folk ballad about the "Ship That Never Returned" and he used to sing to her the Captain's wail:

> "*Just one more bag of the Golden Treasure*
> *It will last me all my days* . . ."

To which she invariably responded by calling his attention to the title and the wail in the closing verse of that interminable song:

> "*Oh she never returned—she never returned.* . . ."

No hope. He plunged to the eyebrows. He was a lover of Charles Lever, and this last venture was a monotonous row of little pine cubicles called "The Dempsy Addition" to Wichita —two or three close-packed blocks of homes all being built at once in strictly modern fashion—and all (including the new home) mortgaged to the hilt for the Grand Coup.

But the Grand Coup did not work that way. It worked like the guillotine. It came quicker than the collapse of the Florida Boom or the Stock Market smash of '29. It busted him. There is perhaps no word in the English language adequate to describe how completely and absolutely busted he was.

He tried to save his home, which, in his love of flowers and shrubbery, he had made into a garden. He carried mail as a postman to try to save it—and a dog bit his boot off. He took a job as a postal clerk. He disposed of all the farm property he had. He kept us living there for several years and during that time took a law degree from the boom-born, depression-killed Garfield University. It was a hopeless fight. Everything was simply swept clean, and in 1893—with a large and similarly busted part of the population of Southern Kansas, he took his family into the newly opened Cherokee Strip of Oklahoma Territory.

Those intervening years taught me something about booms, smashes, depressions, and the wreckage thereof. In the hey-day of the Wichita boom, hopes ran high. The walls of what seemed to me palaces and cathedrals and stately piles of masonry were begun in all directions. "Dempsy" was only one of many additions. Some of them were nearly finished—some never passed the first tier and some were just spacious foundations. The blight hit them like the spell over the palace of the Sleeping Beauty. They were as much abandoned as the ruins at Casas Grandes. They were more than abandoned. They were forgotten. Weeds and brambles grew over them.

It was pitiful for somebody but it was paradise for the play—and vandalism—of ragged urchins. We used them for fortresses and labyrinths and mountain climbing and duck-in-the-hat and run-sheep-run—but they were also a source of revenue for marbles and tops and circuses. We cut the lead and copper pipe out of them and broke the iron grilles of fences and doors and, together with the buffalo horns and bones which still bleached on the prairies, carted the miscellany to the junk-man where they were current at so many cents to the pound—and nobody had interest or care enough to stop us.

It was still a day of westward migration. Past the big house on Seneca Street, all day long, strings of prairie schooners—self-contained small economic units on wheels—trekked creaking into the new country. They were usually emblazoned "Colorado or Bust" or "Oklahoma or Bust." They contained families, bedding, chickens, and farm implements. Sometimes cows trailed behind and nearly always there was a yellow dog in the shadow under the running gear.

Also Indians—mostly Osages—were brought up from the Territory to District Court for their sins and streamed by in the opposite direction in gaudy costumes at term time. That road was a constant and colorful pageant of a changing age to a boy of any imagination—like the road that Sir Launcelot rode to Camelot or Chaucer's road to Canterbury.

It was a two or three year siege in Sam's big house on its spacious lot. We kept a horse, a surrey (left over from better days), and two cows. We raised chickens and pigs—slaughtering the latter at a glorious autumn season of cracknel and head cheese and pigs' bladders to make into balloons by distilling coal gas. You stuck the bowl of a clay pipe filled with coal dust and tamped with wet clay into hot coals. You tied the bladder to the stem. That filled the balloon.

Between the preservation of meat and ample fruit and vegetables, and the nuts that we took from the wooded flats of the

Arkansas, we were kept well fed, but there simply wasn't any money.

The cows went out on the river meadows with the Town Herd—gathered in the morning and brought back and distributed to every near-by home in the evening—and riding on that expedition every day in summer was real sport. Modified cowboys, we were, and if the "little dogies" were only waddling old milch cows, we roped them just the same and practiced bare-back Roman riding and swimming with the ponies in the flooded river. The thrifty Meads used to send from Chillicothe boxes of neatly worn clothes and with these—cut down considerably, mother kept me—and herself—decently clad.

There were good free grade schools and two good libraries and my mother had managed to acquire a wheezy old second-hand melodeon—quite aware of its terrible cacophony, but with her firm chin clamped on the idea that "You are going to read and know good music even if you never play it." At that horrible yellow keyboard I spent an agonized hour a day for five years and, as for performance, "ever more came out by the same door where in I went"—but I did learn to read and, at least a little, to know good music. With the library it was different. I had to be driven out of doors. Without understanding any of it, I had read all of Shakespeare at ten and most of such "classics" of that day as Scott and Dickens—not too glamorously—but I read Huckleberry Finn five times, consecutively, and without intermission. Just when I was beginning to get the feel of English prose some neighboring kid introduced me to Frank Merriwell, Nick Carter, the whole Beadle series, and I did not read another thing worthwhile for a decade except in school—but I'll bet I know my Burt L. Standish better than Gene Tunney does his Shakespeare.

At Greenwich when I was about four years old an incident occurred which both my mother and Bernie Baruch insist is characteristic if far from flattering.

She says she heard clods and bricks thumping against the front door. Opening it she found me backed up to it crying but yelling defiantly at a circle of angry and outraged small takers of vengeance:

"Everybody in the world is a rink-stink but Hughie Johnson and he's all right."

Perhaps NRA and this book had its antecedents.

Mrs. Johnson with Tootie and Toughy

At the Presidio

The Great Race

"Home—home on the plains—"

# Chapter II

## CHEROKEE STRIP

"Oh, Bill—here's your mule."
—*Shibboleth of the "Great Run."*

THIS whole chain of events came to an abrupt end with the Oklahoma Hegira. My father had been appointed Postmaster at the then non-existent, but expectant, town of Alva. He took my mother, my two baby brothers, the whole post-office paraphernalia, and some household goods ahead in a box car which, switched to a siding, was for a week one of not more than five human habitations in the place where that town was planned to be.

The Cherokee Outlet was an early Polish Corridor—a long strip of land 60 miles wide guaranteed to the Cherokees as a hunting path from their reservation to the western buffalo grounds. By 1893 all the buffalo were gone. The Cherokees ranged no more. The strip had been returned to the public domain, and now Grover Cleveland had decided to throw it open for settlement to relieve the terrible depression of 1892.

The whole Outlet had been cleared by troops of all its inhabitants. Only officials and employees of the Federal Government and of the railroads remained. Except for "sooners"— the early chiselers of that great adventure—hidden in cañons and coulees with their eyes on choice "claims" the strip was uninhabited, and troops ringed it with a cordon. Woods County alone was sixty by fifty miles square and Alva was its only townsite. On the north and south borders of the Strip were congregated the flotsam and jetsam of the great economic collapse of the early 90's. Refugees from Kansas, Missouri, Iowa, Colorado, Nebraska, Arkansas, and the South were packed in a solid rank around the whole Cherokee Outlet— waiting for the guns of September 16th, which would release the flood to race for homes and town lots. Every man was left

9

to his fancy as to the quickest and most convenient conveyance—thoroughbreds under jockey saddles, standard-breds hitched to sulkies, bronchos under stock-saddles, buckboards, buggies, and prairie schooners—one man had an ostrich.

No boy ever thrilled as did I over the lot assigned to me. I didn't go with the box car. My father intended to buy a "claim" and farm. He had bought a team of mules and a wagon and there was also the horse and surrey. Two rather elderly deacons of his church wanted to seek their fortunes in this country new. One had a light "runabout" and a pony. The other offered to drive my father's wagon. The first was a carpenter, and if the other was not a walrus, he looked like one and, as it turned out, acted not dissimilarly. I was to drive the surrey under their protection and care.

Eight miles out of Wichita there is a little brook and a shady ford. Here—the carpenter-deacon being in the lead—the little caravan rested. The carpenter (who took pride in his craft) pulled from under his seat a neat little oak chest nine inches square and as long as your arm, carefully mortised and tenoned, the lid screwed down. With exquisite care he removed eight bright screws and then the lid and there, nested in oak sawdust, were four little brown crockery jugs in perfect alignment. With the same elegance of motion, he removed one, wiped it to scrupulous and shining cleanliness with a bandana, drew the cork, put his thumb through the handle, flipped it over his forearm and in the good old way in such matters, threw back his head and gurgled like a rill.

Without a word (but with great decorum) he passed it to the Walrus—and those two old coots never drew another sober breath while I was with them. We should have made twenty miles a day to reach the "Strip" in time for the Great Race—we made fifteen miles the first day, eight the next, four the next.

The stock was not fed unless I fed them. The harnesses were "thrown on with a fork" and never taken off unless I took them off—and the principal sport was baiting me. The Walrus invented the aphorism, "If I had two boys like you, I'd give the devil one to take the other," and the carpenter used to chase me clumsily around the wagon with his buggy whip.

On the afternoon of the 15th, while they were snoring, I sneaked the gray mare into the surrey, drove to the nearest town, left the "rig" at a livery stable and went and sat on the station platform waiting for a train without the least idea of when it would come, but knowing that it could go to only one place—Kiowa, Kansas, eighteen miles north of Alva on the Santa Fe—the edge of the "Strip" and the principal jumping-off place. The train came—crowded to the guards—and without a cent in my pocket I elbowed into a coach. I expected to be kicked off at the next station, but the conductor did not come for a long time. When he did, we were only a few miles out of Kiowa and I wheedled him into letting me stay.

I slept that night with other packed humanity on the station platform. As far as eye could see to east and west there were campfires—like a bivouac. The air was full of dust and particles of buffalo grass pawed up by thousands of horses, mules and—presumably—one ostrich. You could see the videttes of the cavalry along the border. People were yelling all kinds of nonsense and whoopee all through the night. There was one of those senseless yells that seem spontaneously and for no reason to take human fancy which somebody would let out every few minutes all along the South Kansas line—"Oh, Bill, here's your mule."

The morning came with the crystal clearness of that high dry plain. The air smelled good—of camp fires, of burning "buffalo" chips and cedar—of coffee and sizzling bacon, and pungently also of horse, mule, and stable generally. A man was cutting off slices of "boloney" and cheese and munching crackers on a bedding roll beside me. Suddenly he saw that I had neither bed nor breakfast. He asked me about myself, laughed, and fed me. I remember him for his tremendously large Adam's Apple—which traveled further and more emphatically up and down than any I have ever seen—and for his kindness. I never saw him again.

Within an hour that crowd was stirring like a circus entrainment—packing-up, greasing axles, striking tents, rubbing down horses and finally harnessing, hitching up, and saddling. I had intended to hop a ride, but learned that the railroad was to run trains of flat-cars at sixteen miles per hour—a little faster than a gallop or exactly what is called in the cavalry "extended gallop" and that anybody could ride free.

From one of those "flats" I saw the great race into the Cherokee Strip.

High noon. Guns boomed. Cavalry pistols cracked. They

were off to the greatest race in history. Some people ran a mile; "stuck their stake" and then raced to the Land Office at Alva to file. Others "staked" fifteen miles in and raced three to file. There was no way to know exactly what quarter section you claimed or how many others had staked the same claim. It was a disorganized method and, of course, a day of deadly six-shooter argument. In a few minutes you could see people—or rather dust spurts—strung out to the horizon in all directions like clouds in a mackerel sky.

When the train came down the bluff and across the bridge to Alva already hundreds of horsemen had beaten it. Men began to detrain and run on foot long before the train stopped. It was like a mob breaking up and fleeing fearfully before machine-gun fire.

I ran with the rest to the public square where my father had opened his shack of one-by-twelve boards and was ready for business with his Post Office. But my mother and her two babies were still in the box car at the siding in the cool drip of the railroad water tank. I rushed back there and was tearfully welcomed, then back again toward town, found an over-turned wagon which some thrifty Kansas farmer had filled with watermelons (many of them had broken), gorged myself and was very sick for days.

A tent village of 7,000 people rose like mushrooms over-night. It was a wide-open town, saloons in every block—the capital of a county as big as some small states—yesterday vacant, to-day with a family or person on every worthwhile one hundred sixty acres.

The water at Alva, flowing through a gypsum substratum, was a clear crystalline saturated solution of epsom salts. A well furiously sunk for forty feet by relays of volunteers provided it to long queues of parching tenters who came with buckets, but a wise and far-seeing entrepreneur, who had set up a tent-latrine and charged admission, reaped a real harvest before midnight.

There were fights—both fist and gun—over disputes and claims all that night. Men had staked lots near the Post Office and refused handsome offers for them only to find out, when surveyors appeared, that they were on the Public Square.

The population were ashes of a busted agricultural empire in the early autumn. The land could yield nothing until spring.

How these people survived that winter is a mystery. They burrowed into the ground and lived in dugouts. They trapped quail, poached on government timber reserves and traded fence posts for provisions in town. They collected government bounties on coyote, puma, and wolf scalps. Some became very adept at this. By judicious coloring, soaking, nicking, and stretching, old Dad Shirley could get twenty-four "scalps" from the pelt of one coyote. He and others also pieced out by digging up willow wands and selling them to amateur settlers for peach tree slips. There were millions of prairie dogs on those plains—vast villages of chirping rodents, living in holes burrowed sometimes 40 feet deep and (so many thought) accommodating as "boarders" rattlesnakes and prairie owls. In fact the latter denizens lived in *abandoned* holes. In the next legislature a man brought in a bill to change a name from Prairie Dog to Prairie Squirrel. He said he wanted to save his self-respect on that winter's diet.

There were beautiful government timber reserves of cedar trees in the Southwest. The government had appointed a swarm of young Southrons as deputy marshals to guard them. But fence posts were a necessity and split cedar would pass for coin at stores and saloons. The settlers grew very bold. The young marshals were quick on the trigger. There were killings on both sides and consequently outlaws. That region became a rendezvous for outlaw bands and a sporadic warfare persisted there for months.

I saw some of that—a killing and several wounded men—grewsome for a kid but part of the color of a last oasis in an encroaching desert of civilization. I read a book by Marquis James the other day in which he told about Gus Hedwiger, a law officer, and Dick Yeager, a bandit. Gus still lives—a great guy. I knew them both. Marquis says that Dick was not a Big Shot Outlaw. He was. But then Marquis admits that he was only 4 years old at that time. I was all of eleven.

For some reason that I never understood spring brought a great immigration of quail and jack-rabbits. That helped, and the next summer there was produced a wheat crop and a good one, but it was two or three years before the people of that country literally had any money. They bartered at the stores—traded game, pelts, chickens, eggs, butter, cheese, turkeys, skins, pigs, calves, and steers for calico, overalls, saddles, plows, and tobacco. Wheat was the only cash crop, except for larger shipments of cattle and hogs, and these did not come for some time.

Yet that country built up quickly. In a few years it was moderately prosperous with the strength that lies in a self-sustaining, home-owning, land-tilling community. It was one way out of a depression—an economic miracle that could not happen today. If we could magic back into existence a virgin Cherokee Strip and people it on one September day with half-a-million of our unemployed and their dependents, they would be helpless before snowfall and dead before spring.

And yet there are, within a radius of fifty miles of New York City, abandoned farms, or farms to be had for a song, which offer as much relief as did that new country if only this generation had the same urge and capacity to subsist itself as did that elder one. These farms are actually slowly being peopled by immigrants who do have that urge and are making themselves comfortable. I doubt whether any sufferers from this depression are as much up against it as that wreckage of 1892. Perhaps we are doing too much for people.

But, generally speaking, the day of that most rugged of individualism is as dead as the dodo—extinguished by time and change. Industrial America is a great unitary machine in which the cogs and ratchets are human specialists. When the machine runs they move merrily; when it creaks, slows, and stops—they stop too, and there is nothing whatever for them to do. When parts of the machine fail they are likely to be scrap on the junk heap except where some of them can be salvaged or thrown back into the furnace to be melted up in another shape—and that is a painful and difficult process.

In this early Alva there was no school system. With three or four other fathers, mine hired a piano tuner to teach seven children. There were no pianos and, as a pedagogue, he was a fine piano tuner. All I took from this learning period was expertness in using a bicycle pump to squirt water through a knothole at teacher's prominent ears from the back of a rough pine shack.

Then more fathers and mothers hired a lawyer with some pugilistic attainments to teach more and better children in a pine and tar-paper wickiup called—euphemistically—the Union Church. He was a good teacher, but he had too many pupils of too great variety and his discipline was primitive. I was growing fast and—on one occasion—he sat upon my prone form and pummeled me with his fists. I probably deserved it and, in this and other ways, he worked a fair primary education into my head.

My father took the lead in having a regular school system installed and a good brick schoolhouse built which burned to the ground on the night of its opening and was promptly rebuilt. It provided a kind of High School of which one other—Ella Beagle—and I were the first graduates.

There was no church edifice except "The Union." So my father went up to a busted and almost deserted Kansas town and bought a big one—a relic of the boom—splendid and complete with belfry and baptismal tank and moved it bodily to Alva. It was the first decent building in the town. Not content with this he started a campaign for a State College, pushed the bill to a point where he felt sufficiently assured to engage a President and an architect. *He actually started those buildings while the bill authorizing them was still being debated.* That was a precedent for action in the two principal incidents to which this book is devoted—the Draft and NRA.

That President of the "Northwest Normal School" was a godsend to me. I was fourteen when he came and opened his college in the second-hand church, awaiting the new building on the hill. The haphazard and fragmentary education on which I have touched was wholly disorganized. He was a scientific educator and took a very special interest. He built where it was weak and guided where it was not so weak and enabled me to get through West Point four years later. His name is James E. Ament and he presides now at the National Park Seminary in Washington. I have never known a teacher to compare with him. I proudly hold the diploma of that little college although by an unorthodox route—2 years' credit for my 4 years at West Point. Later I got credit for three years at West Point to add to one on a B.A. degree at California—which made pretty good use of four years at the Military Academy.

The Cheyenne and Arapaho Indian reservation was not far away to the south. Among the Cheyennes were not a few old braves who had been at the Little Big Horn and even squaws who had participated in the celebration afterward and who remembered and would talk guardedly about the advance of the Seventh Cavalry toward their camp. Of course, a boy would cultivate these fascinating savages, and I had friends in both tribes. They came up to Alva every autumn for about two weeks' stay. The only one I recall by name was Red Cloud, but he was old and haughty and had no time for wide-eyed white boys.

My father ranged cattle out toward the White Horse Hills and during school vacations I had to work with these herds, with wheat and broomcorn harvesting and with fall plowing. Cleveland was out. McKinley was in. The post office job was gone and we lived in a very comfortable sod-house on the high prairie west of town.

Alva had a militia company—B of the 1st Oklahoma Infantry. I wasn't old enough, but enlistment regulations were not strict and the captain gave me some years that I had not yet lived so I drilled twice a week and had a hot blue uniform and an antediluvian Springfield rifle—with belt and triangular bayonet.

That captain was a newspaper editor and as good a drillmaster as I ever saw afterward in twenty years of regular military service. His only defect as a soldier was that he was yellow passing all understanding. When the *Maine* was sunk and Teddy Roosevelt recruited the Rough Riders, the territorial militias were given quotas and so was Alva. This drill-ground hero hid the notice in his desk and disappeared—never to be heard from again.

The squad in which I drilled found out about this by accident and kept it a secret, intending to present ourselves at Guthrie the next day as Alva's quota—avoiding selections and the insistence of older men. Some of them got away with it, but my father caught *me*. I raised so much disturbance at home that he promised to get me the West Point appointment for the next year. As it turned out, I was the first bona fide Oklahoman graduate from West Point, though several had gotten as far as "plebe January." The educational facilities in the early territory—as Mr. Coolidge said of business conditions in 1931— were "*not* good."

# Chapter III

## WEST POINT

Mother and lover of men. . . .

—*Swinburne.*

MY FATHER was Chairman of the Democratic State Central Committee but the Territorial Delegate to Congress—old Eat-a-Mule Callahan—was a Populist on a fusion ticket and insisted on a competitive examination. That method, as then used in rural districts, populated West Point with young school teachers. It was not (as now) the West Point entrance examination that was used. Generally—and certainly in this case—they gave a school-teachers' examination in the common branches. They were full of trick questions in parsing, obscure geography, and such mathematical profundities as "Multiply 16,768,543,-762 by 267,345,987.61." There were also spelling inquisitions based on orthography of which "phthisis" is a mild example. I didn't have a Chinaman's chance of first place.

To get to Guthrie from Alva, you had to go to Kansas. Coming back into Oklahoma from that state on my trip, I saw several obvious candidates with the old rural pedagogue aura and arms full of books. I got their names and Kansas addresses by talking to them. Some even boasted that they were putting something over on this Oklahoma "Pop" and one or two that they were over-age. Of these one did have a bona fide Oklahoma residence. He had just been visiting in Kansas.

He was a "slicker." He was dressed as he thought an Oklahoma Populist ought to look. He regaled and terrified me by boasting of his championships in Southwest spelling bees. He recited the names of all the towns in the state of Zacatecas. He parsed the longest sentences in the Bible in a kind of machine gun staccato so rapid that you couldn't follow him. He stated the famous ox problem, which lies in that dim field between algebra and arithmetic, and then solved it orally. He finally

ran through feats of mental arithmetic like "2-1/17 × 17 + 5 —
3 x 630—Answer that! Instantly?" and when nobody could he
would and then say, "Ask me one?"

It was just like a duellist giving his adversary a sample of
what may—and probably will—happen by shooting sparrows
out of a flying flock with a pistol. I have never seen his equal
in just that degraded form of mentality and he passed that six-
hour test with a mark of one hundred, which was twelve points
above his nearest competitor and thirty points above me. Two
or three were dropped physically. The Kansas brigade were
omitted upon my challenge—and I was appointed "alternate."
That meant that I might get in if the other fellow failed to pass
West Point—a pretty narrow chance against such a mental
acrobat—so narrow in fact and involving so much expense that
I could not afford to go to West Point in March, 1899, to take
the examination for entrance in June.

This time my father *did* successfully work whatever influence
his chairmanship gave him. He obtained permission for me to
appear in September if my principal failed to enter in June.
Then he went to work on vital statistics and obtained evidence
that the peerless pedagogue was—as I recall it (which may be
wrong)—about thirty years old. It was even said that he was
married and had a family of four children. I don't believe this.
All I know in fact is that he didn't appear in June and that I
went to Highland Falls in that month to prepare for the September examinations.

It was the first time I had ever been one hundred fifty miles
from my family. So innocent were we all of what had gone on
in the world outside that wilderness that when my father let
me order a new suit from a mail-order tailor, I selected a soft
blue cheviot with an invisible red check—*and had it cut as a
dinner jacket*—that was my traveling costume. I had to have
four hundred dollars for fare, tuition, and entrance deposit and
most of this I hid in the sole of my very yellow, very exaggerated, and very new "toothpick" shoes. In a little beehive trunk
I carried my militia uniform, *thinking I would need that at the
Academy!* Thus arrayed and thus equipped and accoutered, I
started east. It is a wonder I ever arrived.

Changing trains at Chicago, I encountered what I could now
tell at a block for an ex-convict and a yegg, who informed me
that he was a "litografur," and that if I took a later train, *we*

would stop at Buffalo, see Niagara Falls, and save one whole
Pullman fare by occupying the same berth. This seemed fascinating and we did it. To regale me in Buffalo he took me into
Canal Street, where we met two young ladies who seemed
gorgeous to me and whom he said (and they said) he had known
for years. This seemed all right and I had my first glass of beer
with reckless abandon, but an inward certainty that my soul
was being damned—but I never revealed what was in my
shoe.

It was very late. I do not know what might have happened.
What *did* happen was that a gruff, sour, dark looking man in
heavy soled shoes came up to our table and asked for a word
with me alone. He got it all out of me in about three or four
questions, scared me almost to death by telling me who—or
rather *what*—these convivials were. He went back for a word
with them. They went away from there quickly. He took me to
the station and saw that I—and nobody else—got on the sleeper
when the train came through an hour later.

All the big cramming schools at Highland Falls were closed—
none expecting thirty September entrants—usually there are
two or three. So an old and very able crammer named Denna
reaped a harvest. He was a magnificent old fellow with more
than a trace of Mohawk blood (of which he was very proud)
and a habit of showering one with a gentle spray as he leaned
close and enunciated such trick-spelling words as mattress thus:
"M-m-m at—tres -s-s—ah—um." Not much came out on the
"m-m-m"—but, with the sibilants, a *geyser*.

He had analyzed every entrance examination for thirty years.
If he would accept you at all he guaranteed to get you in—or
money back, and if he failed I never have heard of it.

At this time the old code duello—complete in all particulars
except fists (instead of pistols for two and coffee for four) was
and had been of obligation at West Point for a century. Of
course candidates thought they had to copy it and discover an
inherent chivalrous punctilio that had lain dormant for the
seventeen or twenty-two years of their previous life.

So just before the examination I had a fight with a friend—
very dramatically with cartel and seconds—in a little glade in
Pell's Wood among the goldenrod and poison ivy. He was considerably the better man. In addition to two black eyes and a
swollen lip, I rolled face-down in poison ivy. When I appeared

before the examining board, my face looked like a well softened abalone with two slits for eyes and a pulpous fold for a mouth. In addition to which I developed acute appendicitis and, refusing to risk entrance by an operation, lay for two days and nights with my abdomen packed in cracked ice. But I was up bright and early on examination day and somehow I got through. It was the most creditable examination I passed for a good many years—thanks to Mr. Denna and his salivary sprays.

I expected to have an easy time at West Point. The system marks every cadet in every subject every day and tells him his mark at the end of every week. At the end of the first six weeks the whole class is graded into about twelve sections from No. 1 man to the ultimate goat. Every preferment at West Point and throughout the Army depends on these marks and every cadet is avid to get them promptly on Saturday.

But I was so innocent, careless, and certain that I never even looked at mine during those six weeks. When the great gradation was read out, I collapsed. There were some hopeless souls who had done worse but not many—and it was almost inviolate tradition that the lowest forty on "General Transfer" were lopped off in plebe January and sent home on the theory that this six weeks' trial pretty much separated the sheep from the goats figuratively and (in West Point argot) literally.

I hadn't been studying but I studied then. Regardless of the Saturday afternoon and Sunday holiday I began right away. I had lost six valuable weeks of fundamental beginning.

By dint of very great effort, by January, I had climbed halfway up the class and except for Mathematics, English, History, and Law (in which I seemed to have some natural aptitude and climbed higher) that is pretty much where I stayed. Proficiency in anything except Mathematics was not at that time considered anything to boast about at West Point. History, the classics, etcetera, were called "spec" subjects which meant that you had to "fly-speck" or memorize your recitation. Mathematics was pure reasoning. The tendency was to make a man believe that what he could not prove was necessarily not true. I too imbibed the fallacy and never rid myself of it until I was well along in my later academic and legal course at California.

Perhaps I have now gone too far the other way. My experience of great mathematicians is that they are more like great chess players than great logicians. It is an adroitness in the permutation and combination of those essential axioms which cannot be proved at all—like 2 + 2 = 4.

I concede that it goes on to such sublimities as the mathematics of astronomy and wave motion but not by any freedom of intellect—only by astonishing dexterity. Is there a God? Has man a soul? If you cannot prove it mathematically it is not true. Tycho Brahe and La Place and Descartes were genii. Baruch Spinoza was a "speckoid." That was West Point opinion in my day. It made human turnips out of perfectly good young men. It is a little better now, thanks to Douglas MacArthur's tour as superintendent, but it was pretty bad while it lasted. I recall a brilliant "math fiend" who "got-by" on a recitation in history which I wrote on my cuff as I heard it. "Alexander was one of the greatest of Theban kings. He went from the Red Sea to the Suez Canal digging artesian wells and erecting mummies to his ancestors, many of which remain to the present day painted in beautiful colors." This boy was great on conic sections and hyperboloids of revolution but I never saw a sentence disclosing in so few words so much ignorance.

I was a very bad cadet. My room-mate graduated at the foot of his class. We had a little club of about ten other "indifferents" which we called the Salt Creek Club. The motto was "Never bone today what you can bugle tomorrow"—"bugle," being any device to keep from reciting. We assumed a superior sophistication toward such classmates as Douglas MacArthur and Ulysses Grant III, who were extending themselves to "come out one." We called them "nice boys" as distinguished from our group who were called (and like to be called) "tough." We studied as little as possible, smoked cigarettes surreptitiously in sinks and bathrooms, read and ponderously discussed "advanced" writers and the literature of revolt, strove assiduously to make life miserable for tactical and cadet officers, called ourselves "Tammany," played politics to keep nice boys out of elective class honors—and generally conducted ourselves in a manner which we thought was "breaking it off on the tacs" and "raising hell."

It was a sort of sophomoric bravado and resistance to constituted authority—an asinine uppityness which I have seen and pitied in many young soldiers since. I tried to warn my own boy about it when he entered twenty-one years after I graduated—but such a group is a tradition at West Point. There is one in every class and, although the three West Point men on his mother's side of the family were all model cadets, he used to sing, "*Voici le sabre de mon père*" when I or my classmate, the Commandant, lectured him—and delighted in doing over again almost exactly what I had so fatuously done twenty odd years before.

After all, it may be well. The nice boys were painting the thing as they saw it for the God of things as they are. We were working just as hard (and under much greater punishment) to play the part our tradition outlined. Nearly all of us got through, joined the Army, "got religion," and barring Douglas Mac-Arthur and one or two others, our military records—nice boys and toughs alike—all look about the same. But oh the heart-aches for proud parents—the blistering of feet on hot "area" punishment tours—the lost leaves and missed football games and gold chevrons never worn. It just wasn't either considerate or smart.

"September members" didn't have a very happy time for the first six months. They had missed the terrible gruelling of plebe summer camp and that rated them something lower than plebes —an almost incredible degree of degradation. Beyond coming close to being discharged for excessive demerits—so close indeed that I had to go two months with next to none or pass over the dead line—nothing distinguished my plebe year.

I was an indifferent if not a worthless yearling—my room-mate and myself both harboring an ideal of keeping heads above academic waters by the absolute minimum of study or even recourse to textbooks—notwithstanding I, at least relatively, excelled Thos. J. (Stonewall) Jackson, Philip Sheridan, Ulysses Grant or George Custer—at West Point.

At the end of the second year, a cadet gets a three months' furlough. I went to New York, spent all my money, but man-aged to get back to Alva to visit old friends and a boyhood sweetheart, who, in the meantime, had found another beau whom she later married. One of their sons came to Washington when I took over NRA and he got a job in five minutes.

My family no longer lived in Alva when I went home on furlough, because (as I verily believe) it had become too much civilized for my father. He was ranching and he said that the Alva country was too thickly settled and too thoroughly fenced. Whatever the reason, he had removed his family and herds to

Okmulgee in the heart of the old Indian territory—as tough a region as there was in the United States.

Okmulgee was the capital of the Creek Nation. When I first saw it, it consisted of the old stone Council House with chambers for both the House of Warriors and the House of Kings of the tribal government (modelled on our bicameral congress), and Parkinson's store and hotel, one or two other native stone store buildings—and almost nothing else except the cottages of the very few whites and jumbles and jumbles of negro shacks. When the Creeks lived in Alabama, Georgia, and Florida, negro slaves used to run away to the milder bondage of the Indians. Upon emancipation the Creeks had to make "freedmen" of their slaves. Intermarriage followed and the negro blood submerged the red in three or four generations. Later I saw exactly the same phenomenon among enlisted Seminole Negro-Indian scouts attached to Fort Clark, Texas.

A great, barefooted black buck came into Parkinson's store while I was there. The floor was littered with broken packing cases. He was offered the job of clearing it away for a quarter, but he drew himself up in majesterial dignity: "Don't you know dat I'se one of dese here kings?" That was in 1901.

In that year my father came home with two pop bottles filled with something he had skimmed from the surface of a creek near Bartlesville and it was palpably petroleum. Then Sapulpa was just a box car at a railroad junction.

At the end of furlough I went back to the Military Academy a trifle more sophisticated and with a little better conception of the responsibilities of a cadet.

Mine had been the last class that was really hazed under the old system. There was little levity about that. It was an institution of a hundred years' standing. The idea was to make a plebe's life so tough that it would shell out the weaklings. It was carried out with great dignity and punctilio. For so much as raising eyes to an upper classman or from the table in the mess hall the punishment was usually some form of physical exercise persisted in to exhaustion and for any serious recalcitrance—a fight. These conflicts were conducted under a code. The upper classman was selected with careful attention to equality of weight and size, but he was an athlete in training and the plebe almost never won. Every fight was with bare fists to a knockout. If a man failed through cowardice it was he end of his cadetship. He went to Coventry. Being immured in those gray walls with no other contacts than cadets, he was suddenly thrust out of their ken and none spoke to him or acknowledged his existence except on duty. Nobody, so far as I know, ever stuck it out.

Latterly—and largely due to a few brutally cruel men—the system had lost some of its dignity. Abuses crept in. Douglas MacArthur was "eagled" over crushed glass till he fainted. The deaths of two men who had been discharged were publicly laid to these thugs and a new administration determined to stamp out the century-old system.

It did not come easily. In my "yearling camp" (sophomore summer encampment) more or less mutinous occurrences were frequent. One evening at the mess hall when the Army officer in charge came in to inspect supper, he was greeted with a "silence." The roar in the cadet mess hall is deafening. The instant this man came in it ceased as abruptly as gunfire on Armistice Day and you could have heard a pin drop. He went into the kitchen and it burst into full volume. He came back and it died again.

He marched us out to stand at attention for an hour and then began a star chamber process such as West Point had never seen and the worst punishment ever assessed there—of which I got my share.

When the class of 1902 came back from furlough that year they were in a sullen and rebellious frame of mind. One night and quite spontaneously, having received what they thought was an affront in orders at dress parade, they and members of the other classes rushed to the parade ground, built a great fire, loaded the reveille gun with stones, dragged it across the parade, trained it on the Superintendent's door and dared him to come out. That was too much for me. I knew that I would be among the first suspected, so I went to my room and took a witness. That was one scrape I evaded.

This mutinous uprising shook West Point to its foundations. As I recall, eleven men were either dismissed or turned back to the next class. Dozens of men were transferred to a status but little better than that of prisoners for the remainder of their cadetships. It did the trick. It wiped out the old plebe system. It outlawed the modified code duello as the basis of plebe discipline and generally marked a new era at West Point.

Second Class (or Junior) year was then the easiest and most pleasant at the Academy. It passed almost without incident for me except for a narrow squeak from being "found" in Chemistry. There was a rule that anybody who made in daily recitations an average of 2.5 out of 3 would not have to take the final examinations. I was so far above this when General Review began that I simply stopped studying chemistry, having made an arithmetical calculation that there was no fear of an examination even if I made nothing on further recitations. That reckoned without the Professor—old Sammy Tillman—who changed the rule in respect to me and one other, and gave the stiffest written examination recorded in the Department. I at least did better than Whistler who said that NaCl was a gas and got fired for it, or the other unnamed cadet on the football squad who was permitted to continue playing if he could make fifty per cent on a special Chem. test. The instructor being called to account—he was a football enthusiast—explained the passing grade in this way:

"I asked him what TNT is and he said Tatanium—and that was wrong. Then 'What is the chemical symbol for table salt?' and he said he did not know—and that was *right*—score fifty per cent."

I suppose every member of a class feels the same way, but if there was any better class at West Point among the seven I saw I did not so rate it. At the head of it was Douglas MacArthur, the handsomest young man I have ever seen. He isn't exactly a gargoyle now, 35 years later. As a boy he was brilliant, absolutely fearless, and a top-hole baseball player. In the Funston Expedition, he repeated Robert E. Lee's daring scout of the Mexican positions back of Vera Cruz, risking life and probably torture on a very thin thread. He acted as special assistant to Secretary Baker and was Chief of Staff of the Rainbow Division, later commanding one of its brigades and finally the Division. Here he scintillated. His command post was usually in the front line and over the top with the advance waves. Even on an early visit to France before our troops came he went out with a trench raiding party and captured a German Colonel. His citation for the D.S.C. read something like this—"On a field where gallantry was the rule, his gallantry was conspicuous." By incredible marching he almost beat the French to the capture of Sedan. He came home to be Superintendent at West Point,

Commanding General of the Philippines and Head of the Army (Chief of Staff). I would like to see somebody tie that record. The only handicap Doug. has had was that there were not enough years between 1899 and 1934 in which to do more things excellently well.

Ulysses Grant III graduated near the top of that class and has had a distinguished record on his own merits ever since. There were plenty of others who reached national distinction like Campbell Hodges, Pat Lynch (Administrative Officer, NRA, C.O. Troops in China and high in the councils of the Infantry) —but I like to remember men distinguished only as soldiers and so left unknown and unsung in that anonymous war.

Jim Shannon, as a cadet, was a deeply religious man and the best two-fisted fighter in the Corps. When he was selected and sent out to a bare-fisted plebe fight *à l'outrance*, his only preparation was to go to his room and pray for divine guidance— presumably as to how best to get the plebe groggy in the first round and treat him as a cooper does a barrel for 8 or 10 rounds. He was always in training and he regarded the plebe system at West Point as a sacred thing.

The first time I saw him after graduation was at Raspadura Cañon deep in Mexico, where I stayed with him for a few days. He had gone in in command of about twenty old-time Apache trailers, who had been on the government payrolls as enlisted scouts since the days of Geronimo. There are no such trailers among the younger Indians. Jim asked me how old I thought his orderly—a glum-faced sinewy old bronze barbarian —and I said "thirty." He was sixty-three and his name was Chicken. We had to censor letters and Jim showed me what this old buck had asked Jim to write to his squaw:

I hear you cry all the time. You quit that crying. I hear you lend my buggy to Cochise. You don't lend nothing. Chicken.

When Jim crossed the border with his braves they struck a trail on a rocky plateau where Jim could not see a scratch. They followed it without even dismounting and, at a little hill-crest, dropped to the ground and pointed out to him a Mexican encampment. Jim saw that it was only a few harmless, straggling wood-cutters and signalled to take up the march—but he wasn't experienced with Apaches of the elder tradition. He didn't realize what he was up against till he looked closely at one of them. The man was breathing almost stertorously. His eyes were beady—like a snake's. Water was running out of the corners of his mouth.

The whole band was defying Jim. The "war-path" meant just one thing to them. They only knew they were in enemy country—they didn't understand the respect due to shoulder straps.

"You stay here," his interpreter threatened, "we killum all." And that is exactly what they were proceeding to do. Jim had to resort to the threat of his automatic and that night, in camp, two of them, stripped and (probably crazed by marajuana) began doing a knife dance in front of his tent while the rest stood around glowering. It was a pretty close thing for Jim Shannon, but what they did *not* understand was the efficacy of an almost professional "shock-punch to the button," which Shannon could deliver with either hand and with perhaps a little prayer to his particular Saint of Personal Encounter. Jim quickly stretched both of them on the ground and after that had no more trouble.

Nobody in the Punitive Expedition had a better mess than Jim's. Those Apaches kept him supplied with game, wild honey, and delicious dishes of strange fresh herbs. They were used to guard the thin signal corps telegraph wire which lay along the ground—the only dependable communication for some hundreds of miles back to the States, and what they did was magic. The wire was constantly being cut—in the beginning.

The first time they went out to locate an interruption they found that fifty feet had been removed on a flinty hill with no visible trace of foot or hoof prints. Jim said the trailers never hesitated but took him on a twelve mile chase leading to a little adobe *jacal* with a pile of grain in a corner. Against the protest of a very much frightened peon, they kicked the *maíz* aside revealing fifty feet of wire, a pair of pliers, three rifles and about 200 rounds of ammunition. Then they went outside and scattered before Jim could call them back. He rode after one party and nothing happened. His whole command dribbled back into camp during the night. About a week afterward, the Mexican government lodged a protest that *American troops*—these savages wore uniforms—were straggling outside the lines—and *scalping Carranza soldiers*. Jim kept them pretty well in hand after that, but there was very little wire-cutting from then on. Jim was a second lieutenant then.

One of the most promising young field officers of the A.E.F., Colonel James F. Shannon, was killed in action in France three years later.

In that class also was Tom Selfridge, the first man killed in an airplane. He had been working with Alexander Graham Bell on tetrahedral kites for aërial photography and was early detailed to work with the Wright Brothers. He was killed in the first airplane crash in history in a demonstration flight at Washington.

Football fans will not forget the record of that All-America Blond Berserk, Bunker, who once tackled a hurdler by grabbing him in mid-air by the ankles and swinging him for a full length loss with the motion used by a shot-putter, or that old-time center Boyers, who I veritably believe came to West Point in a silk hat and with a full grown beard from some place in Ohio at the age of about thirty.

In those days the Navy, who are now so much concerned about Army eligibility rules, used to play their stars for six years on the ground that "past midshipmen" (graduated and gone from Annapolis to their posts of duty and assimilated to the rank of second lieutenant in the Army) were still officially "midshipmen" and so eligible. In the first Army-Navy game of the second series (1899) they brought one of these—who had proved a gridiron sensation for several years—back from the China station (or so we believed) to make a monkey out of Boyers—playing in his first year of varsity football. The score was 17 to 5—Army—although we had not won a single game that season. Boyers figuratively wheeled that big commissioned gob around that field in a perambulator although Boyers was about half his size. It is a sister service, but I think the Navy——

This fond garrulity must cease.

# Chapter IV

## TEXAS AND THE FRISCO FIRE

---

"But I remember comrades—old playmates on new seas—
Whenas we traded orpiment among the savages—

. . . . . . . . . . . . . . . . .

Where lay our loosened harness?   Where turned our naked feet?
Whose tavern 'mid the palm trees?   What quenchings of what heat?
Oh fountain in the desert! Oh cistern in the waste!
Oh bread we ate in secret! Oh cup we spilt in haste!
                              —*Song of Diego Valdez—Kipling.*

---

UPON graduation I went first to New York to spend two weeks
and all my equipment money—about $800 saved through four
years as a cadet. My old roommate lived in New York and I had
become engaged to his sister. We had some real fun with that
money while it lasted—about 3 weeks—but it required two years
of the most stringent skimping and miraculous management on
her part after we were married to pay off the debt I had to incur
to replace it.

I had to buy nearly $1,000 worth of uniforms on credit. I
earned $108.00 a month. We lived on about $40 until that debt
was completely wiped out. It seems incredible, but the record
is all there in a little red morocco book, which she regularly kept
and where one may read how a small roast lasted a week, and
how to feed a fairly husky cavalryman on not more than ten
cents for breakfast.

There were two terrible setbacks. Once the Commanding
General came to the post and everybody was ordered to call on
him in full dress uniform—gold lace, gold belts and all. Among
thirty officers there were just two full dress uniforms. We could
go only two at a time, and then dodge rapidly around to the rear
and change with the next relay. I wore a major's uniform and
carried my hands behind me to hide the trefoil insignia of rank
on my sleeves. That night we got orders to buy full dress *at once.*
With all trimmings that set the Little Red Book back *five months.*

29

The next similar tragedy had to do with an order requiring every mounted officer to purchase a horse of certain specifications. That also came just about the time the book was in balance. From the moment of that blessed event to the present day, I have not been in debt—that long lesson was enough.

After the glorious three weeks of theaters, cabs, and orchids that caused all this, and being fully busted, I went back home to Okmulgee. The whole countryside had changed. My father was in the oil business and so was every one else. He knew so little about it that he drilled five wells on a town lot and pumped himself dry in a few months, but he was making real money again. The whole area was humming and the town was rapidly changing from the huddle of huts it had been two years before to a typical mid-continent oil-town with its full complement of mushroom millionaires. I stayed there two months and then, full of anticipation, went to join my regiment at Fort Clark, Texas—twelve miles from the railroad and twenty-five miles north of Del Rio on the Rio Grande. It was an ante-bellum post, put there to guard the marches from the Comanches. I lived in one of the oldest adobe houses—built eighty years ago. Indeed there were only a few modern quarters there—no conveniences—the slenderest communication with the outside world. But as I look back. it was a young man's paradise and I had more fun in the years i was stationed there and at San Antonio than in any of my life. Built on a slight rise from a mesquite-covered limestone plain of illimitable extent, it guarded one of the finest and largest never-failing well-springs in the country—Las Moras River flowing through some underground limestone channel into the open.

The mesquite was full of quail. The Pinto was full of fish. Ducks came in season to near-by lakes. You didn't have to go far for bear, deer, or javeline. There was no prohibition and the First Cavalry Mess and Club was one of the best-provided in the Army. You could buy a polo pony for five dollars and among all the fifteen regiments of cavalry, there was none like the First.

In those days there were plenty of old Indian fighters among officers, enlisted men, and pack trains and the regiment had not served east of the Mississippi since the Civil War. There were old men in the pack train who had served as models for Remington and they had lost none of their saddle-cultiv. ted gauntness and nothing whatever of their salt.

In the early days of Indian fighting, when winter came, a regiment just "holed-in" and hibernated. There was no communication with the outside world for three or four months. That did not mean that there were no bitter winter scoutings or even winter campaigns—there were—but, at many stations, no supply trains could get through. When spring came and the wagons arrived—especially those of the Post Trader—there was usually a celebration of sorts and there is somewhere in the archives (I have seen the yellowed document) an actual order dated in April, 1872, thus:

The debauch, which has been protracted at this station for ten days, ensuing since the arrival of the Supply Train, will now cease.

By order of Col. Doe
Richard Roe, Adjutant.

As a cavalry regiment the First left something to be desired just then. It had just come back from guerilla warfare in the Philippines where each troop had been isolated in control of some *barrio*—the Captain usually acting in civil government, the troops as gendarmes. It had not been a life conducive to all the habits of good society. Those officers had been little satraps to native communities. The mess was full of fresh and lusty tales of gu-gu fighting but many of the younger officers had never seen as much as a squadron drill or maneuver mounted. They had been pretty well separated from white female society for some years. It was largely a regiment of bachelors and there were only two or three officers' wives in the garrison—at first there was none at all. Among that bunch of wild Indians of young subaltern days some were killed in the World War— one at Zamboanga before the war—horribly. A Moro Juramentado caught him unarmed in the market and cut him to pieces with a kriss—in the presence of his daughter, 5 years old. Some died in bed, but the rest have become mostly plump old colonels with the solemnity of church wardens. I wonder if, in their dignity, they ever think now of the hell they used to raise in Texas.

As I have said, the club was above reproach and there was all outdoors and over eight hundred horses to absorb anybody's youthful ebullience. Across the creek was a typical frontier town rejoicing in soldier saloons with such names as "Bucket of Blood" and "Blue Goose" and everything that goes with them —everything. In January, 1904, I went back to New York and got married to my classmate's sister—and that was a timely end to that *phase*.

My wife had lived four years at Fort Clark, where her father (a Civil War veteran) had been stationed when she was a little girl. Other officers' brides or wives were flocking in. The First Cavalry was settling down. It had a good old colonel and several veteran majors and captains of the plains and Indian fighting days. They knew what discipline ought to be and they finally got it to the *n*th degree.

There was a salt tang to those old soldiers which has been largely lost to the Army—for better or for worse. Some of them wore Congressional Medals of Honor won on the plains. All of them had known the bitterness of long winter campaigns, the isolation of prairie posts, and the constant vigilance of savage warfare. I used to listen by the hour to old Mrs. Benteen, of the Seventh Cavalry, and especially to the story of Custer and the brave squadrons he led out from Fort Lincoln to extermination on the Little Big Horn—the shock to waiting widows and families, the fatal cowardice of Reno and the part her own husband had tried to play in coming to Custer's rescue.

There were well-springs of plains history and tradition there that were never tapped and that are now gone forever—more's the pity.

In these months of hard work and hard play the First Cavalry became what I of course shall always regard as the best regiment in the Army. There is not a horse in it now—nothing but fast tanks and armored cars—it is completely motorized. Somebody was singularly lacking in sentiment not to select one of the younger regiments instead of the First Dragoons with its century old record and the names of cavalry battles from every war from 1833 to the World War emblazoned on its banners.

Jefferson Davis was an adjutant of that Regiment and Albert Sidney Johnston once commanded it. No less than fourteen general officers in the Civil War and no less than twenty in the World War had served a novitiate beneath its guidons. Among the latter generation those I knew were General E. J. McClernand, whose father was the General McClernand of Vicksburg and the Civil War. He was my colonel for many years. General Malin Craig, Chief of Staff of the First Army in the Argonne, had a distinguished record in the World War and throughout his whole service. He was my captain during most of the many years of my lieutenancy. He is one of my dearest friends. General Harbord, who led the division comprising the Marine Brigade at Belleau Wood and who brought order out of chaos in the service of supply of the A. E. F., was the major commanding my squadron during my later service. Before that General Joseph Gaston was my major. General H. J. Breese, then a brilliant captain, was a buddy of mine as was General G. V. H. Moseley—also then a captain. General Booth commanded one of the troops. General Lloyd M. Britt, one of the finest soldiers I have ever known, was also a major then. He wore the Congressional Medal of Honor which he won when his troops were in a tight spot before a superior force of Indians, by entering their camp alone at night and stampeding and driving off their herd of ponies, leaving them helpless. General De Rosey Cabel, who averted a dangerous situation at Nogales during the war, was a captain and lived next door to me at Fort Clark, Texas. He was a much older officer and always took a fatherly interest in me. He was a peppery little man with bristling moustache and shoe-brush hair and once when I was relieving him as Officer of the Day he took me to one of the cells in the guard house where a man was raving in delirium tremens.

"That, young man," said he, "is what whisky will do." I looked at him askance and perhaps a trifle astonished. He liked his toddy as well as the next. He bristled all over,

"I mean *bad* whisky!" he amended. "Bad whisky—*Bad* whisky—*very* bad whisky."

A fine old generation of gentlemen, almost all graduates of West Point in classes now nearly forgotten. They pass the tradition down by the examples of their simple, frugal, honest hard-lived lives and they thus have given new waves of younger officers, year-by-year, the temper and stability and fire that will always give comfort to this country in the integrity of its officers' corps.

This is just the record of one fine old regiment. There are many more exactly like it, and that is how the country got Lee, Sherman, Jackson, Grant, both Johnstons, Sheridan, Custer, Jeb Stuart, Thomas, Pleasanton, Jeff Davis, Hooker, McClellan, Meade, Shafter, Pershing, Liggett, Bullard, Bliss, Harbord, Craig, MacArthur and hundreds of others.

West Point and the First Cavalry are, of course, institutions, but to me they seem like persons—rather stern—wholly gracious—bearing some strong clannish or even family relationship to me and for whom I must do whatever I try to do with all that is in me—for fear I would hurt their *"feelings"* otherwise. I suppose that is because although they *are* institutions, they are built on the comradeship and performance in public service of men for generations back.

There were enlisted men in the First Cavalry who despite the formalism of that relationship were as dear to me as many officers. My first top sergeant—Volmer—a plains veteran, who fathered me with amused affection and taught me more about practical soldiering than can be learned in schools—old Buffalo Brown, an Indian fighter of repute—Louis Dorn, whom I met this spring at Agua Caliente and who is as able as they come—but this is garrulity again. There were Mulvaneys and Sergeant Quirts in the First Cavalry too—and even mightier than they. But this isn't the place to talk about them.

In April, 1906, earthquake, fire, and devastation struck San Francisco like a bolt from the blue, and within a few hours after the first shock the First Cavalry was entraining for the Coast.

B Troop (Captain Pat Murphy), to which I was attached, was hustled to the Presidio and was given charge of several thousand refugees huddling in Army tents. It was a troop of rookies—fresh faced farmer boys. But we put each one in charge of the destinies of several hundred people and began the task of census taking, feeding, sanitation, and order. There was almost nothing that we were not at first called upon to do, including officiating at births, of which every mild secondary tremor, which continued for days, seemed to produce a new crop.

Within a few days after it was known that the government was giving refugees food, clothing, and shelter and would continue indefinitely to do so, hoboes from all over the country began to flock in and present themselves as "refugees." It was hard to check up and we didn't want to refuse any real sufferer. They clogged up other camps—but not the Presidio Camp.

We had invented a card index census—housed in a file made out of tent pegs and "one-by-twelve" boards. We soon knew everything, and had tabulated everything, about everybody in camp. The cards were so systematized that we could call *somebody* from any destroyed neighborhood from which any late arrival claimed to come. Then we started an employment bureau and proceeded to clean out our camp at the very time when other camps were filling up.

Because of the way that worked, I was made assistant to the assistant of the quartermaster of Permanent Camps—an organization charged with the "supply of sufferers from earthquake and conflagration on the Pacific Coast." I was a second lieutenant of less than three years' service and in the Old Army nothing could be lower than that. But (as sometimes happens) on the day I joined, the quartermaster was ordered to the General Staff—the first American Brain Trust. His "assistant" became quartermaster and I stepped up by one "assistant." The next day the new quartermaster was taken to the hospital suffering terribly, and I was acting quartermaster just as the job began. They didn't replace me because my chief was very able and nobody knew how sick he was. He never came back to that job, which was a big one for a kid, feeding, sheltering, and clothing seventeen thousand destitute people.

All that terrible summer we worked organizing and running that service of supply. On July 1st, the $3,000,000 appropriated by Congress ran out, and the Army had to be withdrawn. The San Francisco Civilian Relief Committee was not ready to take over and the War Department loaned several officers (of which I was one) to complete the organization of permanent relief.

We did it but it was the Reuf-Schmitz administration and before winter, in spite of all we could do to protect the situation and ourselves, that administration got so rotten with graft and peculation in relief funds that—one by one—we all requested to be returned to line duty.

I was very loath to go. The Federal Government had appropriated $3,000,000 but private donations were more than $7,000,000. Not far from Golden Gate Park there was the Alms House track. It was quite possible to go far with that $7,000,000 as a basis to eliminate slums in San Francisco. Was it to be used to put up unsightly temporary shacks in all the city's parks, to replace army tents as the temporary shelter for remaining refugees or, using it on an equity basis, could we borrow, say twice as much with the city's guarantee and put up permanent modern housing to abolish slums? Our plans had gone far in that direction. We had tentatively made arrangements for building material at a special and very low price. We had the support of union labor and promises of marked concessions in wage scales on this work. We had even made some progress in architectural plans which anticipated the German *agronomes*— i.e., apartment houses at low overhead and low room costs with a provision of small garden tracts to try to make workmen self-sustaining. It was an ideal situation for that sort of sociological experiment because we also had plans for special rapid-transit communication to the industrial district of San Francisco. But it was utterly out of the question with that political crew in command. I left disappointed about that, but an idea had been well developed by study and, at least on paper, proved practicable.

Out of that experience added to his, Mr. Baruch and I in 1931 drew up an elaborate plan for the relief of the unemployed and the destitute in this country which I still think is better than any yet advanced, and the housing idea was the basis for the plan prepared in 1933, authority for which we included in Title II of the Recovery Act where it still lies dormant to any practical result.

One of the pathetic incidents of the fire was the abandonment of dogs. I owned and took to San Francisco with me a beautiful collie—a product of the Morgan kennels. One day, inspecting the Presidio Camp, I encountered a shifty-eyed bum leading what I thought was my dog on the end of a telegraph-wire leash. I immediately went for him. The dog was suspiciously cool but I was angry and did not stop to observe. My own "Lad" would have devoured me. The man was entirely apologetic when I asked what he was doing with my dog—said he had found it wandering loose in the street—and quickly turned it over. The dog did not seem especially enthusiastic. I had raised my dog as a pup on a bottle. It was not until I had returned to my quarters in "East Cantonment" that I discovered—due to my own Lad's astonishing advent with an unusually enthusiastic welcome—that what I had on the end of my wire leash was a perfect "double"—so perfect that even side-by-side they could scarcely be distinguished.

When my troop went back to Fort Clark—months before I was relieved—I sent both dogs back in care of my stable sergeant. When I arrived only "Lad" swarmed over me. The other dog of that unprecedented team had perished in the Texas heat.

I shall never forget Texas. My boy was born at Fort Clark, and I left no little of youth and laughter there.

# Chapter V

# ISLAND OF LUZON

---

"Well, he may be a Brother of Wm. H. Taft,
But he ain't no Brother of mine."
—*The "Little Brown Brother"; misanthropic song of the U. S. Volunteers, 1901.*

---

MY REGIMENT was promptly ordered to Philippine service and we were back in San Francisco within a few months. The Philippine government was changing its money from "Mex" to the new Conant currency and the mint in San Francisco was literally shipping to it five million dollars in nickels and dimes. Some unkind fate detailed me away from my regiment to convey this shipment. At the mint they offered to let me count the millions and millions of pesetas and medio-pesetas—for which I was to receipt. That was a joke. You couldn't have counted it in a year. What you did was to weigh it on scales so fine that an absent two and a half cent piece had once been discovered. It was deadly serious to me. Although I had never seen what even a million dollars in small coin looked like, I insisted on a military guard from my regiment to take it to the dock—all cased in oak boxes. The cavalcade required ten motor trucks and was a sight for gods and men. I nearly had heart-failure while these boxes were swung over-side in nets. But I checked them into the "magazine"—the last hold aft on the Transport *Thomas*—saw the steel hatch battened down, posted a sentry in a chair sitting over it and went to a well-earned rest.

I had difficulties with my Colonel about that. He wanted me to do ship duties like all the rest of the shavetails. I flashed my orders from the Treasury detaching me from his command and with my little guard of four (detailed from his men) insisted that we were immune from his control—a proposition to which he had to accede although he used to walk around my single sentry sitting on that hatch with what little white hair there was on his bald head bristling.

On the night before we got to Manila the quartermaster of the ship sent for me and said—in the Colonel's presence:

"Mr. Johnson, we must open Hold Number Five to get the Manila mail on deck tonight and I thought you would want to be there to see that your money isn't interfered with."

"Hold Number Five—Hold Number Five? My money isn't in Hold Number Five."

The Colonel's voice piped up like a clarion:

"Mr. Johnson, if you have had my soldiers sitting over an empty magazine night and day for twenty-eight days, I'll have you court-martialed."

Well I had with my own eyes seen those oak boxes go down into the magazine and not into Hold Number Five, but you know how it is with human frailty. *I wasn't sure.*

To make a long story short, of course the money was in the magazine and the quartermaster was wrong. But the Colonel never forgave me. He marched his regiment away and left me sitting on my millions of dollars in nickels and dimes. It was not an army matter and nobody in the Army would help me. I was just stuck there. Finally, I went out on the docks and, out of my slender pocketbook, hired native stevedores who—ten at a time—two to a box—slung those heavy caskets on bamboo poles and carried them to the Philippine Treasury where I had the devil's own time to get anybody to receipt for them and finally got somebody to accept delivery of so many cases "*said to contain* 5,000,000 pesos, in pesetas and medio-pesetas." I have been waiting ever since for some claim that one or more boxes were short of change.

The regiment went to Camp Stotsenberg, Pampanga, Luzon. All twelve troops were together for the first time in half a century.

What a post that was! To the west and just beyond the parade ground was a range of mountains with Pinatuba—the principal peak—standing up like a dog's tooth. Up there lived the Negritos—Dravidian dwarfs with negroid characteristics—the most primitive people in the world, having neither houses nor the institution of marriage. They file their teeth, sell their children, and sleep where night overtakes them, but they are the finest of hunting companions and guides and they are bowmen of deadly accuracy. I used to go hunting with their chief, Lucas, whose death was recently discussed in a syndicated press account—so famous had he become. In every other direction was jungle—rank and lush. Back of the cavalry stables was a mile of sandy plain—then jungle—then the barrio of Tacunda—there were others like Sapun Bato and Decapolis in other directions— dens of vice the like of which civilized countries do not know. Here were native "houses"—long rambling structures built of palm leaves. In the front was a "parlor" with benches all round where the brown ladies displayed their charms—then back of that a long hall with little cubicles on each side.

In those days a private got $13.00 a month—it was enough for about a five days' hooter and, there being few other amusements, hooters were not infrequent.

So impatient had the previous commander become that in one unguarded moment and with a little profanity he had wished "somebody would burn that den of iniquity to the ground." With two regiments and two batteries changing station with each other, there was a double garrison at Stotsenberg. The outgoing lads in true Army hospitality wanted to show the newcomers the sights—and our men had just had a double pay day. The net result of all this was an early morning holocaust of the barrio of Tacunda. Of course, that was riot and arson and could not be condoned.

Having read Blackstone under my father's guidance as a boy and made the most of the West Point law course from intense interest, I was by way of becoming a guard house lawyer—a very doubtful distinction in army circles—anyway I was assigned the duty of finding and convicting the ringleaders. It was a terrible job. Including native dialects it was sometimes necessary to have three interpreters to interrogate one witness, for example—English to Spanish to Tagalog to Negrito. But we finally found the men and obtained the convictions in spite of intimidation and sequestration of witnesses and many other Oriental wiles.

The convicts were very bitter and they had many confederates. On the night that they were to be transported to the military prison and when I was officer of the guard, they contrived a very clever escape which they had long planned and timed for my tour of duty.

We discovered the escape within ten minutes—and then rode three nights and two days without rest or sleep—only to be convinced of the foolishness of such an exertion in an island where two white men cannot move without creating native gossip. With only a sergeant left from the squad of seven with which I started, we stumbled into the Constabulary Station at San Fernando Union. The *teniente*—a Spaniard—laughed and put out a telephone alarm. Within an hour there was an account of every white traveler on the main roads of Northern Luzon, and within two hours natives had captured the fugitives in a rice field. These men—and one of them was a barrel-chested German—had escaped through a hole sawed in two inch nara floor planks carefully beveled and disguised with soap and dust and that hole was about ten by twelve inches. I had always heard that a normally proportioned man can go through any hole he can get his head through. Nobody believed it until the largest prisoner—to absolve his guards from complicity—repeated the feat.

In that tropical station you started drill before dawn, worked all morning, went to the club before lunch, slept until four, played polo until dark, dined, and sat around the club all evening—the day's work involving three showers and changes of uniform and considerably more than that number of Scotch and Tan San highballs.

The barrios continued to give trouble. The Army, under the influence of some misguided morality organizations of the old school, did little or nothing to control the ravages of the virulent social diseases of the Orient. My own troop was largely comprised of recruits from farms—fresh faced young innocents set down in that stews where every soldier's *lavandera* was a potential mistress and center of infection. It was a shocking thing to see one after another of these boys go to the hospital with something that might shadow the rest of their days.

As far as a second lieutenant can, I began to make things as disagreeable officially as I knew how. Being able to get no assistance through technical instruction, I sent to the "States" for texts, studied those diseases exhaustively and, so far as that troop was concerned at least, installed crudely a little of the system worked out later by our Medical Corps, which during the World War protected our soldiers and left the most enviable record in 1917–18 for the American Army that has been known in modern or medieval war records.

But it caused trouble. Finally supreme authority in Manila sent a high-ranking lecturer who talked to the whole assembled regiment. He described the ravages in horrifying details—but of preventive or cure said nothing. When I made bold to call his attention to that from the floor he said, "Oh, yes, I forgot" and then launched into an hour's dissertation on the certainty of chastity as the only preventive or palliative. The men looked scared and desperate. The lecture did more harm than good. Chastity is, of course, all right, but nobody ever saw a barrack which lent itself to the régime of a monastery and this is especially true in a tropical climate in unmoral surroundings with none or few uplifting influences or diversions of any kind.

It was not long after this that the Army took the subject under administration with an iron hand. During the war it cleansed and kept clean of this scourge more than 4,000,000 men—with almost negligible exceptions.

I always thought that that splendid accomplishment of the Medical Corps ranks with what Gorgas, Walter Reed, or Lazarre did and that it has never been sufficiently acknowledged. It is a historical incident of vast significance.

My tour of duty was broken by an assignment to command a war strength composite company of infantry at Baguio in the head-hunter country. Every regiment in the islands had contributed fifteen or twenty men to this detachment and had sent its offscourings. I have never seen such an undisciplined outfit in all my service.

The men went A. W. O. L. at will. There were no drills and hardly any duties. They had no company fund to supplement the harsh army ration and no wholesome amusements at all.

It was fun straightening that situation out. We substituted a new system for the regular army summary courts. If a man was absent, I gave him a choice between depositing $5.00 to his own credit with the Treasury (on which the government paid him 4%) or taking summary punishment and, for the latter purpose, I started to build a road around a rocky hill with soldier labor under an old-time hardboiled army Provost Sergeant whom I had brought with me. There was small room for choice. We didn't build much road, but it wasn't long before some of our toughest hombres were getting to be capitalists. There were no more pay-day sprees and absences because they didn't get anything in their pay envelopes. It all went to their credit. It is remarkable to observe the growing self-respect of a man as he begins to reckon up his deposit slips.

It was a heterodox method but it worked, and I never have been able to see why it has never been adopted in army discipline. It is a lot better than taking away a dollar or two in petty fines which are no deterrent at all, and then caging a man up in a prison cell for a week where he loses his self-respect or at least his horror of incarceration, and upon five convictions for minor offenses discharging him dishonorably. *During all my Army service I never sent 10 men before a court-martial.*

Baguio was an attempted duplication of Simla—a summer capital and a beautiful place. The Igorrotes are, physically, one of the finest races in the Islands and if taking heads was part of their ritual, they at least did it with conscientious thoroughness. They reduced gold and silver ore and cast the metal cleverly into images and utensils. They even smelted copper. They also ate dogs as a delicacy. There was a dog market there and you would encounter far out on mountain trails husbandmen driving yokes of three or four to ten terribly emaciated curs to market. Buyers fed them rice until they were fat to bursting and then, with rice wine, they might form the *pièce de résistance* of a canyow—which is headhunter whoopee—the principal characteristic being the most realistic pageant-dancing I have ever seen, and I was thoroughly familiar with Amerindian dances.

These dances are primitive dramas usually winding up in mock lethal duels over a woman between, say, a man with a head-axe and another with a net and spear.

At semi-official dinners minor Igorrote officials gravely appeared in stiff shirts, black dinner jackets, a gee-string and nothing else at all. The valleys of these mountains were so steep and the hills so high that people on one slope did not speak the same dialect as people on the other and in the frequent forays between them most of the heads were taken, dried and kept to form a ghastly frieze over the door lintels of their not too primitive homes.

Military service there was interesting and very pleasant. Baguio was so high that you had to have fires at night, always slept under blankets and were as much removed from the tropics as you would be say in the Georgia hills in the early autumn—the pines and soil are very similar. The military post was built on the brim of the gorge of the Bued River and you could look down that precipitous cañon with a pair of field glasses and see every type of vegetation from the pines of the north temperate to the rank jungle of the equatorial tropics.

It didn't last long because it was only a tour of duty. I was relieved by a classmate and went back to Stotsenberg.

The captain of one of the troops had been a long time ill and without a lieutenant. It was a troop of rookies with weak non-coms. Without his knowledge, conditions developed there of the worst sort the Army knows and that but rarely. One day as the regimental officers were leaving headquarters at noon, five shots rang out from the barracks of that troop. We all ran back to encounter a rather dazed sergeant with a smoking rifle in his hand. The first officer to arrive was Conrad Babcock. He did as brave a thing as I have seen. He pointed his finger at that man and said, "Drop that rifle." The madman started to raise it but the habit of discipline (he was an old soldier) was too strong.

We seized him and went inside. The place was a shambles. One man ran by us holding his intestines in him with his fore-arm. The first sergeant lay on the floor with the crown of his head as neatly blown off as if it had been clipped with a slicer. Altogether, by firing into a crowded barber shop, this sergeant had disposed of five men with four quick shots. At the direction of the colonel, I examined him within five minutes of the last shot. He sat squatting like a savage with the aura of that dreadful thing still on him but, while he was as mad as a hatter, he answered every question with an acumen and clarity far beyond that of the average professional soldier of the old school.

That troop was thoroughly demoralized. The colonel ordered me to take it out on a practice march next day and to keep it going hard till I thought it had calmed down. The men under the leadership of six "bad actors" were sullen and rebellious. The non-coms were afraid for their lives. They tried to tell me where to camp—a horrendous breach of discipline. That was because they had a rendezvous with a "bino" dealer. We did not camp there. They did not know how to go into camp anyway and a tropical storm was coming up.

It took three hours to get them into camp—it should take 20 minutes—and in the meantime the bino vender had arrived and skulking behind the dog tents had done his work. They didn't have any supper because the whole kitchen crew was drunk. I finally picked out half a dozen old soldiers and proceeded to clean out that camp.

We tied the ringleaders, face up, on bales of hay. We routed out the drunks and got the tents ditched and sodded just as the typhoon arrived, and the pelting rain beat all night long on the men tied to the hay bales. We put on double guards. On the next day's march the mutineers carried their own saddles and packs and we led their horses with the troop. For about three days I hazed those toughs till they came to me and wanted to be good. It was the only manhandling I ever did in the Army but it was a thorough job—an unpleasant experience —the only one like it I ever saw or heard of in the regiment— but there was no more trouble with that bunch. The colonel transferred to it some old non-coms from other organizations. There was excellent raw material there and it eventually became as good an organization as there was in the regiment. Some of the tough boys turned out to be good non-coms.

There was some revolutionary unrest among the natives —there was never an open outbreak. One or two men were ambushed and murdered—at least one of them was—the other disappeared, but, as to this one, his fate was conveyed to us in about as clever a way to deliver a message and not get caught as I ever saw. Our telegraph line to Manila stopped working. An officer named Frank Keller was sent out to find the break. The wire had been cut and spliced with hemp and in the hemp was a message saying what was going to be done to that soldier, by whom and where.

But curious things were always happening to Keller. There was an old colonel of great ability, but somewhat unrestrained conduct—not *our* colonel. He claimed his family to be of direct English ducal descent and he had such mannerisms as he thought a British duke would indulge. It was at least a family distinguished in American history and so was he on both good and bad sides of the record. He had a fancy in quiet periods of shutting himself up in his nipa bungalow out on the Manila road, getting excellently drunk and staying that way in seclusion for some days.

All those houses are built up on piling so that the lower sill of the window is about as high as a mounted man's head and one day Keller was riding by these windows glancing toward them perhaps as Launcelot did toward the windows of the Lady of Shallot. But he saw no magic mirror. He saw the flushed face of this libidinous old coot with a three days' growth of beard and the old man was motioning to Keller to dismount and come in—in a kind of silent, solemn, and mysterious manner.

Keller found the pompous old fellow weaving around with an old-fashioned, long-barreled, Bisley model six-shooter in his hand.

"There is a very large snake," said he with deliberation, "under my bed—very large—*very* large. It would give me no concern whatever, sir, if he would just remain coiled. But he does not *do* this. He is restless, Mr. Keller, extraordinarily restless. Indeed, I have never known a more restless snake. And when he undulates sir—'undulates' is, I believe, the word—he bumps the bottom of my mattress and disturbs my rest. There is nothing left for me now but to do away with him, but I did not care to fire a shot here in the barrio without a witness—now, Mr. Keller, if you will kindly stand by——"

Keller knew what might result from shots in a barrio, especially as natives rushing in would see a white colonel in the condition of seeing snakes.

"Now, Colonel," he said, soothingly, "let me look at your gun first. Just sit down for a moment——"

The old man flashed into ducal and military indignation.

"Stand at attention, sir. Salute me, you impertinent young shavetail."

Keller stood. The colonel knelt, took careful aim and fired three booming shots in swift succession. *The whole bed stood up on end and revealed, lashing and threshing in its death agonies, a veritable, substantial, concrete, and palpable 12-foot house python.*

They were quite common in those old houses and altogether harmless. Indeed they usually kept out of sight in attics and rid the place of all kinds of lesser pests and annoyances.

This old gentleman had many enemies so he used to keep a "black-book" in which he entered the foibles of gossip about other officers, especially his seniors, and he kept sources of information open at all times for he had ample means.

Finally the War Department got tired of his idiosyncrasies and determined to make an end of him. They sent him to a post in command of another colonel—senior to him—a stickler for discipline and propriety, a bachelor who asserted that no soldier should marry, a boaster about his own conscience, and something of a prig. He knew what he was there for and within three months he sent for the colonel of the snake and, with great punctilo, said:

"Colonel, I have the honor, sir, to hand you a set of court-martial general charges of conduct unbecoming an officer and a gentleman, with three specifications in that you have on three separate occasions been drunk in your quarters in violation of the Articles of War."

"Very well, sir. Thank you, sir. And now may I have the use of an office and a stenographer—not for long, Colonel—not for long—possibly not more than ten minutes."

"Quite willingly, Colonel. Of course, you are aware that you have a right—though you are not required—to make any statement you may desire and I am glad to add, sir, that I will be happy to give it every consideration."

"This isn't going to be exactly in the nature of a statement," replied He-of-the-Snake, "and I am *convinced*, sir, that you will give it *every* consideration although I am not so sure that you will be happy in doing so."

With which enigmatic assertion he saluted, "about-faced," and returned shortly with a general court-martial charge and 29 specifications alleging improper relations between the Colonel of the Conscience and the latter's cook, complete with a list of witnesses and a digest of the evidence. That was the end of that.

We passed through a cholera epidemic, than which nothing is more terrifying or ghastly. The natives died in swarms but due to our sanitary service and rigid discipline the First Cavalry only lost one man and he was infected while on leave.

Everybody was a little sad when we were ordered to California for station but two years in the Islands are enough. We were glad to see the Golden Gate loom up at dawn after a voyage of twenty-eight days, not counting some visiting in Japan and Hawaii as diversions.

# Chapter VI

# YOSEMITE AND SEQUOIA

---

"This is the forest primeval."
 —*Longfellow.*

---

OUR SQUADRON of the First Cavalry took station at the Presidio of San Francisco—one of the oldest military stations on the Pacific Coast. It was the first time the Regiment had ever had a post at a large city in the sixty-four years of its existence.

It was great. Nobody had much money but in those days you didn't need much and relatively—for me—I was rolling in wealth. I had begun to write short stories, articles, and juveniles. They were terrible trash but I was making—sporadically—considerably more than my army pay and in one glorious month I had nine of these pot-boilers accepted by the principal magazines of the country. I was really getting an audience.

Sometimes there was leisure to write but more often not. I was soon in one of the latter seasons. Our squadron was detailed in summer to guard National Parks—Yosemite and Sequoia. The second squadron was at Yellowstone. Two troops marched up the San Joaquin and into the Valley by way of Merced. It was just a vacation for most of the officers. Usually at a post like that one is adjutant, one quartermaster, and (in those days) one commissary and so throughout the whole staff hierarchy. But our major, under some sort of old Army obsession, would have none of this. I had to take all of these jobs and, in addition, operate the post store—which was something more than any Army canteen. It also sold supplies to tourists and did a thriving business, the profits from which kept these two troops well supplied with "extras" all the rest of the year.

It was a night-and-day job. It included also the whole strategy and tactics of fighting forest fires which at that season were frequent and very dangerous because they threatened the immemorial big trees in the Merced and Tuolumne groves.

There is a real strategy in fighting them—studies of the map and winds to guess just what course they will take and where your first and second lines of defense shall be—control of back-fires at strategic spots to leave the big fire nothing to feed upon when it arrives—lookouts far behind your lines to take care of the great blazing pine cones which, lifted by the gas from their own flames and caught in the winds, may float like a fire balloon for a mile or more—provision against long resinous roots where fire may smoulder for a week burrowing under your trenches and breaks to start the fire again a week after you have withdrawn your forces and reported the fire out. One fire on Bald Mountain, north toward the Tuolumne, broke out that way five separate times. We had to have all the troops in the garrison out on that one—once for three days and nights without sleep. American regular troopers may "soldier" on a job of cutting lawns or kitchen-police, but never when there is a real job to do and a fight to fight. They would get just as enthusiastic about these fire fights as I ever did. One of them chided his captain once for not taking a fire in his charge seriously enough and added to the gayety of the whole regiment by saying: "That ain't the way me and Lieutenant Johnson goes at it."

But it was a wonderful experience—not only for the practice in running a "general store" for three years, but also for the administration of a world in miniature. My family lived in a comfortable cluster of big hospital tents so close to Yosemite Falls that the wind sometimes deluged them with mist. You were in and out and over that Valley like a bird dog in covert from Hetch-Hetchy, the Finger Peaks, and the Muir Glacier to Merced—out of doors half the time and in an office the rest. I made a study showing the fallacy—from the standpoint of economy—of the use of tentage that had been practiced for twenty years and, in this way, got a garrison of cottages built. It wasn't what I wanted. Using soldier labor, native timber, and cedar bark, I had designed and built a lodge type of house at no cost at all and we could have built the whole garrison that way with much more appropriate architecture and at one-third the cost, but in those days the Army didn't do things that way.

Up to this time I had never been in the presence of the mighty and I knew there was no preferment without that but now I saw my chance. It was the summer of the Great Bull

Moose Defection. We got word that in search of complete rest and diversion Supreme Authority was coming to Yosemite— not as the tourists do—but to seek the absolute seclusion of the wild country north of Hetch-Hetchy where none but the more adventurous of the Sierra Club often ventures. He was bringing with him a notable party of generals, ladies, and aids. But I was warned that the Great Man being himself a famous woodsman and a "trooper tough" in Squadron A, desired nothing taken but a little bacon and cornmeal to fry fish and the simplest kind of accommodations.

Now we knew something about the northern Park. There is no forage for animals. When you go up there you are cut off from bases of supplies and rations. This party included ladies—and how people do eat in that cool dry air! The net of it was that the least I could figure was the entire pack train of fifty-five mules, a small mountain of forage, an escort of four-teen soldiers to supply orderlies, grooms, cooks and guides, and tentage and kitchen gear galore.

We were ready bright and early with our itinerary carefully plotted. It was my chance to make a reputation for efficiency right under the eyes where it would do the most good, and I planned that trip like a campaign. It was a terrible flop.

The Chief sent Major (later Major General) Lassiter to look over our small mountain of supplies and there and then I got my first reprimand, which was a scorcher. I was reminded of the Great Man's woodcraft and his expressed wish to rough it. Only by stubbornly maintaining my knowledge of the Park and this particular little-known tour was disaster averted. Paren-thetically, we had to send back for two more pack-train loads before that dismal journey was complete.

We got started up the cañon wall an hour late. The first day's trip was scheduled short—to Soda Springs—as was always done, especially since the next one was long and very rough. We unloaded and unmantaed while the sun was still high. We started to make camp. But the "old woodsman" was displaying unusual vigor. I got orders to pack up and make the next camp.

Now the old Army pack mule was of a peculiar and decided individuality. He would plod patiently under any load and over any road however long, but once those packs came off—that was a day's work and it took more than soothing words to con-vince him otherwise. Once on another trip, I saw a regular stampede of protest and one particular rugged individualist among those mules led a cargador a merry chase through the cedar-brakes, on the Merced road near the Valley rim—she kept just out of reach for two hours and finally, being cornered, stepped gingerly out on Glacier Point—an overhanging shingle of rock projecting twenty feet out from the top of a 3,000 foot abyss as sheer as the wall of a hotel room. Old Rosie got as far out as she could get and then just posed there with her long ears flopping forward brooding over the awesome sublimity of that chasm. The exhausted cargador just put his arms akimbo to catch his breath and then said: "Why you scenery-loving son of a ———". It was inappropriate to Rosie's sex but it well expressed the general idea.

We finally got the train loaded and made Rattlesnake Lake at sunset—a high glacial gem clear as crystal and cold as ice—with a storm coming up rapidly over the northern peaks. We were approaching the crest of the Sierras. The camp had been selected by the best government scout in Yosemite—an old Indian fighter, mountaineer, and plainsman of 50 years' service —and we unloaded again.

The Chief cast his eye over the scene and I got my next withering. There were two very tall dead pines in the grove. Did I not realize the utter tenderfoot trick I had done? They might blow down in the night and hurt somebody. Anyway one of the ladies wanted to camp on the other side of the lake. Just then it began to rain in torrents.

It was supreme authority and there could be no answer except the traditional "Very well sir," but low in the ranks of the cargadores and military escort there were curses not loud but deep and the pack mules went on a more fervid strike than any NRA has ever seen.

When we finally got around the lake it was dark. There was no dry wood. The cooks couldn't get the fires started. Everybody was very hungry and very cross. About ten o'clock we managed some burnt bacon and rain-sogged biscuits. This ended the first day and the second was like unto it.

We were north of the gorge of the Hetch-Hetchy—almost as sheer and deep as Yosemite itself and gouged out by the same sort of glacier in the same way. Consequently, we were clear out of touch with our base when I began to divine that we were not on a trip solely for diversion. The Chief used to like to have everybody gather around him at the camp fire to hear his reminiscences of men and events and it was easy to see what was on his mind. One evening he sent for me. What communication could we make with the Valley? How could we get in touch with events at the Chicago Convention? If, after a long deadlock between Taft and Teddy, a compromise should suddenly be made on one who had been the latter's protégé and the friend of the former, how could that news be relayed promptly into the heart of this wilderness?

To make a long story short, we had to use every available horse-soldier in the Valley to create a line of relays that kept us in constant twenty-four-hour service over precipitous and dimly marked trails for the message that never came—and was not even bruited.

I like to draw a veil over the rest of that trip. Not knowing how to row, I almost drowned dear old General Crozier in his canvas boat in a glacial lake south of the Finger Peaks. I tried to cook up a conspiracy to be recalled and replaced by another shavetail from the garrison on the plea of the sudden visit of an Inspector General, but got caught at it and descended several more pegs in official favor. The trout wouldn't bite for anybody but an old cargador who made his flies to suit weather and his own shrewd observations. He made them out of pieces of his red-flannel undershirt or the ribbon on his old brown hat and this nearly scandalized the party which was provided with the best tackle that money could buy. I finally got orders that this old man must fish no more. Nobody but Supreme Authority could fish—and he never caught anything, although the lakes and streams were teeming with fat and gorgeous Loch Levens and Rainbows. They were too well fed to strike—except at the delicious cuts from old Long John's undershirt. We finally dragged back into the valley after two (for me) miserable weeks but I did not get any letters of commendation to file with my military record. All I got was a kick about the mess bill which I think was forty cents per day per head.

That pretty much discouraged me on the idea of cavalry soldiers as national park rangers and taught me—for the nonce at least to "put not your trust in princes." Two years later I was Superintendent of Sequoia Park myself and I spent the whole summer writing a brief on why the government could not afford a regiment of cavalry to police parks when at about three per-

cent of the cost it could get better service from a few Forest
Rangers. That was a fully documented and devastating showing. It would never have done to give it the light of day. And
that was the last year in which the War Department ever
loaned cavalry to the Interior Department for that particular
purpose.

The sequoias fascinated me. These are the *gigantea*, much
larger and older than the *semper virens* which seem to grow
anywhere. These true big trees apparently grow only in
altitudes between about 8,000 and 12,000 feet. *Some of them
are more than 5,000 years old.* They have been growing there
since before the dawn of history. Some were big trees when
Jesus walked the earth. They are a perfect cylindrical column
—some rise for more than 100 feet without a branch and then
their great arms reach up to scanty foliage. They are a favorite
target for lightning and it is a marvel that any survive but, in
them, life is more tenacious than in any other organism. I know
of one that is just a shell for twenty feet up—burnt out to the
heart. But they heal and fill in and go on living. The wood is
brittle and when felled they break like a dropped slate pencil,
though how anybody could have the heart to cut one down is
beyond me. Some sort of freak colony did go to Sequoia years
ago, and began to fell them. I saw these ghastly stumps fifteen
years later—and they were still bleeding.

I took and sent to the Interior Department some pictures of
ideographs that we found on the rock wall of a cave near the
trees at Sequoia. They were painted on the granite and quite
distinct although I had to trace them in red chalk to get a photograph. The Digger Indians who were the resident aborigines
when white men came knew nothing about them except that
they had "always been there." On analysis it appeared that
they were painted with a pigment steeped from the little cones
of the Big Trees. It is the most indelible of fluids.

The first time I ever saw one of these trees, I came upon it
suddenly and unexpectedly riding around a sharp bend in a
trail. It stood in a grove of big sugar pines—there is a russet
color of the bark, richer than anything else I know—but this
massive column rising straight dwarfed the pines and seemed
simply *incredible*. It produced in me the same kind of sensation
that a sudden view of Yosemite or the Grand Canyon does—
awe to the point of physical sensation—almost terrifying.

The biggest tree is the General Sherman, of unbelievable dimensions—unbelievable and, I thought, inaccurate. There was a theodolite, a level and other surveyors' instruments in the camp equipment and I amused myself by checking the official Interior Department figures—and they *are* exaggerated, but, although I reported it, they were never changed. It doesn't make any difference, the General Sherman Tree is the biggest and oldest living thing on the earth's surface.

On one march back from Sequoia we made what I think is some kind of a record for cavalry hikes. Almost 350 miles in nine days, in the heat of September, up the San Joaquin Valley —brought every horse, pack mule and wagon in and not a sore back among nearly 100 animals.

The first time I ever saw the breath-taking chasm of Yosemite, I was riding in from Awanee far ahead of the troops in an old four-mule Daugherty wagon. I always had to do that because I was quartermaster and had to prepare camp and procure supplies for the half-squadron to arrive two hours later.

The driver was an old time mule-skinner named Peterman, who was a constant delight to me. He would jog his mules along for an hour at their steady implacable seven-mile trot without a word and then say something like—

"He didn't though," which ended up some story he had been telling *me an hour before* and not a word since. He had a sweet voice and he would sing—"She wore a tulip"—and then after jogging along for five or ten minutes—"A big yellow tulip"— and so through the verse which might take half an hour.

He didn't warn me about our approaching arrival at Artist's Point on the Valley rim—and you never suspect the presence of the Valley there until you are on its very edge and then—its stupendous grandeur actually affects you as a slight tap on the solar plexus might. Peterman hadn't said a word for an hour when—"whoa!" and he jammed his foot down on the brakes. I gasped and Peterman looked on with a pleased proprietary air as though he owned the great Valley and me. After a while he began pointing things out with the air of a gracious host.

"See all them big half-caves in the rocks over there across the Valley from Half-Dome? Well, them's the Washington Arches. I've worked all through that country"—I was too engrossed to listen.

"See all them green woods up toward Bridal Veil Falls? Well, I've worked all through there too." And, after a while:

"See them meadows along the Merced?" (They looked from that height like green clippings alongside a white thread.) "Well, I've worked all through there too and back of the camp and right up so close to Yosemite Falls you could feel the spray."

I suddenly realized what he had been saying and it didn't seem to make sense. So, I asked him: "What do you mean you *worked?*" We jogged on down the Valley wall and after half a mile he disclosed that, through all that geography, he had engaged in amorous adventures with waitresses in the tourist camps.

And this was the only memory or emotion stirred by a revisit to that sublime gorge—

"A primrose by a river's brim,
A yellow primrose was to him
—and it was nothing more."

# Chapter VII

## THE BORDER PATROL

EARLY one Saturday afternoon at the Presidio in 1911, when every officer of the squadron (except myself) and most of the men were in town "on pass" and I was about to go there, a message came from Department Headquarters out of a clear sky directing our squadron to entrain by ten o'clock that night for an unstated destination, but with full field equipment for indefinite service.

How we ever did it, I do not know, but by ten o'clock horse, bag, and baggage—and with no absentees—we were on troop trains headed south. Some troops went to Yuma, some to Calexico, and I think to Tia Juana on the California border. Some went to Tucson and as far east as Douglas and Agua Prieta but "B" Troop went to Nogales, Arizona.

For weeks nobody knew why we were there. Old Diaz seemed firmly in the saddle. We had not even heard of Francisco Madero. At Nogales, Sonora, just across the line, there was a garrison of the old Mexican army with some officers who had attended American service schools, and we fraternized with them in a high old time.

We had to patrol as far east as Huachucha and as far west as the edge of the Yuma Desert with an outpost at Oro Blanco but these were just larks.

That was the country of the exploits of Geronimo, and "Army Doctor" Leonard Wood and "Captain Lawton" are still living as young men in the memories of some of the old sour-doughs in those hills. I located in a box cañon a mound which had been a cabin where a family had been massacred, and in a fight with the marauders six troopers had been killed.

I had read about it in some memoirs and it was a thrill to find it and the half-obliterated hummocks of old graves, and even a few corroded and empty old Springfield carbine shells.

We did not know what we were patrolling for. There were plenty of renegade Mexicans at Oro Blanco, and I had to ride there to arrest one once, but they were harmless, cheerful people and there was no sign on either side of the border of the concentrated hell that was about to descend on the Mexican republic. We even made excursions as far as Arivaca, which was Wolfville of the Red Dog feud made famous by Alfred Henry Lewis. I know of no place that I would rather live than in the crystalline light of that arid but fascinating country.

That didn't last very long. An old First Cavalryman named W. C. Brown (whose initials never lost their usual meaning in barrack rooms) came down on an inspection trip and was scandalized. An order issued forbidding our officers from crossing the border on any pretext. He must have discovered something that we could not find because, almost immediately, new troops—infantry, artillery, and signal corps, came pouring into Nogales, Arizona. Just before the Madero revolution flared up everywhere in north Sonora, that kindly Mexican garrison insisted on giving the augmented American officers' corps a dinner on the American side—since we could not cross to theirs.

W. C. approved, and asked me to prepare a good-will speech in Spanish and memorize it, which I, with great labor, did. But it didn't turn out to be that kind of a dinner. I include it here because it happened to result in the first of my few famous attempts at international diplomacy—like razzing Hitler, the Soviets and Villa in Mexico—later when I was Administrator of NRA.

There was an excellent restaurant in Nogales and a famous border character—"Montezuma Mamie"—ran a really good hotel. We were asked to rendezvous at the latter and it turned out that the purpose was potent and copious champagne cocktails. Everybody expecting that to be all on the vinous side, partook. But it wasn't all. There was another stop on the way to the restaurant and then the dinner. Never was there such a dinner—eleven courses and the proper wine with every course—lots of it, excellent and insidious.

Toasts began early but they were neither literary nor earnest; they were short and to the point like:

"*Que pasa con Capitán Flores?*"

"*Esta bueno.*"

"*Quién está bueno?*"

"*Capitán Flores.*"

which meant almost exactly the same thing as

"What's the matter with the old W. C.?"

"He's all right,"

"Who's all right?"

"Old W. C."

and much talk about "*compadres in armas*" or, *in nostorum linguam*, "brothers in arms."

Major Brown was rapping for order. I knew that he was contemplating speechmaking. I also knew that there was about as much chance as there would be at the average class reunion dinner at two o'clock in the morning. I was beatifically puzzling how we could ever be brothers in arms with these Latin aliens, and how the speech might be replaced by some snappy Spanish toast that would satisfy the Major and yet permit me to get back in my seat before somebody threw something at me.

Suddenly just as the Major got at least momentary attention —an idea—scintillating, coruscating, vibrant—struck me and before I could reflect on this solution of the Brothers in Arms problem, the Major had introduced me and I was on my feet saying in Spanish:

"Here's to the day when the American flag will fly from the North Pole to the Isthmus of Panama—then we can *all* be brothers in arms."

The effect was more than electrical. It was paralyzing. All their officers who could, rose quickly, bowed stiffly and walked out of that room. The Major gave me one withering glance and departed. I felt hurt and much aggrieved. It really was an ingenious thought. The other lieutenant of my troop, our surgeon, and a couple of doughboys stayed there perhaps half an hour talking it over.

Finally I went out for a breath of air. There was a board sidewalk raised perhaps three feet above the dusty street as is common in western towns. I walked to the edge, peered over and then rubbed my eyes. There was a fully accoutered soldier of my troop—prone and wearing bandoliers with two hundred rounds. I walked down the sidewalk and there was another and another and then I saw the first sergeant squatting over them.

"Sergeant—what the hell?"

"We heard de Lieutenant got into some trouble wid dem spig officers and dey is comin' over for to clean up on him, so we just come down to stick around."

Well, I got those men back into camp at the double and into their bunks within ten minutes. I went back to town and found that something like that was indeed in progress across the border. We got the Deputy Marshal, who was popular everywhere, to go across and quiet their wounded feelings by saying that I didn't speak Spanish (which was near enough to the truth) and that somebody had played a practical joke. It was the closest shave to big trouble that I ever had in the Army. Suppose there had been a scrap . . . !

Nobody has ever quite learned what went on behind the diplomatic scenes that year. There was a mobilization of the National Guard at San Antonio and much whispering about Japanese and even British intervention. The revolution blazed out and swept southward. Diaz was out. Madero was in and, while there were some short respites, the First Cavalry has practically been on that border from that day to this.

Over at Douglas, Arizona—opposite Agua Prieta—where K troop was stationed something really did happen. Captain Julien Gaujot was in command and as some bucolic Texas editorial said at the time quite seriously: "Some men are *sui-generis*, but he is *sui-generiser* than any other officer in the Army."

In Samar when "hell-roaring" Jake Smith went out to stop treacherous massacres of American troops incited by a "Black Pope" with fake priests, Gaujot caught several (as I recall eleven) of the latter red-handed and hung them. That got him into serious trouble—but not too serious.

He had an antic wit He had an official scow at his station in Samar and in his little independent principality there were two solemn village elders who regarded him as a sort of king. He got hold of a Navy Admiral's gold laced white cap somehow, made what looked like sea-glasses by lashing two beer bottles together, and instructed one old chieftain in their use. Gaujot used to be punted up the sluggish bayous reclining beneath an

umbrella, fanned by dusky retainers with this old village head-
man standing in the bow, very dignified and self-important,
peering through his "binoculars" clad in the Admiral's cap and
*nothing else whatever*, singing out whaling and other nautical
warnings and commands in a curious English which Gaujot had
taught him verbatim, like: "Thar she blows and spumes"—
"Six points on the stabbud bow" and dozens of others. The old
fellow was getting the thrill of his life. He thought it was some
kind of official ritual.

Behind Gaujot always stood the other burly savage chief,
also clad in nothing but a police helmet—the old gray kind—
wearing a big tin star—tacked on his breast and twirling a club
as Gaujot had taught him to do.

Gaujot even had his quartermaster requisition and set up a
lamp-post in front of his quarters—the only one yet seen on
the island, I suppose. This for "Old McGillicuddy" (as Gaujot
called him) to lean against twirling his club, while Gaujot was
within dispensing justice.

When Gaujot joined the First Cavalry he came, as captain,
to a troop which had not been very prudent with its ration al-
lowance. In those days a troop was allotted a certain sum of
money to be spent at the commissary to feed it for a month.
The improvident mess sergeant had used the whole fund by
the 25th of the month. They were "trying out the new skip-
per." The sergeant came to Gaujot in great perturbation.
"Well," said Julien. "Well-well-well." And then, after deep
thought, "Sergeant, are there any carpenters in the troop?"

"Oh *yes*, sir." The sergeant was efficient and expectant.
"And cabinet makers too—one wood-turner, I believe sir."

"Well isn't that great—excellent—perfect? And here we are
in Yosemite with whole mountains of hardwood."

"Yes sir,—yes sir," said the sergeant, somewhat puzzled
but expectant, "and what are the Captain's wishes?"

"Well," said Gaujot, "I was just thinking that, since you
have 65 soldiers and no food for six days, you might have these
artisans make some wooden bills, to tie on the men so they can
go out in the paddocks and pick with the chickens—it's better
than anything *you* have to offer."

There was a Diaz garrison in Agua Prieta. The Maderistas
came in superior number and surrounded it. All their fire
raked the streets of Douglas, Arizona. Gaujot started to ride

between the firing lines when his nervous trumpeter called his attention to the fact that "Both sides are shooting at us." "I believe the ——— ———s are," was Gaujot's only comment. The trumpeter thought up a new one. "They'll kill old Dick"—Dick being Gaujot's beloved horse. "I hadn't thought of *that*," he said. "Take him back."

Gaujot dismounted and walked on foot alone to the Maderista trenches. He had the choicest collection of Spanish profanity I ever have heard and, for sheer Rabelaisian ingenuity, Spanish profanity leads the world. He either charmed them as virtuoso or bluffed them completely, because what he said was that if one more projectile crossed the border into Douglas, Arizona, he would bring K troop across the line and clean them out from one horn of their half-moon trenches to the other. Anyway they ceased firing. Then he walked in the teeth of rifle fire into Agua Prieta and made the half-lit defenders come across the border and intern.

It was one of the maddest pieces of fearless effrontery in border history but, of course, it instantly created an international incident. All Washington could do with Gaujot was either to courtmartial or give him the coveted Medal of Honor for conspicuous gallantry in action—above and beyond the call of duty. They did the latter. I asked him what possessed him. "Oh, I got so tired of seeing my brother wear one of those things around as a watch charm—and he now a civilian" (all of which was true) "that I reckoned I'd have to go and get me one of them for my own self."

Shortly after this our squadron was finally ordered back to San Francisco and from there to the Presidio of Monterey. My captain was Malin Craig and he had what in the army is called "drag." He used it now to get all the horses in C Troop condemned or transferred and to get authority to purchase and train a complete remount. We were close to the Salinas rim-rock country, one of the best horse-ranges in the United States, and by careful selection we bought up a whole coal-black troop of young, untrained horses. Malin turned their breaking and training over to me. We used the French Saumur system and had the men drilling again in three months. You could pick that troop out in regimental line because the horses' heads were held at least four inches higher than the other troops. It was the show troop at the Panama-Pacific Exposition.

We were scarcely well settled there when out of a blue sky came orders for me to proceed to Cambridge to take a three-year course at the Harvard Law School. I never knew why. I had been counsel or Judge Advocate in three courts-martial of more than routine importance—the Tacunda arson case, the case of a big commissary scandal at the Presidio and then as counsel for a very gallant officer of rank tried on twenty-nine specifications of drunkenness on duty over a period of years. As a matter of fact he was guilty of twenty-eight of them and not guilty of one. The court found him not guilty of the twenty-eight and guilty of the one, so I could not claim great kudos on that but, anyway, here was the order.

We got this officer off without dismissal on his record of unfailing gallantry. There was a letter from Teddy Roosevelt about his utterly intrepid action at San Juan Hill. I introduced as a witness a very old and retired leather-skinned top sergeant with an arrow gash across his cheek who told of an obscure cavalry charge against an Apache ambuscade—and finally brought guffaws from the stern-faced court itself in telling how he had seen the lieutenant—he was an old major now but not to the veteran sergeant who loved him but had not seen him for 25 years—sitting alone at a table at the Post Trader's playing solitaire when the Apache Kid—a drunken half-breed and cold-blooded killer—came in half-drunk and sullen and leered down at the lieutenant threateningly. Finally, with his hand on his gun he spoke:

"Nobody but soldiers and sons of b——s play that game."

"The lieutenant, he just looked up and grinned and he says, 'Well *I'm* a soldier—sit down and take a deck.'"

I did not particularly want to go to law school. But I was still a second lieutenant and when there came an explanatory letter from General Crowder saying that he wanted for judge advocates legally trained officers of military experience and that, if I distinguished myself sufficiently, he would give me a vacancy as major in the Judge Advocate Corps which would occur as I graduated—if ever. That put a very different aspect on the whole matter. It meant about a twenty years' jump in promotion.

Things happened with lightning rapidity. The European war broke out. My orders were changed from Harvard to the University of California. Then I was told that, if I could not contrive to finish the three-year course in nineteen months, I would have to leave without a diploma. By the time all this happened the first semester was a month old. Dear old Dean Jones at California told me that, far from permitting any such doubling up, it would be unusual and difficult even to admit me so late in the semester. But he was sympathetic and the War Department had made a special request. He finally relented on the doubling up too, for a purely experimental period in that first year. I went home and immediately began the hardest nineteen months I have ever put in—harder than either NRA or the draft—a solid average of eighteen hours a day, during the regular course and two summer sessions, I also took some academic courses. In the Law School I had all A's. They commuted my four years at West Point, gave me a B.A., let me make one of the graduation orations, and a year later, gave me a J.D. with honors. It was the first time I had ever really worked in my life.

I had intended to take a short vacation but that was the spring (1916) in which Villa raided Columbus, New Mexico. General Pershing was ordered in after him. My leave was canceled and I was given orders to report to Pershing as Judge Advocate at Namiquipa, Chihuahua, some six hundred miles south of the border, and left the University on the afternoon of graduation to assume that duty.

# Chapter VIII

# PERSHING AND PANCHO VILLA

---

*"La cucaracha; La cucaracha, Ya no puede caminar"*
*—The Cockroach—marching song of the Dorados.*

---

I HAD been in General Pershing's command in both the Philippines and California. Indeed I had been visiting from Berkeley with some officers of my regiment at the Presidio Club the night the ramshackle old house that had been assigned him as quarters burned up and brought to him the bitterest tragedy of his life. I left the Club to go back to Berkeley with Mayhew Wainwright, who, five minutes later, saw the fire and rushed into the house to see if anybody was left in that danger. He saw the nurse outside on the lawn with Warren. She did not know where Mrs. Pershing was with the other children. So Wainwright rushed back calling in every room through the dense smoke. When the fire was out, they were found smothered under a mattress in one of the rooms where Wainwright had called for them.

I knew the General for a stern disciplinarian and a great soldier. The first time I ever saw him was thirteen years before in Oklahoma City where he was serving as Captain on the staff of old Sam Sumner and I was a new second lieutenant on my way to report for first duty at Fort Clark. He had always been an inspiring military figure and a boy's ideal of how a real cavalryman should look and act.

When he got the assignment to chase Villa he was a sick man —broken by a tragedy to his family which had been enough to unnerve anybody—and ready to retire. That sudden call to a difficult duty was his salvation.

The Twelfth Cavalry was stationed at Columbus, New Mexico, which is just in the angle of the niche which that state makes into Mexico. At the southern angle of that niche is Gibson's Ranch. The road up from Casas Grandes forks just south of here, one branch to Columbus, one to Gibson's ranch. That regiment was commanded by Colonal Slocum who had been quite friendly with Villa, and the legend was that Villa had once said that if fate ever forced him across the border to intern, he would seek out Slocum to surrender.

There were warnings of the coming raid—that Villa (broken at Celaya and again in Sonora and writhing in rage because Carranzistas in the latter campaign had been permitted to cross American territory to fall on his rear) was coming north for his revenge on the gringos. He had murdered one of two American cowboys on his northward march. The other had escaped and crossed the border to tell a story of six hundred bandits hurrying north—killing as they came.

But Colonel Slocum was still convinced that this was the long expected surrender and with many of his men left Columbus and went south to Gibson's Ranch to meet his friend. Villa did not take the left fork of that road to Gibson's Ranch. He pushed forward on the right fork to Columbus, leaving Slocum outflanked and on a limb and in the night he descended on Columbus like a cyclone.

He murdered the sentries, looted and fired the stores and hotel, and turned his men loose to unbridled pillage. The few remaining American troops were taken utterly by surprise. The officers were in their homes in the town and for a time the men were leaderless. At last, however, they began to rally in the shadows beyond the blaze of burning buildings and to pick off, one by one, the dark figures dancing drunken sarabands against the fires. This went on for some time, with steadily increasing volume and to the extent of considerable slaughter, before the befuddled raiders knew what was happening to them. When they learned, a panic seized them and they started south pell-mell. They were pursued by the rallied troops, and as long as ammunition held out, they were slashed to pieces. Then the cavalry turned back and the raiders trickled south to a rendezvous at a place called Las Palomas.

There Villa waited expecting an attack and determined to meet it. There was an old treaty of the Indian days permitting pursuit of "barbarians" across the borders on a hot trail. That was largely to prevent Apaches and Comanches from finding sanctuary from close pursuit by riding across an imaginary line. But the Mexican government objected to any further excursion. The days passed in international bickering and meanwhile the United States was concentrating all available mobile troops at Columbus. There was a railroad from El Paso cutting across Villa's line of retreat at Colonia Dublan but by the terms of the final understanding that railroad could not be used by the Americans, which meant that all supplies must follow by trucks or wagons. Finally, nearly two weeks after the raid, Pershing's punitive expedition erupted across the border. Meanwhile, Villa, apparently unaware of all this and grown weary of waiting, had started south again. His raiders were in no small part peasants impressed by terror and forced to accompany the Dorados. They were gradually dispersing on the southern trek.

In a recent movie, Wallace Beery—who is my favorite movie actor—portrays Villa as an almost child-like barbarian with a heart of gold. It is very accurate in other respects, but such was not Pancho Villa—he was a cold-blooded killer to whom murder was an obsession—probably psychopathic and with scarcely an attribute of human sympathy in his make-up.

Pershing covered all possible avenues with parallel cavalry columns which did some of the most extraordinary marching in the history of mounted operations. He, himself, practically without escort and exposed to every danger and privation, kept abreast of the vanguard fuming at the delay and even the timidity of some of the chiefs of columns and pushing ahead relentlessly. Villa amused himself by harassing and flaunting the Carranza garrisons on his way. At Guerrero he staged a miniature battle with them. One of his staff pointed to small specks of distant horsemen coming over the crest of a far hill. Villa thought they were his own stragglers. They were Dodd's Seventh Cavalry in the van of the American advance. At almost the same moment Pancho was struck in the leg by a badly flattened ricochet from the Guerrero garrison and while he lay writhing and screaming he learned that the American pursuit was upon him.

He could no longer ride. They placed him in a buckboard. He tried to commit suicide with bichloride in a bottle of gin. He took so much that it came up as soon as it went down. The conveyance caromed crazily on the rough road. The pursuit found bloody bandages along the way and thought they were within a few moments of a capture. Suddenly the wheel tracks and all signs of spoor vanished into thin air. The whole pursuit swarmed southward to day after day of fruitless bushbeating, to utter exhaustion, to ambush and treachery at the hands of the Carranzistas at Parral, but to no sight, nor sound nor sign of Villa.

Then intimations began to come from Washington to desist —strange orders never yet explained. The expedition withdrew slightly in a column from Bachineva to the border—and dug in. About that time a highly educated Japanese doctor serving on Villa's staff came in and for a consideration revealed Villa's condition and hiding place. That country swarms with Japs, and Villa had simply turned off the road and gone to an adobe *jacal* in the hills. But now the expedition was tied down by inexplicable instructions to let Villa alone, and he was as safe as he would have been in his native Durango. Carranza garrisons had orders to fire on Americans moving in any direction except north, and we had orders not to fire unless fired upon— which made some very nasty situations. A group of us narrowly escaped slaughter in the town of Casas Grandes one Sunday when we rode through to see the ruins—*not* riding north.

All kinds of rumors were rife. The line of communication six hundred miles long consisted only of truck-trains on roads that were being rapidly ruined. It was said that Carranza was concentrating troops to cut it—that ten thousand Yaqui Indians were on the march to interpose between Pershing at Namaquipa and his base at Columbus. One day at Carrizal two reconnoitering troops of black cavalry were literally cut to pieces by Carranza machine guns. That night at Namaquipa we burned all surplus supplies and prepared to march on Chihuahua City.

This time the orders from Washington over the slight signal corps ground wire were stultifying and devastating. We did not march on Chihuahua. We simply withdrew to Colonia Dublan. But first we raided every hacienda from Bachineva to Dublan in search of Columbus marauders who were to be identified by Villa traitors. We rounded up the whole male population of these haciendas—twenty to fifty from each place, took them to the nearest camp, examined them before a screen behind which some Villa turncoat gave a signal that the particular man was or was not at Columbus. If he was we took him and sent him to New Mexico for trial.

The troops now settled down to a weary time of watchful waiting. There was absolutely nothing to do. It was open season on Americans outside the line of outposts. Several amorous soldiers prowling like tomcats around the adobe villages got their throats cut for their pains. Finally an old but very powerful negro sergeant scratched at my tent flap. He said with great secrecy that he was Joe Blackburn, serving incognito to escape some ancient trouble. Whether he was or not, he knew the whole game of professional boxing from showmanship to ring technique. He said there was much real talent in the expedition. He pointed out that we could make a big enclosure out of 'paulins, light the ring with gasoline lanterns, charge one dollar admission and give the troops an interest.

It was thus that I became a boxing impresario. The program far exceeded expectations. We put on two bills a week. Never before or since have I witnessed such fights, especially among negro contenders. I have seen both contestants and the referee, all three, "out" on the canvas at the same moment. Men came in armed squads from all over the expedition to see or to participate. There were never enough oil-can cases for seats. The purses got bigger and bigger. They began to attract high grade professional talent from the States. The fund was so rich that we were able to buy baseball, football and other athletic equipment to supply the whole expedition. From that time on there was plenty of interest.

I was impressed with negro prowess. We had two black regiments. They furnished vocal music and they took nearly all athletic prizes. At one mixed field day comprising all athletic events, they came so near to a clean sweep of *all* firsts, seconds, and thirds, that my enlisted assistant whispered into my ear:

"They're just too damned physical for us, Lieutenant."

I veritably believe that but for the color line there would be few white contestants in either opera or athletics.

The most engaging personality of my Mexican service was my tent-mate, Georgie Patton. He came from a distinguished Virginia family. His father used to own Catalina Island. He went to V. M. I. before he came to West Point and what cadets call "tin-soldier antecedents" do not help a plebe at all. But when the yearlings asked Georgie what he was going to be, he always said, "First, Adjutant of the Cadet Corps and then Chief of Staff of the Army, sir."

No words can convey the sacrilege of such an announcement, to an upper classman at West Point! Humility is the indispensable attribute of a good plebe and humility in Georgie Patton is as inconceivable as hair on a frog's leg.

He barely got through the academy—it took him five years instead of four. His spelling was about like George Washington's—but in knowledge of the poesy and history of all nations I have never seen his equal. Perhaps D'Artagnan was his peer in romantic military idealism, but I doubt it. And on the sheer strength of his soldierly figure and carriage he *did* become Adjutant of the Corps.

He had an antique idea that to be a good cavalryman, an officer should be expert in swordsmanship, pistol shooting, swimming, walking and horsemanship, and he proceeded to make himself so.

For the first Olympic games in Stockholm the government declined to finance an Army team. In fact, there was great difficulty in getting it even to grant Georgie leave to go. But *he went* on his own initiative, and at his own expense. And in the modern Pentathlon, which was an event including all that Georgie thought important to an Army officer, *he won every event except* a Swedish cross-country run so designed that any but a Swedish horse and rider would have the utmost difficulty.

He used to sit in his tent by the hour practicing "trigger-pull" with either hand on a pistol fitted with a spring and a rod which would dart out at a swinging pith ball at which he aimed.

We used to call Georgie a Sears-Roebuck cowboy, because he wore a pistol cartridge belt low about his hips with two pearl handled forty-five revolvers in holsters, one on each groin—he never used an automatic pistol.

Before the motor-truck supply trains were originated the Punitive Expedition lived on the country. This required each officer to go on a roster from which one was selected every day to go with the eleven Dodge passenger automobiles at headquarters and an escort of as many soldiers to neighboring haciendas to buy or commandeer corn—*maís* as they call it in Mexico.

In northern Chihuahua the country people rarely live in separate houses. A hacienda is a big adobe hollow square with cell-like rooms opening on a patio of which the big oaken exterior doors are closed and barred at night. At one of these ranchos near Namiquipa, Georgie suspected that one of Villa's chieftains—Candelario Cervantes—and his band had their *queridas* (sweethearts) and that they came down from the *sierra pura* once or twice a week to visit.

Cavalry patrols had raided the place two or three times, but it stood on a level plain. Five miles away the road approaching it ran around a big butte protruding from the near-by mountains and just back of the hacienda a deep ravine broke the plain and led westward into the heart of the mountains. No patrol could cover the distance from butte to gate in less than 15 minutes, and that was enough to insure the escape of Señor Cervantes—out of its rear gate and up the cañon into the trackless hills. The patrols always found the bag empty.

But Georgie had imagination. He figured that by rounding that butte at top speed of his eleven autos he could reach and surround the hacienda in *seven* minutes.

On this next foraging expedition he carefully instructed his drivers. They were to round the bend, stepping on it to the limit. The leading six were to go straight to the rear of the square covering the ravine, the next two were to go to the far corners, the next two to the near corners and another with Georgie in the front seat with his pistol drawn was to do the front gate.

Everything went exactly according to plan. As Georgie's car swerved up in a cloud of dust he saw that the gates were closed, but he knew he had trapped Cervantes *because two peons were at work at the gate, skinning a cow*. In spite of the unusual advent of Patton and his men—*they did not look up*.

Before Georgie could get to the ground the gates burst open and, like "Boh Da Thone and his gang at his heels," out burst Candelario Cervantes' band of ten bribones—with Cervantes in the rear, yelling and firing their Winchesters from their hips —all for Georgie!

But they could come through the gate only one at a time, and our Sears-Roebuck cowboy stood calmly by a fender and potted these dorados—one at a time and nearly every one right between the eyebrows—ten of them.

A good cavalryman keeps only five shots in his six-shooter —hammer on the empty chamber. As Cervantes dashed out, Georgie's pistols were empty. Cervantes saw him fumbling at his cartridge belt and backed him up against the wall, peppering the air around him with Winchester slugs. But a man doesn't shoot a rifle well from horseback. Georgie got his flannel shirt full of adobe dust from the wall above his head but he also finally got one gun loaded and Señor Cervantes stayed not on the order of his going.

Some old scout had told Georgie that you don't get a fleeing horseman by firing at *him*. Even if you hit him, his horse may carry him away. The trick is to shoot *the horse* in the stifle joint—all of which Georgie duly and accurately did.

Down came the horse, Cervantes got behind him and trained his rifle across the flat-horned saddle—but not swiftly enough. The ambidextrous Georgie got him first.

Then he tied each *ladrone* face up across the hood of each automobile and went his rounds for corn. Georgie staged his return to camp magnificently. He drove up in front of General Pershing's tent with a flourish, scratched on the tent flap, entered, saluted and began to make his report.

"Visited San Luis Rancho—ten hectoliters of corn—La Hacienda de la Familia Sagrada—ten hectoliters of corn— Santa Rosalita Rancho—got ten hectoliters of corn, Candelario Cervantes and ten men——"

"What the——"

"Right outside the door, sir; may I keep his silver mounted saddle, sir?"

This happened just as I joined at Namiquipa but that is the way they told the story at headquarters, and I know that most of it is true. Georgie got thoroughly riddled by machine gun fire when he commanded the tanks at St. Mihiel, but he is as big and husky as ever, and if he doesn't get to be Chief of Staff in due course, it won't be for lack of trying to deserve it.

When the Mormons, driven back from New York to Nauvoo, Illinois, and finally to Nebraska, trekked westward again they intended to shake the dust of the United States from their feet forever. Utah was Mexico. But before they got settled there the treaty of Guadalupe Hidalgo had made that the United States. Later some of them made another hegira into Chihuahua. They were kindly received. What they did in these *Colonias* is marvelous. Colonia Juarez was a gem of a little town at the foot of the Sierra Madres. Riding over a little rise after hours on burnt and saffron prairie and hills to look down on a broad valley checkerboarded with green fields under a perfect system of irrigation, you suddenly get the impression of having been transported from Chihuahua to New England.

They fascinated me. Mormons in Mexico did not seem to have been taken into confidence on the new revelations about monogamy when Utah became a state. The old Bishop at Juarez had a number of families. I went to their church services whenever I could. The sermons were made by one of the elders sitting on the daïs and rushing forward to speak "when the spirit moved." All the sermons were pretty much alike—about the Angel Moroni appearing to Joseph Smith in "the meridian of time" and the admonition to go forth without staff or scrip to preach—every man is supposed to do it for a year of his life. The delightful informality of their prayers was striking.

"Oh God! General Pershing is here today with us and he has several members of his staff here too. The next event in this celebration will be a picnic and we hope to have the General and his officers there and we would like to have you come and bring your Son, our Lord Jesus, etcet., etcet."

They had been very prosperous until Villa began levying on them. They were a peaceful people. The state government left them to their own institutions and kept police and even Mexican courts out. The Bishop settled cases civil and criminal. They had no jail because they didn't need one. The whole of Mormon history is interesting and may suggest a lesson. If that whole harassed people could trek clear across the great American desert—some of them walking with all their possessions in wheelbarrows or carts or travois—and carve out of nothing the thrifty communities that they have erected, without even so much as communication with the outside world, isn't there some relief for our destitute that we haven't yet discovered— let's buy the five northern states of Mexico!

My job with General Pershing was review of court-martial cases. Some of the men were "going primitive" and there was an increasing number of cutting and shooting cases. This was not an onerous duty, however, and General Pershing was ever alert to keep his staff busy. He gave me a real assignment—to conduct a study and inquiry as to why, after trying every form of government known to man, Mexico had never had any peace except under the force of a well-organized military oligarchy.

It was a peach of an assignment. It involved a comparative

study of the whole body of constitutional, administrative, state, and municipal law of both the United States and the Republic of Mexico. We sent for Mexican lawyers, judges, business men, legislators, and farmers. It came to the definite conclusion that the trouble was the insertion of an Anglo-Saxon Constitution under the body of a Civil Law structure of statutes and customs and that the two mixed no better than oil and water and resulted in governmental chaos.

The Madero outbreak was supposed to be an agrarian revolution, but the peons I saw did not yearn for more land. If they lived in villages there were the *ejidas* or appurtenant common lands where each could raise enough *maiz* and keep enough goats to last the year—and that with little enough labor. They liked to sit in the shade and play music or lie in the sun and they were peaceful and content. You can't help liking them and wondering if they are not a whole lot wiser and happier and better off than we are in our constant restless striving to do something to "better ourselves." I doubt if there was ever a real popular uprising in Mexico. They are adventurous and it is a grave error to suppose they are not brave. Some of them like to go to the wars but not—I think—to work any political reform.

But the point important to the rest of this narrative is that this study for General Pershing soaked me through with the theory and practice of Federal, State and Municipal political structure in the United States and that was the whole basis for all that was done in the invention and administration of the Selective Service System during the war, of much of the final organization of the War Industries Board System and of not a little of NRA. I enjoyed every minute of that job and worked on it diligently for weeks.

At the moment of its completion, my mother-in-law died at Fort Leavenworth. I had to go on a short leave of absence which took me to Washington. I saw General Crowder and he ordered me not to return. I became Assistant to the Law Officer of the Bureau of Insular Affairs in charge of civil litigation arising from our Island possessions. That job consisted in writing briefs for cases in the Supreme and Circuit Courts of the United States and was one of the most poignantly interesting tasks I had ever had. That was in the autumn of 1916. For us, the war was just around the corner.

## Chapter IX

## CROWDER AND THE DRAFT

---

"They also serve who only stand and wait."
—*Milton.*

---

RELATIONS between the United States and Germany were growing steadily more strained. General Crowder had been interested all his life in the subject of mobilization. He required several officers to study the history of the various attempts at conscription in this country and in England—especially in the Civil War on both the Confederate and the Federal sides.

One day the President came to the War Department. He wanted a bill drawn to organize a large army and he wanted it by next day. General Crowder divided the work. My job was to write the sections dealing with raising the army. Various memoirs have ascribed to various people credit for "selling" the President the idea of selective conscription in the face of Anglo-Saxon prejudices since the appearance of these tribes in history. I know nothing about that. There were plenty of advocates. Doubtless they all did their share. I had then never talked to the President in my life. I only know that in drafting this bill, we had no instructions whatever as to how that army was to be raised, and at a long venture, without more than five minutes' consideration, I wrote "The President shall have authority to *raise by draft*, etcet., etcet." That bill was pigeonholed for future reference, but that language was never changed.

General March wrote a book saying General Crowder was opposed to conscription. As a matter of fact, the raising of armies by Selective Service—and not by volunteering—was Crowder's especial hobby for years. He was kind enough to give me fulsome credit for the success of the draft. Nobody can ever use that to take from him the full measure of personal responsibility for the astonishing success of that great enterprise. His laurels are too many and varied to be hurt by such sniping.

His Distinguished Service Medal *should* bear no fewer than four bars—for organization of the Cuban government—for complete reorganization of the legal system of the Army—for the Selective Draft—and for herculean accomplishment as Ambassador to Cuba.

My work on the draft was on his responsibility and subject to his guidance. As Papa Joffre said of the First Marne: "Suppose it had been a defeat—*who would have borne the blame?*"

When a man works under another man's guidance and responsibility the greatest of his accomplishments are merely leaves in the civic wreath of his boss.

It is just like an expert muleteer with a championship six-mule jerk-line team. Nobody has a right to say: "Old Long John is *just the driver*—that off-lead jinny is the whole show."

General Crowder was responsible for the draft. Furthermore, without him I would probably be rejoicing in the exalted title of "C.O. San Juan De Bac-bac" or some other outlandish station—writing impassioned articles on drill regulations and lapsing into the final stages of a rotund human turnip.

Events leading toward war were rushing forward like a flood. Within a few weeks the task of drawing a complete bill that really meant business was assigned to General Crowder's office. Many hands and minds worked on that document, but the essential language of the conscription section was never changed. Part of the final draft was lifted by Congress out of the regulations, which we prepared some time later in the Provost Marshal General's office. Another part of it was written in the Judge Advocate General's office. It is a matter of small moment. The bill was finally passed, but that passage was largely engineered by a Republican, Julius Kahn of California.

Long before this, however, came the question of how such a new and unprecedented law was actually to be executed. During the Civil War it was done by military force, under military officers in military districts.

The registration was made by a house-to-house canvas by men in arms. That required nearly a year (our registration was over in twenty-four hours) and outraged the whole population. I recall hearing my mother recite a poignant bit of doggerel of the period portraying Henry Clay's widow wailing over the snatching by the soldiery of her frail, drafted son—the sort of thing that inflames popular passion—but I have been unable to locate it. The actual draft was by the jury-wheel system in local communities, and was said to be rotten with "fixing" and favoritism.

The Civil War draft was a failure, utter and complete. It threw the city of New York into a state of anarchy and riot. A rich man could buy his way out of it. A poor man was subject to all kinds of graft and racketeering in the method of selection. It did not produce forty thousand bona fide drafted men for the Union Army.

The General Staff in 1917 had worked out a plan for "raising by draft." It was written on many score of foolscap pages. It bristled with bayonets. It adhered to the principle of the draft by force. It was only a slight modification of the principle of the Civil War draft, and postmasters were to execute the registration by sending out postal cards. When you remember the difficulty of getting intelligent registration cards even with instructed officials making the entries, the absurdity of this is apparent. We had to print the instructions in twenty-seven languages and dialects.

General Crowder asked me to prepare a substitute. It was written on five pages. It eschewed all use of military force. It threw the entire execution of the draft back on the local communities in counties, or in cities, in blocks of such number of precincts as would comprise thirty thousand population. It made the governors of the states responsible and utilized to the fullest extent the existing institutions of state, county and municipal government. The entire state mechanism of registration for elections was the foundation of it.

It was instantly attacked on the ground that there was nothing behind it except the force of public opinion, which was by no means unanimous on the subject of the war. The answer was that if public opinion in such a country as this could not be persuaded to support a war, this country could not support that war.

This was the essence of the principle later used in NRA and it is the only principle upon which NRA can become anything more than the great mess into which it is now rapidly drifting because of failure to understand that principle.

Mr. Baker, the Secretary of War, immediately adhered to this point of view, rejected the General Staff plan, approved

our plan and assigned to General Crowder the duty of executing the draft in accordance therewith under the ancien
title of Provost Marshal General. That title was more o
less meaningless in this case since we had nothing whateve
to do with spies, deserters, military intelligence or militar
police, but General Crowder favored it for its historical asso
ciation.

The General's time was almost completely taken up wit
the multiplying duties of the Judge Advocate General's office
and he instructed me to go ahead with all preliminary worl
possible in advance of the passage of the Act, which was onl
in the early stages of Congressional debate and already meetin
determined opposition of those who clung to the shibbolet
that there can be no draft in an Anglo-Saxon country. I wa
given the Old Post Office Building at 7th & F streets, and wen
down there with a single assistant, Captain Dowell, and tw
clerks, Alvin Brown and Captain Fullam.

We wrote complete regulations for the registration. We wrot
letters to every governor, mayor and sheriff explaining in deta
exactly what was to be done and what their duties would be
We worked out with the Public Printer, Cornelius Ford, th
exact content and shape of each of the forty million forms tha
would be required and with the Post Office Department a
exact schedule of mailing to get these to every place in th
United States at the same time.

The debate in Congress had become bitter and stubbor
In the midst of it Connie Ford—very much disturbed—came t
me with evidence of a vast miscalculation in the printin
schedules. There was not the required amount of paper an
card stock in the country.

We took our war very seriously. We computed that a wee
lost here might be a week lost at the very crisis, and here wa
a chance of losing six weeks over a matter so prosaic as printe
paper forms. Connie Ford was especially impressed with th
possible effects at some future military crisis. Several hundre
thousand dollars were involved. Printing in advance of th
Statute was absolutely illegal, but we figured that we didn
have thousands—much less hundreds of thousands of dolla
to forfeit, so that the worst we could lose was our jobs ar
maybe spend some weeks in jail. We knew that if we went
more responsible officials who couldn't afford to take the r

sponsibility we would be turned down. Anyway, we shook hands solemnly and swore each other to secrecy.

Connie thought he could keep his employees from knowing what it was all about. The danger was that somebody would tell the enemies of the draft in Congress and they would obsolete the whole work by some change in the law. I gave the order. Connie turned on the presses and began to buy paper and card stock in train-load lots.

The secrecy business was a joke. Nobody had ever imagined the bulk of that printing job. Soon storerooms and the very aisles of the great Government Printing Office were overflowing. Connie said that there was no more room to work. There was about as much chance of concealing our draft preparations in the G. P. O. as of concealing a bull in a china shop. Finally we took secret counsel with City Postmaster Chance of the Washington Post Office, where all the country's surplus mail sacks came to depot. He was as much impressed as we had been by the need for both speed and secrecy. He suggested that we begin packing, sacking, and actually addressing the forms to each proposed local board, promising to hide them in Post Office storerooms until the Act should pass. But once again we reckoned short of our bulk. The printing job was only half through and all the surplus mail sacks in the country were absorbed.

It was then that we decided on a move which disclosed what I have always regarded as one of the most beautiful demonstrations of the patriotism and trustworthiness of American officials of every grade. We wrote about four thousand unknown mayors and sheriffs telling them frankly and exactly our predicament. We asked them to secrete the forms in vaults, send the sacks back at once and say nothing to anybody. *Until the very day of the passage of the Act not a single one of those confidences was abused.*

The day the Act passed somebody alarmed the Secretary of War by a calculation showing that our plan of complete registration within two weeks was all wrong and, basing it on a showing that no such national organization and preparation of printing and mailing forms, regulations, and instructions was humanly possible in less than three months. The Secretary immediately sent for General Crowder and he for me with an ominous message.

I did not know what to say or how he would receive our infraction of every law and regulation on the subject, but the main point was that, at that very moment, with the ink not dry on the new law, every hamlet, village, town, county, and city—no matter how remote—was organized and instructed, ready and fully equipped to conduct that registration on twenty-four-hour notice.

He was as apprehensive of the Secretary as I had been of him, but he might have saved his fears of that ingenious, efficient, and vigorous Minister. Mr. Baker was delighted.

The next job was to inform and convince the country of just what was necessary. With Woodrow Wilson's prestige and personality it could only be done in his name. General Crowder assigned to me the task of preparing that proclamation and warned me that it was probably love's labor lost, because the President had theretofore insisted on writing his own state papers.

There were so many fine technical points here that it seemed necessary that certain language be preserved verbatim. So, regardless of the press of other things, I took two days off literally to soak myself in the style and writings of Woodrow Wilson. This is part of the result in the draft proclamation; our suggestion was approved with only one insertion, which resulted in a grammatical solecism and had to be omitted. One of my proudest possessions is this manuscript with that penned alteration:

The power against which we are arrayed has sought to impose its will upon the world by force. To this end it has increased armament until it has changed the face of war. In the sense in which we have been wont to think of armies there are no armies in this struggle. There are entire nations armed. Thus, the men who remain to till the soil and man the factories are no less a part of the army that is France than the men beneath the battle flags. It must be so with us. It is not an army that we must shape and train for war; it is a nation. To this end our people must draw close in one compact front against a common foe. But this cannot be if each man pursues a private purpose. All must pursue one purpose. The nation needs all men; but it needs each man, not in the field that will most pleasure him, but in the endeavor that will best serve the common good. Thus, though a sharpshooter pleases to operate a trip-hammer for the forging of great guns, and an expert machinist desires to march with the flag, the nation is being served only when the sharpshooter marches and the machinist remains at his levers. The whole nation must be a team in which each man shall play the part for which he is best fitted. To this end, Congress has provided that the nation shall be organized for war by selection and that each man shall be classified for service in the place to which it shall best serve the common good to call him.

The significance of this cannot be overstated. It is a new thing in our history and a landmark in our progress. It is a new manner of accepting and vitalizing our duty to give ourselves with thoughtful devotion to the common purpose of us all. It is in no sense a conscription of the unwilling; it is rather, a selection from a nation which has volunteered in mass. It is no more a choosing of these who shall march with the colors than it is a selection of those who shall serve an equally necessary and devoted purpose in the industries that lie behind the battle line.

The day here named is the time upon which all shall present themselves for assignment to their tasks. It is for that reason destined to be remembered as one of the most conspicuous moments in our history. It is nothing less than the day upon which the manhood of the country shall step forward in one solid rank in defense of the ideals to which this nation is consecrated. It is important to those ideals no less than to the pride of this generation in manifesting its devotion to them, that there be no gaps in the ranks.

It is essential that the day be approached in thoughtful apprehension of its significance and that we accord to it the honor and the meaning that it deserves. Our industrial need prescribes that it be not made a technical holiday, but the stern sacrifice that is before us urges that it be carried in all our hearts as a great day of patriotic devotion and obligation when the duty shall lie upon every man, whether he is himself to be registered or not, to see to it that the name of every male person of the designated ages is written on these lists of honor.

We did not proceed immediately to registration merely because we wanted ample time for due notice to all concerned. But we did proceed precisely on the original schedule, and by breaking law and regulations we saved at least six weeks which, when translated into terms of the situation on the Western Front in the spring and summer of 1918—the destruction of Byng's Army, Château Thierry, Belleau Wood, St. Mihiel and Soissons—entitle one to some comfort in the reflection that "they also serve who only stand and wait."

But there was little standing and waiting on that job. After the registration would come the draft, and the whole country had to be organized into systems of draft boards—more than four thousand of them—nominated by governors and appointed by the President. The whole body of draft regulations had to be prepared, the great lottery arranged for, and the complete system for mobilizing and transporting the selected men to camp completed. It was a greater draft on time and energy than NRA. For weeks at a time, I worked on four to six hours' sleep on an office sofa.

In the meantime, our staff had grown from three men to an adequate personnel composed of some of the ablest men in the Army and the legal profession. We were handling a vast correspondence under a rule that required an answer to every letter in twenty-four hours—a task that would have been utterly impossible had not the system been absolutely decentralized with no authority in Washington to exempt or even consider the individual case of a single man. We were invading ten million homes with an inquisitorial process. The whole matter lay in the hands of a man's neighbors and, except in a limited class of cases, which we later whittled to nothing, there was no appeal beyond those local and district boards.

The registration was one of the most spectacular developments of the war. It was completed in a single day—nearly ten million men with a succinct census of their availability. More than that—within twenty-four hours afterward we had almost complete national returns of the result. The news of that didn't do the Kaiser any good. It was, as the President had said, evidence of a nation which had stepped forward in a single rank and "volunteered in mass."

The great national lottery to determine the order in which each man should be called to the colors was the next job in the "selling" campaign. Due to Civil War precedent, there was more skepticism about the fairness of a drawing than any other incident. We had provided for this by having numbers on the registration cards corresponding to a scheme for drawing numbers on slips of paper in capsules out of a glass bowl in Washington—only ten of them, and nobody in the country knew why these numbers were on the cards. Thus number 1 when drawn would fix the order of going of registration cards, one, eleven, twenty-one, thirty-one, forty-one, etcet., and also of one hundred one, one hundred eleven, one hundred twenty-one, etcet., and of one thousand one, one thousand eleven, one thousand twenty-one, etcet., and so forth for each digit.

On the very eve of that lottery we discovered a mistake made in sorting the cards by one whole state, which invalidated the plan. We had to draw ten thousand numbers out of that bowl, and to switch the plan in ten hours. We sat up all night getting ready to do it, and the drawing went off on exact schedule without one mistake—that the country knew about. One of the capsules holding a number did fall on the floor and adhered to the high heel of a lady spectator's shoe. She didn't find it until about midnight after she had gone home to Chevy Chase. She realized at once what had happened—drove all the way back to the Senate Office Building, gave us the capsule, and we dropped it back into the bowl where it was duly fished out. The public atmosphere was so jittery just then that any error would have upset confidence in the whole show. We were ready for the actual selection and mobilization of drafted men, and actually did send a man to camp during July.

There was a serious fault in the first Draft Regulations. The War Department had first to determine how many men it would require during a given period and then request the P.M.G. to furnish them. The latter had then to begin to call men for examination and keep on calling them until the culling out of the physically unfit and those with claims to exemption had yielded the requisite number. This was a long indefinite process and, if we had not changed it in December, 1917, the system could never in this world have furnished in the spring of 1918 the millions who turned the flush of German victory into disastrous defeat.

Under the old system, it became necessary for us to know at once the immediate requirements for the army because even after we knew that, it would take weeks to select them. In July I had suggested in a memorandum, the immediate examination of a sufficient number to produce one million availables, and that memorandum went to the President. It came back splattered with an ink notation to the effect that our contribution would be chiefly money and supplies and that the country would be shocked by, and would never stand for, a draft of a million men. Counting all services more than 5,000,000 men wore our uniform in 1917–1918.

The President's statement was, however, in entire accord with Allied thought at that time, as has been repeatedly reflected in many memoirs. The Allied military missions here felt that we could neither arm, train, equip, nor transport an army—that our attempt to do so would interfere with the availability of our raw and manufacturing resources to them. So we started the piddling process of examining and sending men to camp in driblets on particular calls. Upon the draft organization had also fallen the task of transporting men from the four thousand locations of the draft boards and setting them down at sixteen concentration camps. That schedule was worked out by us with the Association of Railway Executives and served throughout the war without a hitch. I believe it to be the greatest traffic performance in the history of transportation.

The first drafted man was sent to camp before the end of July although the big drafts did not begin to move until September. That, however, was no fault of ours. We were completely ready by August 1st. The camps were not. I went to Yaphank early in September to see the first contingents come in. A bitter breeze blew from the sea and there were neither stoves nor blankets to take care of men who, on War Department orders, had come with a minimum of baggage and insufficient cover. It was disheartening.

As the summer and fall campaigns developed in Europe and Russia collapsed, it was more obvious to us than ever that we *must prepare* to furnish instantly men in far greater numbers than anyone had yet imagined. We decided to revamp the whole draft system from stem to stern to meet this anticipated contingency.

I first called a conference of the more effective draft boards to get firing-line experience and called on every other board for a summary of experience and suggestion. Armed with a digest of all this material I retired to a secret hideout in the Woodward Building with a highly competent staff, and came out four weeks later with the complete new regulations and forms of the questionnaire system which was absolutely new.

In essence, it did this. It drew out all pertinent facts bearing on exemption of every registered man in the country by a self-conducted survey rather than by an inquisition. It provided for an immediate examination of the whole pool of registrants, regardless of War Department requisition. It classified men in such fashion that, even among availables, only those who could go with the least disruption of domestic and economic ties should go first. It abolished completely the system of voluntary enlistment in both the army and navy, but provided for limited volunteering within the pool of available registrants. It created a reservoir of several million fully qualified availables which could be drawn off at a moment's notice in whatever number the military situation might require. It made available for service behind the lines men of limited physical availability in places where they could serve without danger to their health or continuing obligation to their country. This was a vast departure from precedent because, before this, if a man were only to be a pill-roller in an apothecary department he had to be physically perfect. Finally, it classified every man according to his occupational specialty and, in view of the increasingly overwhelming demand for technicians in that war of science as well as arms, this was one of its most valuable aspects. We could now on twenty-four hours' notice literally honor a draft for one hundred one-eyed pigioneers with wooden legs.

It wasn't done a moment too soon. At the very instant of its completion European missions were here with charts showing with arithmetical certainty that at the rate of casualty, and in view of the relative number of German and Allied reserves, allied collapse on the Western Front was a matter of weeks.

We were short of nearly every item of equipment for such vast forces as were then required from us, but the cry was, "Send us men in their undershirts—we'll equip them."

The President's reply was instant, determined, and courageous. *We began to draw men from the ranks of civil life at a rate of nearly half a million a month*—ten times as fast as we ever could or did do it before. Except for our change in system, this would have been a total impossibility. It released trained combatant troops from all the Allied lines of communication and sent them to the front by the hundreds of thousands. It raised the strength of the A.E.F. so far and so fast that within a short time it *outnumbered the largest force that the British ever had in France*. But above and beyond all, was its effect on German morale and strategy as a demonstration of the illimitable manpower resources of the United States and of our ability to raise and transport it to a foreign field three thousand miles away— a thing theretofore believed on all hands to be impossible.

It has been recently said that our CCC mobilization surpassed it. That statement overlooks entirely the fact that while we were shipping four or five hundred thousand drafted men into the camps an equal number of trained soldiers were being shipped out of them and also the fact that commercial traffic is now stagnant, but then it was taxing to the very limit the whole transport system of the country. The CCC mobilization, excellent though it is, was not even a pale shadow of that war work.

Of course, these vast inroads into our pool of availables caused us to think of the future. We were creating labor shortages in some industries and localities. Yet many of the men with low order numbers, many who were deferred for purely domestic reasons, and many who were employed on jobs that women could fill in what had been declared by the War Industries Board "less essential" industries, were not engaged in any pursuit contributory to the great aim and purpose of us all. I prepared a memorandum on this for the War Council suggesting that men in any of these categories who did not, within a reasonable time, faithfully take on employment essential to the winning of the war should be advanced to the head of the list and taken at once for military service. We called it the "Work or Fight" order.

At that time dear old Sam Gompers was President of the American Federation of Labor and in a hot spot. Also I had as an assistant Dean Wigmore of Northwestern University, the great authority on the Law of Evidence. In his exuberance, he told Sam about what we had cooking on the stove. The "Work or Fight" memorandum opened with an attack on men with low order numbers or domestic affiliations, who stood in saloons and pool rooms watching their contemporaries marching away to war.

Old Sam asked me to call on him, which I did. The first thing he did was to dive down into a drawer and pull out a file of letters from the more radical labor leaders attacking him for too great complacency and the next thing he did was to ask me to consult an old gentleman named Sullivan in the Council of National Defense.

Mr. Sullivan at once assumed a dramatic attitude. The saloon and the pool room, according to his views, were the poor man's clubs, and also, as he saw it, there was no shortage of labor. This was such palpable bunk that I resented it but Mr. Sullivan was very firm. He said that with his influence at the White House no "Work or Fight" order would be emitted. We had a hot little scrap in that torrid pasteboard building.

But Old Joe Cannon was in my office while that "Work or Fight" order was being written and he was enthusiastic about it. It was approved by the War Council, but came to a lingering death in the White House. Through Mr. Burleson, old Joe, after some weeks, demanded action and we got it—hot, scorching and straight from the Great White Father. This was a political question—no business of the War Council or of mine. Well, some newshawk managed to get a copy of that memorandum—and said in his Sunday story that this drastic Work or Fight move was being considered at the White House. The editorial comment approving the idea all across the country was instantaneous and unanimous. Within twenty-four hours the "Work or Fight" plan was adopted on direct order of the President. It did not get many men for the Army, but it put drones to useful work by the hundreds of thousands. In any new national mobilization it should be a part of the original plan.

I need not recount here the complete success of the selective draft. Except for two big mistakes of mine it functioned perfectly and there was never any question or delay in the supply of millions in man power. I even was able to work out a method whereby we persuaded nearly two divisions of resident British subjects to go across to Canada and enlist. And we raised our army without any serious disturbance of family or industrial relations.

But there was one very large plump and fuzzy blue-bottle fly in the national ointment. In spite of the fact that this country for two years had been supplying in overwhelming quantities nearly every kind of implement and munition of war to the Allies, when we ourselves entered the lists our munitions program faltered and at last almost completely failed.

The real reason for this was the cocky American proclivity for trying to improve on everything anybody else has ever done. We were making some of the machine guns with which the Allies had fought their fight. But this was not enough for our production planners. We had to design and then make a better one. Their airplanes and their motors wouldn't do for us. We had to plan new ones. Even the trucks which we had been making by the thousands to supply their lines must be revised on

American military lines and, most astonishing of all, the French 75 mm. gun which had proved the most effective artillery weapon in the world's history wasn't good enough for us. We had to redesign not only the shell, but the gun itself. Finally we called in some efficiency experts of the Taylor System to redesign our whole Ordnance Department which was responsible for the vital arms and ammunition program. They redesigned it all right but they completely paralyzed it in the process and it did not recover for a year. Nothing more tragic happened during the war.

Senator Chamberlain of Oregon—a conscientious and sincere statesman—early charged that the War Department had broken down. He did this in a speech in New York which incensed the President so far beyond expression that he cast back the short and ugly word. It was given out that the Senator would reply on Senate Floor and both houses of Congress attended. If there has been a more effective speech on that floor, I have not read or heard it. It was delivered in a purely conversational tone. It leaned over backward to be fair and moderate. It outlined the failure of supply. It quoted letters from mothers who had lost their sons, relating to hospital conditions in the camps during the meningitis epidemic—not critical letters but resigned and patriotic letters, hoping that something might be done to save other mothers' sons. It brought audible if suppressed gasps not only from the crowded galleries, but from the equally crowded floor. It covered the whole field of supply. It suggested a ministry of munitions such as the British had installed and it produced such an effect that if the Senator had cared to press it, he could have passed a joint resolution under suspension of rules there and then.

He had no such intent. He asked only for a remedy of a bad condition. The Government was prompt with a reply. It would coördinate its own efforts within itself by a complete War Department reorganization of supply under a new division called, Purchase, Storage and Traffic, and by implementing the hitherto rather futile War Industries Board with real authority over the whole economic system. Best of all it practically put B. M. Baruch in charge of the whole economic mobilization.

General March, vibrant with energy and ambition, had just returned from France to become Chief of Staff, and he began to strike out on every side. Several supply chiefs were replaced and three men who had had some spectacular success with organizational and administrative jobs were added to the War Department Staff. One was the late Edward Stettinius, who supervised the British purchasing program for J. P. Morgan and Company. The high reputation of the great Goethals was utilized by making him Chief of the new Division. I was put in charge of Army Purchase and appointed to represent the Army on the War Industries Board, now in complete control of industry. So far as the War Department itself is concerned, all this didn't mean very much. The Bureaus dug deeper into their century-old prerogatives.

## Chapter X

# BARUCH, GOETHALS, AND THE MOBILIZATION OF INDUSTRY

---

"Her brilliant, if pitiless, war industry had entered the service of patriotism and had not failed it. Under the compulsion of military necessity a ruthless autocracy was at work and rightly in this land at the portals of which the Statue of Liberty flashes its blinding light across the seas. *They understood War.'*
— *Von Hindenburg, on American industrial mobilization.*

---

IF THERE was ever a job which I didn't want, that was it. When General Pershing had come up from the border to accept his great assignment to the A.E.F., he received carte blanche to pick any officers he desired for his staff, and he told me that he had selected me for the same job I had with him in Mexico— Judge Advocate of the A.E.F. Of course, I was delighted.

Plans for the draft registration were then complete. But no such assignment came. General Crowder had said nothing to me. Quite by accident I encountered General Pershing on Connecticut Avenue one day walking with his boy Warren, and he then told me that, when he had asked for me, Crowder had specifically requested, as a personal favor, that I not be taken until registration was complete. I swarmed back to Crowder greatly aggrieved because I had not even been consulted. He said he had thought it would upset me, but assured me that he and General Pershing had an arrangement for a new request as soon as registration was complete and that he would then let me go. The request came, but the promise was never fulfilled, although to my certain knowledge the request was later made five times. I am not saying this critically. Each time it came we were just entering the threes of some new reorganization, and no individual preference can be respected in a war. I mention it only because the disappointment that it entailed caused me to abandon my twenty-year army career as soon as the war was over.

Late in 1917, a commission as brigadier general was offered me as Deputy Provost Marshal General. I was thirty-five years

old and less than nine months before I had been a first lieutenant (acting captain), and this was unusual promotion, but I
relinquished it in favor of a much older officer, Colonel Kreger,
because I knew another request was coming from General
Pershing, and this proposed Brigadier job would anchor me
to a Washington desk for "the duration."

I might better have taken the rank. Three months later General March sent for me and told me he was going to change my
colonel's eagles to stars and appoint me in charge of Army
Purchase in place of General Pierce. I told him my story about
General Pershing, that I knew nothing about industry, and that
I did not want the job. He assured me that I would do what I
was told to do—which was obvious—but he softened the blow
by saying that he was not going to sit in a chair when a war was
going on, and that when he got things going here he would take
me with him back to France. I had been surfeited with similar
promises, but there was nothing for me to do. That afternoon I
had a letter from the President asking me to represent the War
Department on the War Industries Board and the next morning
I met a man who was to become closer to me than anybody—
Bernie Baruch, to whom the President had just given unlimited
powers for the mobilization of American industry and for the
coördination of all public and Allied purchasing programs and
the protection of the civilian population.

The President's letter follows:

THE WHITE HOUSE
WASHINGTON

*May 14, 1918.*

*My dear General Johnson:*

The Secretary of War having recommended to me that I designate
you as the representative of the War Department upon the War
Industries Board in succession to Brigadier-General Palmer E.
Pierce, who has been sent on foreign service, I take pleasure in desig-
nating you for such duty and desire that you report to Mr. Baruch,
Chairman, War Industries Board at your earliest convenience.

Very sincerely yours,
[s] WOODROW WILSON.

Brigadier-General Hugh S. Johnson, N.A.
Office of the Chief of Staff,
War Department,
Washington, D. C.

General Goethals, who had been recalled from retirement to be Quartermaster General and who had masterfully put that department in order, was to be my immediate boss in the War Department as Chief of Purchase, Storage, and Traffic. I was to be chief of the Division of Army Purchase, but in my functions on the War Industries Board I was independent of anybody in the Army—even the Chief of Staff—reporting directly to Mr. Baruch. Thus I was directly concerned with the whole problem of mobilizing American Industry for war. But it was not a perfect organizational set-up, and it sowed seeds of trouble. Both General Goethals and Mr. Stettinius occupied positions senior to mine in the War Department and General March was not of a temperament to welcome extraneous control. He was a twentieth century Richelieu, and all one has to do is to read his book to be sure of it. Yet while I was subordinate to him in the War Department, the Board of which I was a member could give that Department instructions—not so hot!

The supply situation was as nearly a perfect mess as can be imagined. There were at first five, and later nine, separate purchasing agencies embarked on what was planned to be a thirty-billion dollar program. Nobody knew what sized army they were buying for. Each bureau had its own buying program, no two were the same and no one was the right one. Yet when a soldier went over the top, his clothing must come from one of these, his equipment from another, his first aid kit from another, his gas mask from another, and so on throughout the whole category of his supplies. In the markets, these bureaus were competing with each other ruthlessly for price, facilities, transportation, and delivery. They so clogged up the efficient factories and the whole industrial region north of the Potomac and east of the Alleghenies that they practically paralyzed them by shortages of labor, fuel, raw material, power, and transportation. It seemed a hopeless tangle.

In order to place and provide for the long-range program of raw materials and facilities, the War Industries Board simply had to have a statement of gross requirements, and these departments could not furnish it. It was absolutely necessary for that Board to forecast some kind of a supply program to parallel the manpower program, but there was no supply program to give them. The bottleneck upon which all this depended was available overseas shipping. I thought this was my first job, and we started to work on it at once. I knew that I did not know enough about industry then to approach that task, but kindly Fortune sent me just then one of the ablest industrialists in the country. I secured the services as assistant of Gerard Swope, now President of the General Electric Company, then Vice-President of the Western Electric Company. He put his finger on the limiting factor, which was ships, and we began at once to try to work out a program of supply on that basis. A considerably increased tonnage of ships had been released by the Allies, by the Dutch and by charter arrangements with other countries.

In the meantime, we began to consolidate the purchase of every item procured in more than one bureau in that single one of the bureaus that was best fitted to handle it. Generals Pershing, Moseley, and Dawes were able to do this job easily in France, because they were three thousand miles from political Washington and had plenary authority. It was a very different thing at home, partly because the program was many times larger, but chiefly because we were at the seat of political government and these reforms trod on the toes of bureaus, some of which were a century old and all of which were as jealous as the diplomatic corps of their protocol, prerogatives, and functions. Somehow it was done, but not without agonized writhings and enmities, some of which have never entirely disappeared.

The tentative supply program on which we were working caused even more trouble. While it was still in a purely formative state General March, by accident, saw it in Assistant Secretary Crowell's office, and he hit the ceiling. He sent for me, and asked me if I thought I was running the Army. That shocked me like a bolt from the blue. I did not even know what he meant then, and I do not now. I only know that it caused a row that finally required the Secretary of War and the Chief of the War Industries Board to settle, and that the Chief of Staff took that document into his custody and did not release it to supply departments for weeks, during which time the supply situation descended into confusion worse confounded.

As the summer advanced it was so badly unbalanced that just to take up cargo space we were shipping incomplete parts of things, the complements of which might not reach France until weeks later. It is my recollection that although we did send ample steel and semi-finished products abroad, yet for all the hundreds of millions we spent for artillery ammunition, no American-made high explosive shell was fired on the Western Front, and only some ten thousand rounds of shrapnel. Regardless of the fact that we were the greatest manufacturers of motor trucks, the supply of trucks for the Argonne offensive gave out completely, and the lines of communication were clogged with wrecks with nothing to replace them—a condition which would have probably stopped our advance had the Armistice been delayed. The airplanes with which we were to "darken the skies" over the Western Front never even speckled it. The artillery program for which we had built and contracted factories galore materialized only in parts. We bought most of our effective guns in France and England. Finally General Pershing cabled back that if he could not get the supplies he had requisitioned when, where and as he wanted them, the American advance would have to stop—a cable which was not disclosed to the responsible War Industries Board, and was discovered by accident days later by Bernie Baruch, who promptly began to make the fur fly.

In the meantime, General Goethals called me into his office one evening and in his usual chuckling way—nothing ever fazed that grand old Roman—confidentially commiserated me on the fact that he and General March were sailing next day for France—leaving me, he said, to hold the bag—he to take General Harbord's place in S.O.S. and General March for some unspecified job—presumably Pershing's. That trip never started because somebody prevented it but at one time it certainly was so imminent that Goethals had packed his bedding roll.

When the War Industries Board swung into real action after Baruch had been given real coördinating authority, some order began to appear. In August, I went on an inspection trip to every industrial center. It revealed one thing clearly—that if someone with ultimate and instant authority to straighten out messes in the field—right on the ground—were to retrace my route, hundreds of bottlenecks to production could be immediately broken. B. M. Baruch at once dispatched George Peek, Gerard Swope and, I believe, General Williams, to do just that and they did it with a vengeance.

It is not serving the public interest to withhold the observation that the American Army Supply System just didn't work. It didn't work because there was no proper coördination and organization of purchase bureaus. I can say this because part of that coördination was my own responsibility. I have often reflected that in the organization of the whole nation for the draft, starting with nothing, we turned in an almost perfect job, but that in the reorientation of an existing "going system," we never really rang the bell. The cause is not far to seek—the tremendous tenacity of life of a government bureau. The draft system was a temporary emergency improvisation, and we did it mostly with kids. There was no hierarchy or vested rights in federal functions. The supply system was just a cluster of jealous and ancient bureaus. They fought the exterior control of the War Industries Board at every step, even after we had contrived a plan of integration that put their men in control of practically every economic unit. We did, by major assault, concentrate purchase activities in single units, but as soon as the war was over the old chambered nautilus is back just where it was before Sarajevo; and there methinks it will remain in spite of hell and high-water.

The War Industries Board between March and September, 1918, after Baruch was given real authority, whipped the production channels into line. The great masses of army material at last began to flow through the production lines and if, as everybody expected, the war had gone into 1919, we could have deluged Europe with metal, gas, and explosives. The War Industries Board had kept up and increased the tremendous supply of our Allies and added our own almost equal requirements for war material. It had protected the civilian population, checked the mad up-swing of prices and finally placed so firm a hand on the whole industrial system that it was prepared to disgorge in 1919 enough war material to supply a much larger army than we formed. That experience gave us as intimate a view of the fundamental pattern of American industry as it had ever been given to any group to enjoy. It brought us into close contact with all industrial leaders. It was such an experience of how to do what had to be done, as is vouchsafed to few.

From that experience I went away with one outstanding lesson burned into my brain—governmental emergency operations are entirely different from routine governmental operations. This country is so vast in every aspect that when any central authority steps in to control or direct its economic forces, coördination of such efforts is the principal problem. Lack of it is so dangerous that it may completely frustrate the almost unlimited power of this country.

We repeated the early war mistakes in the Recovery Program. It was not coördinated in the beginning and it is not coördinated now. One effort tends to cancel another and, until this condition is cured, we are pretty apt not to make our billions of spending fully effective. It is the crying need of this moment.

Yet let no one belittle the accomplishments of American Industrial and Manpower Mobilization of the Great War. Coördination began to come when the President on March 4, 1918, made the War Industries Board the real control agency of industrial mobilization.

We came into the war separated by 3,000 miles of sea water from the scene of action. The Germans did not consider us important except as a financial Santa Claus to the Allies, because they did not regard successful mobilization by us as possible and the Allies thought much the same thing. No major overseas operation had ever been conducted so far from base.

The Central Powers were coming to a new peak of strength. Ludendorff said of the condition of January 1, 1918—"We had never been so strong in comparison with our enemies." Their submarines had sunk 3,000,000 tons of Allied shipping. In the first quarter of 1917 they destroyed 2,000,000 tons, 800,000 tons in April alone. Great Britain had only 6,000,000 tons available. In October, 1917, Caporetto made Italy a military liability. Mackensen had wiped out Roumania as a war factor. The *Gallipoli* attempt had failed. Russia was out. The war had a distinct cast of German victory. The Allies had passed the peak of their man power, and exhausted their credit for munitions here.

Five days after the declaration of war there was introduced in the House a bill authorizing $5,000,000,000 for our Allies—eventually we loaned them a total of $12,000,000 for war purposes alone. In actual out payments on account of war we spent $49,000,000,000. The net war cost to us was $36,000,000,000. In the fiscal year 1918 alone we planned to spend $24,000,000,-000 and would have spent more had the war not ended in November.

General Pershing sailed on May 28, 1917. Within a few days he cabled for 1,000,000 men and asked for preparation for

3,000,000 more in anticipation of a 1919 campaign—which would have required, with replacement and troops in training, 5,000,000 men as a total.

On May 18, Congress authorized us to register 10,000,000 for the draft, and we did it within 17 days. Eventually we enrolled 25,000,000 men for possible service, and at the date of the Armistice had nearly 5,000,000 men under arms, with 1,500,000 fully qualified and ready for call to the colors.

These men were made available without great harm to industry by close coöperation between the Provost Marshal General's office and B. M. Baruch on the War Industries Board.

We called to the colors and absorbed 1,000,000 men in 90 days and in one month alone—400,000 men. We stepped our overseas shipments up from 70,000 a month to 300,000 a month.

With a very small ship-building capacity at the beginning, we increased it 10 times in 10 months and, at the end, it equaled the *ship-building capacity of all the rest of the world combined.* From a nine months' average time for building a 3,500 ton ship we so speeded production that we once turned out a 12,500 ton ship in 28 days—60 days became standard. We actually built 10,000,000 tons of ocean going shipping—nearly twice the available shipping of Great Britain in the first quarter of 1917.

Nobody has ever adequately appraised the Herculean job General Pershing did in France. He practically reconstructed the harbors of the southern ports and constructed a railroad system clear across France to the American lines on the northeast salient. He did the greatest supply and organization job in the war. He commanded 2,000,000 men with great distinction and there is no blot of error or disaster on his record. We have not sufficiently honored that man.

We cut 17 days from the experienced turn-around for cargo ships and absorbed all the available shipping of the maritime world.

Under Mr. Hoover, in face of a short crop, we fed our Allies. Clemenceau once said, "In 18 months the United States sent us 5,000,000 tons of food and fed 12,000,000 Frenchmen for a year and a half!"

Our industries supplied our own country, our armies, and our Allies with all the raw material that was required for victory, and under the most difficult conditions increased that supply in an ever-growing flood.

The record is a complete refutation of Mr. Lloyd George's criticism that "Wilson made war timidly."

There has been nothing like it in the history of this world. It was a great schooling for the new national effort of which NRA was a part.

We didn't sufficiently honor Baruch, Crowder, Pershing or Harbord. We don't honor performance. In England they would be dukes or something—but imagine anybody trying to pin the title of "Duke of Missouri" on Jack Pershing or "Marquis of Manhattan, Kansas" on Jimmie Harbord!

# Chapter XI

# THE PATHFINDER DIVISION

---

"The King of France went up the hill with twenty thousand men.
The King of France came down the hill and ne'er went up again."
*—Pigges Corantoe.*

---

IN THE meantime, my chance came. General Pershing had asked for me again. General March wanted to see the last of me. Bernie Baruch had promised to let me go when I could show him a successor he could accept, and I now had Gerard Swope. I will never forget the day I went to "the Chief," as everybody still calls Bernie, and said, "I've got the man who can fill my place a lot better than I ever did." I did not need to expand on his industrial attainments, but there were other considerations. Could a civilian work with the military? "Oh," but I said, "Gerard is a diplomat—suave, smooth, discerning." "That's right," said Bernie, "Gerard is so suave and smooth and discerning that he could seduce a house-fly—I guess he can handle the Army."

There was a vacancy in a Brigadier General's command in the Eighth Division, then under immediate orders to proceed from the camp at Palo Alto, California, to embark for France. I took the next train after my assignment and arrived at my station—*with flu*. I was the senior Brigadier and so my brigade was slated to entrain first. This misfortune deferred it five days. The other infantry brigade went first instead and got to France. I was left in command of the bulk of the Division but those five days were fatal.

I got the rest of the Division aboard troop trains finally, but news from overseas was not encouraging for active service. I have a letter in my files from my friend General Harbord written early in October in response to one of mine expressing a belief that there would be no 1919 campaign, and that my chance for active service was over. As late as that he scouted the idea and he knew as much about the military situation as anybody. But the late news did not bear that out. The Austrian front had crumbled. The Germans might resist behind the Rhine, but what Ludendorff called their "home front" was breaking to pieces. The country no longer supported the war.

I have never in my service seen such troops as the Eighth Division, and especially my own brigade. It was a Regular Army Division—one of the first formed and ironically enough called the "Pathfinder" Division.

But it blazed no path to France. After an unusually complete and extended training and just as it was ready to sail, the necessity arose for troops for the unfortunate and futile Siberian expedition. Many of these were taken by drafts from the Eighth which unfitted it for embarkation to France until it should be again recruited and trained. But this process enabled company commanders to retain their best men and to hand-pick the replacements. The result was the tallest and most physically perfect soldiers I have ever seen and an officers' corps perhaps more fully trained than that of any division in the Army. Their divisional song was a parody on "Over There," viz.:

> *"On our bunks we're sitting,*
> *Doing our knitting*
> *Dropping stitches everywhere.*
> *And we swear, we declare,*
> *That when it's over, the war's all over,*
> *Col. Dead-Eye Dick[1] will lead us over there."*

They did not know how accurate the prophecy would be. (The other Brigade arrived after the Armistice and was in the Army of Occupation.) Their hopes had been so long deferred and so frequently disappointed that their eagerness amounted to scarcely repressed fervor. There couldn't have been more realistic bayonet work—a form of military exercise which involves growling, grimacing, and a sort of self-exaltation approaching frenzy. The Germans taught us those dramatics and the performance of troops at this was supposed to be some index of their state of mind toward combat. If that is correct these men were Berserks.

We got them to Camp Mills on Long Island, and finally to Hoboken and aboard a convoy of transports. It was a strange

[1]Referring to a one-eyed officer whom they didn't much like.

fleet—new ships with super-structure incomplete and decks mere staging. It was some ghastly blunder. This was a fleet not yet ready and really bound for Halifax to be completed. We were recalled and sent back to camp. A day or two later we embarked again. It was the day of the "fake armistice." Once more we were ordered back to camp. We marched in at 1 A.M. in a drenching rain. The straw tent floors had all been taken up, leaving a sea of mud. I heard a man in a signal battalion bellow out, "*So this is Paris.*"

Three times this march up the hill and down again happened. Then came the true Armistice. I shan't forget that night. The men had been in quarantine against flu for weeks. They were West Coast boys and most of them had never seen New York. They had been bitterly disappointed. I expected discipline to dissolve. I decided to address them and tell them that an armistice was only a truce and that I had just come from the General Staff and would see that they got to France in any event. There were about twenty thousand of them and we could only get four thousand at a time into the auditorium. We scheduled the audience in five relays. When I stood up before the first relay to speak my piece a ghastly sensation came across the footlights. *These men didn't want to go to France.* They knew the war was over even if I didn't. They were respectful, even indulgent, and gave me a faint and ailing cheer, but that pep-talk of mine was the sickliest thing I have ever heard. We got that first relay out of there as soon as we could and stopped the rest—and the bayonet stuff next day! The fine Berserk frenzy had vanished like water on a red-hot stove. The men went through the motions with about as much fierceness and *élan* as wet wash on a clothesline in a slight breeze.

Then we embarked, but only to go to Newport News and Camp Lee at Petersburg, Virginia, where I took command of some sixty thousand similarly disappointed and disillusioned warriors awaiting demobilization.

In going over the organization at Camp Lee, the military intelligence officer told me of the case of a prisoner in the Bull Pen under the alias of Hirshbergh who had been an associate of Trotsky and whose sentence of ten years in Atlanta for draft desertion, criminal syndicalism, and a score of other offenses was on my desk. His dossier showed him to be a graduate of the University of Jena with doctor's degrees from two other universities.

By some underground telegraphy he knew everything that was going on and, altogether, it was a most interesting history.

I sent for him and he came in chains, guarded by two sentries —sullen and with arms folded as military convicts were required to stand. In those days a General in command of so many troops was surrounded with as much formality as a king. Against the protest of the guard, I ordered him unshackled, asked him to sit down, and ordered the guard out. He was as fine a specimen as I ever saw—classic features, and a body like the Discus thrower. He told me a great deal about the theory of communism, but the striking thing was his reply when I asked him how, in the then temper of the United States, there was any chance for such a movement.

"Did you ever see in a sunbeam, in a wood on a still and sultry day, millions of midges hovering in a swarm?"

"Yes."

"Did you ever see them suddenly move over to one side or the other, say three feet—all preserving the same distance and relative position?"

"Yes."

"What made them do that?"

"Well, a breeze perhaps."

"I said, a *still* day—but did you ever see them move back after just a few minutes?"

I was very clear as to that.

"Well, what made them do that? I'll tell you. There are mass movements in human psychology—just as there are inexplicable mass movements in all sorts of life."

He cited the migration of ocean eels and salmon and seals— the great tribal movements of the barbarian invasions and made a persuasive case that such a movement toward Communism might occur here or anywhere else at any time. It was not very circumstantial, but it was a striking thought.

Demobilization was a sickly job. It was there that I confirmed my opinion that my active military career was over. I had spent twenty years from the age of sixteen trying to learn to be a soldier. My kid brother, who had never even seen a soldier in his life, after two months' service, was carrying messages as a staff officer into the beleaguered machine gun garrison on that fateful day at Château Thierry under direct shell-fire, and I hadn't heard a shot fired in anger. All I had done was to sit around officers' clubs and hear other men talk about struggles fierce and wild against plains Indians, Spaniards in Cuba, and gu-gus in the Philippines. I determined not to suffer that again about the World War. I was wrong about that—not more than 40 or 50% of regular officers got to France.

I went to Washington to help General Crowder liquidate the draft and to get records together for Bernie Baruch's final report, but in a few weeks I resigned. I had been offered very remunerative employment by several large industrial companies, but I was too bewildered and sick at heart to have enough interest to make a decision. I went down to a quiet place on the Delaware beach near where this book is being written, to lie on the sand and try, if possible, to get my bearings, just as I am doing now after a somewhat similar whirling experience 15 years later.

There was only one interesting interlude which bears on the main subject of this book. Of the War Industries Board, Bernie Baruch said, "It's a dead cock in the pit. Let's turn industry absolutely free. Everything that made us possible is gone—the war-spirit of coöperation and sacrifice—the vast purchasing power of government—the scant legal authority we have had— and the support of public opinion."

But there were others who felt that the sudden post-war business paralysis could be avoided by "self-government in industry under government supervision," a clear forerunner of NRA. The President actually appointed an "Industrial Board of the Department of Commerce." George Peek was literally drafted to head it, and I acted as his General Counsel. We began at once to consult with the steel and other industries to agree on a stable and much reduced price level. We even got an agreement with the steel people which was preserved by them for years. But it suited my friend Carter Glass, the Secretary of the Treasury and in charge of railroad purchases, no better than its inheritor (NRA) suited him, and it blew up when the President agreed with him.

Mark Requa (war-time Oil Administrator) and I worked hard on an NRA idea in those bewildered times, but it was all vanity and vexation of spirit. It was necessary for me then as it is now to forget the great national effort and my part in it and go back to work to earn a prosaic living.

The night we got off the ships after the fake armistice was

signed, I turned my face to the wall of my little shack at Camp Mills and bawled like a baby for the frustration of twenty years of hope for a military career—and began to wonder if this was not the end of that chapter. A few weeks later, I threw those twenty years of training and service over my shoulder and in February resigned from the Army at the age of 36 to start all over again without the slightest idea of what I could or would attempt to do to earn a living.

# Chapter XII

# SWORDS TO PLOWSHARES

---

"... unmerciful disaster
Followed fast and followed faster."
—*The Raven—Poe.*

---

THE men on the War Industries Board became very close
friends. Especially George Peek and I, who had worked on its
reorganization for industrial mobilization, seemed to chum together pretty well. He also had been offered flattering posts,
among them the presidency of several of the country's most important corporations. He had made his success in the farm implement business, of which Moline, Illinois, is the chief center.
But he didn't want to go back to that. He had his eye on something else.

John Willys was at the climax of the mushroom growth of
his many ventures. In some form or other his various direct or
auxiliary companies at that time took tribute from every automobile made in the United States. But there was no cohesion
or organization whatever among this great cluster of manufacturing corporations. George wanted the job of supplying that
lack, and he thought he had some sort of understanding with
John Willys about it. But John (foreseeing too far the motoriza-
tion of farms) had just bought the old Moline Plow Company—
which George had known very well for years as a competitor—
and his advice to Mr. Willys was that it was a terrible lemon,
that on conservative accounting it had not made money for
years, and that it was still slipping fast. This alarmed Mr.
Willys and he asked George, as a first step in his more ambitious
schemes, to go out there and see just how bad the ruin was. This
George did—and took me with him as assistant and general
counsel—in September, 1919.

We started to make an investigation of that company, but
it was no easy thing. It required a reconstruction of the books

for ten years past and a complete overhauling of a sprawling organization with 23 branches in all parts of the United States. In the meanwhile, the post-war inflation boom was carrying its business to peaks it had never known before. It was entirely inadequately financed to carry this business, but Mr. Willys wanted to expand it as rapidly as possible and assured George he could have all the money he needed for that purpose. We went booming ahead on borrowed money through 1920 and right up to the cataclysm of 1921.

During the period of westward expansion, while the farm implement business had ups and downs, it was among the most stable in the country. There were always new farms and vast areas to be equipped. There was a constant replacement business from the east. There were never any disastrous years.

But all this had changed during the years before the war. There were no vast new farm areas. Agriculture was in the grip of a creeping decline when the war gave it one final and potent shot in the arm. But when the collapse of post-war inflation came in 1921, the hardest hit industry in the country was agriculture and the next was the farm implement industry. That collapse was no respecter of persons. It caught everybody and everything. It caught John Willys and blew up the vast financing of the proposed new and enormous "Willys Corporation," and on this he had relied to keep the Moline Plow Company afloat. It caught that company with a new, heavy high-priced inventory, an enormous debt, and a portfolio full of farm paper that had always theretofore been regarded as "sound as wheat in the mill," but which now turned into worthless chaff by millions.

It was a catastrophe, and at the bottom was the almost utter collapse of agriculture itself. George came to a typical conclusion: "There can't be any business for us until the farmer is on his feet. There is nothing we can do here—let's find out what is the matter with agriculture."

We spent a year on that job and jointly wrote a pamphlet called, "Equality for Agriculture." In simplest terms it proposed to remove the agricultural surplus from the domestic market, sell it abroad for what it would bring, thus permitting the tariff to protect American prices for domestic consumption, and then to spread the loss on the surplus over the whole crop by means of an equalization fee—all of which would have elevated the *average* price considerably. It was based on a proposition to restore the pre-war parity of farm purchasing power. It was the essence of the McNary-Haugen Bill, which was passed twice by Congress and twice vetoed, and if there has been a single argument ever advanced in the long campaign for farm relief from that date to this that was not contained and discussed in that document, it has not been called to my attention, and I do not believe that it exists.

We took it to Washington in the early days of Harding, and sold it lock, stock, and barrel to the elder Wallace, Secretary of Agriculture. We advised him to call a conference of leading bankers and industrialists, which he did. Some of them, and I can name Jim Bell, Fred Wells, and Ogden Armour, became convinced of the practicability and necessity of that plan. I understood Charlie Dawes also to approve it. But we made the mistake of taking it also to Herbert Hoover, who was intent on building export trade and would consider nothing that would raise the cost of American industrial products. He collared these converts and turned them "about-face." Although Secretary Wallace had specifically requested that everybody come back with his own opinion and that discussion by groups be postponed, Mr. Hoover had sent for Julius Barnes, who controlled the conference and led it into a caucus for the purpose of condemning the whole idea. He was in the export grain trade. They came back to that conference with Julius Barnes as their spokesman and damned that plan from cover to cover. Not so, however, Otto Kahn, who thought that it ought to be tried, and B. M. Baruch who, as a shrewd trader and elder economic statesman, believed that it offered power enough if capably administered to sustain the purchasing power of American farm products. It would have worked then when we still had an export market for farm products.

We then suggested a conference of economists. This conference generally approved the basic idea. Over this issue Mr. Wallace and Mr. Hoover clashed.

Congress had just completed an extensive study of the cause of agricultural depression, conducted by Congressman Sidney Anderson. He was also chairman of a great convention of farmers, industrialists, bankers, and labor leaders on the same subject, called by President Harding in fulfillment of campaign pledges. We went to Mr. Anderson with this discussion of the effect of the tariff in view of surplus production on agriculture which had been carefully omitted from his Congressional study. Of course, whatever one might think of the particular plan we proposed, the export surplus was the *only* controlling fact in the problem of farm distress. He frankly told us that if we tried to raise this point in that convention, he would steam-roller us— all of which he faithfully and artistically did.

But it takes more than that to stop George Peek. He never did stop. He took up the cause of farm relief or "Equality for Agriculture" sunk his teeth in it, spent largely of his own fortune and all his time for twelve years of bitter battle. I do not know his equal for tenacity. George supported Al Smith on that issue. He did more to deliver the rock-ribbed Republican States of the Mississippi Valley to Franklin Roosevelt on that issue than any other ten men in or out of politics. He stayed by the Congressional battle in every session. He piloted the McNary-Haugen Bill through two defeats and two victories, and he did more to secure farm cohesion on the Adjustment Act than did anyone else. If anybody is entitled to be called the Father of Farm Relief, George Peek is the man.

When the Moline Plow situation had come by sad stages to the point of inevitable liquidation, George could not bring himself to assent. He resigned and left the salvage job to me.

My seven years with the Moline Plow Company were simply seven years of unrelieved hell and disappointment—a seven years' fight to save a company doomed to destruction from the first day we saw it—doomed as well by its own financial weakness as by its economic circumstance. It was in the hands of creditors at all times after 1922, one reorganization following another, receivership hanging over it always, and liquidation inevitable after the first brave attempt of its bankers to save it.

By my side throughout this whole seven years of desperate fighting was Robert W. Lea—as loyal, honest and able a man as ever trod shoe leather. I have never been in any big industrial job of single responsibility that he was not with me. He was President of the Implement Company and took Dudley Cates' place as my NRA "Assistant for Industry." When I think of the sincerity and devotion of Bob Lea, it does not seem possible that there can be in the world such meanness and furtiveness and self-serving scheming as I have on some occasions encountered elsewhere.

I learned about bankers from this experience. The Old Moline Plow Company's list of creditors might have served for a Who's Who in Banking in America. There were seventeen of them—the cream of the lot. Their interests were finally centered with the Chicago First National Bank. The old wheeze about the borrower who could tell the banker's glass eye from his good one because of a slight gleam of human sympathy in the former certainly did not apply to *that* management. Frank Wetmore was the President. He was a very Ulysses of his craft—a great banker who never made any money himself because he thought his job a trust. He treated me as a father would. I always thought that the Moline fiasco hastened his end. Mel Traylor and Ned Brown were his principal aids and both have distinguished themselves throughout this depression by courage, ability and a fine sense of public responsibility. Only Ned Brown—Edward Eagle Brown is left of that devoted trio. If I wanted the most competent, distinguished and disinterested advice and help in working out the banking problem in America I know just where I would go to find it and it wouldn't be in Wall Street. I'd wire for Ned Brown to take the next airplane.

There is probably no more complex manufacturing and distributing business than that of farm implements. This is because of the enormous diversity of product, the rapid shift of demand depending on crops and seasons, the bucolic character of the distributing organization, the primitive state of the intermediate credit system as applied to farm implements, and the savagery of competition throughout the field.

When you add to these natural and normal difficulties of the business the burden of trying to operate a great concern with the hot breath of the sheriff on your neck night and day for seven years, it may not be pleasant, but it is an industrial, financial and commercial schooling which (as Frank Wetmore once said to me) no man could get in forty years of normal business experience.

There was one pleasant aspect—and, as I recall it, only one—and that was the labor relationship. Plow manufacture is a craft. There are no blue prints to guide the shaping of a plow. Just what warped surface will make it bite into different types of soil and level off to do its work derives from no mathematical formula yet discovered, but from craftsmanship. The earliest artisans came from Sweden to Moline and the craft was handed down in home-owning families, proud of their art. There were sometimes three generations working in the same shop. During my entire time at Moline there was never a complaint from the men. One operator of a drop forge earned as much as fifty-six dollars a day, and people used to come from afar to observe his skill. When the shops, for the first time in their history, were practically dry of production and Moline got its first real dose of stark unemployment, the employed in our company, from the president down, contributed ten per cent of their gross income to feed, shelter, and warm their comrades, who were out of work. That was an unemployment relief plan which worked at least to the extent of preventing suffering.

After George Peek left, we undertook a bold plan. We closed and sold out every shop and branch that had not operated at a profit. We threw ruthlessly out of our catalogue any implement that had not been sold at a profit. We concentrated every effort on sales in the southern hemisphere—Argentina and South Africa—in order to straighten out and make equable our highly seasonal production curve and give employment all year around. We reduced our number of types and styles to a starvation minimum. We restricted our field of business to an area within one thousand miles of the main factory. To this we added the most daring policy of all—we would only sell in carloads or half carloads and only for spot cash. In this way we saved so much in cost of distribution and loss in manufacture that we were able to advertise that *we would sell at ten per cent less than the best cash and quantity deal of any competitor.* The saving really amounted *to more than fifteen per cent* to merchants on the usual terms of the bulk of their purchases.

The whole implement industry regarded this as sheer madness. Implements had never been sold on a "Short-line." You had to sell *all* implements or none to give your dealers an all-year business. You couldn't sell from the factory, because you had to give "service" to farm implements, etc. That kind of advice frightened me, but we were at the end of our rope. With us it was "root, hog, or die." We rooted.

From the sales of discarded plants and inventories we had been able to make substantial payments on the long-over-due debts of the old company. That meant scrapping a promising automobile subsidiary, selling a fine modern tractor plant, disposing of a great eastern harvester factory, eliminating a wagon line and, in fact, decimating a great and very old general-line implement company. I went abroad and tried to sell the harvester business in France, and to negotiate a continuing business with Russia, but all I got out of that was a good look at French industrial methods and an introduction to the Soviet business régime. The unit of the old company we had left we capitalized at only three million dollars—thirty thousand non-par shares—on assets of which nothing was cash, but neither was there any debt. The bankers wanted to sell this little unit, but could not get a bid in real money.

I was so sure that I could make it go, in spite of dire predictions of disaster (and even charges of mental unbalance for proposing such a plan) that I got some friends who had confidence in me to make available one million five hundred thousand dollars. Then we offered the creditors either their share of the whittled-down company in stock, or cash at fifty dollars a share. Over ninety per cent of them took cash, and we were on the spot on our own responsibility and in the last ditch. I gave every key man a share in our potential profits, if our plan should work. The total of these shares I gave away was three times anything I could hope to gain for myself. But this was a desperate chance and I thought that each deserved an opportunity for modest competence if we could win with it. They all went at it in a kind of Berserk frenzy—*and it worked*.

We began to make money and pile up cash from the very first month, and we kept on making and piling up cash. The simple control and accounting system devised by Alvin Brown was one of the quickest, best and most accurate that I have seen anywhere. The little new company made money every year for four years, and its balance sheet began to look more like that of a bank than of an industrial company.

The organization was working so well that I began to have a great deal of leisure. The Attorney General of Illinois appointed me as Special Assistant to represent the state of Illinois in the long-drawn-out Lake Levels case—seven states against five in the original jurisdiction of the Supreme Court—an experience I enjoyed more than anything else in that dreary period.

It was a case resting on engineering rather than law, and I spent a year studying lake-transportation, sewage disposal and the hydrology and hydrography of the Great Lakes and Mississippi systems. My partner in that litigation was Cy Dietz, a former football star at Northwestern—a character known and loved throughout the state of Illinois. He was as near and dear to me as a brother. He was killed in a riding accident while serving on the Illinois Supreme Court.

I had begun to do a few special jobs for Mr. Baruch—examining companies in which he had been asked to invest. That kind of work attracted me. On the first three jobs I did for him —concerning highly propagandized companies of very large capitalization—I had the good luck to call the turn of their sorry future with at least the accuracy of the Prophet Isaiah.

Then B. M. asked me to come to New York and associate myself with him—a thing I wanted to do not only out of my love for him, but because the work was of a kind that I preferred above everything. Chicago and Illinois had just won the Lake Levels case before Special Master Charles Evans Hughes—it was later reversed in the Supreme Court. There seemed a good prospect of selling the Moline Implement Company. I was more free than I had been for a long time. I jumped at the chance and came to New York. That was in the fall of 1927.

## Chapter XIII

# BARUCH, AL SMITH, AND THE COMING OF THE DELUGE

"There is something rotten in the State of Denmark."
—*Haml.t—Shakespeare.*

A GREAT many skilled observers and clever writers have tried to give the public a trustworthy impression of Bernie Baruch. I have seen none succeed, and I am not going to try. I once heard a famous portrait painter say that he could not do it even with a brush and paints on canvas, because of the infinite variety and shades of expression constantly flitting across that aesthetic mobile face.

He is the most faithful, kindly, and considerate man I ever knew. Nearly all the people who serve him have been with him twenty years and many of them thirty. At his South Carolina home a whole negro village has lived for thirty years on his bounty.

Of all who owed the most outstanding war positions to their associations with Woodrow Wilson, he and Cary Grayson remained actively faithful in word and deed throughout the great President's life and, after his death, to his memory. Not one word of Bernie's generous bounties is ever permitted the public. He is not, as is commonly supposed, one of the country's very wealthy men. In nearly all his *grands coups*, like the industrial development of Texas Gulf Sulphur, he has "carried" to comfortable affluence many people on a pure basis of friendship. In his buying and selling of stock he operated alone—never in a pool. He bought what he bought outright, and I can say as absolute fact that after the war he did it chiefly because he liked to use his undoubted genius for trading,—now he does not even do that. He is "out of the market" and has no further interest in making or amassing money.

All of this brings up the question in everybody's mind—what is this genius? That is a question to which, after a closer association with him than any other contemporary has had, I do not know the answer. For the processes of his judgment are apparently *not* analytical. It is true that he is the keenest observer I know—almost clairvoyant. From the expression of a man's face and his approach to his subject, Bernie gets that man's number at once and nearly always with complete accuracy.

When you sit down to explain something to him, you will be sure to find him coming in with a question which anticipates your discourse. He is away ahead of you. He is a very poor expositor himself because his racing mind always outruns his expression and because he assumes in his listener a basic knowledge or an apprehension of the subject equal to his own— and not one out of a hundred has it. Herbert Hoover once said that he liked to advise with Bernie because of the swift directness with which his mind goes to the heart of a project, but that he is the most inarticulate smart man he ever knew.

Bernie's judgments come forth spontaneously like lightning with no supporting brief of argument, and often he could not make such a brief even afterward. I have known only one other mind like his, and that was General Goethals'. Both would sit and listen intently for awhile—both would interrupt with a spontaneous answer and in a great majority of cases both would be surprisingly near the truth.

Of course it is neither intuition nor instinct. I think it is a subconscious, or at least an unconscious process of reasoning with lightning rapidity. Both men were markedly ruminative— sitting for long periods of time in silence and, as I conjecture, letting their minds roam freely over all aspects of a general situation so that when some particular phase of it is presented as a problem, the solution of it springs fully developed out of some unobtrusive brain cell where it may have been stored for weeks. Of course, there is also stored there as varied an experience under heavy responsibility as comes to any man and a very large gleaning from constant reading and study and writing in the field of world and national economics.

I know what the guiding impulse of Bernie's life is now, even if he doesn't and even if nobody will believe me. It is pure, unselfish and self-effacing public service. He does not want office. I know that he was twice offered and twice declined the portfolio of the Treasury under Woodrow Wilson. I know that many of his powerful friends were prepared to insist on it being again offered to him by Roosevelt, and that he forbade them with language no less unequivocal than General Sherman's, "If nominated I will not accept; if elected I will not serve"—which always seemed to me considerably less enigmatic than "I do not choose to run."

When Mr. Wilson brought him to Washington during the war everybody said, "He is just a Wall Street gambler." But he was very much more than that. He probably knew more about railroads and non-ferrous metals than any other man in the country. He had not only foreseen the war but also the necessity for a vast industrial mobilization to an extent nobody else had imagined. He also had a fine sense of public morals and obligation. Knowing that he was to be brought into contact with industry, he liquidated his entire interest in industry and put most of the avails into Liberty Bonds. He closed up his business and got out and stayed out of the market.

Once, before he joined the government, when the Germans had just sunk another American ship and there was a violent flurry in the market, a "leak" from the White House was suspected, and Baruch was questioned by a Senate Committee (figures apocryphal) thus:

"They say you made a million dollars."

"Oh no I didn't; I made *five* millions"—and then, in the gasp of astonishment which followed, that quiet cool voice went on: "but you don't know me very well, I see—if I had known about that news in advance I wouldn't have made five million—I would have made fifty."

When he joined the government, he concentrated everything that was in him on the vital concerns of his country. People soon stopped calling him a Wall Street gambler. They saw with what amazing tact and absence of friction he handled one great problem after another. They saw with what love and loyalty the greatest and the least in the vast organization of the War Industries Board followed his leadership. He has maintained these attachments ever since. At W. I. B. reunions they flock to him from all over the country and for no other reason than to see his luminous figure and to be with him once again.

Finally when he at last took the helm of industrial mobilization with plenary authority from the President, they saw with what lightning rapidity order came out of what had been hopeless chaos and confusion, and that industrial mobilization in America had at last begun to work. That experience, that organization, that method are of the very essence of the background of NRA and NIRA—the basic thought was, if Industry can thus act as a unit for the purposes of war, why cannot it also act as a unit for the purposes of peace?

Bernie Baruch has never ceased to be grateful for that opportunity to serve. He has never lost his boyish pride in the dignity, honor, and trust that came from his ability, public spirit, and patriotism. There has never been any real criticism of that vast administration. To maintain that position, to serve again—not in public office but in any way he can be helpful—is the single guiding principle of his life now.

With these opinions (which I have never changed) I went to work for Bernie, and in the first week, in one of his seemingly clairvoyant flashes, he laid down for me the organic chart for our efforts. It was a prophecy of what was to come and it proved as accurate as a mariner's chart—the inflationary boom, the inevitable collapse, the unbearable burden of the debt structure, the foolishness of foreign loans, their eventual repudiation, and the coming of the deluge. He did not attempt to time it. He said that could not be done, but he gave me two certain criteria.

"Watch automobile sales and the construction figures—this whole false fabric is built on the unprecedented conjunction of these two big credit-inflated booms—when they slide, the whole structure will collapse." I did just what he told me to do as a cat watches a rat hole.

That was why he saved out of the wreck the bulk of what he had, when so many other fortunes vanished.

But in 1928 the time had not yet come. The two critical booms showed no signs of softening. Bernie bought and sold securities with his usual acumen, bought and developed companies—always with his lines of retreat left open and his weather eye on the gathering clouds. I did none of these things, because I did not then know and do not now know anything at all about playing the stock market. He "carried" me in some things in which I made more money than I had ever made in my life. I dropped it later in the Big Smash—not so much in the stock market as in companies I tried to develop and couldn't get out of. But it was very pleasant while it lasted.

Those years with Crowder and B. M. were an education in practical government and economics. In the Selective Draft I had a chance to play on the key-board of state, national, and local government. In the War Industries Board I had an unprecedented glimpse of the very vitals of the American industrial machine and a part in making it work for a great national purpose. But that was a general view. In the Moline Implement Company I had bitter years of intensive education in sole personal responsibility for the financing and operation of a great industrial enterprise. I learned also how to recast, liquidate, reorganize and refinance the same—to deal with overwhelming debt—to escape the sheriff. But with Bernie I had all that and a great deal more. My job was to get into the inside of one great faltering concern after another to try to find out what was the matter with it—or to examine some industrial whited sepulcher to find the dead men's bones and all uncleanliness within and there were plenty of sepulchers in those days.

It was an active and intense existence. It frequently involved long searching studies of some particular industrial art directing experts in an attempt to reach a right conclusion in advance. To mention just a few of these investigations in, or just preceding, my service with B. M. they were: the hydrology of and transportation on the Great Lakes and the practicability of governmentally financed inland waterways; several hydro-electric projects; sanitation and sewerage of great cities; the mechanical retting of flax and the re-creation of an American linen industry; the art of rayon production; artificial refrigeration by the Birdseye and other processes and a new use for dry ice; radio direction finding; color-photography; the production of chromium and high alloy steels; the feasibility of a new great iron and steel combination; the manufacture of non-woven and seamless rubber-backed carpet; air-cooling and conditioning; the manufacture of fertilizer; the commercial practicability of the remarkable adsorptive properties of silica-gel; the distillation and liquefaction of coal; several projected petroleum enterprises; the hydrogenation process of refining crude oil; the moving picture industry; rock asphalt and road material; financing of installment and commercial paper; banking; all forms of transportation; the paper and pulp industry; several department stores; a general survey of distributing systems for farm products; the glass industry and three processes for nonshatterable glass; the publishing industry and the management and liquidation of a trade paper combination; the French process for preventing rust and heating and destruction of cereals in storage; a new process for food preservation without vitamin destruction and the manufacture and sale of soft drinks. This list is only partial but it includes those things which I studied in something more than a superficial manner. All this was in addition to the daily grind of reports on balance sheets and income statements of companies listed on the Stock Exchange to try to arrive at some idea of the worth of their securities.

I doubt if anybody had any more direct or complete access to sources of information than B. M. and he always gave me a free hand in the consultation and use of such scientists and experts as I might need. I was for several years the only Research Staff which he permanently maintained. That and what went before was a great training for service in NRA because these studies covered a considerable segment of the whole of American industry and the experience with government linked the two together.

But Bernie's thoughts and my work were largely devoted in 1928 to something much more fascinating—the general situation, both economic and political. The 1928 campaign was coming on. We both felt that Mr. Hoover's plan to maintain prosperity by foreign trade financed by loans to "backward and crippled countries" could lead only to disaster. My studies showed that, in spite of fabulous and inflated profits to a few large groupings, the bulk of manufacture in the United States was operating in the red, and that very certainly, at the height of our "prosperity," no less than three million employables were without work. Even then the farm situation was desperate and the whole tenor of the economic thought on which Mr. Hoover seemed to rely indicated a belief that anything done to help agriculture would handicap industry in expanding export trade. The latter expansion Mr. Hoover believed (and frequently said) was absolutely essential to the maintenance of domestic prosperity.

We felt that export trade should be regarded as a necessary but secondary consideration—that, if there could be a balance of benefits between Industry and Agriculture and among all consuming groups, there were unlimited possibilities of expansion in the domestic market with promise so rich that, if we tripled our exports (which was out of the question) at the expense of domestic balance, we would be the loser as against a sane activation of our domestic markets.

After the nomination of Al Smith, Bernie offered his own services whenever they might be needed and donated all of mine at his own expense. I took a desk at Democratic headquarters in charge at New York of the agricultural activities of the campaign. Our man on the firing line was our old friend George Peek. By this time he was recognized by farmers of the Mississippi Valley as a determined, able, and disinterested leader of the cause of farm relief. He had battled for it unremittingly without hope of personal gain for seven years, spending his own fortune and all of his time.

Unfortunately, Al made one or two unguarded remarks at Albany before he had been able to turn the full of that protean mind on the farm problem, and our adversaries made the fullest possible use of them in the Farm Belt during the entire campaign.

George in Chicago and Bernie and I in New York worked day and night on that problem. Nobody ever wrote a speech for Al. In the first place he made only one speech from manuscript during the entire campaign—his acceptance speech—and he vowed he would never do it again. In the second place he has his own way of saying things, and no one does it better. But his speech on agriculture had to go back to a long and complex history. Some of the principles had become Farm Belt shibboleths with which he was not familiar—and these had to be preserved in Al's discourse. So with great pains and care I prepared a memorandum telling the whole story of the debasement of American agriculture. From that work I had a chance to see Al's system on speeches. He took me into a room in the Biltmore Hotel and sat there for hours absorbing that memorandum as a sponge drinks up water. He asked questions that searched that structure to its bones. Every once in a while he would stop to tell a story, and he always *acted* the characters so poignantly that you could see them vividly as in the wrong end of a telescope.

Finally he said: "Well I've got it—take it over to Barney Shintag and tell him to fix up *the envelopes.*"

That was the first time I had ever heard about "The envelopes." These containers, prepared by the searching analytical mind of Barney Shintag, had typed on the outside of each of them an illuminating and highly condensed heading of some main part of the speech. Inside of them was a newspaper or Congressional Record clipping, or other document bearing on that heading. Al held these envelopes between his fingers and his "Wa-a-l, let's look at the record," gave him the momentary breathing space necessary to collect his rapid thoughts and memories for the new head of attack. It took a few seconds to open the flap, and that was always enough for Al.

He went to Omaha. He delivered that Farm speech in a masterly manner and went away with the Corn Belt in his vest pocket. It threw consternation into the enemy's camp. But we had all reckoned without Bill Borah. The Hoover High Command threw him into the Twin Cities and there, at the very top of his forensic form, he delivered the speech that defeated Al Smith. It must have cost him many a pang thereafter and even at the moment of delivery. For the whole burden of his keening was the almost divine humanity of Herbert Hoover in insisting that Germany after defeat be fed by one hundred million dollars out of the United States Treasury, and how could the farmers think that this Great Heart could ever fail to feed their needs as well! If he did not weep, he seemed to. "What a slimy creature," he almost sobbed—or words to that general effect, "is he who would dare to suggest that this Angel of Charity and Patron Saint of Farmers had kept farm prices *down* after the war"— that he *did* keep them down was a perfectly demonstrable fact of which Mr. Hoover had actually boasted on the record.

Now the weak point of all this was that ten years before, when Mr. Hoover had asked for those one hundred million dollars, Senator Borah had arisen in the Senate and denounced him, accused him of conspiring with the packers against farm prices for hogs, and said that after weeks of investigation on his oath as a Senator he could not trust Mr. Hoover with one hundred million dollars.

But Senator Borah's speech set the prairies on fire and took them away from Al. It promised nothing, but it hinted much. We all know that Senator Borah was sincere in his belief that Hoover would act for the farmer at last. He was simply disappointed. We knew what that speech had done and we tried to get Al to go back at him. There was material enough, but Al is a believer in a paucity of speeches on one theme. "One subject—one speech," he said, and nobody could budge him except for a little parenthetical aside.

We could not move Al on another subject on which we had spent weeks of study. Mr. Hoover's speeches were simply economic essays with holes in them as broad as barn doors. On his own figures, it was apparent that his formula could lead only to almost immediate collapse, and he was fast and loose with his use of those figures. He was boasting about the miraculous replacement of labor with machines, but when he came to account for the replacement of that labor he said that it had gone into banking and hotel and garage keeping—he might have added bootlegging and racketeering, but he didn't.

But the employment figures in the occupations he named did not respond. The probability of the loss of new foreign loans; the stark staring fact that we were financing our entire increase in export, the allied payments to us, and a large part of German reparations by continued loans; and, finally, the certainty that we were skating on the eggshell of disaster supported only by paper profits on an inflated stock market—all the stigmata of approaching dissolution—were so plain that, without getting into the realm of technical economic conjecture, it was possible to write a blasting speech in barnyard language that anybody could understand. Even if it could not swing the election, it would make a record that no one could dispute. It was right up B. M.'s alley and the manuscript reads like a few chapters of one of the major prophets. I have never admired Al more than when, after wrestling with it for two or three hours, he said: "Aw, hell, General, I don't know anything about this kind of stuff and if I tried to do it everybody would say: 'At last Al's letting somebody write his speeches for him.' They gotta take me the way I am or not at all."

John Raskob delivered part of it, but of course that was not the same thing at all. That manuscript proved that there had been a steady march of unemployment which was growing in 1928; that not half the industrial enterprises of the United States were operating at a profit; that technological improvement and mass methods were creating an industrial surplus quite as threatening as the farm surplus and that disaster was upon us if we did not activate the *domestic* rather than the *export* market by improving the condition of agriculture, increasing the purchasing power of workers, and shortening the hours of labor. B. M. and I have always been proud of it *because it was written in 1928, called the turn on the collapse, and states a philosophy that has been demonstrated through the years and is just as good now as it was then.*

Mr. Raskob used only parts of it and I do not like to quote anything that was not actually publicly recorded, so I shall quote him instead of the manuscript. Those parts read, viz.:

During and since the war America has passed through an economic revolution. . . . In my younger days it was an axiom of industrial administration to produce at the lowest possible wage and the longest possible hours for labor. Beyond bare necessities the buying power of labor was nil. . . . Under Wilson, for the first time our government adopted as a definite labor-wage policy, a flat upward revision of all rates. . . . The elder Barons felt that the Day of Dissolution had arrived. . . . There followed a home consumption of manufactured goods that no economist or business man had ever dreamed possible . . . the war passed but wage scales did not drop . . . the industrial attitude had undergone a fundamental change. We had created a vast new market on our own doorstep by doing economic justice to wage and salary earners.

Mr. Hoover's economic plans are pretty clear . . . promotion of American trade abroad on a greater scale than has ever been achieved . . . if a nation . . . competes in world markets it must be in a competitive position on costs . . . labor is the overwhelmingly predominant element of cost . . . Mr. Hoover is at pains to show that we pay labor from two to seven times the wages paid by competitors. . . . In relatively few instances are we in foreign markets on a sound basis of competition—i.e., competitive price yielding profit. . . . 60% of our exports are raw material . . . 40% are agricultural yielding no profit . . . 10% are machinery depending on invention and not low cost. Mr. Hoover's plan for our economic future is hopelessly inconsistent with his fundamental tariff policy. In opposition to a bill for restoring profit to agriculture . . . he wrote: "it would subsidize the British Empire . . ." In our rapidly increasing industrial efficiency and use of automatic machinery *we are already threatened with over-production and unemployment. We must find increased consumption—new markets.* It is the most serious cloud in our business sky. Mr. Hoover has nothing to offer except export markets at the expense of farm relief. Such a conclusion goes far to impair my confidence in the business genius of Mr. Hoover . . . he is wrong on the most serious question before American business.

We have seen a fabulously rich and unsuspected domestic market spring up under our very feet by the simple expedient of giving wage and salary earners fair pay and shorter hours . . . business-like administration of our domestic markets will uncover new strata of prosperity. The search for export markets should go on but we should not follow Mr. Hoover's plan to sacrifice for them our most promising field ... it is time to organize our prosperity at home ... partial restoration of agriculture to economic equality would unloose such a flood of buying as to tax our facilities.

Continued low (farm) prices will increase the already tremendous exodus to cities ... in my opinion it will increase unemployment *and threaten a human catastrophe in the near future. Our economic system cannot withstand such a violent shock. Even Mr. Hoover's proposal to spend billions in public works (1928), evidently to offset what he foresees— will not suffice to handle this situation.*

The first requisite for prosperity is consumption, and that requires purchasing power. Payrolls shot up 100% under Woodrow Wilson (1916–1920). The wheels of industry started turning as never before. This proved the path to prosperity.

The Republicans believe that prosperity resides in concentration of benefit of political action on particular economic groups ...—the doctrine of Alexander Hamilton ... —it may be appropriate to transition from a wilderness of raw material to a highly organized industrial community—it is indefensible today.

*The Democrats believe that prosperity lies in maintaining equality of benefits, thus broadly increasing the consuming power of our whole domestic market. This is the only sound economic principle for an integral domestic market of 115,000,000 people.*

If, at any particular moment of time when we have a segment of population in a depressed economic condition (e.g. pre-war labor— post-war agriculture) *the simple process of elevating the depressed segment will give an immediate impetus to business progress. The Republican policy toward agriculture plus Mr. Hoover's prescription for industry threatens prosperity today.*

Such were the principles of this philosophy in 1928, when they were *prophecy* and *foresight*. Such also were they in 1932, and after 15 months of NRA in 1934, when they were *hindsight* and informed an effort to retrieve the grievous errors which neglect of them had caused.

There was no excuse for what happened in 1926 to 1929. In retrospect it is as incredible as any of the phantasmagoria related by Mackay in his history of the world's popular illusions. But the very government was behind that mass madness and if anybody of substance had got up in the market and cried a warning, he would have been torn to pieces as a calamity-howling destroyer of "prosperity." It just had to run its course.

When the collapse came, it came as Bernie had always said it would come—like a deluge. The story that it started in Europe is a myth plain on the face of every trend chart. We had been carrying Europe on our shoulders, and when we collapsed the world collapsed with us. We had indulged not merely an economic debauch, but a seven-year impregnation with false stimuli. We did not have just an upset stomach and a bad headache, we had cirrhosis and complete physical wreckage.

It is painful and unnecessary to recount the period of the Great American Deluge. After eighteen months of it, B. M. said:

"Let's just get out of everything and begin studying the world and domestic fiscal and economic and political situation to see if there is any suggestion of a way out of this morass."

That is exactly what we did. We charted and measured and compared the beginning, sequence, and existing state of the depression in every country. We studied the fiscal and economic history of this country from before the war to our then moment. We examined the condition of banks and the effect of recent fiscal policy. We went more deeply into the agricultural situation than we had ever gone. We drew up a comprehensive plan for the relief of the destitute. We studied the effects of prohibition repeal. We analyzed the budget of the United States in intimate detail and drew up a plan to save a billion dollars a year in ordinary expenditures. That got us into a little squabble with Mr. Mills over Treasury estimates of revenue and expenditure which resulted in a downward revision of estimates by the Treasury of some four hundred million dollars.

I doubt if, with so many resources for study, so few interruptions, and so impersonally and disinterestedly, men outside of a college or institution ever made so thorough a study of the underlying facts of an economic situation. And much as I respect, admire, and know the usefulness of academicians, I would take Bernie's final judgment on an economic problem every time. Their ability in that field may flash brilliantly in books, but his has been tested against all other judgments through the vicissitudes of forty years on the firing line against the best there is on Wall and Threadneedle streets. This is so not only personally, but for the country. As far as he is concerned, it rests soundly on the excellent preservation of his own economic skin, his record on the War Industries Board, and his advice (which was not followed but which *is* recorded) at the Peace Conference as Chief of the Economic Commission. His great public record stands unimpaired by time and change.

Among his most remarkable actions was his brave and tenacious insistence that the allied demands on Germany could only wreck the commerce of the world. On the proposition that you cannot enslave a militant people 60,000,000 strong, he recommended a gross war charge of $6,000,000,000, based on actual reparation and he accurately prophesied what would happen on the adopted formula.

The conventions of 1932 were approaching. After the Smith-McAdoo embroglio at Madison Square Garden in 1924, which split the Democratic party when it might have won, B. M. had taken a determination never again to support a pre-convention candidate. His philosophy was very simple. "Why should I? I don't want public office. I don't want anything from the party. I only want to serve it." There were many who expected more of him, and one, I know, who didn't believe him, but I was with him almost night and day and I know that what I have said is the literal truth. There was Bert Richie who had been Counsel for the War Industries Board and an intimate personal friend for years. There was Roy Bulkley, who had also served with the Board, and of course there was Al Smith, whose candidacy (if any) had never been disclosed. But B. M. told them all frankly of his position, and they recognized and respected it.

*In June, 1932,* I wrote and circulated privately among friends several editions of the following, two or three dated copies of which are still extant.

By
MUSCLEINNY
*Dictator pro tem.*
*A PROCLAMATION*

The undersigned has temporarily assumed the dictatorship of the Republic. He here reports to the people, first the eight reasons for his eleven acts and then the acts themselves.

I. REASONS

*Reason No. 1:* In the greatest crisis in our history, the Constitutional government was rendered futile by the approaching elections.

Influenced by selfish interests and organized minorities, it frittered away five months while our country descended to the edge of destitution.

*Reason No. 2:* The burden of the cost of all ordinary government has arisen to fourteen billions. The burden of interest to ten billions. The national income has shrunk to forty-six billions, leaving only twenty-two billions to the country to carry on commerce. That is not enough to sustain national life. Government proposed nothing and did nothing.

*Reason No. 3:* In two years government spent and squandered eight billion dollars though its revenue was only four billions. The accumulation of such an unheard-of deficit was made possible by highly improbable Treasury "estimates" of revenue based on exaggerated official forecasts of impending prosperity . . . all that Congress proposed remitted the country to the second largest deficit in the history of the human race—$1,500,000,000 —the largest being our own deficit of three billions in the current year.

Expressed in another way, a failing government "concern" again sought to "get by" its stockholders (the voters) on a balance sheet and "income statement" which it could not have had "certified" by any reputable public accounting firm in the country. Sickened by such trifling, the people so far lost faith in public credit, that the government dared not try to sell its bonds, because these large new issues would so far depress the price of fourteen billions of bonds outstanding as to threaten a general collapse of savings banks and insurance companies. In this dilemma government obscuredly devised a plan to use its debts for money.

*Reason No. 4:* Largely because government, by such methods, had literally beaten public confidence to death, the buying power of our urban population was destroyed. One third of them were in, or on the edge of, destitution. It was indispensable to get employment and buying power widely disseminated among them immediately.

*Reason No. 5:* The condition had gone too far to be cured by the slow process of re-employment and adjustment alone. Local resources for relief of suffering were at an end. Provision had to be made at once to guard against starvation, exposure, and houselessness of the more unfortunate.

*Reason No. 6:* Agriculture had long been oppressed, through the tariff system, by being charged a highly protected price for all that it bought and being denied any protection from world free-trade prices on domestic consumption of its surplus crops. The depression had aggravated this condition beyond human endurance. Our agrarian segment was on the verge of collapse. Government had failed to take one remedial step. Relief could be denied no longer.

*Reason No. 7:* An indefensible tariff policy was ruining the commerce of the world. We had to restore it at once and the government refused to do so.

*Reason No. 8:* The country was facing bankruptcy—in business, banks, insurance companies, railroads, agriculture, and the governments of many states, cities and counties. The slow and destructive process of individual receiverships and scaling down of debts was inadequate. A means of immediate and general receivership had to be devised.

*General Reason:* The combination of these causes threatened immediate ruin to our country. It was a ridiculous if ghastly paradox. *It was entirely avoidable and unnecessary.* In this crisis, and especially in this political year, divided powers were wholly inadequate. *The sole cure was singleness of control and immediate action.*

## II. Acts

*Act No. I:* The President, Vice President, and all members of Congress have been sent to a very pleasant archipelago not under American jurisdiction, where they have been distributed among several islands in small but congenial groups—none large enough to constitute a quorum. They will be treated with every courtesy, consideration, and respect and returned to their proper places and functions promptly on November 10th. All other officers have been retained and, although the Cabinet has resigned, each Secretary is "acting" in his former capacity. There being no government in existence, action was imperative.

The courts are open. The Constitution will, in all things, be respected, with the single exception that these decrees will be treated as duly enacted laws—subject, as usual, to determination by the courts as to their Constitutionality in all respects save the manner of their creation. In other words, *not one single power has been assumed that did not reside in Congress and the President. They could have done all things necessary to salvation without this—but they did not and apparently would not.*

The Conventions and Election shall proceed in due course. For two reasons, the undersigned takes no part in them: first, it has been demonstrated that political candidacy paralyzes an official for courageous action in such a crisis; second, he will doubtless spend the rest of his life in a federal prison.

*Act No. II: I have suspended gold payments for three months.* I did this to prevent any panic due to the vulnerable condition in which government left the fiscal situation. Gold payments will be resumed on August 1st, by which date I shall have re-established the federal credit on an impregnable basis as described below. If there is further delay in this, gold payments may be further suspended.

*Act No. III:* My notes on costs of government showed:

1.1 billion public debt (can't be cut)
1.    "    Veterans (cut 400,000 millions)
2.    "    other departments (cut 600 millions)

_____

Total 4.1    "    (cut 1 billion)

I saved one billion dollars, or 25%, viz.:

(*a*) I decreed that no benefit should be disbursed to any so-called veteran without a clear showing of service-connected disability—nor to any dependent of a deceased veteran except on a clear showing of his service-caused death. This, with concomitant contraction of facilities, saved $400,000,000 and required no surveys or delays. The ethics of this action are perfectly clear.

(*b*) *Other Departments.* I called together the heads of all other spending departments and simply applied the method adopted by every family and business establishment in the country during this emergency. I said:

"Boys, the total of your budgets is $2,000,000,000. We have to reduce that 30%, or $600,000,000. Each of you take your own budget back and reduce it 30%. I leave the method to you, subject to my approval and subject to one single rule—after you have eliminated unnecessary services, spread your remaining spending over as many employees as possible by a complete application of the 30-hour week. That rule is to be universal in all government spending."

A few executives said the job was impossible. These I fired. The revised budgets were brought back to a common conference in a week. After adjusting a few anomalies and shifting certain appropriations from one department to another, the complete saving of $600,000,000 was made. Since the revised amount is greater than these departments spent a few years ago, the country can be assured that there has been no impairment of essential service.

*Act No. IV:* Having cut 25% from the cost of Federal government, I called a conference of governors and said:

> "Gentlemen, the salvation of this country depends in a cut of 25% in the burden of fixed charges. You see what has been done in Federal government. We cannot coerce the states. *But the Federal government is going to have to disburse several billions of dollars in the states to meet this emergency.* It has routine service in many states. The latter will be withdrawn to the limit of Constitutional possibility and the former will be withheld altogether from any state, county, or municipality which does not (*a*) Immediately effect a 25% reduction in spending; (*b*) Apply the 30-hour week to all state employment and contracts as far back through the industrial chain as possible. Much progress has been made and I am assured of a full compliance."

*Act No. V:* Excluding the annual debt retirement fund of $500,000,-000 which I shall take care of separately, the total budget for ordinary government expenses including interest on the debt is 2.5 billions. The present revenue is running at the rate of 1.7 billions. I rely on a 30% increase in business from my measures. Careful and dependable estimates (not "Treasury" estimates) show that such recovery will increase the revenue from the present tax structure to $2,000,000,000, leaving $500,000,000 of new revenue which I must find to cover expenses with absolute certainty, and amply. This new tax I call:

"*The Budget Tax.*" It is flexible in that it levies $2\frac{1}{2}\%$ to 4% on the amount of manufacturers' output of all articles in commerce except plain food, plain clothing and certain necessaries for the poor. We will start at $2\frac{1}{2}\%$; if this does not return sufficient revenue the Treasury is authorized to increase it at the end of any month in increments of $\frac{1}{2}\%$ until it *does* provide sufficient revenue but not to go above 4%, and if it returns more than enough to balance the regular budget it will be reduced by a decrement of $\frac{1}{2}\%$ per month.

*Act No. VI:* "*Debt retirement tax.*" The suspended government said we could default on $500,000,000 sinking funds. But we must establish the credit of the United States beyond peradventure in the eyes of the whole world. While I concede that this might be deferred a year, it hurts the public credit to do so. Since I think returning business in the next fourteen months ought to provide something for this fund in the fiscal year 1934, I am willing to make an experiment now. In this emergency, experiments are justified. I am not sure that the Congress, if in session, or I, in their absence, could Constitutionally legalize beer by declaring it non-intoxicating, but I am willing to try. We drank two billion gallons in 1915. *I have authorized beer and levied a tax of twenty-five cents a gallon.* I call this the *"Debt Retirement Tax."* It will return $500,000,000 unless the Court strikes it down. If not, I shall have balanced the budget to the last cent. If so, returning business may do the job in 1934 without this tax.

*Act No. VII: "The Emergency Construction Tax."* The urban population must be given employment spread in the widest fashion. I *must* give employment. But I cannot again unbalance the budget. I *must* maintain the public credit. There is only one way to do this,—to borrow money.

We *do* have to issue and sell bonds, but in this crisis three things are necessary:

(1) To lend or spend the money only on projects that will yield enough money eventually to pay off the bonds and pay interest on them.

(2) To impound that yield at the source and put it into an amortization and interest fund.

(3) To insure interest and sinking fund on the bonds by providing, before issuing the bonds, for special new federal revenue from a tax large enough to make up for any possible failure of the projects themselves to earn sufficiently to pay charges.

This special bond issue will thus be so well secured that it can be honestly and openly sold to the public without unbalancing the budget and without impairing the market for other bonds. The money thus obtained will either be spent by the Government or loaned to states or municipalities to finance self-liquidating or self-supporting projects or for any kind of project which is itself amply supported by a special local tax impounded at its source.

*Loans or expenditures* will also be made to proper self-liquidating slum replacement or low cost housing projects— *preferably on a semi-rural self-supporting basis like the German agronomes.* I have established an expert engineering and professional commission. All such projects must be certified by it, as to practicability, soundness and necessity,—not on the basis of population nor on any other criterion not responsive to its purpose—but solely on the basis of maximum necessity and maximum effectiveness in providing employment. The professional commission is given absolute decision on these matters. Like the draft boards in the war—it is utterly removed from political consideration and control. I have appointed the most vigorous administrator I can find. He has plenary authority. Red tape is out. This work proceeds at once. A condition precedent to any loan or expenditure is the 30-hour week on all contracts and sub-contracts and even on manufacture of supplies as far back in the industrial chain as possible.

To support this loan issue of two billions a year I have provided revenue of eighty million per annum called: "*The Emergency Construction Tax:*"

(a) A "revenue only" tariff of five cents a pound on rubber to yield $40,000,000.

(b) A tax of one cent on ten cents on all admission tickets over twenty-five cents, to yield $40,000,000.

*Act No. VIII: "The Farm Relief Tax."* Emergency construction will aid only urban communities. We must remove from farms and rural communities the unconscionable tariff inequity.

I am making effective the present illusory forty cent tariff on wheat by causing the Farm Board to buy wheat whenever the price is less than world price plus the tariff of forty cents. It shall immediately export what it buys and not keep any wheat hanging over the domestic market in the foolish manner of the Farm Board. I shall collect a ten cent sales tax on all wheat sold, to absorb the loss on export sales. This will increase the domestic price of wheat about forty cents. (It is now about sixty cents in Chicago and about 1.75 in Paris.) The farmer will get about thirty cents of the increase. The price of wheat will not be fixed. It will fluctuate daily as it does now because the price is, and always will be, made abroad. But, by this means, the tariff will always be added to the domestic price and the ancient humbug of a forty cent tariff made at least partly effective. This involves no cost to the government as the ten cent sales tax absorbs loss on exports and pays costs.

*I shall also proceed to rent and retire from production enough land to reduce the production of other crops to a condition of balanced supply and demand. For this I must provide $200,000,000 a year,* which I shall raise by a Farm Relief tax on the processing of all cereals and all meats of about 6 cents on cereals; 2 cents on meats and $\frac{1}{2}$ cent on textiles.

To make this plan effective I may have to destroy or divert from normal uses some part of the surplus of wheat and cotton now foolishly held over the market by the Farm Board. If necessary I will. This is a war emergency. No surplus will accumulate under *this* plan. Its whole purpose is to get rid of surplus.

*Act No. IX: "The Hunger Tax."* We can no longer leave destitution to chance. We must have at least $300,000,000 per annum of revenue to be sure that nobody goes cold, or hungry, or unclad. I have no faith in Treasury estimates. I have levied a group of taxes which I call *"The Hunger Tax."* It is as follows:

| | | |
|---|---|---:|
| (*a*) | Increase in individual income tax spread over higher brackets | $ 75,000,000 |
| (*b*) | Increase in individual income tax spread over lower brackets | 25,000,000 |
| (*c*) | Additional excises: | |
| | (1)  5¢ a package tax on chewing gum | 30,000,000 |
| | (2)  25¢ a gallon tax on soft drinks | 50,000,000 |
| | (3)  20% tax on furs and jewelry | 60,000,000 |
| | (4)  15% tax on cosmetics | 40,000,000 |
| | (5)  7$\frac{1}{2}$% tax on candy | 20,000,000 |
| | | $300,000,000 |

NOTE: The additional income taxes are spread between higher and lower brackets on a three to one ratio. They provide considerably lower rates than the Senate tax on both brackets. I have not increased corporation tax because I want to start business activity. I have cut out all nuisance taxes. I have cut out all postal increase.

I shall use this "hunger" money as necessity requires, trying to pay as I go *but borrowing against this revenue if necessary,* lending it wherever appropriate or possible, to cities, to states, or even to needy individuals, taking their obligations into a retirement pool, but I shall *give* it where necessary. These taxes will be reduced as rapidly as the necessity for them disappears.

*Act No. X:* Our export commerce has been stifled by an absurd tariff law. A condition has been created that can be cured only through negotiation and not by statutory action here alone.

But we have very many elements with which to trade. I have high hopes of "trading out" expanding export markets in many countries and breaking the world tariff cabal against our country. I have set up Commissions of experts and of business negotiators of known fitness. They are now working under general coördination, guided by the most competent advice I can secure.

*Act No. XI:* We have lifted from our commerce a fixed charge of about 3.5 billions in reducing the costs of government, but we have done nothing to relieve the greater clog of debt. The burden of debt is the prime cause of continued depression. It is going through the most paralyzing and destructive process in the world—annihilation of bond prices, suspension of interest payments, foreclosures and bankruptcies. The uncertainty and frustration surrounding the whole situation is the chief bar to returning commerce. We cannot endure under a cloud of threatened individual receiverships and progressive dissipations of assets. We must do the whole job in one stroke. It is as follows: Gold payments will be resumed on August 1st unless there is a necessity to suspend them further. But from and after the date of this decree, *the gold content of the dollar is reduced 25%. As to clauses in contracts requiring payments in gold of the old standard of weight and fineness, I have decreed a tax of 40% on the total of any payment in dollars in excess of the number of dollars borrowed.* It will be to the creditors' advantage to accept payment of the specified amount. *This tax is not applicable to payments on foreign obligations* except as my international negotiators for restoration of world trade may agree as to war debts. The advantages of this action are:

It should lift one-fourth of the burden of debt and fixed charges from the nation; from states, cities, counties and municipalities; from railroads, banks, farmers and mortgagors in general. It should make imports one-fourth more difficult and exports one-fourth easier. While, in one sense, it may impair the present purchasing power of the *par* value of bonds, it and other measures just taken, should much more than offset this impairment by a prompt increase in the present *market* value of such bonds.

I am glad of these tremendous advantages but I did not do this to secure them; I did it because it was necessary to avert disaster.

*I have also amended the Bankruptcy Act to permit any composition concurred in by a majority of creditors to be declared effective by a System of Commissioners under the direction of the Federal*

*Courts* and I have provided for purchase by the R.F.C. of any farm or home mortgage at appraised value but not more than sixty per cent of the face value, taking back a new mortgage from the original mortgagor at not more than face value of the new mortgage and *not more than* $4\frac{1}{2}\%$ *interest.*

## SUMMATION

I find my justification in results accomplished

(*a*) We have lifted an annual charge of six billion dollars, or $25\%$, from the cost of interest and taxes to the nation.

(*b*) We have taken away $25\%$ of the unbearable load of debt and provided for the prompt liquidation of all private debt.

(*c*) We have increased the buying power of agriculture and removed a considerable part of the deadly disparity between farm and other prices. This should greatly contribute to the facility of exchange of goods between industry and farming and replace our lost foreign markets by a greatly increased and hitherto sterile market on our own doorstep.

(*d*) We have set the money and securities and general credit of the United States on an impregnable basis in the eyes of all the world because we have:

1. Balanced the recurring budget beyond peradventure of deficit.

2. Covered every emergency loan or expenditure with ample and impregnable special security.

3. Amply provided for the orderly retirement of all debt.

4. Conserved a plentiful supply of gold sufficient to cover our revalued currency over $100\%$.

5. Improved both our creditor position and our favorable balance of trade.

(*e*) Provided amply against destitution and launched a great re-employment program which can be got under way at once.

By: MUSCLEINNY
Dictator pro tem

*June 20, 1932.*

Of course the idea of a dictator who sequestered Congress but left the courts open was only to show that what he "did" could really have been done constitutionally by Congress itself.

The interesting point here is that Muscleinny had his brief allegorical existence and spoke his piece *considerably before the formation of the Democratic platform in the Chicago convention* and that, from the principle of taking active charge of events through several of the principal acts that were found to be necessary more than eight months later, *Muscleinny pretty accurately diagnosed the situation and at least dimly anticipated much of the Recovery Program.* Of course Muscleinny didn't just pick his figures out of the air or invent his program on the spot. They were a result of years of work under the direction of B. M. Baruch.

I always had a good deal of sympathy for poor old Muscleinny even if he was all wet on the immediate effect of cutting the gold content of the dollar—even if he didn't realize that no export market for American wheat existed any longer, and even if he was never more than an allegorical figment of imagination. He was right about everything else and, at least, *he knew what he wanted to do and had a plan for doing* it. Also his plan followed the Baruch philosophy, "*You can aid the operation of natural laws. You can't repeal them.*"

Some time later the House Committee on coinage weights and measures consulted B. M. on a plan for purchase and increase and stabilization of the price of silver. We studied that and especially its probable effect to stimulate Oriental Commerce. B. M. expressed an opinion that the purchase of silver and the pegging of its price would not have all the horrendous results that some people were prophesying—that it would not materially increase our Far Eastern trade—that it could be wisely done at insignificant cost with benefit to some of our silver-producing States—that after purchases were made in increasing quantities selling would cease. Succeeding events have demonstrated the accuracy of this judgment also.

# Chapter XIV

# THE ROOSEVELT CAMPAIGN

"Away slight men! You may have been Captains of Industry once, but you are Corporals of Disaster now. A safe place for you may be yapping at the flanks but it is not safe to stand obstructing the front of this great army." . . .—*Notes for a Campaign. Speech later used in an NRA speech at Atlanta, Ga.*

WE WENT to the Chicago Convention as observers and as nothing else. Bernie took with him some friends who were not even Democrats and, of course, Mrs. Woodrow Wilson. He was concerned with the Platform and, two days before it was decided upon, wrote a suggested one himself which was published from coast to coast—shorter even than the one that finally came out of the Committee, the actual platform differed from the Baruch suggestion in no important particular.

Mr. Baruch was consulted by the real candidate-makers on more than one critical occasion, but maintained his attitude of absolute neutrality to the very moment of the nomination, taking a position only on the question of abolishing the two-thirds rule, which he regarded as indispensable to the protection of his native South.

The moment Franklin Roosevelt was nominated, Bernie went to Jim Farley and offered his services and mine without stint or condition. The first question was of the acceptance speech, for which Ray Moley had assembled the data, and we were asked at once to go over this especially in its agricultural aspects. This we did, but had nothing to add except to endorse all that Ray had prepared.

But, as to the campaign speeches themselves, we had the result of our years of study and especially the economic criticism of the Hoover régime and of the world and domestic situations—all carefully printed in galley proof and exhaustively documented.

It broke itself naturally into about half a dozen divisions, and the first of them was an analytical approach to all that had happened in this country since the advent of the Harding régime. I had so much fun writing that first division long before the Convention that I cannot refrain from quoting parts of the memo I made from it, especially as it is a succinct running commentary on the economic events leading up to and through depression from the point of view on which Bernie and I regarded the remedies that must be applied. Nobody used it as it was written so I think I have a right to quote it:

For much that has happened we are all to blame. We followed an illusion. Yet, before we offer help, we must ask: What is the trouble? What illusion? Who bore the banners and who beat the drums?

Seeds of moral and economic dissolution were sowed under Harding and Coolidge. A definite policy was proposed by Herbert Hoover in 1928—accepted blindly by our people—rigidly followed by the President—and it has brought disaster. When disaster came, emergency policy was blundering and futile. Responsibility for the length and depth of this depression is direct and single. Forces from abroad are not to blame. These are weak political excuses which obscure the truth. To cure these causes we must be willing to face them without sentimentality. Our purpose is to point the way to better things.

Let us go back a little way to recall the conditions when Woodrow Wilson resigned his stewardship to Warren Harding. The gold of Europe was in our vaults or destined to them. We were creditor to the nations. We had financed a world conflict without scandal, fraud or politics—an unparalleled record in war government. Our machinery for production was intact and the starved demand of a shattered world reached out to it.

The gallantry of our soldiers and the devotion of our people bespoke the spirit of a great crusade. We were still looked upon as the saviors of Allied victory. We alone had come to the Peace Conference "with malice toward none and charity for all." We stood at such a peak of economic strength of domestic righteousness and of international leadership as had never been occupied by any nation. With this shining heritage, the material and spiritual fate of this country, and of the whole world, passed into Republican guardianship in 1921.

Let us smother our distaste and review hastily the sordid chain of immediate events—the breach of highest public trust in naval oil reserves, in funds for crippled veterans and custody of alien property. Induced by examples of notorious corruption in the shadow of the Capitol, a fog of civic evil seemed to rise throughout this land. In two years, it had stifled the clear moral atmosphere of the war period and smirched our high repute. Government was at once in contact with all that is worst in big business and indeed with all that is worst in our national life. From that contact sprang a brood of bad beginnings.

Politically planned by Republican leadership to "give the wets their liquor and the drys their law," the new organization for Prohibition Enforcement now came to corrupt public office, to debase federal courts, to degrade all law, to destroy most of the great guaranties of our Bill of Rights and to create fierce popular dissension which flared forth in 1928 in response to furtive acts of campaign management which stirred up shameful bigotry and intolerance throughout this country.

It gave our language and our people new and hateful words and institutions—"racketeering," "hi-jacking," "bootlegging" and systematized murder. These new practices financed and created the vast under-cover criminal organization which now affronts our whole country with its audacity and power. We shall never know whether effective enforcement was ever possible. We can only be certain what Dead Sea Fruits it bore in the ruin of an "experiment noble in motive" at the hands of experimenters noble in nothing.

There were other bad beginnings.

*First:* A stupid foreign policy which has estranged all Latin America, combined Europe against our interest, driven our industries abroad, and is rapidly destroying our commerce with the world.

*Second:* Centralization of power which has added billions to our tax burden and which threatens the rights of states, the liberties of citizens, and the freedom of domestic commerce.

*Third:* A consistent lack of frankness in all relations of government with the public which has blotted the record with half-truths, and worse, and has destroyed public confidence.

*Fourth:* The complete art of straddling and an utter absence of clear-cut position on any vital policy except the tariff.

The essence of recent government is materialism without regard to moral loss—all else is words. . . . Government claims that it introduced a "new thing in government," and it is that new thing which has brought this country to its present state. From the beginning of the "great Coolidge Bull Market" our Federal government as such stood behind the mad race of speculation with a goad. At every sign of public doubt or flagging interest, Cabinet officials or the President himself, bent down to lash it on. And from the Federal Reserve System while some futile warning was added its action on rediscount rates can only be interpreted as designed to spur speculation on. It served and abetted the expansion of credit and its concentration in New York until the flood had become tidal and nothing remained

within its power but to open the dykes and precipitate the deluge—
all of which it did. There stands the record and nobody's piety nor
wit can cancel half a word of it.

All this is wrong. The daily fluctuations on the ticker tape are not
a proper chart for the ship of state. Such economic captaincy is too
heavy a responsibility for mortal man. Few have dared to try it.
Foremost among such adventurers was John Law, "Farmer of the
Revenues of France and Manager of the Royal Mint," but his Mississippi Bubble will probably stand in history as a lesser delusion than
the 1929 Boom.

In 1928 all this was still within the limits of control, but signs of
approaching madness were everywhere apparent. We should not
forget that summer. It was a season of high-pressure selling, lavish
spending, headlong incurment of debt—a hey-day of promoters,
sloganeers, and mushroom fortunes—a time of opportunism—per-
sistence in any course, however unsound, if, for the moment, it
promised to "get by." Into this feverish atmosphere was launched
the 1928 campaign. But—in the cool detachment of a Dakota camp—
a canny little New England President had typed on slender slips of
paper: "*I do not choose to run.*"

The world has reason to remember 1928 campaign speeches and
other pronouncements. They were an entirely materialistic series of
economic essays. They laid down a specific formula for American
business with such an air of assurance and expertness that it was
generally accepted with the confidence in which a builder takes an
architect's blueprint. It turned out to be the effective cause of collapse
not only in this country but in the whole world.

It commended the rapid progress of the country toward mass and
machine production. It urged its continuation and said that such
was "the road to abolition of poverty." It clearly recognized and
stated that we were already producing goods much in excess of our
own needs and the question of what to do with this astonishing surplus was squarely met and specifically answered. We were to sell it
to export trade. In this, it was said, lay our sole hope, but there was
nothing to fear. On the contrary we were on the verge of the "greatest
commercial expansion in history."

Baffling questions arose and were snapped out in rapid fire. Would
not such rapid mechanization and concentration of industry displace
millions of workers? Had it not already done so? Had not the production of great surpluses in agriculture prostrated the entire farm
segment of the country? Had not the candidate insisted that the sole
hope for Agriculture was to starve out all surplus production? *If this
was the remedy for Agriculture, how could the magnification of surplus
be a proper prescription for industry?* Finally—and perhaps most

important of all: How could we sell such surplus to export trade when our customers had little gold and no credit and while another branch of this policy insisted that we should raise tariff walls against the importation of foreign goods?

Every one of these questions was met with striking boldness. We could capture the world's markets because, by accelerating mass and machine methods, we could obtain industrial costs so low as to exclude competition, notwithstanding the boast that we were paying our labor real wages from three to seven times as high as our competitors. As to unemployment: "No dangers lay in store" because these high wages would create such consuming power that new demands and new industries would absorb much of the labor displaced by machines in every farm and factory.

This latter conclusion was clearly disproved by current reports from the Department of Commerce, which, *in spite of greatly increased output, showed unemployment creeping up like a tide to engulf prosperity at home.* The tendency was appalling and was clear on the face of the monthly figures of that Department that the Candidate will never be able to explain the speech he made to labor at Newark in which he discussed this tendency so vital to his whole plan and denied and attempted to explain away its presence. He was trifling with the right of men to earn their daily bread. He was trifling with the trust of all of us in his economic genius. He was gambling with the welfare of the United States. *Nobody will ever be able to defend the Candidate's representations to labor on that subject.* . . .

In 1929 we reduced our recent rate of yearly remittances of loans to backward and crippled countries by $561,000,000, or 25%. The keystone of the arch of the "new economics" began to crumble and the world collapsed. We all know what happened. In two months *over thirty billion dollars of fairy gold faded away on the New York markets alone.* It was the deluge. Since the first surge a treasure greater than the wealth of the British Empire has vanished here like water on red-hot iron, leaving no trace.

The Candidate's specialty is deluding the public with nonsense. "Abolition of poverty" was nonsense, but the memory of a whole people rushing after it to their destruction is so recent and so much like the Pied Piper and the children of Hamelin, that we must prick this bubble now. This country is the largest self-contained market in the world. Our export business with the world is normally between 5% and 6% of our total business. In this depression we have lost about half of that export business or not more than three per cent of our total business, but practically 50% of our total business has vanished. It is nothing less than an affront to American intelligence to tell us that an impairment affecting 3% of our total business is the effective cause of the loss of half of it. We must not belittle the importance of export trade but when the Candidate tells this country that the losses of between two and three billions of sales abroad is responsible for a loss of between forty and fifty billions of business at home, something ought to be done about it. We brought this calamity upon ourselves and the world, and the world did not and could not bring it upon us.

It would be fitting, after this history, if the "Economic Marvel" myth were forever laid in its grave. But such is not the case. In the 1932 version the theme is of a marvelous generalship in the fight against depression, or as the current slogan more dramatically puts it—"The war on many fronts." Let us look at that. The first claim is that, when the depression came, government softened the blow. These are the facts!

Shocked by the worst crash in history many industrial companies began to trim their sails and nearly every family did the same. One large corporation announced that it had reduced overhead by forty millions of dollars. But none of these methods appealed to government. Its first message to Congress referred to this prudence as "unwarranted pessimism and fear" which was said to grow out of memories of previous crashes. "I have," said the message, "instituted systematic voluntary measures of coöperation with the business institutions and with the state and municipal authorities to make certain *that the fundamental business of the country shall continue as usual.*"

In its next annual message government addressed this economic tendency to frugality among families and admonished them "not to hoard through fear, but to continue their normal spending and recreation." For pure presumption our political history presents no equal to this—this chiding of responsible industrialists for applying experience in previous crashes and checking plans for the extension of their business at a time when it was perfectly apparent that at best American business had expanded far beyond reasonable limits— the admonition to families not to take some thought of the future in the most threatening economic crisis of our lifetime—these things are only equalled by the impertinence of the attempt now to dramatize them as genius in leadership in a "war against depression." What do corporations and families who heeded that advice now think? How would they like to have the money they then expended on the strength of it? What may the feeling be of those who invested on the strength of the governmental exhortations in 1929 and 1930? What is it that government would have had these people do? We can answer in advance. It wanted everybody to gamble highly— their all if necessary—that, notwithstanding all caution to the contrary, prosperity was just around the corner. And in this let us tender recent government a second preëminence—the greatest and boldest gambler—not only in modern times, but in all history—*with other people's money.*

From the first day of the crash to the present moment the basis of the whole philosophy has been "government at a gamble." No not from this first day of this crash but from the moment of this candidacy. For the economic plan of hazarding continued prosperity on loans to "backward and crippled countries" was a spacious gamble on a hairbreadth chance. . . .

There is nothing the matter with America. There is here a plenitude of every needful thing. There are here 123 million people accustomed to the highest standards of living, suffering a pent-up starved demand of three years of the greatest depression in history. There are resources of all kinds and the world's finest system of plants and facilities for both production and distribution. There is no lack of money. There is enough money and bank deposits today to finance a greater volume of sales at present prices than we have ever known.

Here, then, are all the elements of an active business and a moderate prosperity—save one—confidence is gone. The present stagnation is a malign spell without economic rhyme or reason. The name of that spell is fear—fear engendered by the worst record of bungling mismanagement in the history of this or any other government. The evil genius of that spell is Republican leadership and the way out of it is Democratic victory.

I still think the foregoing summary is important because the President's chief opponents offer nothing different now from what they gave in the twelve post-war years of their incumbency and what they gave is here outlined in brief review. I think it is also important because it is a critical approach to a new policy of reversal of old policy—to the new policy of the New Deal.

I like the last paragraph. I think it is still truth. I believe that the answer is fiscal stability then as now. I will go further and say that then as now, or at any time since say June, 1933, we could have restored prosperity to the country by that formula alone.

Ray Moley and Rex Tugwell came up to B. M.'s house and we went over all the material that B. M. and I had collected and summarized in our years of work. They, with Adolph Berle, had long before worked out the subjects of what they thought would be an ideal scheme of economic speeches for a

Presidential candidate, but they had few facts. From that moment we joined Ray Moley's forces and we all went to work to find for Franklin Roosevelt the data which he welded into the very remarkable series of simply expressed speeches on homely economics which convinced this country that here was the leader upon whom it could rely.

I did not do anything else, night or day, except for 12 days when I went to England to come back with B. M.—over on one ship and back on the next, with just one night in London to see *Cavalcade*.

There was nothing particularly new in the essence or principles developed. We had worked out and expressed precisely the same philosophy in Al Smith's campaign in 1928.

B. M. played a more effective rôle. Headquarters *just didn't have any money*. Sometimes they couldn't even pay the radio bill for the candidate's speeches. They had practically nothing to carry on the campaign in the critical state of Maine. Every time a crisis came, B. M. either gave the necessary money, or went out and got it. Those were quaint and parlous times, but I never had so much fun in my life.

One of the worst jobs was to get Jack Garner to make a speech. Jack doesn't believe in speeches and he is probably right, but the enemy were making much use of his silence. We got him up the dope for a dandy, based almost entirely on his own splendid record. Then we read it with great emphasis before a hand-picked and fully instructed audience of such lusty genii as Amon Carter, who sat around and clapped their hands and interrupted with "Gosh, that's good—gee, that's great," and thus we finally persuaded him, against protests couched in none too sacred language. He had the Charlies Michelson and Hand fix it up to suit him and he delivered it over the radio.

Two of my friends (one of them was Joe Kennedy) who had made suggestions for this utterance were lying on twin beds in a hotel room listening to it.

"After the first paragraph or two, they both sat up and one of them said: "If he goes on like this, in the next paragraph he's going to call them by their real names in Texas language." They had not believed that Jack would make that speech and they both began to laugh and didn't stop until the end of that oration. Nobody on the other side ever again baited Jack Garner to make another speech.

It wasn't all plain sailing. The incumbent Administration managed to stage a gesture toward recovery in consumers' goods, and there was a good deal of worrying. The middle West was by no means certain. There were some "Republicans for Roosevelt" organizations out there herded by Mr. Ickes —well-meaning and enthusiastic. They did not know what to do. But George Peek was out there and he *did* know what to do. To B. M. and George and me, it was the culmination of a twelve years' fight against great odds for Farm Relief and our old "Equality for Agriculture."

George is responsible for more political progress in this direction than anybody I know. The Republican states of Iowa, Kansas, Nebraska, and Illinois have always been beyond my comprehension. The high tariff Republican policy has exploited them for years. The natural line of economic demarcation in all the years before and after the Civil War was between the Industrial East whose market was made at home by the tariff —and the Agricultural South and Middle West—whose market price was determined in Liverpool by world conditions and whom no conceivable tariff could protect. The South understood this. It caused the Civil War. The South Carolina Doctrine of Nullification was caused by a tariff of abominations. But the red-herring of slavery was dragged across the trail in the Middle West. The bitterness of the Civil War kept these natural allies apart for generations. The bloody shirt, waved by every flamboyant politician from Robert Ingersoll onward, took into camp the mid-Western farmers and kept them there till 1932. After an acute experience for years with the sale of the "Equality-for-Agriculture Doctrine" to agrarian Republicans, I will say that George Peek—almost single handed—wrought that miracle.

George failed by a hair to deliver those states to Al Smith, but he wasn't going to fail to grab them for Roosevelt. He not only knew what to do himself and did it, but he knew what to tell the "Republicans for Roosevelt" what to do to get the farmers and then see that *they* did it—all of which he duly and fiercely and effectively did. He was a "Republican for Roosevelt" too, but he had gotten sick and disgusted of "Republicans-for-Farmers" early in the Harding régime and this time he cashed in. The result of his twelve years of effort made two Cabinet members—Ickes and Wallace, and verily he had his reward in another way—winning the election itself—and he wanted nothing more.

I know that many of the principal farm leaders were prepared to insist on his appointment as Secretary of Agriculture and that he decisively forbade them unless the demand should be unanimous—which it wasn't by the absence of one radical group, but George would not relent. It was his way of getting out of something he did not want to do.

I doubt if I have ever been happier in my life than I was when the election returns came in. There was only one fly in *my* ointment—that Hoover carried a single state. I honestly didn't think he would, and I was bitterly disappointed when he did.

## Chapter XV

## THE INTERREGNUM

---

Between the acting of a dreadful thing
And the first motion, all the interim is
Like a phantasma, or a hideous dream;
The Genius and the mortal instruments
Are then in council; and the state of man,
Like to a little kingdom, suffers then
The nature of an insurrection.
                    —*Julius Cæsar—Shakespeare.*

---

FROM the moment of the election, Bernie and George Peek and I went back to our mirth and our employments, and kept the noiseless tenor of our way. I doubt if there were three men in the party more averse to public office or political preferment —especially in the uncertain authority of an emergency administration. I have never been able to understand why so few people credit this state of mind. It is a very simple thing and it springs from experience. There is little reward except the satisfaction that may come from doing the best you can. On the other side of the shield are slander, suspicion, and vexation of spirit. In my own case, I had been through it all before, and upon taking my job, was able to predict the precise outcome. I do not mean to depreciate the honor that was given me, the great adventure I have had, and the chance to put in practice the principles to which I had so long been committed. But in view of so much that has been said or implied, I must relate the state of mind in which I took the job. I expressed it at the beginning and over and over again during my incumbency —all of which is black and white on the record. There is, of course, a large amount of public notice which for an actor or a politician may be an asset. But people also stop on the street to look at Al Capone or a three-headed calf. For a man who wants nothing but a place in the country to read and write and enough to keep out hunger, thirst and cold, it is a great weariness of soul.

There was an interlude at about the end of the campaign. A few weeks before election banks and insurance companies holding railroad securities asked Calvin Coolidge, Bernie Baruch, Alex Legge, Al Smith and Clark Howell to study and recommend a national railroad policy—"The National Transportation Committee."

B. M. was sick for part of the time and let me substitute for him. The Committee also entrusted me with digesting the evidence and preparing suggestions for a report. I spent three months of work and study on that. These were the last days of Calvin Coolidge and I saw a lot of him—an experience which only increased my respect and admiration for him.

I was hot to have the Bankruptcy Laws revised to permit prompt scaling down of Railroad Indebtedness, and I thought a timely and emphatic recommendation by the Committee would help. He was extremely reluctant.

"Don't like the word—bankruptcy." And then seeing a quizzical expression on my face:

"People who have had a hanging in the family, don't like to talk about ropes."

A regular meeting of the Committee was scheduled for the day after election. He offered to postpone it "to spare the feelings of the three Democratic members." They declined the consideration. Al Smith came bustling in a little late.

"Well," he said, "Mr. President—something happened yesterday."

"Yes—some of us can fool all of the people some of the time —and some can't." Which was a neat little way of suggesting that Al hadn't.

I think Mr. Coolidge knew what was just ahead for him. He was much sweeter and more mellow than the Coolidge I had known in the White House—a truly human man with the simplicity of greatness.

The Committee held exhaustive hearings, studied everything that had been written on the subject, engaged the Brookings Institution to supplement all this, received the suggestions of every one affected and conferred with the Interstate Commerce Commission and both Congressional Committees. It would profit anybody in interest to read that short report of the National Transportation Committee and then observe the trend of all political developments in the transportation field since. They follow it as closely as a ship follows its predetermined course.

It began with a brief of all that it contained which is so short and succinct as to be worthy of quotation:

### Conclusions of the Committee

I. The railroad system must be preserved. Changed conditions require new policies but not abandonment of railroad regulation. The development of regulation and of new methods of transport make it unnecessary for Government further to create and foster competition with or among railroads as a defense against monopoly. That is an expensive and ineffective attempt to do indirectly what Government has shown its ability to do directly. Regulation is sufficient, Government policies should be freed of any purpose either to favor or to handicap any form of transportation with relation to any other form. We cannot solve the problem on the theory upon which horses are handicapped in a race. In a fair field and no favor competition should be permitted to decide the result. Regulation should not attempt to "run the business" of transportation. It should concentrate on protecting the public against discrimination and extortion and on requiring the most efficient service at the lowest competitive cost.

(1) Parallel lines and systems are wasteful and unnecessary. Regional consolidation should be hastened and, where necessary, enforced, looking eventually to a single National system with regional divisions and the elimination of all excess and obsolete lines and equipment. Neither holding companies nor any other device should be permitted to hinder consolidation or evade the letter of the spirit of regulatory law.

(2) Unprofitable railroad service should be replaced by cheaper alternative transport methods.

(3) Railroads should be permitted to own and operate competing services, including water lines, and regulatory jurisdiction should be extended to water rates and practices in coastal, intercoastal and lake shipping to relieve commerce of present chaotic conditions. Congress should promptly clarify its intention on the long-and-short-haul clause of the Transportation Act.

(4) Government assumption of all or part of the costs of inefficient competing transport as a defense against monopoly is no longer warranted and should be aban-

doned. As a general principle inland waterways should bear all costs of amortization, interest, maintenance and operation of the facilities for their navigation. If they cannot bear such charges and compete with other forms of transport, they should be abandoned. *The St. Lawrence Waterway should be tested by this rule of self-support and if it fails in that test the pending treaty with Canada should not be ratified.* Governmental commercial operation of the actual facilities of transportation, such as barge-lines, should not be continued.

(5) Automotive transportation should be put under such regulation as is necessary for public protection. It should bear its fair burden of tax but only on a basis of compensation for public expenditure on its behalf, plus its share of the general tax load. Neither tax nor regulation should be applied for any purpose of handicapping the march of progress for the benefit of the railroads.

(6) Wages and working conditions of labor in transportation are determinable by established procedure in another forum and are not within the scope of this inquiry. There should be no heavier burdens on the railroads in employing labor to operate automobiles than on competitors. In the railroads (as in other industries) rates, capitalization, salaries, and wages must all follow changing economic conditions, but none should be sacrificed for the benefit of others.

(7) Beacons, weather service and similar auxiliaries to air traffic should be maintained at public expense, and air transport should be encouraged during its development state but we believe that every such service should ultimately pay its own way.

(8) The Committee has no recommendation to make on pipe lines.

II. The policy of trying to appraise railroad properties on some selected basis of valuation and then saying that they are entitled to earn a fair return on this appraisal should be reconsidered. Where competition with trucks and other methods exists, it will determine rates. In other cases rates must be regulated, but the basis of costs of operation under efficient management is a better general guide than any attempt to preserve capital structures regardless of economic trends. We see no reason why the rate-making rule should not say in plain English that railroads are entitled to make a reasonable profit based upon costs of efficient operation and that they are not entitled to earnings merely to preserve present structure if overcapitalized.

III. The railroads should do much that they have not done to improve their condition without any government help at all. They should promptly be freed of all unnecessary restrictions on the doing of it. It has been estimated that less than twenty per cent increase in traffic would put most of them on an earning basis. In view of the narrowness of this margin of loss and of the very great savings possible in railroad operation, we regard their outlook as far from hopeless.

    (*a*) Railroads should adopt the competing methods of which they complain.

    (*b*) Railroads should coöperate to reduce competitive expense.

        (1) Unnecessary services should be abandoned.

        (2) Metropolitan terminals should be consolidated and unnecessary facilities scrapped.

        (3) Circuitous haulage should be eliminated.

    (*c*) Financial management should be improved.

    (*d*) *Transport methods and equipment should be brought up-to-date.*

    (*e*) In view of what could be done by better management, the general outlook seems far from hopeless.

IV. Regulatory jurisdiction should be extended to the whole National transportation system but applied only to the extent necessary for public protection. The existing regulatory mechanism of the Interstate Commerce Commission is inadequate and should be improved by reorganization without expansion or increased expense.

V. Emergency Recommendations.

    (1) Corporate reorganization can and should be facilitated by revision of the bankruptcy procedure.

    (2) The recapture clause should be repealed retroactively.

    (3) The statutory rule of rate-making should be revised.

    (4) "Adequate security" does not necessarily mean "marketable collateral."

In my opinion all this is so practical and so logical that it charts an inevitable future course and in view of present developments I think it *is* doing so.

Leading figures in the Senate asked B. M. during the interregnum to suggest a basis of economic policy. On that, too, we worked for weeks. It would also profit any student of present trends to read *that* document also in the light of all that has happened since. Anyone who is interested in what happened in agricultural legislation, could, with profit, read George Peek's testimony before that Commission.

All of these documents suggest the amount of work and study that had been given to subjects covering what was later to prove a large part of the Recovery Program and reveal also something of the experience, the common sense, and protean grasp of B. M. on the causes of the ills which beset this country and his suggestions of what to do to cure them. Its main value is its background of knowledge from experience. One trouble with our government is the multiplicity of men who know what they are talking about only through reading and conjecture —which is not to *know* at all. It is like "Tomlinson":

". . . O this I have felt, and this I have guessed, and this I have heard men say,
". . . And this they wrote that another man wrote of a carl in Norroway." . . .

Peter wouldn't let him into Heaven and the Devil wouldn't let him into Hell—but oh how we welcome him in government! In his Senate testimony B. M. proposed:

(*a*) That submarginal farm land be rented or purchased to wipe out unmanageable surplus and showed that it could be done at negligible expense.

(*b*) That the bankruptcy laws be revised to provide a quick and effective reorganization and reduction of the crushing burden of all debt.

(*c*) That the ordinary budget be firmly balanced, that extraordinary expenditures be put on a proper loan basis and properly supported by specific taxes fully covering interest and amortization—much on the "Muscleinny" formula.

(*d*) That whatever is necessary for reëmployment or relief be freely spent from this borrowing.

I want to quote from just a few of B. M.'s public expressions because they are part of the record—they date themselves—

and they show how clearly the principles of NRA were stated before the Act was passed or even conceived.

From his Senate testimony (February, 1933):

The objective in mind of every thoughtful man is to restore to distressed humanity the opportunity to earn its daily bread—to get people back to work again. . . .

We cannot oppose legislation to natural laws. But legislation can aid and hasten and guide their effect. In this crisis the golden rule should be:

Reject all plans which oppose or postpone the working of natural processes. Aid and accelerate the effect of curative economic influence. It is a simple rule, but it is a right one. We have overlooked simple things too long. The artificialities of the Great Delusion were plain. We closed our eyes and went on loaning two billion dollars a year to finance sales to "crippled" countries because we were persuaded to disregard arithmetic.

For four years we have treated the inevitable collapse of our folly as a mere interruption of a dream. We have maintained the boomtime costs of government and incurred destructive deficits solely on the argument that the dream would come again. No other assumption could justify our policy.

We have set every legislative force against the economics of cure. We have used federal credit in a vain attempt to reconstruct or preserve the ruins of phantom values. We have tried to avoid paying for our folly. We have not yet taken one really constructive step. I doubt if we have even recognized the true evils.

This is not progress. This is opposition to progress. The single project to aid (and not to oppose) natural cure is to be found in the principles of the LaGuardia Bankruptcy Bill. It is high time that our affairs should be taking an upward turn and I believe that we are delaying rather than advancing it. . . .

If I were writing such a program, it would be: First (and foremost): make adequate provisions against human suffering; second: put federal credit beyond peradventure of doubt; third: aids to rapid liquidation of debt; fourth: plans to encourage rapid consumption of commodity surpluses and to control productive capacity; fifth: determination of policy on world economics, disarmament, and debt.

"Baruch is too dogmatic," complained an academician.

"Yes," said Carter Glass. "On a proposition like 2 + 2 = 4. Bernie can be dogmatic as hell about that."

In receiving a doctor's degree from Johns Hopkins University eleven days later, February 22, 1933, he said in part:

Humanity in distress seeks a comforter. A hurt child cries for its mother. She takes it in her arms, and by the magic of her love, soothes and sends it back to play. It becomes a man and puts away some childish things—but never, it seems, the need for solace. In a less material age, religion served as a buffer to government and, for this reason, the first article of anarchy is the destruction of faith. There remains, however, in every social system mother government as the giver of all good, the receiver of all blame and the first and last refuge from every evil. . . .

Government flows from the people. For the same reason that water does not rise higher than its source, no government is stronger than the people governed. In our flight from confidence in ourselves to reliance upon government, our position becomes almost absurd. There is hardly a class among us which seems willing to stand on its own feet —banks and railroads, no less than farmers and workers, captains of industry and leaders of economic thought, no less than captains of hunger-marchers, turn in their distress to Pennsylvania Avenue and almost never to Main Street.

Everybody leans against government, blind to the fact that government, by its very nature, leans against everybody. We have reached a point where those who can only lean vastly outnumber those capable of being leaned against and the social structure totters like a building collapsing under too much weight. In the whole fantastic picture nothing stands up straight and our economic surroundings whirl dizzily like blurred figures in a nightmare. Everything seems paradox. People are starving in the presence of too much good; homeless in streets of vacant houses and ill-clad before bales of surplus wool and cotton. . . .

It was in just such a maelstrom in the currents of his life that King Saul, in his confusion, set aside the faith of his fathers and went to Endor to consult the witch. Humanity, in any great distress which it cannot understand, seems always to turn first to the road to Endor. That, I think, is the reason why, in this moment of bewilderment and danger, our modern witch-doctors appear and get credit for their incantations. Wand-waving—promises to magic away the results of human folly—occult spells arising out of the pseudo-science of economics, or technocracy, or some other abracadabra not yet announced— these are to rescue us by virtue of a force outside ourselves—a force usually emanating from some proposed political action.

The same sequence is going on all over the world. Distressed nations

lean against their weakened governments and, when they feel them
sway, the people invariably take one of two courses. They over-
throw their political system in a whirlwind of blood and destruction
—after which invariably comes a despot to scourge them back to
reality and righteousness. Or, they seek to put substance in the slender
reed on which they lean and themselves create a despot at the outset.
Dictatorships are many and we talk of one for ourselves.

But this also is the road to Endor. We need leadership and a definite
program but neither a dictator with no plan to dictate, nor a magician
with a patent plan. . . .

There is no need to dogmatize the details of such a program. It
may be wrong in part. It cannot satisfy all opinions. It need not be an
easy way. It must point the *right* way—the ways proved by the world's
whole experience as right ways as seldom easy ways. After wandering
for three years in a morass of uncertainty, opportunity opens to us.
For a moment we shall stand at a crossroads in a clearing and the fate
of our country and perhaps of a whole world hangs on our choice of a
path. Our course has run so long and so far into by-paths of expediency that any wrong-turning now may take us to a place from whence
there is no retreat except such a one as Napoleon made from Moscow—
leaving the ruins of an Empire in his wake.

But if our program now proposes action in consonance with the
essence of our institutions and runs with and never against the course
of natural law, the country is ready for it. . . .

The people of this country languish for such action. They are sick
unto death of inertia, expediency, and nostrums. They need only to
be shown with a clarity and certainty born of knowledge and experience, the way for them to work out their own salvation.

*There is no longer any necessity for gestures and concessions to any
particular faction, section, or school of thought because our people know
that Fate never put upon one pair of shoulders such a freight of human
aspirations as is about to descend upon the man they have chosen for
this task. Not for his sake, but for their own sake and that of the whole
world, they will demand for him the unwavering loyalty of every man,
regardless of prejudice, party, or selfish interest. They will know that
anyone who does not accord it in full measure is either dull in his per-
ception of danger or derelict in the most sacred duties of citizenship in
an hour of national peril. Public opinion will scourge such a man as it
pilloried slackers in the war. . . .*

Here certainly was a respectable philosophy. But B. M.
did not confine himself to generalities. His Senate testimony
proposed a specific program *and on May 20, 1933, he delivered*

*before the Brookings Institution a speech the essence of which had been worked out long before by many different economists and thinkers and which anticipated every fundamental principle of NRA.*

It has often been advocated that business needs, and should have, a common forum where problems requiring coöperating can be considered and acted upon with the constructive non-political sanction of government. It may have been sound public policy to forbid by law anything that looked to limitation of production when the world was in fear of famine. But it seems public lunacy to decree unlimited operation of a system which periodically disgorges indigestible masses of unconsumable products.

In today's desperate struggle for the scant remaining business, cost and price have become such factors that, in the unstable fringes which surround each industry, a few operators have taken *the last dangerous step in economic retrogression—the attainment of low costs by the degradation of labor standards.* Low costs secured in this way create an unbearable competitive disadvantage to companies of larger vision and a sense of social obligation. These companies have no defense save to follow suit,—thus a whole industrial and labor group is forced to drop to a lower step, from which new level there seems no escape from a repetition of downward scaling. Lower wages—lower costs—lower prices—and the whole vicious cycle goes on. It is the descent into an economic Avernus, from which no mere program of public works can rescue us. It is a process of rapid dissolution, and it is no wonder that the whole of industry seems to have risen *en masse* to find some way to check it as a matter of stark self-preservation. It *had* to do so because of government restrictions on self-defense through coöperation.

The government has fostered our over-capacitated industrial combinations, and even encouraged these combinations to increase production. But nothing was ever done to *regulate* production. Over forty years ago we enacted a law which said: "Every combination in restraint of trade is hereby declared to be illegal." As the Chief Justice said recently: "It is safe to say that no business man after thirty years of interpretation can even now be sure as to what he can lawfully do, although he has been advised of much that has been forbidden."

The oil industry, for example, has repeatedly asked the government to assist in regulating production. The answer has practically been: "We cannot, because the Constitution forbids it, and you must not, because the Sherman Act forbids it." What an astonishing example of complete economic impotency. A possible guide in this crisis may be found in the organization and methods of the War Industries Board which functioned under President Wilson in the World War.

There seems to be a general feeling that some providential and unselfish coöperation will manifest itself and solve all problems without anything more than nominal direction, and—let us speak frankly in this serious hour—without any power of firm and certain disciplinary measures. While we agree fully that Industry must voluntarily accept and ask for coördination, and that any appearance of dictation must be avoided, the power of discipline must exist. At least we found it so in the war experiment.

*The best method of enforcement lies in the power of public opinion.* Further, the indispensable ingredient in industrial control is effective and self-directed coöperation. But, from a vivid and intense experience, let me say that nothing is possible without distinct and adequate authority in whatever coördinating body we create.

On this point I quote my own testimony given two years ago before the Cabinet and Congressional War Policies Commission. In speaking of industrial coöperation, I said: "In many of our conferences the government had the enthusiastic support of some producers and in some the unanimous support of all. But—I venture to think that there is not one of those leaders who would not heartily agree with me in saying that no one—no matter how generous—could consent . . . *unless those willing to agree through high-mindedness knew that the government body with whom they were dealing has SOME sanctions— some control with actual teeth or some disciplinary power to apply to recalcitrant or unwilling subscribers in the event of default.* . . ."

But even at risk of repetition, I must say that the mere existence of these powers *does not impair the principle of voluntary and self-governing action by Industry.* We had plenty of power during the war, but let me quote Newton Baker's testimony before the War Policies Commission in stating our methods of administration; what the War Industries Board did was to make itself (I quote) "the leader of American business, rather than the boss of American business . . . to *send for the leaders of an Industry, seat them around the table . . . tell them the national view, lay out the economics of the situation to them . . . and at the end of the conference they were not only informed of what was to be done, but they were enthusiastic for doing it.* . . ."

With all earnestness let me say that if this policy of enlightened coöperation is not the actual method of the new industrial coördination it must fail.

The primary purpose is to bring about and maintain industrial stability through, among other things,

        (*a*) Reëmployment of labor
        (*b*) Maintenance and increase in wages

(c) Standardization of hours of labor
(d) Control of production
(e) Establishing a fair price scale

If all companies in each competing group do this, the object is possible of attainment, but we must all frankly and clearly recognize that this means higher costs and therefore higher prices. *Higher prices by agreement constitute a danger signal and this brings us face to face with the necessity for governmental supervision.* Industrialists who favor this plan must understand clearly that it involves the imposition by government of a price limitation, agreed upon by industry to be sure, but always subject to government approval.

Another caution seems appropriate. *The purpose is not to invite monopolistic combinations, or to favor any particular group or to preserve the value of unwise investments in uneconomic assets, and it must not be used to eliminate labor by closing down plants. It is an experiment which is worth while making, but the most certain way to insure its failure is to attempt to use it for any other than the purpose for which it is designed.*

In certainly a majority of trades the same rule for hours and wages is applicable. *The quickest method is to bring the uniform cases to swift action by a blanket rule and then to deal with the exceptions.*

The way to determine the general rule is *not* an exclusive resort to research and statistics. It is principally a resort to men. A general rule applicable to 75% of industry could be worked out very promptly by a conference of leaders in industry and labor. With this decided upon in a general way, the next step is to submit it to Trade Associations for their voluntary acceptance or requests for modification. The idea is to get the widest possible areas of industry under the rule at once and then to provide for the exceptions—and by exceptions I mean—

(a) Modifications
(b) Special cases
(c) Recalcitrants

The exceptional cases should be presented, in the first instance by Trade Associations to whatever Federal administrative agency as is named. A competent Federal administration must be set up promptly. It should be composed of a practical and disinterested specialist for each principal industrial grouping.

*It is just here that the mobilization of public opinion becomes important. If it is commonly understood that those who are coöperating are soldiers against the common enemy within, and those who omit to act are on the other side, there will be little hanging back. The insignia of governmental approval on doorways, letterheads, and invoices will become a necessity in business. This method was used with success in 1918. It is a short cut to action and to the public support, without which no such plan can succeed.* . . . (This should lay forever the repeated assertion that the Blue Eagle was an afterthought.)

"This is an emergency worse than war, and calls for volunteers from that class of whom Woodrow Wilson wrote:

> "They turned aside from every private interest of their own and devoted the whole of their trained capacity to the tasks that supplied the sinews of the whole great undertaking. The patriotism, the unselfishness, the thoroughgoing devotion, and distinguished capacity that marked their toilsome labors, day after day, month after month, have made them fit mates and comrades of the men in the trenches and on the seas."

(Unfortunately in NRA we got no more than a handful of the men to whom Woodrow Wilson referred.)

*Almost exactly three years* before this Brookings speech, B. M. had *proposed the NRA plan at Boston on May 1, 1930.* Several other men had voiced similar opinions.

*What business needs is a common forum where problems requiring coöperation can be considered and acted upon with the constructive, non-political sanction of government.* It may have been sound public policy to forbid by law anything that looked to regulation of production when the world was in fear of famine but *it is public lunacy to decree unlimited operation of a system which periodically disgorges indigestible masses of unconsumable products.*

*No repressive, inquisitorial, mediocre bureau will answer*—we must have a new concept for this purpose—a tribunal invested like the Supreme Court, with so much prestige and dignity that our greatest business leaders will be glad to divest themselves of all personal interest in business and there serve. Like the Supreme Court also it must be absolutely non-political.

*It should have no power to repress or coerce but it should have power to convoke conference, to suggest and to sanction or license such common-sense coöperation* among industrial units as will prevent our economic blessings from becoming unbearable burdens. Its sole punitive power should be to prescribe conditions of its licenses and then to revoke those licenses for infringement of such conditions.

*Its deliberations should be in the open* and should be wholly scientific, briefed like an engineer's report, and published to the world. Such a system would safeguard the public interest and should be substituted for the blind inhibitory blankets of the Sherman and Clayton Acts. . . .

It is not government in business in the sense which is here condemned. *It is only a relaxation of the grip government has already taken on business by the Anti-Trust Acts. There is no fallacy in restricting ruinous excess production*—a policy which the Federal Government is now vigorously urging on Agriculture. Yet if there is nothing in the change of concept from bureaucratic precedent to that of an open forum where business can practice group self-government, acting on its own motion *under sanction of non-political, constructive and helpful tribunal*—then the idea is not practicable. *But that there is a possibility of such industrial self-government under governmental sanction was clearly demonstrated in 1918.*

Many difficulties suggest themselves. In the first place anything done in the elation and fervor of war must be accepted as a criterion only with caution.

*In the regulation of production price is one consideration. That is a subject which is loaded with dynamite.*

There are other obvious reservations. *The thought is* revived at this critical moment because it seems worthy of consideration as an aid in a threatening economic development or unusual extend and as an alternative to governmental interference and vast extension of political powers in the economic field—an eventuality which, in the absence of constructive action by business itself, is almost as certain as death and taxes.

Mr. Raskob's speeches in September and October, 1928; B. M.'s Boston speech, 1931; Muscleinny's decrees and B. M.'s "platform," June, 1932; the memorandum of July, 1932; B. M.'s Senate testimony and his Johns Hopkins and Brookings Institute speeches, and the Transportation Committee Report, February, 1933—in these ten documents quoted or cited in this book—dated by their publicity—will be found the development of the economic philosophy of the 1928 campaign and of almost all that happened since. Of a part of this philosophy NRA was a concrete expression. I do not mean to give the impression that the group of authorities here mentioned was the only group that had these thoughts. Beginning as far back as 1919 there were many economists and thoughtful business and labor leaders who talked and wrote and urged part or all of the same philosophy. I do not happen to have access to these other expressions and I do have these documents in my own files. I make the point at all only to answer the repeated claim that NRA was an after-thought or an unexpected brain-storm conceived in the confusion of early 1933. It is important also because it represents consistent, philosophical, economic *pioneering*. Many of these expressions now seem trite, but what I have quoted was *the very birth of them.*

# Chapter XVI

## RUGGED INDIVIDUALISM VS. BALANCED ECONOMY

---

*"Ah! when shall all men's good be each man's rule."*
*—The Golden Year—Tennyson.*

---

THERE is something about this depression that doesn't speak
well for what we call our common sense. We have suffered for
five years. And for what? The fields are just as green and fruitful, the skies are just as blue as they were in the 1929 boom,
when everybody was going to get rich and poverty was to be
no more in the land. The birds and the beasts seem to be faring
about as well as ever—except those in care of men—and, so
far as one can see just riding through, there is nothing much
the matter with the country—until we get to the Lords of
Creation—the vaunted human race.

If we saw a squirrel starving to death in a knot hole in his
nut-filled hollow tree, we wouldn't believe it. And yet here are
125,000,000 people—granaries full, factories shut—but with
millions of workers idle and hungry and shabby and afraid of
the future and of everything and everybody about them—and
money galore in banks and depositories. It just doesn't make
sense. It is too much like a dark huddle of jungle savages
dying, by swarms, of Asiatic cholera, because nobody ever told
them to wash their hands before eating. It is a shocking thing.

Although tariffs and selective taxes and Adamson Acts and
many other devices affect the natural laws of supply and demand, yet during the depression and up to March 4, 1933, few
legislative steps were tried and the argument was "Let things
alone and they will get all right because they always did, and
because you cannot interfere with natural laws." That is the
same philosophy that kills the savages. It is the philosophy that
opposes vaccination for smallpox or the use of a parachute
when you jump out of a balloon. We can and do daily interfere
with natural laws. It is fair to say that if we had let things

alone for a few weeks longer we *would* have had to call somebody in—the undertaker and the riot squad.

We have mechanized our industries and specialized our people. Families are no longer self-contained, economic units that can be put on wheels and trundled into a new environment to start things over again. Our nineteenth century safety valve of cheap or free new lands and a constantly expanding country has ceased to exist. The old order of our frontier days is gone forever and by no man's designing. All this had brought benefits, but it has also brought great griefs. The roaring, clacking engine of our industry and commerce has become a vast and highly active machine of which no individual is more than an integrated part. Each performs a specialized function. In most cases living income comes as a matter of determination by a power with whom there is no bargaining in any true sense. The individual worker accepts the wage scales decreed by employers and is thankful, and his separation from the particular ratchet in which he revolves may be a tragedy. At his doorway there is no longer an open road to high adventure in a new and brighter country, and even if there were such a road, his specialization has unfitted him to take it.

In March, 1933, we had almost achieved economic collapse. Of the credit and product and hoarded reserve of domestic industry and labor and agriculture (indeed of all our people) *too much had been concentrated on production—too little on distribution and consumption.* The people's financial resources were thus squandered, either through their own unwise investment or the equal madness of their bankers. The results were a grotesque speculative structure of values; an elephantine production and service plant; a creeping paralysis of consumption and employment which began as far back as 1926; a decay of agriculture which began even further back in 1921; and an interior cavity in domestic absorptive and resisting power which started coincident with this diversion and impairment of the proper income of all people, but which was concealed until 1929 by an expansion of all kinds of credit—an expansion like a bubble—the skin of which became so tenuous and thin in 1929 that no power on earth could have saved it.

If you want to know where the consuming power of America went, you need only look around you and see it congealed in icebergs of unnecessary building and un-needed plants—and in the dead leaves of the worthless securities which financed them, and our fatuous foreign loans. Suppose that, instead of so freezing such vast sums a prudent part of them had been distributed in wages and dividends or conserved in cushions of credit invested in more stable securities—does anybody doubt that we would never have suffered this Gethsemane?

But suppose anybody *had* foreseen it all in its precise and exact value as late as 1928, and—seeing it—could have convinced the nation? What could have been done about it as the law then stood? Precisely and exactly nothing—except perhaps to have precipitated an earlier and slightly less violent collapse. Why? Because our law and institutions were such that neither industry, nor labor, nor banking, nor finance could effectively act in unison.

But no prophet crying in the wilderness could then have convinced the country. Old slogans would have killed new thoughts. "Let nature take its course"—"rugged individualism"— "competition is the life of trade"—"combinations to restrain it are unlawful"—"liberty of contract"—etc., etc., *ad nauseam.*

Well, if we could not have avoided the collapse under the old rule of "let us alone," it is certain that we could not have attempted a rescue without a complete change of formula when disaster left us stunned and helpless. How could we reverse our situation? Obviously, by a plan to obliterate its causes—an amendment to the rule of *laissez faire.* We were face to face with an effective demonstration of the fact that economic development had outstripped our political system and we had to act at once.

In such a state of industrial organization as had grown up here, rugged individualism may have been rugged but it was not individual. It was unchecked independence of great groups. It may have been rugged individualism for these groups, but it was not so for the man who works, or the consumer. The great economic machine had no governor. It moved under no restraining influence and, when eventually it creaked and slowed and came to a stop, it was so poorly assembled that all the king's horses and all the king's men have not as yet been able to put it together again.

In March, 1933, we could no longer afford to sit and do

nothing about millions upon millions of frugal hard-working people who had been cut off from their livelihood. We could no longer say "Let them work out their salvation." Economic and mechanical progress has outstripped political progress and taken that salvation completely away. *Any human economic and political system has failed when people can no longer live under it by their own efforts.* For five years a very large proportion of our people have not been able so to live. *We must substitute for the old safety valve of free land and new horizons a new safety valve of economic readjustment and direction of those great forces. There is no other alternative to shipwreck. The need for immediate and effective action is still upon us, and the need for wise direction will always remain. We are permanently in a new era.*

Up to 1933, we thought that both our industry and our agriculture could depend on foreign markets to sell their products. We did not admit that, if only we could give the agricultural half of our population a fair price for its products, we could create—in our own backyard—one of the richest markets for industry in the whole world. We did not fully realize that, if only we could see to it that the working segments of our population—employees of all classes and grades—get a fair wage for their labor, we could create in our own country the best market for our farm products that we could expect if we combed the whole round earth.

We did not concede that we must try to balance production and consumption and that the best way to increase both is to *push them up together.* The way to do that is to try to balance and correlate the income of great groups. We must not let too much of profit and the people's credit and savings run into unwise speculative obligations of debt for the purpose of increasing production. We should try to direct more of it toward the uses of distribution and consumption, so that farmers and workers and *all* producers can constantly consume more and more in order that there may be more employment, more business, more profit, and that the people of this bountiful country can enjoy to the full the fruit of their own labor and the resources which are now locked away from them. We did not act on the principle that *it is the distressed and backward economic areas which topple the structure of prosperity, make depressions, and that the exploitation of any class is a downward drag on the progress of the whole people.*

If we could have perfect balance among all producing segments—agriculture, capital, industry, workers in industry, the services, and the segment engaged in transportation and distribution, there would be almost no limit to our consuming capacity. Of course, that is Utopia and can never be attained. My only point is that all law, all administration, and all popular effort should be directed toward that goal instead of away from that goal. I think that the *essence of the New Deal is to point toward that balance.* I think that the *essence of what preceded the New Deal was to point away from that balance.*

Savage wolfish competition without any direction whatever, has proved to be one of the most destructive forces in our economic life. When it got savage and wolfish enough it began immediately to gnaw upon the living standards of wage and salary earners and hence of farmers, and that happens to include over 85% of our population. When times are fabulously good the great prosperity of the few filters down to the many and tends to obscure this tendency. But in normal times and especially when depression such as that which began five years ago comes upon us like a blight and millions of men begin tramping the streets, looking for any kind of work that will afford a crust of bread for their families, the whole aspect changes.

Plants finding a scant market for their products begin frantically to seek for any possible method of reducing prices and the most obvious methods of all are to reduce wages, speed up machines to produce more in a shorter time, and extend the hours of work to the limit. Most humane employers do not want to do this—but a single great competitor can force it, and, like a rotten apple spoiling a whole barrel, one plant or one locality which adopts this method can bring it eventually to a whole industry.

That very thing was the worst of this depression. It began to have its destructive effect almost immediately in 1929. Early in 1930 President Hoover made strong efforts to arrest the dizzy downward spiral in wages and employment but one company after another in savage competition for the rapidly declining business, cut wages and lengthened hours. As each did this, its competitors were obliged to do likewise until all did it in industry after industry. This descent into the maelstrom went on for four years. The great "share-the-work" movement started by Walter Teagle helped to arrest destitution, but unless share-the-work is accompanied by maintained wages for the shorter week, it is simply an enforced contribution to relief funds by the class least able to contribute.

Another thing—apart from savage competition—too great a share of prosperity went to too few people. Just because a man has a million dollars he doesn't actually consume very much more than a man who has a thousand dollars. The very rich do not buy forty dollars' worth of ham and eggs for breakfast. If we want to preserve economic activity we must find a way to let everybody buy at least a half-dollar's worth of ham and eggs. This is the same old theory that 1,000 men with ten dollars each are a better market for any product than one man with ten thousand dollars and 999 men with nothing at all, or even than 500 men with five dollars apiece, and 500 with fifteen dollars each. This is a point of vital importance, which the Old Deal advocates persistently overlooked. That does not argue any effort to distribute wealth. When you try that you only distribute poverty. It does mean an effort *to distribute opportunity.*

When the President's Recovery Program finally got under way, employment and wages in this country were at a low point. Fierce competition and disproportions among great segments of consuming power were starving us in plenty, freezing us in warmth, and destroying us behind bulwarks of financial strength.

There is no virtue in sitting and taking all this and never striking back. Even the good Lord only mentioned turning one cheek and, when he found men in the court of the Temple fattening on the faith of a distressed people, he used the knotted end of a rope. This country had tried sitting and taking it for five years, and now it is trying to do something about it. That is the reason for NRA, AAA, PWA and all the loan and fiscal acts. We are here concerned only with NRA.

The most obvious, immediate way to erase the effect of the depression on wages and hours was the NRA project to decrease hours, to speed work and to increase wages to maintain purchasing power. The whole idea of shortening hours and raising wages has been attacked on this argument:

"The principal element of cost in any article is the labor cost. Increases in that cost by higher payments to those benefited simply increases price to the whole people whose capacity to buy is already so limited, that it may be assumed that they are buying all they can. The result can only be reduction in the tonnage of consumption and hence of manufacture and hence of net employment."

There is no doubt in the world that there is much here to give us pause. Dr. Sachs and I considered it prayerfully when we blocked out the NRA program. We relied, however, on PWA to activate the heavy industries at once and thus increase the *total number of available purchasers*. We relied on AAA to increase farm purchasing power immediately and thus still further add to the *number of purchasers*. These added to NRA additions would so far increase *volume* that we thought (and I still think) the increased labor cost could be absorbed without much increase in price. The President specifically asked industry to take this gamble. But we also relied on the principle just mentioned, that many men with a little each is a far better market than one man with much, and all the rest with nothing.

In other words, the argument against NRA just quoted would be stronger if *everybody had a job*. It doesn't make much difference to a man who has nothing at all whether the price of what he wants is high or low. We did not favor mere spreading of work *with no increase of hourly pay* for a reason already stated, but we *did* believe (and I still *do* believe), that a prudent and scientifically determined shortening of hours with no diminution of weekly pay can create new consumption which (even though the price be higher) will make far more tonnage than would be the case with fewer people with small employment and a vastly greater number with none at all. "Believe" is a weak word. It's a dead moral certainty. I must hasten to add that this implies no support to the idea of a 30-hour week with no decrease in weekly wages, indiscriminately applied. Its proponents say:

"You still have 10,000,000 unemployed and you have not reëmployed as many as 5,000,000 by all your efforts. This work must be divided and workers' incomes *must* be increased. NRA can't do it under the Codes as now written, because they only cut the work-week from 52 to 40 hours. 'Tain't enough! We are going to apply the 30-hour week to every company in this country by a statute. That will employ everybody and with everybody employed at high wages there will be both production and consumption and prosperity will return with a rush."

This would be tantamount to a 25% decrease in hours and a 33⅓% increase in the labor element of all costs. When you carry that 33⅓% through all states of production and distribution you would get somewhere near a 30% increase in price, and unless you put on rigid maximum price control, a much greater increase. But you would not by this means have increased the purchasing power of the agrarian population. You would have decreased their consuming power and so would you have decreased the consuming power of foreign customers and of everybody in this country to the extent that they depend on profits, salaries, incomes, professions, rents, pensions, or insurance. To what full extent this reduction of available market might go it is impossible to say, but it seems probable that the net result would be a sudden and catastrophic decline in consumption, production and employment.

I am fully aware that so much of this discussion as opposes the indiscriminate 30-hour week is applicable to what NRA has done, but there is this overwhelming difference. We did not pick our "figures out of the air." The efforts for improvement under NRA and the Blue Eagle were a result of exhaustive studies by Dr. Sachs, extending over years and brought up to date of the then existing economic conditions, especially with reference to farm prices and the general industrial situation. They were designed to attain and preserve a balanced economy of production and absorbing power as among many segments and they have proved to have been not far from right. *It is an untruth supported by nothing that prices have increased as fast or as far as purchasing power under NRA.* Agricultural purchasing power had already advanced, exports had been made easier and imports harder by the currency control. Interest and incomes were being restored by the banking policy and the new loan laws. PRA and NRA did no more than to try to bring wage earners up abreast of the rest. But *there is now no similar advance in farm price and other income to balance so drastic a change as would follow a 30-hour week with 40-hour wages throughout all industry.*

The second principle which the quoted criticism of NRA overlooks is that the increase in labor cost occasioned by NRA is by no means a constant *percentage* of total cost. If I have three clerks in a store at $300 a month cost, and if the three sell only $3,000 a month, that labor cost is 10% of total cost. But, if I sell $30,000 a month it is only 1% of total cost. Exactly the same principle applies to manufacture. Therefore, if by spreading purchasing power we can increase *volume of trade*, it by no means follows that cost or price will increase as fast as purchasing power and, as a matter of fact, *it has not done so*, although a rapid speculative rise in prices in June and July, 1933, almost ruined NRA before the Recovery Act was signed. It was due to the monetary policy, fear of the AAA processing tax and a too great apprehension of increased costs due to NRA.

Nevertheless it would be just as foolish to deny that the advocates of "let-us-alone" have anything at all on their side of the argument, as it would be to say that the principles just discussed are the end of the story. The truth lies in between. This middle course—as I shall try to show—was the real doctrine of NRA.

Critics also say: "Any method of limiting production is unsound. It is an economy of scarcity while what we want is an economy of plenty"—and then they tear into provisions in NRA codes limiting machine hours, usually citing the extreme case of some individual manufacturer who has suffered, but neglecting to mention the thousands who have benefited. They add, "Every new machine which lowers cost by reducing man power increases consumption through lowered cost. Now, NRA exercises control over new labor-saving machines—that is the foolish New Deal "economy of scarcity"—in AAA and NRA —*anathema marenatha!*"

These academic critics call themselves the Apostles of Plenty.

Of course, labor-saving machinery does reduce costs but it also reduces employment and, even if it raises the wages of those who remain employed, it leaves mass-purchasing power lower. In the long run I will admit that any opposition to it opposes the irresistible march of human progress and would be futile. But explosive and disruptive eliminations of employment should certainly be examined carefully as long as millions are still tramping the streets. Water is necessary to a man, but a neat little form of torture ending in murder (not unknown to the military) is to force about a gallon into him through a tube when his stomach is already full.

It is simple historical fact that shortened hours and higher wages—without any NRA at all—have been a constant concomitant of increased use of automatic machinery, beginning with 96 hours a week down to about half that on the advent of NRA.

As long ago as 1928, no less a rugged individualist than Herbert Hoover told the nation at Boston that, after increasing our per-man production in industry by 40% in a few years, we were producing more than we could consume at home and that we would *have to sell to export*—"*or else.*" And that was at a time when we were setting so close to "two cars in every garage" that we were almost ready to call in the carpenters— a time when inflated purchasing power was at its maximum. NRA has taken the position that some *regulation* of new labor saving devices is advisable, but it has never prohibited new installations. It has said only, "Let's look at them first, and if the government in consultation with the industry feel that they would now do more harm than good, let's postpone them."

For several years prior to NRA it had been my job for Mr. Baruch to keep in contact with new processes in industry from a purely practical point of view. No man who had lived through those years in that kind of a job could fail to agree with Mr. Hoover's 1928 Boston prophecy—not with his remedy of export trade.

I don't know how many *thousands* of thousands of years man required to get off his "all fours"—how many more *hundreds* of thousands to use polished stone implements—how many more to bows and arrows—how many *tens* of thousands to smelt metal—how many *thousands* to use gunpowder— how many *hundreds* of years to the French 75's. But I do know how many *mere years* it was from telegraph to wireless and from steam engine to motor bus and from gas to electric light, because *these far greater advances were all in my life time*, as compared with those early æons of such slight progress. My point is that scientific improvement is a movement not merely *progressing*. It is *accelerating* at terrific speed. And now, with research and scientific institutions multiplied and the scientific population raised to the tenth power, with the mass of classified knowledge behind them rolling up like a snowball—the things which are just over the horizon to boost the present per-man rate of production are appalling in their threat. Man as never before is "heir of all the age in the fore-most files of time." Economic progress has hopelessly outdis-tanced political advance and scientific improvement is far beyond them both. It is a badly unbalanced team and it must be supervised. Continued shortening of hours is and will con-tinue to be a necessity. Continued use of machinery and proc-esses replacing more and more men is inevitable. But we can't let any uncontrolled and volcanic effect of either or both of these trends produce a new set-back. *Let us balance one to the other and use such flexible supervision as NRA to prevent a catastrophe.*

The "economy of plenty" is not plain sailing. We have had it in agriculture ever since the war when, in order to feed our allied friends (who will not now pay even for what they ate—much less for the consequence to us of our efforts for them) we increased our production of cash crops to an astonishing degree. We had plenty with a vengeance when they stopped buying. The theory of the Apostles of Plenty is that that disaster resulting from too much surplus will starve out the surplus-producing acres down to a balance of supply and de-mand—but in twelve years *it hasn't*.

And if it *did*—what? Must we go through an indefinite period of peonage and destitution while starvation proceeds to balance the account? The farm tragedy in the United States is one of the most sickening chapters in our economic history. We can't sell more bread than people will eat, or make women go back to five and six petticoats to consume our cotton. Production of surplus beyond consumptive requirements has always destroyed price. Destructive price destroys wages which destroys consuming power which again destroys price down to the very depths of the 1933 pit.

Neither is it true in industry that excess productive capacity dries up when bankruptcy overtakes the marginal producer. Somebody simply buys up the ruin at a slaughter price and thus relieved of much of the overhead of interest, depreciation and taxation goes merrily on producing at a new cut-throat price. Why I know one old buggy plant that has been through liquida-tion over and over again. It still runs and most appropriately it is now making *hearses*.

The Apostles of Plenty must temper their doctrine. The answer is not to produce as much as you can at the lowest cost you can get, especially if that low cost comes out of wages or too abruptly out of employment. That simply starts the descent into the economic Avernus—cut employment, cut consuming power, cut production and so cut employment again. We simply must supervise these trends.

Always the answer is *"balance"*—balance of supply to demand, balance of prices at fair exchange parity throughout the whole economic structure, and balance of benefits among great economic areas. You cannot even move toward this balance in this modern muddle without *some* direction. NRA offers one way to get that supervision in industry just as AAA offers it in agriculture and the various securities and fiscal acts in investment and banking. These statutory makeshifts are not the final answer. Everybody knows that. They are hasty and imperfect. *But* the very heart of the New Deal is the principle of concerted action in industry and agriculture under government supervision looking to a balanced economy as opposed to the murderous doctrine of savage and wolfish competition and rugged individualism, looking to dog-eat-dog and devil take the hindmost. This Utopian balance will never be achieved—there will never be perfection. But every plan should try to achieve it instead of trying to prevent it.

The whole plan of recovery hinges on the same question of degree and balance. Anyone who will take the trouble to work out the curves of any of several basic commodities charted for price and superimpose them over a period of years will observe that in normally prosperous times they draw together like a hard-twisted rope but, in periods of exaggerated depression, or boom, they begin to spray out like separate strands of frayed rope. The exchange value of the commodities of lower price has been impaired and this immediately impairs consumption of producers in that group, and so *drags down price and production of all.* It really makes little difference whether prices and wages are high or low *so long as they fluctuate uniformly and together.* When they fluctuate together the *exchange* value of each man's efforts is preserved and all can enjoy the fruit of their efforts. When they do not fluctuate together the exchange value of the laggard group is depressed, and that depression of one great segment tends to pull the whole structure down. In our present shattered balance, five years have shown that we cannot depend solely on rugged individualism and "let-us-alone" to restore balance. We cannot get along without team work and control. With this thought in mind both AAA and NIRA were written and administered. They may have departed at times and in places from these principles, but they never departed very far and at least they knew what they were trying to do and—right or wrong—went some distance up the road toward the goal of doing it.

Of course, I *know* that I made many mistakes and blunders. I have sought unsparingly to confess them in this book, so that they will not be repeated. I know that the *law* isn't perfect. I know that the integrations of the various Emergency Administrations isn't complete, and, in my opinion, much improvement could be made in policies toward debts—public and private—taxes, spending, and money. But how anybody could expect anything else under such a complete readjustment as our economic structure must undergo is beyond my comprehension. To my mind the President has approached and administered this thing in the only way it could have been handled —"try and err and try again, but never let it get so far out of hand that you can't bring it back to try once more." That's what he has done and he has done it more quickly, safely, and effectively than any other man I know or have read about could possibly have done it. In the back of his mind, as he has frequently said, since the very beginning of his campaign and constantly throughout his administration, is exactly the idea I am trying so much less successfully to say here—the idea of a balanced economy as opposed to rugged individualism, savage competition, and "let-us-alone."

This idea of spreading purchasing power, elevating groups of depressed consuming power for the health of the whole to the end of enormously increased production and prosperity —indeed to the sole avenue of escape for our system from bitter destruction—that idea is not new with the Democratic party. The quotation from Mr. Raskob's speeches in 1928 contains the essence of all that has been said on that subject since. It was repeated emphatically by the candidate in 1932. It has been enunciated over and over again in the NRA campaigns. It is the very vitals of any recovery program that is not sounding brass and tinkling cymbals. A recent book of the Brookings Institution is heralded as unsetting these theories of NRA. It actually supports them. It showed, among other things, that $\frac{1}{10}$ of 1% of all American families enjoy an income greater than 42% of all American families, that 21% of all families received $4\frac{1}{2}$% of income, and that 71% received less than the average. There is nothing new about this. NRA was conceived on similar statistics. But this does not argue that we should rush to produce as much as we can. It argues that we must try to iron out these disparities as quickly as we can and thus increase our power to consume for thus only can our productive capacity be utilized.

You can't float a ship without water, and you don't sell goods to the busted part of any community.

# Chapter XVII

# NRA VS. ANTI-TRUST ACTS

"We sought to prohibit price fixing when it would result in monopoly ... which is the only kind of price fixing to which objection has been raised on this floor."
—*Senator Robert F. Wagner, June 12, 1933.*

BEFORE going further with this narrative, it will be well to consider briefly the evolution of the philosophy on which NRA was based.

Before the war, American business was a honeycomb of water-tight industrial compartments. Each cell was jealously guarded. There was a maximum of competition and a minimum of coöperation. Ruthless and untempered competition was decreed by the Sherman and Clayton acts. The war changed that. The world went mad. The nations entered a contest to see which could pour the greatest mass of its young manhood and the largest amount of its money and property into the fire in the shortest space of time. That was the way to win the war.

The old honeycomb machine of the United States couldn't produce things fast enough in this race to destroy everything. We had to scrap it. And in the short period between April, 1917, and November, 1918, we literally tore it apart and put it together again. On the call of government and under the pressure of patriotism the old individualist battlers royal became an organized squad—all marching toward the sound of the guns.

We did not repeal the Anti-Trust Acts. *We simply ignored them.* Competitors pooled their resources, their trade secrets, their facilities. Industries organized themselves into groups and figures with the speed and almost the precision of a highly drilled chorus on a musical comedy stage and government took charge of both production and consumption and to a large extent, prices. It worked. It poured forth such a flood of product

172

tion for the uses of war as the world had never seen in one country. It won the war.

Woodrow Wilson dispersed the 1918 model Industrial Control Mechanism with a single edict before the year of the Armistice was out. But much of the change in the underlying pattern of trade and industry which had resulted from it, remained. The country had learned that coöperation and organization pay. It had learned that high wages and short hours create wider domestic markets—richer than any market to be sought elsewhere in the whole world. It was freely said: "If coöperation can do so much maybe there is something wrong with the old competitive system."

As the War Administration broke up, its Chief made a memorandum suggesting the possibility of a High Court of Commerce and Labor for peace, and a few men who had seen it all made specific suggestions that the Anti-Trust laws be amended to permit industrial organization and self-government by coöperation. The public interest intended to be conserved by those laws was to be protected by providing for a revocable government permit of any particular act or course of conduct which, without such permit, would be illegal under the Anti-Trust Acts. The permits would be withdrawn in case of abuse. That idea was very prevalent but it ran into this snag.

What political authority could be entrusted to issue and revoke such permits? The Federal Trade Commission had been set up with some such thought in mind. The assertion was made that it had become more of a policeman and an inquisitor than an administrator. It was manned by officials of the legal or academic or political type rather than by men adept in business, labor, and consumer problems and having something more than a legalistic concept of economic necessity. It was urged that these circumstances had turned aside the original idea of its creation and that any similar political supervisory unit would arrive at the same end. It was alert to tell industry what it could *not* do. It would never say what it *could* do. The slightest coöperation, planning, or industrial control was practiced at peril. To this good day the policy, philosophy, and action of that body is repressive of coöperation—and, while it is of great value in its own field and will always be required in that field, it could not in its present concept add anything to the attainment of a balanced economy. It does not believe in any brakes

on such wild industrial racing as ended in the 1929 debacle.[1]
It believes in *laissez faire* on an individual basis. Instead of
being a curb on monopoly, it has become the Mother of Monopoly. It must be made very clear that I do not criticize this.
The Commission is carrying out the law of its creation. There
is still a conflict of opinion as to how far that law was amended
by NRA. We shall speak of that in another place.

Several resourceful alternatives were suggested to carry
out the post-war proposal, the principal one being the High
Court of Commerce and Labor already mentioned. It was to
have all the dignity in business and labor that the Supreme
Court maintains in law and generally. It was to be made so
desirable and honorable a post that the very elder statesmen
of business, labor, and economics, would aspire to it just as
the very cream of the legal profession aspires to the Supreme
Bench.

By the time this idea developed we were in the very back-
wash of the high idealism of war. We were on the road to
"normalcy" and little green Washington houses and little black
bags and Tea-pot Domes, and Ku Klux Klans. Bootlegging and
racketeering had begun. Nobody seemed to be seeking the
rarefied atmosphere of any High Court of Commerce. The war
heritage of organization and coöperation in industry and trade
remained—but subject to no restraining influence and informed by no common purpose for the public good.

The hold-over war organization of industry began to work as
we came out of the depression of 1921, moving toward the
1928–1929 fantasy of economic whoopee which preceded and
induced the collapse of '29 and the succeeding four years of
economic hell. In all those years nobody again mentioned
Codes of Fair Competition.

We had supervised coöperation in the war because we had to
have it or suffer defeat. There was a "let-us-alone" gang then
also, but we swept them into the ash can and there was no
longer any sentiment for the old slogan of "Let-us-alone" be-

[1]It is interesting to note that there were two Federal agencies set up to prevent just
such an event as the 1928–1929 boom and crash—the Federal Trade Commission and
the Federal Reserve System. In the 1920–21 inflation the latter did intervene—perhaps
too violently. But in 1928–1929, beyond a few spineless gestures, nothing was done to
prevent disaster. That was because politics informed policy and politics was gauged to
the upward swing of prices on the Stock Exchange. It was one of the most unfortunate
maladministrations in our fiscal history.

cause all knew that government intervention was the sole salvation. When that pressure was gone, "Let-us-alone" rebounded into light and became the guiding principle of government administration from the depths of 1921 to the giddy peaks of 1929.

"Let-us-alone" and unhampered individualism worked well enough during the formative days of individual pioneering—nothing else would have worked—but it did not work when we had to meet the war crisis and after-the-war reorganization of trade and industry. It had become a relic of old days and, as things turned out, a very dangerous one.

"Let-us-alone" and every man to himself is one thing when every man can *be* for himself, but it is a very different thing when progress has organized it out of existence but statutes still retain it.

At the adoption of the Constitution almost everybody worked for himself—the boot and shoe industry was the village cobbler, the textile industry was the housewife and the weaver, the steel industry was the forge and the smithy, the electric light industry was the candle maker, and so forth through the whole gamut. In such a scene we invented the doctrine of rugged individualism.

This condition lasted in the Mississippi Basin until the Civil War. Even then as small factories and group employment invaded the Valley, there was always an escape for a man out of work. The road to free lands in the West was always open and —most such men still being aware of how to plant and reap a crop, build a log or sod house, skin or milk a cow and slaughter a hog—they had no need for either sympathy, doles, or regulation of industry when things went wrong.

But even preceding the World War that condition began to vanish. No free and fertile lands remained. Men were already specialized. Colonies of city men transported to the dry farming country of the High Line of the Northwest had to be rescued from famine.

If you set a modern white collar man and his family down on a rich virgin prairie with a team and tools, they would starve to death in a month. In a great depression like this there is little for the modern specialist to do but perish from tramping the streets hungry or else to ask for charity. That is not the American heritage of liberty. It is liberty to starve—and it is the only alternative for millions if we go back to the old system.

In the post-war rush toward more mechanization, greater industrial centralization and more refined specialization—to the average small merchant, artisan or clerk, rugged individualism ceased to mean anything but disaster.

I need not recount here the statistics of that vast coalescence —the growth of the chain store system crowding out small shops—the expansion of facilities in great groups of industry eliminating lesser factories—the death struggles of the survivors reflected by corporate returns even at the peak of 1929 showing fifty per cent of industrial establishments operating in the red—a constant contraction of independent establishments of every class—even the professions tending toward service in great legal department stores, engineering associates and medical clinics. There is no question about it—the war showed the way and the unchecked flight from economic individualism had gone so far by 1929, that any reasonable projection of the curve of its then trend would have shown in ten years an almost complete elimination of any kind of living in the United States (except possibly in agriculture and that is doubtful) which would not have come from investments, wages, or salaries.

There is now much talk about the desirability of a return to the good old Anti-Trust Acts and the safety of the Federal Trade Commission. They talk about the mild control of NRA, as encouraging monopoly, oppressing small enterprise, and thus threatening people with economic serfdom. We shall discuss some of these things in detail later; here it is enough to say that *NRA will have to move on a broad front and at terrific speed if it can beat that record of the destruction of individual enterprise made under the full force of the Anti-Trust Acts, the negative powers of the Federal Trade Commission, and the most active business period in our history.*

It is black on the record that the unchecked competitive plan under the Anti-Trust Acts was destroying small enterprise of every kind at a most astonishing rate. It is a shorter record but equally certain the NRA has exactly reversed this killing process. Competition down to reasonable cost is still as free as air but the public does not want and cannot afford competition of bankrupt stocks and it is now protected against the flim-flam of being enticed into a store by a window display of some popular product being sold for half its cost and then inveigled into buying other things at a good fat profit. There is a curious—almost maddening confusion in terms when superficial observers begin using the words "monopoly," "price fixing," "anti-trust acts," etc.

The Anti-Trust Acts prohibit combinations in restraint of trade. But NRA specifically permits such combinations with government sanction and supervision. *There is not one single Code that is not a combination in restraint of trade,* and if Codes are not permitted so to restrain trade then NIRA ought to be repealed tomorrow. It doesn't mean a thing.

*But both NIRA and the Anti-Trust Acts do prohibit monopoly* —there is no question about that. The only real question that has been raised comes from the assertion that price agreements and combinations in restraint of trade *are of themselves* monopolistic. *That is the very heart of the question that plagues NRA.*

Of course price control *can* be used as a weapon of monopoly. It has frequently been so used and that use of it was the very reason for the Anti-Trust Acts themselves. But that was price control *downward* in an effort to destroy competition and practiced by powerful combinations for the specific and determined purpose of oppressing and wiping out small enterprise and individual initiative, and transforming all business in the country into a gigantic corporate cluster under private control—an unthinkable and intolerable result. No such thing exists or is attempted or could exist or be attempted under any code. NRA price stabilizations are all for exactly the reverse purpose—to prevent cut-throat and monopolistic price slashing, to maintain small industry, to continue employment, to abolish economic murder. There is only a fragmentary element of cases where this is not true—i.e., cases in which small industries can pay code wages and actually undersell large ones and whenever and as often as this happens relief is given at once. There was never a more ghastly, nonsensical, and destructive anomaly than the charge that price controls under NRA tend toward monopoly. The trend is in precisely the reverse direction. So far as that particular argument is concerned it is a silly sophistry inimical to the public welfare.

Furthermore, while there is price stabilization in many codes, there is actual price fixing in only three or four cases and in those, such as Bituminous Coal—it was absolutely necessary to support the labor dependent on that industry and to prevent bloody and implacable economic war. That became so apparent and unavoidable during the Bituminous negotiations that I called the President's attention to it and obtained his personal approval to negotiations on that basis.

Of course there are two other aspects of this subject which are rarely mentioned but which are really matter for grave concern. In the first place there are parts of industries which have been built up on *low prices derived from sweated labor*—such as sweat shops, dependents on home piece-work and child labor, and other cases which will be described at another place. When *they* are forced by NRA to pay living wages, they cannot continue to exist. They say, therefore, that NRA *oppresses* them. But as to this the President, in giving NRA its marching orders, took the bull by the horns. He said that *no industry which depends for existence on less than living wages has a right to continue to exist.* And on that phase of my administration I stand or fall. These were not only my orders—they were also my convictions. I will concede that all the regional differentials under NRA are not scientifically worked out. I know there is a wide field where readjustment is necessary. But that is no argument for permitting the return of the scandalous labor conditions revealed by NRA.

The second question is *whether the consumer has a right to the lowest prices that any kind of competition can provide.* The Anti-Trust Acts say yes. NIRA says no. And there is the white-hot center of the dispute. Everybody is a consumer. Nearly everybody depends on *some* enterprise in the competitive field. Consumers are not entitled to low prices achieved by the degradation of human labor and if they were entitled to them they would be fatuous to accept them, because once the principle is admitted it applies to all human labor and all human labor consumes. Nor are consumers wise in seeking the low prices of economic slaughter—especially at a time like this when explosive and disruptive changes in the existing structure throw more and more people out of work.

On all these considerations, NRA came as a blessed alleviation of the dog-eat-dog rule of the Anti-Trust Acts. This does not mean that there is no competition or even any improper limitation of competition under NRA. It means only that competition must keep its blows above the belt, and that there can be no competition at the expense of decent living. The only price limitations in NRA outside of three (or at most four) special cases, are limitations against making a practice of selling at less than cost of production for the purpose of destroying competition or of preventing competition based on the degradation of human labor.

This is a point so poignant, so important to the welfare of all people, so obvious and irrefutable that it is a stark pity that there are no words strong enough or clear enough to make it crystalline and compelling. The zeal of advocacy of the Consumers' Advisory Board has done more to obscure this vital principle than any other single influence.

Here I want to acknowledge a blunder in setting up the Consumers' Advisory Board as I did. NRA was not the only (or even a principal) element of increased prices to consumers. Far more effective were:

(a) The monetary policy deliberately designed to boost the whole price structure very materially.

(b) The AAA deliberately designed to raise food and cotton prices not merely by some fixed increment, but to raise *and keep* them at their pre-war *ratio* to industrial prices so that, after the first zoom to parity, they were to continue to advance just as fast as industrial prices advanced.

(c) State and national spending and taxing policy (which out of a national income of not more than 40 billions was taking no less than $33\frac{1}{3}\%$) which was bound to result in increased prices.

The Board representing consumers should not have been set up exclusively in NRA where it felt a duty to "*Make a record*" and attack *every* Code on general principles, and without regard to other influences affecting prices, and especially when, in its argument, it cited price increases which were resultants of all these forces, and on that ground opposed reasonable provisions of NRA price stabilization which were responsible for less than a tithe of the advances cited.

The Consumers' Advisory Board should have been independent of all administrations, should have been a sort of liaison among all, and should have been a composite of labor, economic, industrial and popular representation. Thus constituted, it should have sought, and have been placed in a position to seek, some composition of all diverse policies for the best interest of the people as a whole and then (instead of attacking everything) it should have supported that composition. I never heard of the Consumers' Advisory Board supporting anything in NRA. The President himself is the real representative of Consumers, i.e., of the whole people of the United States.

The solution of these as well as most of our other economic problems is so to manage controls in the codes and elsewhere that, on one hand, the consumer is not injured by any invention and on the other that labor and small enterprise are not destroyed by return to cut-throat prices or any oppression.

That is why the government sits in every Code Authority and that is why it must forever continue vigilantly to do so. But there never was any theory or principle that the Consumers' Board was put there to amend or frustrate the purpose of the law under which it was created. It was put there to fulfill the law.

Our philosophy was that competition by price cutting below cost for the purpose of driving competition out of markets must necessarily come out of the wages of labor. *Nobody in NRA and least of all myself ever favored arbitrary price fixing.* But so far as I know everybody in NRA while I was there opposed economic slaughter through the price-slashing route. The press reports Mr. Donald Richberg as now opposing price stabilization and the new Administrative Officer of NRA, Mr. W. Averell Harriman, as saying that he proposes to see that rules against selling below cost are abolished and adding that such was the invariable recommendation of the Industrial Advisory Board during my régime. As to Mr. Richberg, he was General Counsel when these codes were approved and, as he himself has said, never was in disagreement on policy. I do not know what considerations wrought his change of heart—if any. Although I understand that he now asserts that some codes under criticism were never able to get the O.K. of the Legal Department of NRA, the records will not bear him out.

I can scarcely credit what Mr. Harriman and Mr. Richberg are supposed to have said as accurate reporting, because, as to the assertion that the Industrial Advisory Board took any position against NRA price policy, the whole record will disclose that it is without the slightest justification in fact.

My good friend Henry Wallace, in his lucid book *New Fron-*

*tiers*, registers some disagreement with NRA policies. He thinks there should not be price stabilization without unlimited inquisitorial powers in government over all books in Industry. He also thinks that *"cost of production"* is not a proper basis for price stabilization.

With much of what he says, I agree, but not with all and to make the difference clear, I am going to try to say exactly what I was striving for in NRA.

Nobody ever fought price fixing as hard as I did in the Petroleum Code and in many other places. Petroleum was a special case. All they needed was *production* control. That attained, price would take care of itself. The only price fixing that would then be needed there would be *maximum* price fixing to protect the public. Precisely the opposite consideration obtained in Bituminous Coal. In other words, there is no iron rule. But our goal was clearly this:

There should be no secrecy about prices. They should be posted openly. Sellers should be free to change their prices instantly and at will, but actual net prices at which goods are sold should be as available to the public and to competitors as are daily prices on the stock or commodity exchanges. There should be a general rule against predatory price slashing with a fundamental principle that consistent sales below cost of production are at least prima facie evidence of a destructive tendency and an unfair practice. When such a tendency appears, any member can complain to the Code Authority which, with government representation, hears the complaint and if subversive and unfair competition thus appears, then in the industrial self-government to which NRA has always been dedicated, and under direct government supervision to prevent abuse of power, the Code Authority can order a stop to it. That order after appeal to an administrative NRA tribunal should be enforceable in the Courts.

That is—and since the beginning consistently has been—the sum and substance of NRA policy on price control. If it has changed, I do not know it. As I have said before, there are special cases and special emergencies but this is the standard rule, and I make bold to say that when that policy is abandoned, NRA will have passed into the hands of its enemies and should be immediately rescued or else completely abandoned.

In the distributing trades costing is simple. Cost is net invoice cost plus, under NRA, a maximum of 10% to cover expense. No merchant can consistently maintain a policy of selling for less than cost. If he does so, there is smoke enough to indicate a fire that should be extinguished, and after an extensive inquiry extending over years I know of no legitimate merchant who sells at an expense of less than 10% on cost.

Now this is not price fixing at all. It is a method for preventing monopolistic price slashing. And it does not require, as Henry Wallace suggests, any inquisitional power over all books and accounts in general. It requires access only to cost figures, and then only to particular costs in a hearing on a particular complaint.

There is under NIRA unlimited power in government to complain against and to investigate any instance where prices seem improperly high with an adequate remedy in case it finds such to be the case.

I have an idea that my friend Wallace would not dissent from this policy and that his remarks are really addressed to abuses of or exceptions from it, but if such is not the case—(and while it is not an argument)—*tu quoque* applies to AAA—*it is the biggest price-fixing attempt in the history of the world.*

I do not say this in any critical sense for, as he points out in his book, I was co-author of the very price-parity formula on which he is operating. It is justified by a scalding emergency—the threatened destruction of the whole agricultural community as we have known it. All of which leads me to say in passing that there is no more thoughtful and moderate-minded man in the administration than Henry Wallace.

There is a school—I had, inaccurately, almost said "of thought"—in NRA that has prevailed since I left it which insists that any provision against predatory price slashing is "economically unsound" and "unenforceable" and "rendered unnecessary by the wage-fixing rules." I fear that they have prevailed and that new NRA legislation proposed by the Administration will follow this so-called view. It is a ghastly paradox and I will fight it with all I have to give. Here we have self-styled reformers echoing the shibboleth of some of the most reactionary influences in this country. It is a shivering inconsistency, explicable only by the almost bucolic innocence of practical business experience in its proponents and chief champions. Of course it is espoused by those of NRA who represent the most predatory of interests. For reasons already stated, if this academic fatuity is to prevail, NRA should be folded up and put away in lavender or—better and far different—set to guard the harem of rapacity incarnate. It will have been completely emasculated.

Wallace is also right in saying in effect that you cannot act to stabilize prices unless you have some control over production. During the war we had the most effective price control ever known in economic history, but there we had complete power over both supply and demand.

However, organized Industry under a well administered Code *will* control production. It can do so where agriculture unorganized and in some five to six million separate units cannot do so. No industrial producer who knows all about the price and inventory situation in his industry is going to over-produce in the face of an unmanageable surplus and a downward price trend. It will not necessarily require any quota system to attain the end of controlled industrial production. All that is needed in industry is full, accurate, complete, and honest information on prices and inventories. With that in hand we shall never see another such phantasmagoria as we saw in 1928–1929.

It is not so in agriculture. Who can persuade—who can herd into one corral—the individualistic, the obtuse, the recalcitrant, among 6,000,000 separate farming enterprises—however well informed?

When the Revolution came every member of a village community was an individualist—the blacksmith, the weaver, the tailor, the butcher, the baker, the candlestick-maker—and *the farmer*. Economic progress has compounded them all—all except the farmer who remains today as in 1776 he was. There is no way to get his fair share of modern economic integration except in such a way as Henry Wallace is, without too much certainty, trying. It is the only salvation for agriculture.

There is no great mystery about costs—much as the accountants may dispute. Every able manufacturer knows not only his own costs but, in close approximation, the costs of his competitors.

I speak from experience. There is no more varied industrial product than farm implements. Yet regardless of the speed and efficiency of plants there was a time when I—relatively a tyro—could walk through a competitor's sample floor and tell, within reason, what it cost him to make anything from a manure spreader to one section of a peg tooth harrow and there were men on my staff like Bob Lea and Harold Dineen who could tell within 1% and bet money on their judgment.

On the NRA policy as I have defined it, an effective stop to monopolistic price cutting and preservation of small enterprise, will follow price posting as a matter of course.

The net of all I have just written is to urge that price fixing is not necessarily monopolistic and under NRA it is not monopolistic at all. But there remains the other assertion that *any combination in restraint of trade is monopolistic in and of itself*. As previously remarked if it is, NRA had better be abandoned because *every* code is a combination in restraint of trade. For example the Petroleum Code's provision to limit production is restraint of trade, limitations on machine hours are restraints, agreements against child labor and sweat shops and in favor of maximum hours and minimum wages are all restraints of trade. So are agreements not to use particular kinds of advertising, or secret rebates, or credit terms which might ruin companies not financed to grant them, and so forth and so on through the infinite variety of NRA code provisions.

But these things are *not* of themselves monopolistic. A monopolistic combination is an easy thing to concoct. But whether a combination is monopolistic or not, is a question of fact. Code combinations are not conspiracies of a few companies. They are open to a whole industry on absolutely equal terms to great and little companies. It would be impossible to create a combination of that kind that could be monopolistic. It might be repugnant to consumers' interest or be otherwise objectionable. But the word "industry" comprises *all* competitors in a particular field and if all competitors in an industry operate under the same code rule, that rule could not possibly be monopolistic.

NRA contended that neither price fixing nor fair trade practices authorized by NIRA are under the ban of the Anti-Trust Acts, unless they are monopolistic or oppressive, *in fact*. Some of NRA's enemies contend that *any* price fixing or *any* combination is inherently monopolistic. That, of course, means that the deliberate Act of Congress known as NIRA is simply a nullity.

They go much further and insist that price fixing was not authorized by NIRA. Senator Borah says this specifically. If any man ought to know the contrary to be the case, he is that man. Before the Act was passed, he introduced an amendment requiring that codes *should not permit price fixing and combinations in restraint of trade.* I happened to be before the Conference Committee when that came in approved by the Senate, but rejected by the House. I pointed out that it would completely nullify the Act, and it was stricken out by the Conference Committee leaving only the words prohibiting monopoly and oppression. The fact that the Conference Committee's report was adopted after this history is conclusive that the President was given authority to approve both price fixing and combinations under Codes of Fair Competition so long as they should not be monopolistic. On this subject, Senator Borah himself on the Senate floor, four days before the law was passed, said exactly what NRA then believed—I do not know what it believes now. I think that all it stood for is being scuttled.

"This therefore is the situation, Trade Associations may meet and formulate codes and these codes may contain combinations in restraint of trade. The codes may fix prices. I take it, therefore, that it is proposed to leave free power of code makers to do these two things, and if they see fit to fix prices by the codes there is no inhibition in the Bill against it. It is thoroughly understood by business men generally that this is the effect of the amendment."

I have never heard any able lawyer dispute this conclusion. The only legal limitation on price fixing and code combination is that neither shall be used for monopolistic or oppressive purposes.

But to return to our story—during the whirling, industrial period between the war and the depression, the rapid growth of domestic demand due to post-war higher wages and shorter hours, encouraged the creation of bigger and bigger industrial units, greater and greater industrial capacity, and vast profits accrued—not to "little fellows" but on paper, at least, to these great economic clusters. There was economic planning a-plenty but the planning was done by executives of vast corporations. Even that might have saved us but there were too many plans with no cohesion, coördination, or control and with no regard for industry as a whole, or labor as a whole, or even for the country as a whole, but only for the competitive victory of the particular industrial unit—rugged individualism of gigantic artificial corporate persons, but no rugged individualism of any natural person except in his rôle as a servant or master within them.

And because, for each of them separately, there was no incentive—nor even any leeway—to do otherwise, they separately plowed so much of gross profit and the people's savings back into increasingly excessive capacity and distributed too little of it as wages and dividends to sustain the buying power of the rich domestic market which the war changes had created on their own doorsteps. They literally starved that market to death. This has been recently denied and the denial backed by a bristling marshaling of imposing figures showing how little accumulated surplus in industrial balance sheets would have aided consumption if they *had* been distributed. They are entirely beside the point. They neglect to say how much of popular savings and credit was also thus frozen and they came from the "economist" of a bank which was as responsible for as much of this delusion as any.

The biggest and most expensive industrial plant or apartment house or office building in the world is a liability instead of an asset (worth less than zero) unless it can earn money. It can only earn money if it can maintain a profitable market for its product. If there are too many of them in any given market area none can earn money. In the period of 1922–1929, non-existent earning power was capitalized by withdrawing or withholding money (consuming power) from the public and freezing it forever into the steel, bricks, and mortar of an astonishing excess capacity-to-produce, in practically every industrial and commercial activity.

The record of this lunacy is too recent and too astonishing for any economist of an affected bank to attack with any statistical abracadabra. It burned the candle at both ends in that it destroyed the consuming power of the American market by congealing it in bricks and mortar at the same moment that it was destroying the earning power of industry itself by overcapacitating its productive facilities. It was sheer, stark madness and it was a direct and inevitable result of the Anti-Trust legislation.

Take the steel plow industry as a single example which could be paralleled by a hundred others. There is one plant in Moline, Illinois, which could turn out all the steel plows required by the whole of American Agriculture. Yet that capacity is multiplied no less than ten times in the United States.

Nothing like that could have happened if, during that crazed period, the industries of this country could have taken counsel and united action under governmental sanction and supervision. It happened because they were doomed by the law to unchecked and uncontrolled competition—doomed by the law not to take common counsel, not to regard each industry as a unit and not to regard the country as an economic integer in which every citizen had an interest and every employer an obligation. They could not have saved themselves because any company that lagged in the fight for a new capacity, constantly increasing production, and the other fellow's market, would go to the wall. The laws of the United States simply said: "Root hog or die— Devil take the hindmost," and the Devil took it all. "The bigger they are, the harder they fall," and this structure first became monstrously big and then fell with a crash that shook the whole world.

A volume has been published by a private institution for study of economic trends which affects to show that there is no over-capacity to produce all that the people of this country *want* to consume. Of course, in a state of perfect balance among various economic segments, there is hardly any limit to what this country could consume of *some* things. For example it could not consume more than it needs of wheat or animal fats, or tobacco, or drugs, or agricultural products generally.

But this is altogether beside the point. We are so far from equitable balance among various segments of our people and there are so many barriers to the exchange of goods and services that it might as well be said that if we had 200,000,000 more people here, we could consume as much as we could produce with our present capacity, as to say that there is no over-capacity because if such and such other facts were present, we could consume all that it could produce. These facts are neither present nor immediately attainable. There *is* an overwhelming excess of productive capacity in this country and its presence can also be charged as a crime of *laissez faire* under the Anti-Trust Acts. As B. M. Baruch said in his Senate testimony:

"I am not speaking of 'over-production' which is a mere co-relative of 'under-consumption.' I mean *excess productive capacity*.

I mean the vast plants which (though idle now) sometimes seem to me like masked batteries of machine-guns waiting to lay down a new barrage of production whenever buying reappears. We must find means to control production, especially of farm and mineral output. It is a stupendous development throughout the whole world—sugar, silk, rayon, wheat, rubber, coffee, tin, iron, and copper. I know of no exception."

You can't have recovery without amending the Anti-Trust Acts because you must prevent a repetition of 1922–1929. You can't do that without control and you can't have that control under Anti-Trust legislation. Those Acts have failed in every crisis. They had to be forgotten during the war to enable the country to defend itself. When they came back to memory in 1919, they set the stage for what happened up to 1929. They contributed to the boom and they were helpless in the crash. Without amendment, following the principles of NIRA, they will go on (as they did) to create the very condition of monopoly and erasure of individualism which they were conceived to prevent and in the future, as in the past, they will have to be abandoned in any crisis economic or military. Unless so amended, they have no place in the mechanized, highly organized and integrated civilization in which we live. *There is no more vital and fundamental issue before the country than whether we are going to control modern scientific and industrial development to our use or suffer it to our destruction.*

The only forces that *can* control it are industrial self-government under Federal supervision and the only plan that has ever been presented through which that control can be applied is NRA. If we scrap NRA, it will be just like releasing on a roomful of school children a flock of mechanical man-eating Frankensteins—irresistible and ravenous. If we follow and develop and perfect NRA, it will be like harnessing them, putting brains into their brazen skulls and driving them in a powerful team to pull us out of the mud of this morass.

# Chapter XVIII

# PREPARATION FOR ATTACK ON THE NRA FRONT

---

"One sentence will undoubtedly be remembered till our Republic ceases to exist:—
*No duty the Executive had to perform was so trying as to put the right man in the right place.*"

—*McMaster on Thomas Jefferson.*

---

FOR four years of the depression men hoped and fought, but about March, 1933, they lost hope. Industrial management sought to abdicate. There may have been men in this country who thought that we should continue to do nothing about it— still to sit and suffer, but I do not know who they were. There was hardly an industrial, economic, financial, commercial, or agricultural leader who did not advance some idea of governmental intervention. A snowfall of paper plans drifted about the Capitol, and there was not one of them that would not, in some measure, have modified the Anti-Trust Acts.

Some of the plans emanating from very throne rooms of industry were fantastic; for example, that every factory in the United States should (under government subsidy and on a given day) suddenly blow the whistles and start up at once on the 1929 rate of production—the idea being that this would instantly restore 1929 employment and consumption, and bring back the rare old, fair old, golden days just as the Kiss of a Prince Charming awoke not only the Sleeping Beauty, but also the whole retinue of the Enchanted Palace. It overlooked our loss of foreign trade, the fact that the consuming power of agriculture was still paralyzed, and the wreckage of debt and bankruptcy from the great delusion. Another plan provided for immediate government loans of billions to all industry on deferred priority on the theory that this would pay off prior liens and release purchasing power. There were others proposing a complete dictatorship, and the immediate adoption of the

Fascist corporate state. One which is being again put forward is that factories start, and the government will buy all that the people do not buy.

Haven't we had enough of unmanageable surplus? If the presence of it hanging over a market will destroy agriculture, why will it not destroy industry? What all such plans fail to realize is that it is not a loss of industrial turnover of 8 or 10 billions a year that keeps us down. *It is a loss of 40 billions.* We can't restore *that* by anything the government can do directly. Even this government could not entertain any such outlay. We must seek to activate our private economic mechanism—not to substitute a political mechanism.

All these plans seemed to present insurmountable obstacles and none to meet the problems just discussed. Out of the paper drifts, there soon began to emerge the new financial, banking, bankruptcy, and loan-lifting legislation, the Farm Act and the Recovery Act. We are here concerned only with the latter, but we must always remember that it was intended to be only part of an integrated legislative whole which President Roosevelt had sketched in very broad outlines during the summer of 1932.

The economic cataclysm of March, 1933, cried out that if anything were to be done under the various emergency acts, it must be done quickly. As monetary, farm, debt, and industrial legislation began to take shape a new peril began to appear. It was less obvious in form than the deep collapse, but even more threatening in substance. Industry began to rush to speculative production and prices entered an upward spiral which threatened a run-away. The cause was clear enough. Many people thought that threatened currency depreciation, increased wages under NRA, and the processing tax would instantly be reflected in an exactly proportional increase in the whole price schedule. They hurried to turn their money into goods to take advantage of this expected artificial rise. Nobody knew the extent of possible effects of the new projects, and all manufacturers likely to be affected tried to "beat the gun" by producing as much as possible before the processing tax could become effective, and before labor wages should be raised by conditions expected to be contained in the codes. Warehouses began to fill up with cotton gray goods, sometimes purchased by men who were not even in the textile business. Everybody was stocking up on all staples and a false industrial activity started with a bang.

Except in isolated cases, wage scales, under this impetus and *before NRA*, were *not* improving and employment was not increasing proportionately with production. Purchasing power was lagging far behind the mass and cost of production. In short there was threatened a new mountain of undigested and indigestible goods and—of course—a new wave of unemployment and despair. The country was in no temper to stand such a setback of hope and expectation.

In every past recovery, improvement in wages and working conditions has always conspicuously lagged behind improvement in prices and production. This has invariably produced a temporary secondary reaction punctuated by decreased consumption, sagging prices, strikes, labor unrest and finally improved wages. But in this case, the price and production increases were so steep and so strongly stimulated, the depths from which they rose so disastrous and the wage-lag so stubborn, that then, as never before, speed and action were absolutely necessary. The Recovery Act was included in the general plan for the very purpose of eliminating any lag at all in wages and employment and of remodeling the usual trend to the end of producing a steady recovery at an equable and uninterrupted rate. But the extraordinary phenomenon of speed in increased price and production had created an emergency which would brook no delay.

Long before the actual Farm Bill was presented, B. M. and I had been discussing these problems with George Sloan and Nelson Slater of the Cotton Textile Industry, the packers, and Jim Bell of General Mills Co., trying to get some spontaneous industrial support of what had been proposed in the campaign as the economic policy of the new administration. It did not seem to succeed too well except with the Cotton Textile people. They responded at once and to this good day they have not faltered. But in the light of my experience with the industrialists I have never doubted that we could have reached prompt and complete agreement with both millers and packers.

A little later Secretary Wallace offered B. M. Baruch the job of Administrator of the Agricultural Adjustment Act, later accepted by George Peek. Bernie felt that someone better known to farmers should take that job. The incident is interesting because if the task had been accepted there is no doubt that both George Peek and I would have gone along as assistants with B. M. and the NRA effort might have been better directed.

All this happened to be in connection with the proposed Farm Bill—a subject on which Mr. Peek and I had spent much study and he much effort. George Peek was at last called in on that, and so were B. M. and myself, but not until after Henry Morgenthau and Rex Tugwell had given it cast and direction. Our idea was that the way to restrict the surplus production that for ten years had ruined agriculture was to rent or purchase (and let lie fallow) the surplus-producing acreage, which could have been done at that time at not too great a cost. We had worked out a complete plan for doing it. That idea suffered shipwreck on the proposition of Dr. Mordecai Ezekiel that it is economic law that you cannot rent any land except at the gross value of its potential product—for example, that an Iowa farm, producing 25 bushels of corn per acre at fifty cents a bushel, could not be rented for one cent less than twelve dollars and fifty cents per acre. We had conducted a practical survey which indicated that all surplus producing acreage in the United States could be rented at an average of three dollars an acre. But you could not get by the dictum of Dr. Ezekiel: "That is not the economics of the situation."—And this to George Peek, who has made his living in the corn-lands from so far back that he would hate to hear the tally of years so much as mentioned!

One day, walking into the President's office, I was deeply engrossed in a warm discussion with the good Doctor and not realizing that we were clear inside that office I replied to his "That is not good economics" with a rather ribald remark about good economics and it fell on one of those curious silences that carried it clear across the room. I saw the President's eye twinkle and I almost swallowed my tongue.

On the meat situation, we had a simple proposition that, for giving the packers the privilege of sustaining the price to consumers by exactly enough to support the increased costs and permitting them to consolidate their multifarious distributing systems to reduce cost or distribution—all under governmental supervision—they were to pay farmers the pre-war parity price for animal farm products—and part of the savings in distribution—with several more or less technical provisions to prevent shifts to substitutive foodstuffs.

I don't know what rock that split on. Some talk there was of killing little pigs and sterilizing sows and plowing under cotton— all of which the Democrats had scornfully condemned in the campaign. By this time—in spite of ten or twelve years sporadically, the past several months intensively, spent on this problem—the whole subject had become too technical and esoteric for my comprehension, and I went back to New York convinced that Dr. Ezekiel is one of the best mathematicians in the country.

It was not very long after the friendly passage at arms with Dr. Ezekiel over the farm bill that one day when B. M. Baruch and I were returning from a hunting trip in South Carolina we met Ray Moley in the Carlton Hotel, Washington. He said that the draft of an Industrial Act was an immediate necessity and, recalling our many studies of the subject, our frequent talks with him, and B. M.'s experience in the mobilization of Industry, asked if I could not be loaned to him to draw up such a bill. At that time, neither he nor we had the slightest idea that anybody else was drawing up such a document. Mr. Baruch readily assented, and I went over to Ray's office that afternoon. Indeed I never went back to New York from that day to the end of my service except to get my clothes and rarely even so much as saw my own family.

Lew Douglas was the fair-haired boy in Washington at that time. Our studies of the Budget had been of service to him. We had spent a year on them and as previously related had forced a recast of the expert Treasury figures. We had loaned him Alvin Brown who had worked with us on those studies—a boy whom I had "brought-up"—one of the keenest and quickest analytical and practical minds in this country.

I cannot let this incident pass without a remark or two on Alvin Brown. When I went down to the Old Post Office Building with only three assistants to organize the draft, Alvin was one of them. Having worked his way through college and George Washington Law School, I found him employed as a stenographer in the Judge Advocate General's office. At that time the administration of Federal water law was largely in the War Department. In off moments he had made a digest of it and it was the only authoritative work extant at that moment on a little known subject of major importance—one of the most accurate bits of analytical and logical summation I have seen and I had specialized in that subject in law school. General Crowder agreed with this estimate of it. I took Brown with me and it was he who organized and directed the immense and important paper work of the draft, covering the entire nation and directly or indirectly affecting every home in the land. It was a perfect job.

He was just a boy and at the moment national recognition was about to come to him he confronted me and said: "*You* may have to sit behind a desk, but *I* don't and I'm going to this war." I used everything from persuasion to profanity, but there he stood, a callow kid twenty pounds underweight, quiet (he never raises his voice) but adamant. Finally, I said, "The hell you will," and called up every Recruiting Office and the Adjutant General and got them to agree to reject him—he could have been accepted only on a waiver of the physical defect of marked underweight. But I forgot about the Air Corps. Next day he came in grinning in the uniform of a flying cadet. He learned flying so easily and had such cool, calm nerve that the next I heard of him he was a principal instructor in aerial gunnery and—like many another too efficient flyer—failed to get to France because he was "too sorely needed for instruction here."

By these acts he had forfeited his civil service status, on top of which he had perpetrated matrimony, against my earnest advice, and when the war was over he was just another ex-officer out of a job. I had gone to my new assignment at Moline, but I could not begin bringing in, in high executive capacity, my former associates without industrial experience and merely on my estimate of their intelligence. He solved that in his usual decisive manner. He simply appeared in Moline one day and demanded his *original job as my stenographer*. Of course he got it.

Within a month the general sales manager—one of the old school of implement salesmen—had been called upon by George Peek for a complete survey of sales performance and he didn't even know how to begin. I tried to help him and called Alvin in to make a preliminary layout. In a few days Alvin was in charge of that work and it was another masterpiece of analytical survey. Nothing would do but that I must let him go as assistant sales manager, which with simulated reluctance I did. To make a long story short, within a year he was Comptroller, Treasurer, and Stock Manager of what was then a large and important industrial company. His monthly figures were always in within three days after the end of the month and I have been told by accounting firms, that excepting only Mr. Filbert's work in the Steel Corporation, there were no reports in the country to compare with them. They were not just cold figures recording the facts—they were *interpretations* of those figures telling what trends they revealed, what shortcomings they disclosed, and they were always right.

When I left the Moline Implement Company, Alvin also left. His needs were few and he wanted to rusticate. He had made his share of the profit in the sale of the Company and it was a modest competence. He received all kinds of flattering offers— one of them to supervise the investments of one of the larger fortunes in this country. But he went to Bethany Beach, Delaware, with his wife and children, rented a cottage and lived there simply in beach-combing costume, reading, writing, and thumbing his nose at the world.

He came back to me only when Mr. Baruch decided that we were going to take economic and governmental figures apart to see what was the matter with things. Although he worked on everything, Brown's particular study was of the Federal Budget and I veritably believe that he knows more about it now than anybody else. But the moment I came to Washington in NRA, Alvin pulled his old stunt of applying for a job as stenographer. He was so unhappy that I finally persuaded Lew Douglas to let him go. He is Review Officer in NRA. It is his job to analyze Codes and on one short sheet to show wherein they are inconsistent with established policy. He is the best informed and one of the ablest men there. He is a genius on organization. He certainly knows ten times as much about what is in all the codes and in NRA policy as any other man. He has one of the best minds in NRA but he makes no concessions from truth to expediency, diplomacy, or politics, and I rather shrewdly suspect that he won't be able to stay there. Two Richelieus of the new NRA dispensation in Washington do not want him ostensibly because he does not grin at them like a Cheshire cat with a set of false teeth—but actually *because they never were able to put anything over on him and never will be able to do it.*

But to get back to the birth of NIRA. Lew Douglas said the President wanted a short bill drawn up in the broadest of terms. I wrote the Recovery Act on a couple of sheets of legal cap paper and I have always thought and still think that it was far superior to the involved and obscure statute with which we are now struggling. I wish I could write it over again.

On the main points of the bill, I felt relatively confident. It was a subject which B. M. and I had been studying off and on for years. For nearly a year Alex Sachs (who became the first Chief of our Research and Planning Division) and I had conjectured roughly on the steps and action necessary to success. Mere activation of the consumer's goods industries, we felt quite sure, would not be enough. Even that would not be an easy thing to do unless we could change the gloomy outlook of the country but we thought we knew how to do that—in exactly the way it was actually done.

But a cursory glance at the figures on unemployment showed that the bulk of unemployment was in the heavy or capital goods industries which were in almost complete collapse, and that, unless substantial reëmployment could be had there, a mere activation of consumers' goods must certainly fail because it left a disparity too wide and too deep in the consuming population of the country. We computed that plenary authority to lend or extend from a three or four billion dollar appropriation, money for the purpose we had in mind relative to heavy goods, on any terms the President might choose, taking away all restrictions placed on R.F.C. and the Federal Reserve under the old law, would do the trick.

In drafting the statute we preferred to—and did—give authority to *construct, finance or aid in the construction or financing of low cost housing and renewal and repair of homes.* (A provision which lay dormant for a year and a half.) We later roughly set up a program on these powers which we then thought would reëmploy 1,000,000 men in capital goods industries by October 1, 1933.

Our conclusions were:

(*a*) That a shortening of hours and increase of wages coupled with the repression of prices to only such increases as would accommodate increased out-of-pocket costs due to improved hours and wages—relying for profit on increased volume rather than increased price—would help to institute and sustain recovery.

(b) That, to be effective, such a result would have to be produced in an extraordinarily short space of time.

(c) That, while it would not be too difficult thus to produce the required results in the consumers' goods industries, it was a much more difficult job in the heavy goods industries.

(d) That by vigorous and immediate administration it should be at least possible to put 3,000,000 men to work on consumers' goods and 1,000,000 men in the heavy goods industries within from three to four months after a start had been made.

To my mind Alex Sachs is one of the best men in the country on this particular kind of work. Like few others of his profession he has a record of prophesying correctly. Over and over again he impressed on me the absolute necessity of activating capital goods in unison with consumers' goods and warned me that *any other result meant failure*.

These were deliberate studies which began to take definite form in charts and graphs early in the year, becoming more definite as we were whipping the Act into shape. But as passage of the Act dragged through Congress and as the extraordinary speculative or beat-the-gun boom began to cast its shadow forward, it became very apparent that, without a great amount of action anticipating the statute, there was little hope of avoiding a new buyers' strike, a new and serious secondary reaction, with disastrous effects on the Recovery Program, the extent of which it was difficult, at that time, to gauge.

In more detail our plans on this front were: In the first place, the armies of the world are rapidly being mechanized and motorized. This puts men behind steel shields instead of opposing to shell, shrapnel, rifle and machine-gun fire nothing but soft and yielding human flesh. It so increases speed and mobility in getting to critical points on any battle ground, that a very few men, so equipped, can do the work of a very great many under the old armament. It so increases the fire-power of any group of soldiers from a corporal's squad to a field army that the figures would not be believed if I quoted them. Finally, to send an army out not so armed against one that *is* so provided is like sending naked men with bows and arrows in a canoe against a modern battleship. It is a life-saver, a home-saver and a necessary element of defense. Furthermore, *this is an expenditure that this country will have to make sooner or later.* We wrote into that Act authority to make it now in this necessary emergency spending, instead of spending a far greater amount on barely disguised doles, and then having to spend this money also. Such expenditures were practically all designed to go directly into the heavy or durable goods industries for steel, motors, electrical equipment, tractors, caterpillars, and machinery of all types.

We wrote in a provision for vast naval construction which—to our astonishment—was never even questioned and which is now in effect, although I fear that it is not progressing very rapidly. We never even discussed that Naval provision with anybody. I simply wrote it in on a gamble much as I had written "To raise by draft" in the Selective Service Act fully expecting to see it torn out by the roots. It was never seriously contested.

Our studies showed that, while there is plenty of apartment house, hotel, and office construction, that is not true of small independent housing. They indicated the argument and difficulty to be expected in city slum clearance with real estate people and city government and the delay of demolition but showed the facility and usefulness of the so-called German "agronomes." Our plan was to go thirty or forty miles outside of the great industrial and commercial centers, buy up tracts of land, allowing three or four acres to each of several thousand families for fruit and vegetable-raising, cow, pig, and chicken keeping (the elements of self-subsistence) and then to construct both large modern apartments with cheap-per-room overhead costs and also small cottages. These linked to the urban centers of employment by special economical rapid transit facilities, we thought would alleviate the distress of complete or partial unemployment and also put a basis of individual stability under families victimized by the depression. There is a difference between such installations and so-called "subsistence homesteads." The idea here is not completely to ruralize surplus industrial workers, but to keep them geographically available to industrial jobs and also give them a source of food beyond their wages and thus to provide a safety valve against suffering due to unemployment. It differs also from plans to decentralize and ruralize industry itself—which would revise a natural law and, in my opinion, be a long, difficult, and perhaps impossible project.

This plan had another important advantage over slum-clearance. The government would not have to wait on real estate boards, the doubtful inducement of cheap loans, or any other discretion outside itself. All it had to do was what it did in the war. Then, within a few months, the government built miniature cities which eventually housed something like 4,000,000 men. Under this idea the government could make and execute its own plans (which are not difficult) and then proceed *without asking leave of anybody*. Complete and unlimited authority to do just that was written in Title II. We felt that it would provide a great deal of the employment so sorely needed in the building trades.

This idea grew out of the plan I had made in connection with the use of relief funds for the San Francisco fire in 1906. Of course, its success depended on a type of architecture and construction that would result in good houses, but houses erected on such a basis of economy as would place their cost within the reach of the people we were trying to accommodate.

There was also written into that Title (II) plenary authority to loan or spend money for railroad electrification, equipment, re-equipment of rolling stock and rights of way or elimination of grade crossings on any terms of interest or priority which the administration might see fit to exact. We had already negotiated on that with a few railroad presidents and also talked about a plan to eliminate grade crossings everywhere by a plan to share the expense of doing so.

To make it very apparent that Title II intended *action* we wrote in the words preceding the enabling clauses "with a view to increasing employment *quickly*."

In order not to hamper administration of Title II in the eventual choice of some one else as administrator, we had, with the President's assent, detailed Colonel George Spalding from the Army where he is regarded (with three or four others) as a fit successor to General Goethals. He is one of the best engineers and executives in this country. We had also secured the services of a great many other outstanding executives and engineers as a preparatory staff anticipating the Act and they were working like beavers.

If it were all to have been done over again, I would have written the statute to provide for an Administrator with a small Advisory Board of the best construction experts in the country, but I would have used as Executive Officer General Edward Markham, now Chief of Engineers of the United States Army.

I would have built the whole decentralized territorial organization upon the basis and the pattern of the existing system of the Engineer Corps, supplementing each district engineer with a staff of civilian engineers, architects, and construction experts. It would have saved enormously in overhead. It would have accelerated speed. It would have removed worry about peculation, favoritism, and graft.

Out of all these projects, and with this organization, we had prepared a plan and gone far enough with work looking toward putting it into execution to convince us that we were justified in the original estimates of reëmploying at the rate of 1,000,000 men in heavy goods and construction under Title II by the 1st of October. This with 3,000,000 which from our studies we thought we could put to work under Title I gave the estimate of 4,000,000 men back at work by October.

We regarded these two plans, NRA and PWA, as complementary and necessary to each other. We thought that if we could not get the construction and heavy goods industries into operation along with consumers' goods, there would not be enough balanced buying power to sustain the reëmployment in commerce, the lighter manufactures, and auxiliary services. This is how we planned. That is how we wrote the act and we confidently believed that with the benefits of agriculture from the Farm Acts, coupled with reëmployment under both Title I and Title II, there would be a sufficient forward surge in purchase and employment to absorb the expected speculative production and price boom (which actually came), and really start normal recovery into a balanced and sustained upward cycle.

Furthermore, from the magnificent job that was being done on the budget, we predicated the whole plan of NIRA on further assumptions which perhaps we had no right to indulge. One was that the monetary policy (whatever might be decided upon) would be definite and stable and the other was that the Agricultural Adjustment Act would be carried into immediate execution with quick effect.

In brief, we looked upon the Recovery Program as an integrated whole which through some central coördinating agency would be driven abreast so that the whole artificial pressure to start an upward spiral of business and employment would proceed as one combined push exercising all force at once and never permitting the frittering away of force by applying it in spaced impulses or, worse, the cancellation of one effect by the effect of another. These considerations are highly important in appraising the rest of the record. There was no such coördination, and several of our premises as just stated turned out to be wrong.

There was one point on which I felt weak—the labor point of view. Although I had managed or been responsible for large industrial enterprises, I had never had any trouble with labor in my life. Apart from the legal aspect I only knew by reading and discussion what the main points of difference were. My only contact with the American Federation had been with Sam Gompers during the war and once or twice during the fight for Farm Relief. He had upheld my hands at every turn and a real comradeship had existed between us during the war. But he was gone and that time was fifteen years removed. I began to inquire for somebody to help me. I had never heard of Mr. Richberg but he was recommended to me as a brilliant unknown. I made further inquiries and was told that he was a subtle and astute lawyer reputed to be a progressive on the radical side, a successful lobbyist, associated with the Railroad Brotherhood rather than the Federation, but was thought to possess the confidence of labor. I sent for him and asked him to work with me on the Bill. We seemed to strike it off at once. I liked him and I thought he liked me. He made several suggestions and we drafted the Bill to include all of these.

We believed that any statute in this uncharted sea must be very flexible. It should try to foresee everything. But, if it attempts to state a specific rule of action for any predictable event that rule will be invariable. Here we were facing an unknown problem for which there was no rule—a virtual reorientation of an economic universe. There could be no invariable dicta. There could be no inflexibility. We must reserve the right to try, fail, change, and try again and to make these alterations instantly upon the discovery of mistakes. It was for this reason that we made authority as wide and as general as possible.

Another point—we could not move on anybody's mere conjecture of what *might* be the effect of a particular plan. For example, some authorities (thinking from the basis of an entirely different statutory structure) conclude that the *"basing point"* system of sales may tend toward monopoly. NRA has to take the position that a large segment of American business *is* done under one form or other of a basing point system without any discernible monopolistic tendency, from this, in practice. It is the business of NRA to see what the defects of such a system are—to correct them and learn by experience whether they are monopolistic in fact.

Now this can't be done by cloistered academic speculation. In writing the Act, the method we invented (for there was no precedent)—*and later used*—was:

1. Industry was to make a proposal.
2. It was to be submitted to a public hearing.
3. Within NRA itself were departments made up of accredited representatives of the three conflicting interests:
   (*a*) Industry.
   (*b*) Labor.
   (*c*) Consumers.

It was to be their business to point out every Code proposal which they thought might bear harshly or unfairly on the interests they represented. They voiced and supported their protest and—be assured—they did it. The Boards not only were to do this themselves, but they were to activate and assist all public or private groups of similar interest to present their cases.

4. These expressed conflicts of interest were then to be digested and the Deputy Administrator was to seek to compose as many as could be composed by conference.
5. The Administrator himself, then, with the aid of the Department of Research and Planning and the Legal Department, was to seek either to get complete agreement of all conflicting interest, which was generally done, or else to narrow the field of disagreement to a point where a final decision to be recommended to the President would produce the maximum of fairness and justice and the minimum of harm to all interests.

Of course we invented this system on the principle of trial, error and correction. It was for this reason that, at his very first press conference, when NRA publicity began, the writer made his prophecy about dead cats and his eventual decapitation. That required no foresight.

I must call attention here to another fundamental of NRA. In view of an uninterrupted course of Supreme Court decisions we did not believe anybody could write the labor provisions into substantive law to be enforced by pains and penalties. We thought they must be left to Code provisions to which industry would agree. Like the Draft Act the whole law is written to depend on coöperation and popular support rather than on statutory compulsion. That is the very basis of NIRA and NRA. It is what is being forgotten today. It must not be forgotten unless NRA is to fail. Those provisions can no more be constitutionally included in this Act now than they could then, and even if they could—they would be even more futile then than now.

Another thing—Code making is one process. Code administration is a very different process. We had many hundreds of codes to make. It would require about the same size of organization to administer all the codes as it had taken to make all the codes. Should we hire and train two organizations? Or should we leave the early codes largely to development by the industries under only very general coöperation, while we completed code making, and *then* turn the whole trained and informed organization over to code administration? I deliberately chose the latter course. I wanted a fully trained and veteran corps for the latter job, and the place for training was in code making. Otherwise, I would have had to double the organization for a few months half-manned with tyros and then fire half of them. The course I took involved a hiatus in effective code administration. Much criticism attended this choice. Perhaps it was wrong. The great faults of NRA were non-compliance and insufficient code organization. If we had eliminated that hiatus we might have escaped both faults. That mistake (if it was a mistake) was mine alone.

If I had it to plan and do it all over again—after an unique public experience of thrice helping to organize this whole nation for the universal application of a somewhat sacrificial public statute—once with the Selective Draft in 1917, once with the mobilization of industry on the War Industries Board in 1918 and once with NRA in 1933—if I had it to plan and do again, I would not know how to organize it otherwise. No one has even suggested to me a better *or even a different way.*

About this time I learned for the first time that there were other bills in the mill arising from various places in the Administration. John Dickinson of the Department of Commerce and Jerome Frank of Agriculture had been working on one. Senator Wagner had another. To make a long story short, the President who had had new drafts of our page-and-a-half bill submitted to him almost daily, got everybody together and told us to lock ourselves up in a room and come out with an agreed bill. We met in Lew Douglas's office—Lew, Senator Wagner, John Dickinson, Mr. Richberg and myself, with a few "horners-in" from time to time. Without difficulty—or at least *much* difficulty—albeit some slight misunderstandings at the offset, which were resolved by Rex Tugwell, we came out in a few days with a document on which we could all agree—but alas for the page-and-a-half bill! It was now as long as the moral law.

During that period, and applying to one of the "horners-in," Donald Richberg told me what I thought was one of the best political stories I have heard.

"Mayor Schmitz of San Francisco, to excuse his frequent nepotism, made a prepared speech citing Napoleon, Alexander the Great, Mohammed and Ghengis Khan as examples of solidifying administration by appointing relatives to all the principal jobs.

"Gavin McNabb, in opposition, recalled Caligula who had appointed his favorite horse to the Aedileship and said that the Mayor had overlooked that precedent which he thought far better than the Mayor's nepotism, because the Roman Emperor had, at least, appointed a whole horse."

I have once or twice failed to look to the question of equine entirety in my own appointments.

Now came the suspense and anxiety of nursing the bill through Congress. Eddie McGrady did most of that although I stayed at the Capitol all of the time. I doubt if his equal exists on a job like that. He called the turn on every vote on every amendment and as I recall he missed accuracy only once, and then only by one vote.

Bob Wagner extended himself in preparation of this bill, sponsored it in the Senate, and it bears his name. He has done more in intelligent labor legislation than any other statesman of recent years. He afterward served as Chairman of the National Labor Board and did a pioneering job.

After the President asked me to take over administration and before deciding on the exact and final form of the bill, it was necessary to learn something about its possible reception.

B. M. arranged for me a meeting in New York of the principal labor leaders, some leading industrialists, Felix Frankfurter, and Leo Wolman. We went over the fundamentals of this whole plan and were in general agreement.

It was my intention to keep a close and friendly coöperation between labor and industrial leaders at all times. We started well. As I shall later show, that continued for several weeks.

I asked Leo Wolman to come with me. I had known him during the war and seen his work, which was and has continuously been excellent. No man ever had a more faithful and courageous associate. I told William Green of the Federation that I wanted a personal assistant from the Federation who would remain constantly at my side. The Federation named Eddie McGrady who had been their legislative representative. No greater stroke of luck happened to us. He became a bosom friend, a wise counsellor, an aide whose loyalty knows no bounds.

Wolman is a scientific type whose mind goes straight to essentials. He sees the main objective and is impatient of pettifogging obstacles to direct shots at the bull's eye. He is absolutely fearless.

So is McGrady—and as independent as a hog on ice. He knows politics as well as any man in Washington and practices it up to a point where it begins to interfere with frankness and fairness. He is as loyal as the Iron Brigade and I would rather have him contacting Congress for a great department than any man I know. When intra-mural planning against NRA began a year later, the first move was to get and keep McGrady out of town and, for the object in view, that was a very sagacious move.

The Chamber of Commerce of the United States was in session. I went back to Washington and into conference with about thirty of our most important industrialists who had come for that meeting. They did not like some things about the plan, but in view of the fact that their president had not long before suggested the dictatorship idea, their criticism was not exactly carping. Most of them approved and some of them turned out to be the strongest supporters we had.

It is now being said that NRA is practicing a new policy of consulting Industry and obtaining Industrial assistance. I think NRA invented *that* policy before there was any NRA. What NRA did *not* invent was chameleon changes and surrender to particular advisory groups.

I did one other thing which now seems to be significant. I asked B. M. to call together a few of the very Brahmins of Big Industry and we asked them for a show-down as to whether they were going to support or oppose this plan and whether they would come in with proposed codes immediately upon passage of the law. We wanted to start off with such leadership for its effect on industry. One or two were skeptical but most of them agreed. Most who agreed played ball. One or two did not.

More important still we asked them if they would recruit and get for me the very best material in industry to man the new enterprises. Several agreed. But, with some outstanding exceptions, that part of the plan never materialized. B. M. had said on May 20 that the experiment depended on such men and we fully counted on them. But war is one thing and a depression is another thing. We did not get enough of the type of men which was necessary to success, and that was and still is the greatest handicap to NRA.

As I have already related, we set up skeletons of two organizations—one for Title I and the other for Title II. And we had developed outline plans for each. For NRA I started with an "Assistant for Industry," Mr. Dudley Cates; an "Assistant for Labor," Eddie McGrady; and an "Administrative Assistant," Miss Frances Robinson, now known from one end of this country to the other as "Robbie"—whom I regard as one of the two or three most efficient women I have seen in Business or Government. Another is Miss Anna Rosenberg, Regional Director of NRA in New York.

For Title II, I had Col. George Spalding, whom I have already mentioned; Col. John P. Hogan, who had been working on the general plan for weeks; Col. Henry M. Waite, who actually carried on under Mr. Ickes; Bob Kohn, H. H. Hunt, C. G. Kilbourne, Colonel Fleming, several other regular army engineers, and a score of civilian engineers whose names I unfortunately do not recall.

I had been working for weeks on the Cotton Textile Code to have it ready as soon as the law passed. Similar preliminary work had been done in codes for Steel, Bituminous Coal, and Automobiles. The skeleton preliminary organizations under both titles were working night and day because we thought that time was of the very essence of our task if we were to relieve unemployment before winter set in.

In the meantime, certain employers' associations began to contest the labor provisions of the Act. They held a great convention of protest in Washington. They asked me to address them, to explain certain parts of the Act, and then hurriedly passed a resolution condemning them *before they had heard my explanation*. The effect of all this was to hurt coöperation and start the Act off in an atmosphere of bitterness and hostility between management and labor—a result that I had done my level best to avoid and thought I had avoided by preliminary joint conferences of leaders on both sides. It was very unfortunate and it hurt NRA tremendously. I then believed and I still believe that by quiet conferences we could have gotten the great industrial and labor leaders into a relationship of friendly joint action which the law specifically asks for to the avoidance of much of the trouble we have suffered. I believe *this* for two reasons. The first is the truly broad and coöperative spirit of the really big men on both sides, and the second is that I went far enough in "feelers" toward leading men in labor and industry to convince me that satisfactory compositions could be made. The plan now seems to be to serve industry and exclude labor. That won't work.

During about two-thirds of the time just discussed, I had no intention or intimation that I would have anything to do with the administration of either Title of the Recovery Act. I didn't want to. I had a very clear vision of exactly what it would do to me and I wanted to go back with B. M. and try to recoup something of my shattered fortunes which was a clear possibility in the spring and summer of 1933. I was only trying to do everything in my power to carry out Bernie's instructions to do all I could for the President and then come home and go back to work with him. From April until the passage of the Act, I had been putting in between sixteen and eighteen hours a day on this job and I was frequently tired and sometimes disgusted.

One day while I was going over a chart of the proposed organization for both titles with the President, he said:

"Hugh, you've got to *do* this job."

Contrary to gossip, he didn't consult B. M. and B. M. did not suggest this to him. B. M. had other plans for me. My heart sank, but I knew exactly what Bernie would tell me to do. Furthermore, for my own part, I thought and still think the President is in the toughest and most responsible job in our history. There is nothing that he could ask me to do which, consistent with self-respect, and administrative possibility, I could do that I wouldn't do. I told him promptly that I would and further that I would be loyal to him and nobody else in doing it.

There was a curious thing about that. I had no more than returned to my hotel when an Associated Press reporter named Jim Selvage came to me saying that he knew I had been selected. I had not spoken a word to a soul in Washington. I have since learned that I talked too loud over the telephone asking somebody to come down and help me and this smart reporter had put two and two together to make four. The story broke next morning. When it did, I spurned the congratulations of my friends with the remark which was fortunately recorded. "*It will be red fire at first and dead cats afterward. This is just like mounting the guillotine on the infinitesimal gamble that the ax won't work.*"

There was no question about this. There are three conflicting interests in NRA—management, labor, and consumers. You can't fully please any. You can only try to be fair to all while denying to each the full of its demands. When you try to do this in an atmosphere of sniping, reaching for power and intra-mural intrigue, you have assumed an almost impossible job. Of course, the alternative is to support one cause and suppress the other. You can thus concentrate your dead cats on one flank and get the support of those to whom you have knuckled—but that is a cowardly and faithless course for a public servant.

Nevertheless, we redoubled our efforts on all plans. One evening when I had a date to go over organization charts again with the President, I found to my surprise most of the cabinet seated around his desk. Except for the President, there was that about the atmosphere which did not seem particularly friendly. Standing alone in that silent semicircle, I felt like one accused before the Masked Court of the Venetian Doge. The President approved the chart in general except that I had a Division reporting to him and marked "Labor Policies Board." He asked me about this and I reminded him that, during the war, we had found it an absolute necessity to have such a Board of the very highest standing of which ex-President Taft was Chairman and in which Felix Frankfurter was important, to take out of the hands of the War Administrations the formulation of labor policies and the settlement of labor disputes and place them in a purely neutral forum.

I observed that while on the one hand the formulation of the codes by terms of the statute was in the hands of industry and that this might prejudice labor, that, on the other hand, the Department of Labor had a duty to advance and advocate the cause of labor with a result that, if *that* Department were to act as arbitrator, management would regard itself as being forced before a partial judge and would never coöperate. There was no further discussion, but we dropped that Board.

At my suggestion, some months later, the National Labor Board was created and, also at my suggestion, Senator Wagner was appointed its Chief. It was set up independently and not in connection with the Department of Labor. There was one serious fault with it. It had a neutral chairman and equal membership for labor and industry. All should have been neutral. A divided Board throws the casting vote to the Chairman on all vital issues. You might just as well have one man. You don't get the benefit of a deliberative body.

Nothing more was said to me by the President until the Act was signed.

The President was rushing to get ready to go on his vacation. Just before he went, I was called in at the tail end of a Cabinet meeting with all the members of the Cabinet present. I thought one or two of them had the expression of the cat which has just swallowed a canary. I was told—contrary to my previous understanding—that I was to report not to the President, but to a Cabinet Board, who were to control NRA; that the Administration of Title II (Public Works) was to be divorced from that of Title I, and put under *another and different Cabinet Board,* and that the Acting Chief of the temporary and tentative organization which had been working on Title II was to be supplanted for some reason which I do not know.

I was taken aback because I thought it indicated some vast change and a disturbing lack of confidence. But far from being disappointed, I was immensely relieved, because it seemed to me that there was only one course open to me. I thought that I should not undertake this unprecedented job in such circumstance and atmosphere.

Furthermore, I felt that, from *that* moment, success of the plan—at least as we had drawn it—was impossible. Unless Title I and Title II could move abreast in perfect coördination the whole economic basis of the plan as we had proffered it was changed. As it turned out these two efforts did not even move in contact. Mechanization of the Army did not follow. House repair and renewal were not started. Railroad re-equipment and grade crossing elimination languished. That and the industrial-agrarian "agronomes" are just now being seriously discussed—18 months after authority was given to do these things. Public Works moved at such a tempo that CWA was invented to get any considerable money into employment during the winter.

I want to make it very emphatic that I say none of these things in criticism or complaint. The considerations which governed action were doubtless compelling. I am not in a position to judge, because I do not know the problems which others had to meet. I record these facts because they are indispensable to any just appraisal of the accomplishments and shortcomings of NRA, of which this is a history. I have both a right and a duty to state them, because NRA is a public consideration transcending any private concern. But it is a little painful to reflect that our housing plan was submerged and now to see it dragged out as a brilliant discovery and the sole hope of succor.

When I had recovered from this surprise, I made one or two suggestions in the wording of the order, made some notes to change the phrasing of a speech that I had prepared and started back to my office with my mind fully made up as to what I must do.

I was intercepted by Madam Secretary of Labor who apparently saw in my face what I intended. She asked me and I told her frankly that I was going to resign right then, not from pique, but because I felt that a situation had been created that completely changed what I had undertaken to do. She asked me to get in her car and, while we drove slowly around, she pointed out to me that what I purposed doing would make a great upset and interfere with the President's vacation; said that I had an absolute duty to stay at least until his return; conjectured that perhaps some coördination could be worked out; observed that there was an immense social service to be performed any way; and was generally so understanding, friendly, kindly, and persuasive that there was hardly a choice but to agree with her and—as it has turned out—very fatuously, I did. When a man can't subscribe to a plan of action for which he is asked to accept responsibility, he has no business to undertake any part of it—no matter what the contrary considerations may be.

The thing I dreaded most was facing Alex Sachs with whom I had planned so carefully. I did not see him for a day or two, and his reaction was what I had expected—that whatever of social good might be done recovery was unlikely unless, under some coördination of NRA and PWA, the program could still be made to march abreast. I told the Secretary of the Interior that we had prepared plans which I would be glad to discuss with him, but I never received any further word from him. That was all right and above reproach. He had his own responsibilities and I had mine. If there was any coördination to do, it was neither my responsibility nor his. My job was to mind my own business and let other people's business alone.

Before I knew it, I was caught in the maelstrom of my own job and that was that. I had made my first great blunder by not stopping before I started. For this there is nobody to blame but myself, and I am complaining not at all and criticizing nobody but myself.

As I have said, my whole theory of administration was to make NRA a forum of controversy. Nothing short of clairvoyance can prevision the effect of a code; first, because the whole idea is unprecedented; second, because no group of men could be gathered who could know enough about the infinite variety of circumstances in American business to pass in a closet on its problems. The only way to get the truth in such a case is to give every adversary and informed interest its day in court. A third reason was because the codes, like all law, are necessarily compromises, and you don't get compromises in a dictatorial decree.

In getting representatives of the three conflicting interests—management, labor, and consumers, I wanted appointment to be wholly independent of myself, so I asked the Secretary of Commerce to appoint the Industrial Advisory Board; the Secretary of Labor to appoint the Labor Advisory Board, and I appointed the Consumers' Advisory Board after consultation with both sides.

An important function of the task was that of General Counsel. I had worked so closely with Mr. Richberg, our minds seemed to run in such complementary channels, and I so much wanted at all times to preserve the Labor point of view with which I felt sure he was familiar, that I asked him to continue with me as General Counsel.

He was practically unknown except as a radical labor lawyer. I was fully aware of exactly what this would bring down on me from practically the whole of Industry, from the Press, and from other large popular and political sectors—a charge that I had delivered NRA at the very offset into the hands of the labor and the extreme radical side of the argument. But I made up my mind that if I knew such charges not to be true, that if a man were qualified as I thought he was, were as loyal as I believed him to be, and were devoted to the principles of this Act as I thought he was, then I would have to make my choice on those considerations and stand loyally by it in spite of all attacks on him or it, and, if there were any consequences to take them—which I did and am still doing.

Just what I expected happened. Industrial protests rained on me from all sides and even some labor men of the Federation protested. At that time, Mr. Richberg stepped into the limelight more because of the dead cats that were flung at me on his account than for any other reason. I told those of the conservative critics whom I knew exactly what I have said here and insisted that I was responsible for NRA, including its General Counsel. At any rate we did not retreat before that first baptism of criticism.

It was also asserted that I had appointed too many Jews to important posts and Mr. Richberg was cited against me on that score too. Just for the sake of the record, I must say that Mr. Richberg is not a Jew. If he had been it would have made no difference to me. I tried to get the best staff I could persuade to serve, and I did not stop to inquire about whether they were

Jews or Gentiles. I had several able Jews but they were a scant minority and every single one did an outstanding job. Not one was disloyal or self seeking.

Eddie McGrady was my assistant for labor and, after his appointment as Assistant Secretary of Labor, I had an understanding with the Secretary that he should remain with me—an understanding fulfilled until a few months ago, when with no word to me, he was detached in circumstances elsewhere related and he never returned to NRA.

My first assistant for Industry was an old friend and associate of mine—Dudley Cates—formerly of a most liberal mental background but, as appeared after a few weeks, he had developed firm and sincere convictions which were not consistent with the meaning of the Recovery Act as I interpreted it. He has one of the best minds I know and he is conscientious almost to a fault, honest and fearless. When he, too, came to the conclusion that our interpretations did not agree, he resigned. Our friendship remains unimpaired, as far as I am concerned. He acted as any true man should act. When you can't agree with a decided policy, the only course is the course he took. It was the first time in my rather varied career that I ever lost an associate through disagreement.

Women are an important factor in the Recovery Act. Indeed its eventual success will depend on them. In addition to that, the nature of this job requires some person of ability, adept in stenography, and familiarity with all complexities of the job to be always in the office. That person must be one in whom absolute confidence can be reposed, who shall be a witness to all conversation and record such as seems vital. I had seen something of Miss Frances Robinson during the campaign when she worked as a volunteer at Democratic Headquarters. She was recommended to me as having held and excelled in a responsible executive position in RCA and I decided to give her a trial during our preparatory period. Her performance was astonishing.

I learned a lesson during the war—bitterly—and as a result never had a conversation, without an alert and expert secretary in the room, who proceeded, unobtrusively, to take shorthand notes whenever the talk seemed to become critical. These notes were carefully preserved and were only transcribed in case an issue arose. This precaution once saved the government several million dollars during the war and avoided a very unpleasant situation—but that is another story. I continued it during my entire service in NRA—a fact that may be of some interest to various people.

On the first schedule of appointments for which I secured approval I named Miss Robinson as assistant to the Administrator at a Deputy's salary. The petty jealousies arising out of this and the innuendo and slurs that have attended it are probably too well known to require comment or characterization. She rapidly grasped every detail of the Act. She served as liaison with the White House, where she proved acceptable and welcome. She checked and kept all original copies of codes. She handled the numerous calls and requests of members of Congress so far to their satisfaction, that most of them never even tried to see me—a saving of time which was of vital importance. She managed my colossal correspondence in such a way as to give me an almost complete escape from the bulk of it. She worked longer hours than I did and that meant more than sixteen hours a day, as an average of the time I was there, and for certain periods much longer than that.

I also insisted on having a woman, Mary Rumsey, as Chairman of the Consumers' Advisory Board. I got nearly an equal number of dead cats from that mostly on the ground that she was wealthy. One or two of her own associates, selected by her, engineered an even more insidious and contemptible newspaper propaganda against her, even going so far as to attack her sanity. I don't know whether she was wealthy or not. "Some that was ain't." But I know that she did her job. Therefore, I stood by her also against the most vicious kind of assaults. Her sudden death was a public misfortune.

My original deputies and principal assistants were: Bill Allen —very able, two-fisted, upstanding, frank to a fault—a great industrialist and a great associate; Kenneth Simpson, a scientist and metallurgist (he and Mr. Richberg became the closest of friends and coadjutors); Arthur D. Whiteside, President of Dun & Bradstreet; Philip Kemp, an able lawyer with such a keen mind and wide industrial practice that he was invaluable in our earliest and hardest cases; Malcolm Muir—a human dynamo who through his business publications had a very broad grasp of industry as a whole; Major Gen. C. C. Williams, who as wartime Chief of Ordnance administered the biggest purchasing program in history; he took with him the love and respect of everybody; William Pickard, who had been associated with me in a responsible war position; Nelson Slater, with whom I had worked for several years and who is a great friend of Madam Secretary Perkins; Robert Stevens, just about the most promising young man I know in American business life, my true friend who worked here for the sake of the job until he wore himself out.

I hate to do it, but it would be quixotically unfair to fail to mention my own son, Lieut. Kilbourne (Pat) Johnston, who I think earned his spurs apart from his relationship to me, since the new Board after my resignation appointed him as Divisional Administrator. He had an engineering and a legal education (West Point and Columbia Law School) and an excellent Army record. He has been with NRA from the beginning; has worked in nearly every department of it and did much of the organizational planning.

I didn't know what to say when he asked me for advice about accepting this big job from the new Board. If I had said "No," it would have been set down as due to pique. If I had said "Yes," it might indicate that I still wanted to keep a finger in the pie. What I did say was: "You will have to decide that yourself, but if you decide to take it, let's make it a point never even to *mention* NRA in any talk between us"—to which he assented. We never have mentioned it and never will. He costs NRA nothing. He is detailed from the Army where his pay is less than $150.00 a month. Other men in about his category in NRA now receive more than six times as much.

Robert Straus was with me during the campaign and in NRA from the very day we began working on the Act. He is an NRA veteran of veterans. He has my affection and esteem. Earl Dean Howard wore himself out in faithful, efficient, and devoted service. Lindsay Rogers, who knew the garment trades well, undertook that difficult assignment and acquitted himself with his usual brilliance. There were, of course, many others, who are mentioned elsewhere in this book.

Later there came to me Sol Rosenblatt, whom I have known for years. He handled the difficult Amusement Codes—movies, theaters, etc. I know of no other man who could have done that job—certainly no one who could have done it half as well. It was one of NRA's major performances. He came to me for help less often than anybody else. Usually when Sol came in it was to turn in a finished job.

Big George Buckley—God love his Irish soul—has been my friend for many years. He is more than six feet tall—200 pounds of solid man. He has a cool incisive mind and speaks from a world of experience in positions of the greatest responsibility. He handled publicity, but he was always a close adviser on all subjects and a pinch hitter in every time of trouble.

Col. R. W. Lea came to take Dudley Cate's place. He has been a partner of mine for many years. He is an able industrialist of great experience both here and abroad. He handled the purchase of all horse-drawn equipment during the war. We have been through every vicissitude of business life together. When I think of the unfailing loyalty for 16 years uninterrupted by any dissension which I received from Robt. Lea and Alvin Brown and many other such life-time associates and then reflect on some of the things I encountered in NRA, it seems as though these men must spring from a different species of what John Lewis calls the *genus homo*.

In addition to this starting crew in the NRA organization proper, I had veritable towers of strength in the Advisory Boards. Gerard Swope had been my assistant and later my successor in the old Purchase, Storage and Traffic Division of the Army during the war. I suggested his name to Secretary Roper at once. He is one of the ablest industrialists in this country. Our close friendship is of years' standing and he took his duties very seriously. He helped in almost every aspect of the work and especially in breaking industrial log jams at serious crises. He is a leader with genius.

My only previous contact with Walter Teagle was right after the war when he advised me against making a certain business connection—and he was right. He then offered me a job which I didn't take, but would have done it if I had known him then as I do now. There were all kinds of slurs and slams at him in NRA because he was Chairman of the Standard Oil of New Jersey and the Oil Code was up. He religiously never raised a finger to influence it. He is a big man, conscientious in the extreme—considerate, able, and loyal. In all my contacts with American Industry, which are now as wide as anybody's, I know of no more stable, honest, courageous, and public-spirited citizen.

Louis Kirstein is one of the country's great liberal merchants.

I saw him in all kinds of stress and I never saw him do a selfish thing or advise a course that was to his own interest, or that was not as fair to labor as to industry, or that was inconsistent with the President's policy.

I do not mean by mentioning these three men to reflect on the other members of the Board. They all sat through that sweltering summer in constant attendance and in loyal and unselfish devotion. I shall mention them in another place. But these three musketeers were on the job longer and they walked in and out of my office whenever they discovered anything that needed attention.

I had exactly the same kind of relationship with John Lewis, George Berry, and Sidney Hillman of the Labor Advisory Board. What I am trying to say is that between myself and the six men I have named there was something far deeper than the mere official relationship. There was a sort of mutual understanding of the terrific thing we were up against and a consequent comradeship and coöperation that was a little different from many other friendly contacts. I believe that with those six men as a working group you could approach and settle the most serious labor difficulties that could possibly arise in this country.

John Lewis is a man from the sole of his foot to the mane on his shaggy head. His word is his bond and a contract made with his union is a contract. He may not be as gentle as a perfumed zephyr in the heat of an argument but he is as effective as anybody I ever heard on either side. He is genuine, dependable, courageous and true.

George Berry is as different in method from John Lewis as two men could be. He is gentle and polished and suave—but it is the velvet glove on the iron hand. When he is thoroughly aroused the soft Southern drawl goes out the window. He never raises his voice but something clipped and icy comes into it and you know that you are up against a man. He is my close and faithful friend.

Sidney Hillman simply *is* the efficiency of the Garment Unions and the apostle of fair and responsible dealings therein. Sidney is not only blessed with great native intelligence—he is a highly educated and cultured man and he has put himself where he is by the sheer determination and ability of his own efforts. I never had a bit of trouble in arguments with Sidney and they never consumed time. If logic and fairness were against him, he gave in—if they weren't, nothing could move him.

I will treasure the friendship and memory of these six stalwarts to my grave.

Mike McDonough came in a little later at my request. I number him in the same category, as I do also Dan Tracy of the Electrical Workers Union.

My boss during a part of the war was Edward Stettinius, Assistant Secretary of War. In his office I met a stalwart young second lieutenant of the same name. The first Industrial Advisory Board brought down the second Edward Stettinius to be its executive officer. My heart went out to him at first on account of his father and it stayed there on account of himself. He is one of the leading young men in industry and I am glad he has come back to NRA for a second tour.

Father Haas on the first Labor Advisory Board was a gentle reasonable mediator and a tireless public servant. Rose Schneiderman was also a pioneer who knew the labor problems in the needle trades from a lifetime of unselfish effort to better conditions there.

Jack Elliot on the Industrial Advisory Board was a faithful and able public servant and one of my very good friends. Robert Lund did more than any other man to compose differences between NRA and some rather hostile manufacturing associations and has my affection and high regard.

My Chief of Staff—the man who kept the original organization working was John Hancock. John handled the Naval Industrial Program with the War Industries Board during the war—a job much like the one I had in the Army—one of the biggest purchasing programs anywhere. He did the outstanding job of that kind in the war—far more effectively than I did mine. He also resigned at the end of the war and went into industry and finance where he made his name. He whipped and kept in shape our first organization. It was a bang-up job. John never does any other kind of a job. For much of our early success he is responsible.

This was the skeleton of continuing organization with which on June 16th we plunged into the incredible task of trying to get the whole of American industry, by voluntary action, under Codes of Fair Competition in the shortest possible space of time and thus practically to revolutionize the whole employer-employee relationship in America.

For whatever success attended the efforts of NRA with these men rests the credit. With one exception, they were as faithful and devoted as soldiers on a battlefield. To me personally they were as considerate, thoughtful, solicitous, and loyal as brothers. I believe that between myself and everyone there is a strong tie of personal affection that will last as long as we do. Strenuous service under fire is what makes and tests and preserves friendships, and all my harvest of hard knocks was more than compensated by these gleanings of affection.

As to my one lost sheep, I do not grieve. There was a philosophical old captain in my regiment who had a very conscientious top sergeant. There had not been any desertions from that troop in years. One day the first sergeant came and asked to be reduced to the ranks—*three* men had gone "over the hill" the night before. The captain ruminated long. Finally he said, "Three out of 65, eh!—what percentage would that be out of a platoon of twelve, Sergeant?"

The old sergeant laboriously figured it, "About $\frac{1}{2}$ a man out of twelve."

The captain blew a puff of smoke.

"Better stick around, Sergeant. Our Lord himself lost one out of twelve."

Chapter XIX

# THE GOLDFISH BOWL

---

"Are the hearings to be public?"
"We're gonna do this whole job in a goldfish bowl."
—*First NRA Press Conference, June, 1933.*

---

IN VIEW of repeated charges that NRA promised too much in the beginning and *had no plan or policy*, I want to quote verbatim from stenographic records some of the earliest utterances on the subject. We simply had to carry out the *policy that was stated by the President.* There are very few questions raised that are not mentioned in his short but very careful statement (See Appendix).

My own utterances in June, 1933, were viz.:

Of course, the major problem is to try to get people back to work. That is what is on everybody's mind. It is what is worrying everybody. If we can do that, we can get out of the hole we are in.

Another thing the President said was that if we can get employers to shorten the work week and to pay a decent living wage *in fact*, we can look for a better future.

I don't want to say how it is going to work. But I can say that from all we have learned and from the very extensive work that has been done by the leading industries, they understand what the aim is. Sometimes the problem is very difficult, but they are trying to go along. I believe it is going to work. *All that I can say is that I think we are going to put three million back to work this summer.* Anything may happen but I just want to say that it looks very promising.

On the question of organization: What we have tried to do is to set up a minimum organization that could possibly handle this work and try to keep a selected type of men in reserve to do the job. As the task develops the organization will develop. No one can accuse us of delay. In the short time we have had to work since the Act was signed we have accomplished a great deal.

Very excellent work has been done by the textile people. I don't say we will accept that code—there will be hearings on it. Also, there are other industries which are working night and day to get something in the way of a workable plan.

*Q.* Can you tell what number of major industries you know are definitely working on codes?

*A.* The whole cotton industry, the garment and needle trades, the clothing—I know that all the elements of it are trying to work out a plan. Also the whole iron and steel industry.

*Q.* Will the $10 and $11 wage proposed in the textile code create enough buying power? (The rate on the actual code was $12 and $13.)

*A.* That rate is for the lowest class of wages in the industry. That is the basis in all industries in making up the whole schedule of pay.

*Q.* How are these groups to be heard—in what size?

*A.* I would like to have them together in the largest groups possible because they are easier to handle. It doesn't make much difference to us whether they come in together or separately. In these hearings we will listen to anything any minority may say. From our standpoint it is easier to handle one group than six, but it doesn't make much difference—what we want is to have everybody in an industry come in.

*Q.* What is meant by the statement in Bulletin No. 2 that the industries will make their own codes?

*A.* Everyone will be allowed to be heard before a code is adopted. Everything will be done in an open hearing, every interest that has a word to say will have its day in court.

*Q.* Are the hearings to be public?

*A.* We are going to do this whole job in a goldfish bowl.

*Q.* In the effort to set up a minimum wage, do you contemplate a better wage in New York than in the South, for instance, for machinists, or a difference in wages paid to carpenters in Seattle and those in Ohio?

*A.* There are differences in living costs. In the common labor rate between Moline and Chicago there is a difference of about seven cents. Yet I think the people in Moline are better off than the people in Chicago. They live in a smaller town, better advantages for children—these differentials create a difference in the economic structure—that we cannot disturb. I think, however, we also recognize that there are some differences that arise from exploitation, where people are living and working at less than a living scale. We can't have this. We can help there. The thing to do is to lift these wages up where it is practicable, and if we can get everybody to do it we will be carrying out the purposes of the Act as expressed by the President.

*Q.* How does that fit in with the word that the railroads have just asked a cut in wages?

*A.* You ought to be able to answer that one—it doesn't fit in at all.

*Q.* Are you going to do anything about it?

*A.* It is not my baby but something must be done to coördinate efforts.

*Q.* How about the small industries who are being menaced by new people coming in when the industries are already organized and over-producing? Are you people doing anything about that?

*A.* We are going to ask something in the nature of an armistice on increased producing capacity, until we see if we can get this upward spiral started.

*Q.* Has there been a tendency to raise prices before they get their trade agreements in operation?

*A.* I don't think we have been going long enough to know if there has been a tendency.

*Q.* Will you elaborate on that projected armistice you spoke about?

*A.* You know we can make no hard and fast rule but we are going to ask these people to pull together to try and get our purchasing power back. We are going to plead very earnestly with these industries not to use any further labor saving devices or anything further to increase production for the present.

*Q.* Will there be any attempt to organize men in non-union plants?

*A.* Section 7 takes care of that but also it must be put in the code. I have said this consistently and to everyone concerned and the American Federation of Labor agrees with me that this Administration is not to be used for unionizing any industry.

*Q.* How can you have a fair code in the coal industry without unions?

*A.* If the men organize that is all right. My job is to sit here in an impartial way. I have no initiative in this thing. This law has given men the right to bargain collectively. There is no argument. I have a law to execute and I am going to execute it.

*Q.* Suppose the industry does not abide by the code?

*A.* The law takes care of that.

*Q.* If in a certain industry where few men are employed, they organized to take advantage of this act, and presented a code, what would you do?

*A.* The employees present nothing here. The codes are presented for the industry by the employers. If they do not come in they cannot get the benefits of the code. That is the law.

*Q.* For instance, in the textile industry they have what they call designers. Suppose the designers got together and made a code for the designers. Would you recognize them?

*A.* I have no function on that sort of thing. There is nothing for me to do. The law prescribed no duties and creates no rights on that line.

*Q.* Is there any industry that operates wholly within one state? How would you handle that situation?

*A.* That presents a purely legal question. If an industry is contained within the borders of one state they probably can find plenty of smart lawyers to tell them that they would not come under Federal law. I have enough to do without bothering with that. There are two phases to this thing. The first is to try to get everybody started back to work at once and to increase purchasing power. *A limited basic code is what we are asking from these people right now—to include in the first code only minimum wages, maximum hours of labor and what is needed to protect them against chiselers on the fringes of the industry.*

I want to avoid any czaristic appearances. It is industrial self-government that I am interested in. There is a difference between the National Recovery Administration and the War Industries Board.

There our problem was largely administrative. It came to be a centralized administration of American business. This will be different.

It took England 120 years to arrive at the "law merchant," which was codification of commercial practice, thereafter accepted as a part of the common law. We are trying to do that in America in an hour and a half, by agreement. It is no easy thing to re-orient the universe. The whole thing is coming on much faster than I thought it could.

This is being organized almost as you would organize a business. I want to avoid any Mussolini appearance—the President calls this Act industrial self-government.

The first move of an industry is to bring in a code. I am trying to develop the technique of this new thing. Therefore I have certain deputy administrators, just a few at first. A man will come in and deal in a preliminary way with the problem of the industry up to the point of a hearing. I am going to conduct these first big hearings myself.

It will be a new procedure—nothing quite like it has ever been seen before. I don't know how it will turn out but I have definite ideas as to how it is to be carried on. After a hearing and the code has been approved it becomes a sort of "law merchant" for that industry.

Then complaints will start to come in and will have to be treated. As the deputies become adept in treating with this business we will have other men come in. The deputy going on to another code will have to leave behind him a small organization to receive complaints. To what extent it will grow in administration is a matter of what may actually happen. There will be no administrators of an industry, as such, in the early stages.

*Q.* Are you going to permit price fixing in these codes?

*A.* No general rule has been laid down. They don't have to put it in their codes. *In these codes it will be proper to have a provision that they are not going to sell products at less than the cost of production. When they go beyond that in price fixing I would have to step in.* I am not here to institute the organization and operation of these industries. We are here for the purpose of seeing that what they propose to do does not bear unfairly upon the public. That is where the Consumers' Advisory Committee comes in.

*Q.* When do you expect to invoke the licensing power?

*A.* I do not expect to invoke it if I can avoid it. (I never did invoke it.)

*Q.* Will you license all units in an industry or just those that will not go along?

*A.* No—you would have to license them all. I mustn't talk hypothetically—nobody can imagine these things until he confronts them. In most cases industries will come in with codes because of the benefit that there is in the code. The code goes out with every assumption of good faith of execution. Complaints will come in. When they do come in it is because they are accused of doing something in violation of the code. Sometimes they are justifiable and sometimes not. If this code isn't working out the President can modify it or withdraw it under terms of the Act. If he withdraws it—they have lost the benefit of the code. I don't want to use the licensing power in *any* circumstances unless I absolutely have to.

*Q.* Is there any thought of placing men in various parts of the country to watch price situation?

*A.* I had an opportunity of watching the same sort of thing during the draft. Everybody told me "you can't make draft boards go without force." We intended to make it police itself because in a particular community people who were not playing the game would be taken care of by other people of the community. We also want to avoid inquisitorial powers and police functions here. Whoever begins to violate codes will be complained against by the people in the industry itself.

*Q.* In the matter of price fixers—how about retailers?

*A.* The retailers have various reasons for wanting to come in on this thing. They have suffered a great deal from bad practices. As they come in here with their association and their codes, they have a subject that has to be attended to.

*Q.* If you can strike at a manufacturer for price fixing can you also strike at a retailer?

*A.* If the code is set up in the way I described, nobody can say that something was done that is going to hurt any group. If there is anywhere in this a chance for extortion or exploitation it has got to be carried before the President and approved and he couldn't approve of a code that permitted this thing.

*Q.* Are you setting up a Consumers' Advisory Board?

*A.* Yes, it is going to be a committee and we are setting it up right now.

*Q.* How will the same industry in different areas get together on a code?

*A.* Here comes an industry up with a code. That industry is represented by an association. In these trade associations—there are big and little ones—the interest is not always the same. The code has probably been voted on by the majority and the dissenting minorities will be represented at the hearing. They come up to the table where sits the Administrator. Always in the agreement there are three principal interests that we have to consider: (1) the industry itself; (2) labor in that industry; (3) the consuming public. One of our first rules is that the deputy can't have any interest in that industry. At one side of the table sits an Industrial Advisory Board for the Administrator. At the other side of the table are representatives of every element of labor in that industry in an advisory capacity. A third board will represent the consumers. The purpose there is when you get through with the hearing that everybody affected by that code has been represented and that every conflicting point of view has been heard.

There is a question of statistical data that is one for our own organization (of Research and Planning)—we cannot accept all figures that they bring in because they may be self-serving. We must have our own.

After a hearing is complete and the code has been modified to the extent that they are willing to modify it, it goes up for a very thorough study in this organization that we are setting up and after it has been approved it goes to the President.

It then becomes a part of the law of that industry. It took them a century or so in England to build up the law merchant idea and we are trying to build it up in an hour and a half.

My point in making these quotations is that those colloquies, which took place a few days after the act was signed, reveal every basic policy that has controlled and is still controlling NRA. I am sure the reader will find that there was no overstatement, and I hope that this evidence to which scores of newsmen can subscribe ought to answer the criticism that we promised too much or had no plan. As a matter of fact nearly the whole of this book discloses the gradual development over a period of many years of all the essential principles of NRA.

On this sort of general idea we moved into execution the very moment the Act was passed. The Cotton Textile Code was well along, but the lost sheep for which our hearts yearned was the Bituminous Coal Code.

To most of us bituminous coal, though millions are dependent upon it for a living and though its fate indirectly affects business everywhere, seems unimportant. I doubt if one person out of a hundred not connected with the industry has ever even bothered to read its code.

Yet exciting drama could be written out of the strain and struggle and conflict which went into the making of that code. And since this code contained almost every kind of problem that we had to meet elsewhere, it may be worth while to touch on its human background.

In the spring of 1933 the entire industry was moribund. Almost every economic force that touches it had conspired to ruin it. The coal fields have been the dark and bloody ground of industrial and labor warfare for decades—over-capacitated, under-sold, unable to pay even starvation wages, the most sinister clouds on our industrial horizon lowered there.

Some days prior to the passage of the Act, the writer, with Divisional Administrator Kenneth M. Simpson (who was to assist on coal), attended a meeting of representatives of all the warring districts. It began early in the evening and it lasted until 2:30 in the morning and, in all our experience with 400 approved codes, never has anything seemed so hopeless as that.

George Harrington and D. W. Buchanan of the Illinois field, Fred Taplin, a scrappy independent, Charlie O'Neill, J. D. Francis, Ralph Taggart, and John Morrow with a dozen others of the Appalachian field—I shall not try to name all of them— were the very chieftains of these despairing legions. In the background at that time were John Lewis, Tom Kennedy, Phil Murray, Van Bitner, and Henry Warren, leaders of the labor organization of the United Mine Workers. There were, on both sides, the scars of bloodshed in old battles. They recognized the hopelessness of their condition but there was too much bitter history in the background for them even to confer. They frankly said there was no hope of composition on any national plan.

All these men later became leaders of the NRA van—but then I never left a meeting with a heavier heart. The Textile Code was coming along, but the Steel Industry was increasingly coy —developments in the Motor Industry were not encouraging, and from the beginning of the NRA movement to this good day, there was no more discouraging period.

There seemed to be only one chance on Coal. These leaders thought, from decades of experience, that they could never herd their people into one compact. Our answer was:

"You never had the same circumstances before. Under the old law your very efforts to this end were unlawful if not criminal. You never had such a leader as Roosevelt. You never had a whole people demanding such action. You never had a situation so desperate." The rejoinder was of course:

"There are old bitter memories to be overcome. There is a diversity of purpose and aim which nobody outside the industry can understand. Yet, if you think you can sell the proposal to the operators themselves, they will be in National Convention in Chicago when the Act is signed. If you want to risk it you can come there and try."

With more desperation than assurance, we accepted this challenge.

The National Industrial Recovery Act was signed on June 16th. That was the last day of the Coal Convention. But the Army offered to furnish an airplane, which by a close shave could make the distance within the time. No speech was prepared and the early part of the day was taken up with hurried arrangements at the White House, and the bitter disappointment which I have already recorded—the last minute shift of the whole Public Works program, from any contact or cohesion with NRA. We could not leave the flying field until after three in the afternoon.

The plane got away on reports of good weather over the Alleghenies, and with the aid of a miniature staff we began at once on the plane to try to prepare a presentation to the Convention. It was a task so engrossing that nobody even looked out the window for an hour. When I did look, my hair rose on end. Wet wisps of mist were floating and waving by like washing on a clothes line on a windy day. Just as I raised my eyes, one of these ethereal union-suits flapped its legs up and disclosed that we were headed into a mountain not a hundred yards away with no sight of its top and no idea of what lay on left, right, or bottom.

Like the amorous couple in the *Divine Comedy*, we "read (nor wrote) no more that day." We were off the radio beam. We were lost in the mist. We had not enough gasoline to dare to climb over the fog and we fumbled around those mountains for an hour and a half. When we should have been over Uniontown, we located Johnstown forty miles off our course, and precariously threaded our way up the valley of the flood (which seemed about as wide as a notch in a rifle sight) with a fluffy ceiling forcing us so low that we could almost spit on the wet automobile tops on the road below, and the wing tips seeming nearly to touch on either side.

We made an almost horizontal landing on the mesa of the Pittsburgh Port—no speech—Chicago out of the question, and in the pious suppression of men who for an hour or two have been trying to remember whether "Now I lay me" comes just before or just after "Forgive us our trespasses." In that state of perturbation and, in the foolhardiness of a first appearance, I remarked that it had been a hell of a day and rushed to a Pittsburgh radio station and attempted an extemporaneous but impassioned plea to that disrupted Chicago Convention.

It was a sorry beginning. It was a flop. It is a mistake to try to talk without notes over a radio. There was nothing to do but begin those long gruelling sessions—night and day—day after day—week after week—in an effort, by persuasion, sometimes by bluffing, principally by plain horse trading and barefaced poker-playing—by which most of the early great Industrial Codes finally came into being.

In a recent article in a magazine it was said that we faltered and that Secretary Perkins drove us on, that we faltered again and that a coal strike drove us on. These are lies out of whole cloth. We never faltered, and Madam Secretary had nothing whatever to do with it. It was also said in that article and another in the Chicago *Tribune* that I received a defiant letter from the operators in a restaurant, cursed and tore it to bits. That also is a falsehood—no such thing ever happened any more than the equally blatant fabrication that I ever *commanded* a business man to remain and negotiate, or threatened to crack down on Henry Ford. These are libels from which a man in public life in such a situation has utterly no protection. The Cotton Textile hearings were scheduled for June 27.

WORKING ON HIS EAGLE, AGAIN.

The petroleum situation was as bad as that of coal, and there was nothing to do but plunge into both of these situations at once, leaving the coal situation to simmer awhile.

The Cotton Textile Code will always be a high mark in the economic history of our country, first because the coöperative attitude of the industry showed the way and set the tempo for the execution of the entire recovery act and, second, because this industry led the way for all industry to the abolition of child labor—something done here in half an hour that it had taken England eighty years to do and that we by statute and proposed constitutional amendment had failed to do after forty years of effort. That incident is of such epochal importance as to justify quotation from the record. The hearing opened with the following statement:

GENERAL JOHNSON: Ladies and gentlemen, you are about to be witnesses of what may prove one of the most momentous meetings of this kind that has ever been held anywhere. We have presented here from a great industry, with practical unanimity, a suggestion of a method whereby management in that industry, and labor in that industry, have joined hands in coöperation to pull this country out of the difficulties in which we have been for the last three years.

This law permits industries to present here for the consideration of a government agency these arguments. The function of the government is to safeguard the public, to see to it that such agreements as are presented attain the end for which they are designed, but in attaining that end, that they do injustice to nobody.

I am not going into extensive discussion of what we are about to do, because what we shall do will be unrolled before your eyes as these proceedings advance.

On this platform there sits at my right the Legal Adviser of this Administration, and at the end of the table the Deputy Administrator, who in a preliminary way has discussed with this industry its code, without any commitment whatever on the part of this Administration.

In the circle behind this table sit three great committees. The one on the right is a committee representing industry at large. It is Advisory to this Administration, and sits here to watch the general policy of the department, the development of that general policy, and action under that general policy, in the interest not only of the industry which is here presenting this agreement, but in the interest of all industry.

Industries, in a sense, compete with each other, and it is absolutely necessary, if we are to have cohesion throughout this whole effort, that the various agreements presented shall be in harmony with each other, and the function of this group, besides giving that advice, is to see to it that, at every one of these hearings, particularly interested industries, the industry which is presenting the hearing, and all those cognate industries which may be affected by the result of this agreement, are properly represented.

In the center of the circle sits a group representing the consumers, whose duty it is to watch over everything that is done here to see that nothing is done that unduly prejudices the consuming public, with functions very similar in a general way to those of the industrial group. On the left sits a group representing labor.

The industrial group was chosen by Secretary of Commerce Roper, it being entirely inappropriate that any group with particular interest should be named and should control or be controlled by this Administration. In order to carry that idea out, the Secretary of Commerce appointed that group, and in appointing it sought, not to have representation by regions, not to have representation by particular industries, but to have representation of men who, through their leadership, some in larger fields and some in the smaller fields of business, have demonstrated a liberality and leadership which he thought would give confidence to the whole of industry.

The Consumers' Advisory Committee was selected by the Administration from a list of names proposed by Secretary of Commerce Roper and Secretary of Labor Perkins. In that group the idea was to select people who had given a great deal of their time and thought, unselfishly, in the formative period throughout the years which led up to the enactment of the Industrial Recovery Act, to the interest of the consumer. They may be regarded as leaders of thought in that field.

The labor group was chosen by the Secretary of Labor, as representative of a wide choice of all the elements in labor that might be affected by such a hearing, organized labor, as well as unorganized labor, so far as anybody can be said to represent unorganized labor; people who by their lives and work have shown that they have the interest of workers primarily in their minds, and with a function exactly like that of the Industrial Advisory Group.

The effort has been made, in setting up the tribunal before which these agreements can be presented, to preserve a balance to see that every interest is represented, to see that nobody who might be affected by this code can ever say at the end of one of these hearings that that interest was not represented, that anything was done hastily, that anything was done without due regard to every interest that might be affected.

Mr. George Sloan then presented the code and almost immediately the following colloquy between him and myself ensued. I regard it as one of the most significant if not dramatic moments in NRA.

GENERAL JOHNSON: I want to say this to you, Mr. Sloan, I know what you have gone through here over the week; I know with what zeal you have to work to bring this thing together so that we could move forward. Without in any way prejudging your case, I just want to ask you one question that came up in connection with the discussion you had of the Child Labor provisions of your code.

I understood, and it was the understanding, I think, of those who helped prepare the legislation for submission to Congress, that the minimum wage was a minimum wage in fact, and that whatever advantage the industry had out of employment of children in the past was that they paid children less than they paid adults, so that child labor more or less eliminated itself by the elimination of any competitive advantage due to the low wages paid to children; that is, there is a minimum wage and it applies to children as well as adults—is that right?

Mr. Sloan: That is correct, with the exception of the three classifications that were discussed, that is learners for six weeks, and outside yard help and cleaners.

General Johnson: That is something to be discussed in determining this code. If it be true that the minimum is a minimum applying to everybody, then, if there were any advantage from child labor it would not be an advantage to the operators—they do not want that, is that right?

Mr. Sloan: I do not quite get that question, General.

General Johnson: You will no longer have any financial interest in maintaining child labor after approval of this code?

Mr. Sloan: We have no interest in maintaining child labor, that is correct, sir. We make the point that there is, in fact, practically no child labor today.

General Johnson: If it is such a small matter it should be practically out of consideration?

Mr. Sloan: With this code, you will find in sixty or ninety days' time there will be no child labor.

General Johnson: What I am trying to say is this: If anyone wants child labor it is not the mills. There may be some workers who want it for the benefit of their families, but the mills do not want it, because they have to pay a child as much as an adult?

Mr. Sloan: Well, if you refer, General, to the insertion of the specific provision in the code, I would frankly like to have an opportunity to discuss it, and to have the Committee discuss it with representatives of the government, because that has not been discussed in our preliminary conferences.

GENERAL JOHNSON: But the principles are the principles which you believe are covered in your code?

MR. SLOAN: That is correct.

Mr. Sloan and the proponents of the code retired and at the opening of the next session Mr. Sloan requested a moment for a report of the utmost importance on overnight action by the Cotton Textile Code Committee. What they had done was to propose a specific clause in the code to the effect that the employment of minors under sixteen years of age be not permitted during the life of the code.

There was a moment's silence in that over-crowded audience, and then a thunderous burst of applause. The Textile Code had done in a few minutes what neither law nor constitutional amendment had been able to do in forty years.

The President said in his approval of the code:

I have just approved the Cotton Textile Code, subject to certain modifying conditions, clarifying, but not greatly affecting the proposals as submitted.

Many significant circumstances attend this result:

Child labor in this industry is here abolished. After years of fruitless effort and discussion, this ancient atrocity went out in a day, because this law permits employers to do by agreement that which none of them could do separately and live in competition.

In the eyes of the whole public, there was a great conference among the very leaders of our Industry, Labor, and Social Service, presided over by Government. It considered the most controverted question in the whole economic problem—wages and hours of labor—and it brought that question to a definite conclusion. It dealt with facts and facts only. There was not one word of accusation. And most remarkable of all it arrived at a solution which has the unanimous approval of these conferring leaders on all three sides of the question at issue.

I know of nothing further that could have been done. I can think of no greater achievement of coöperation, mutual understanding, and good will.

It would be unfair to omit a word of commendation of this great industry. It has proved itself the leader of a new thing in economics and government. That took faith and courage and patriotism of the highest order. They have their reward in the result they have achieved and the example they have given.

(*Signed*) FRANKLIN D. ROOSEVELT.

In view of the many criticisms of what has or has not been done, I shall, to the end of my days, take comfort in this trail-breaking. There was nothing said in the law about how these codes were to be made—what the organization, or the approach to the problem should be, how management and labor were to be treated, what the goal or where the path thereto. Administration could have been purely negative—a passive attitude of waiting for a move from management. It would never have come. Or we could have moved in to hale the industries before us and, on some preconceived idea of what they *ought* to do, we could have cracked the whip and told them what they *must* do—licensing all companies in interstate commerce—and installing a Federal economic dictatorship. It would not have lasted sixty days.

Any other thing might have happened. I do not know. I only know what *did* happen. We brought the whole of American Industry voluntarily in under the Industrial Recovery Act and we did it (by the PRA) in four months. "Let the heathen rage and the people imagine a vain thing"—nobody can ever take that accomplishment away from NRA and to attack that vast reform of national extent and universal benefit because it is alleged that there were some faults in its execution, is like condemning the sky because it is not always blue.

# Chapter XX

## THE BIG SIX CODES

---

"The highest and best form of efficiency, is the spontaneous coöperation of a free people."

*—Woodrow Wilson.*

---

It was our plan to get the ten big industries—those comprising the bulk of employment—in first. For this I had extended myself for weeks before the Act was passed by such conferences and conversations as I have related. These were Textiles, Coal, Petroleum, Iron and Steel, Automobiles, Lumber, the Garment Trades, Wholesale Trade, Retail Trade, and Construction. The latter four were too complex for immediate action, but the former six would accomplish our first purpose.

Things were not going too well in any of them. The condition in Bituminous Coal has already been described. Something was holding back the Steel Code, which I had expected to have almost as soon as the Textile Code. Lumber was ready with a code, but it asked too much. The Petroleum Industry was a discouraged and disorganized mob. In automobiles the sticking point was the fact that Henry Ford was not a member of the Automobile Chamber of Commerce, and they were apprehensive about what he might do once they had committed themselves to a definite policy. There, at least, was one tangible on which I believed I could act.

It has not been my first contact with the Fords. During the war, when I took over the job as Chief of Army Purchase on the General Staff, I felt the need of some one in Industry who understood production, and my thoughts turned at once to the Ford Company. I telephoned Mr. Ford's office and on the very next train, he sent me the cream of his organization; Mr. Wills and Mr. Hawkins—foremost in popular estimation of the type of men I wanted. Throughout the war this had been his attitude—despite the fact that he detested war as an institution—wholly helpful, instantly responsive.

There had also been one of those unfortunate developments of the draft; a claim of exemption made by Henry Ford for his son Edsel as indispensable to industry had been denied by the Detroit District Board, and appealed to the President. The case was very far down on the President's docket, but the welkin was ringing with popular protests. Under the new questionnaire system, which I have described, all appealed cases went back for reclassification. Edsel was then placed in Class I—fully available for service. But Class I had a sub-class (father of a child) which was not to be called until those without children were taken. At just about that time, Edsel became a father.

It was a cruel thing that people should have criticized that boy. He had nothing whatever to do with the outcome. He had never made a claim of exemption for himself, and the application to him of the new rule was perfectly fortuitous. I wrote that rule and I certainly could have known nothing of the forthcoming happy event. Although it was a very unpopular thing to do, I proceeded to say so with all the force of which I was capable. My admiration for both the elder and the younger Ford has always been unstinted; indeed, Mr. Ford had established the principles of his own NRA, so far as hours and wages are concerned, years before the depression.

On all these considerations I thought a visit to the old gentleman might aid me in breaking the jam in the Automobile Code, and yet I didn't want anybody to know that I was making it. So one evening, after office hours, I took a fast army airplane, arrived in Dearborn before dark, spent the evening with Mr. Ford, left early the next morning and was in my office before it opened. Nobody but the principals knew about that trip for weeks afterward.

I must somehow have misunderstood him, but I thought that he said that he would support what I was doing to the limit and even beyond. Representatives of his Company sat in with the U. S. Automobile Chamber during the formation of the code and right up to the moment of its completion—and then, at the last moment, they suddenly withdrew. That threw both the automobile camp and mine into complete consternation.

I did not know what to do, but I finally decided to make one more effort and again flew to Detroit. I found Edsel in a state of great concern. He told me that they would sign the code at once, if I would assure them that they would not have to bargain collectively with representatives of their men. Of course, I could not do that. An article in a magazine said I once offered to omit collective bargaining and that again Madam Secretary intervened. That also is an absurd lie. That would have been unlawful, was never even discussed and again Madam Secretary had nothing whatever to do with it. Edsel said that his father was ill with a high temperature and hoped that no immediate decision need be made. But I could no longer delay the code. It was submitted without Mr. Ford's signature.

Now it is not necessary for any member of an Industry to sign a code for his Industry which the substantial majority thereof has proposed and has approved. If he violates it, he violates the law, and in order to get the Blue Eagle, he must file a certificate of compliance. No authenticated case of violation had ever been proved against the Ford Motor Company, and yet it has become a shibboleth to say that I threatened to "crackdown" on Henry Ford. That came from a newshawk who is a friend of mine, Bobby Allen, who (I veritably believe) would not consciously do me an injury. Yet he did do the whole Recovery program a vast intangible injury by suggesting that we were going around the country "cracking-down" on all and sundry. Here is a verbatim report of the colloquy on the cracking-down process taken from the stenographic transcript of the press conference in which it occurred.

*Q.* General, how long will Ford have before you take steps?
*A.* I do not know.
*Q.* Before you crack-down on him?
*A.* I think maybe the American people will crack-down on him when the Blue Eagle is in other cars and he does not have one.
*Q.* In other words, you will not give it to him if he will not sign?
*A.* Certainly not.

No violation has ever been proved against the Ford Motor Company, but neither have they ever had a Blue Eagle. It was a simple application of the law and regulations which I was sworn to enforce and indicates no animus at all against Mr. Ford. I have none. However, sooner or later he is almost bound to come up against the Collective Bargaining provisions, and if he persists in his determination as expressed to me by Edsel he will find himself athwart the law of the Land.

The final submission of the Automobile Code was made to me in Detroit. In that case I made such a slip as I suppose might be expected of anybody in such stress. The code contained the famous merit clause. To my mind it doesn't mean anything. Nobody can agree to modify or amend a law or a statute. But the President was determined against even the appearance of doing so. I read this one hastily and said I would approve it. The code was submitted on that condition. Later I saw that it was inconsistent with this phase of the President's policy, but I could not throw it out and keep my word. It is in there still. It has never raised a question of dispute, and it never will, because it is meaningless. But if I had it to do over again, it would not be there.

The Automobile Code was approved with minor changes, and that was Number Two of the Big Six we were after.

In the meantime threatening and misleading activities were being furiously pushed by both industry and labor, and it became necessary for the NRA to clarify its own position which it did on July seventh, as follows:

Circulars and other literature purporting to come from labor union agents have intimated or openly stated that it is a purpose of the National Recovery Act and Administration to unionize labor or that the only way labor can secure benefits under that Act is to join this or that union.

Similar statements purporting to come from industrial concerns have intimated that this or that newly formed company union is the only organization through which labor can get a fair deal under this Act.

Both statements are incorrect and such erroneous statements of the Act and its Administration tend to foment misunderstanding and discord.

It is the duty of this Administration to see that all labor—organized as well as unorganized—gets a square deal, and the Administration is organized to do and will do that duty. The improved labor conditions proposed in the textile industry, which is largely unorganized, are an example of this. It is not the duty of the Administration to act as an agent to unionize labor in any industry and, as has been repeatedly stated, it will not so act. It is the duty of this Administration to require the inclusion in codes of the mandatory conditions of section seven and see that these conditions are complied with, and it will perform that duty.

The policy of the National Recovery Administration respecting the rights and obligations of both organized and unorganized labor is based on the declaration of policy in section one of the Act itself, which clearly stated the objectives of this legislation, in part as follows:

"to induce and maintain united action
of labor and management under adequate
government sanction and supervision."

Manifestly the purpose of the Act is to create and preserve harmonious relationships and to prevent industrial strife and class conflicts.

Labor in any industry has the right to organize and bargain collectively; the law also recognizes the right of individual workers to bargain for their own conditions of employment. But in the execution of this new social policy to which the government stands committed, it is the obligation of the National Recovery to require the payment of living wages by industry as a condition of continued existence and to prevent excessive and unreasonable disparities, in the interest of both social justice and a balanced economy.

Collective bargaining under adequate Government sanction and supervision should hold no fears for the fair-minded industrialist; on the other hand, the National Recovery Administration pledges itself through its Labor Advisory Board to obtain a fair deal for labor in any industry presenting a code, whether the employees are organized or not. It is not the function or the purpose of the Administration to organize either industry or labor.

The following is quoted from the President's statement of policy of June sixteenth, which is and will remain the Magna Charta of this Administration (See Appendix):

This Act is a challenge to industry which has long insisted that, given the right to act in unison, it could do much for the general good which has hitherto been unlawful. From today it has that right. . . .

This law is also a challenge to labor. Workers, too, are here given a new charter of rights long sought and hitherto denied. But they know that the first move expected by the Nation is a great coöperation of employers, by one single mass action, to improve the case of workers on a scale never attempted in any nation. Industries can do this only if they have the support of the whole public and especially of their own workers. *This is not a law to foment discord and it will not be executed as such. This is a time for mutual confidence and help and we can safely rely on the sense of fair play among all Americans to assure every industry which now moves forward promptly in this united drive against depression that its workers will be with it to a man.* . . .

If we ask our trade groups to do that which exposes their business as never before to undermining by members who are unwilling to do their parts, we must guard those who play the game for the general good against those who may seek selfish gains from the unselfishness of others. We must protect them from the racketeers who invade organizations of both employers and workers.

In the meantime we were sitting up night and day with the warring elements of the Bituminous Coal Industry. I have often been accused of bulldozing the industrialists in that and other industries. Just try to do it! There was hot talk in plenty—it was a hot summer.

Take the shaping up of the Bituminous Coal Code—there were ultimatums (from one side to the other, not from us to either) and "crackling oaths went to and from across the fist-banged board," but you do not get a dozen warring districts which have never known peace in our lifetime and the labor in all these districts, together with each other and with their employees to agree for the first time in history by suavity and slickness or by reading economic lectures by a professor. Outside of agriculture labor here is the most individualist group in this country, and all the gentle arts of suasion have for decades been tried and failed.

Once in the white-hot heat of negotiations, we had to fly to Harrisburg to try to help Governor Pinchot, in a state-wide strike where a miniature war was already in progress. We wrote the speech on the plane, delivered it under his helpful auspices and then asked him to fly back to Washington with us to help. But the negotiations would break up if he appeared before we had gotten by a certain newly raised point. It seemed a wrong thing to bring the governor of a great state into such an embarrassing situation, and he too agreed and volunteered to wait in a Senator's office, although it was then almost dark.

We went into immediate session, but that certain point was elusive. The minutes went by and the hours went by. I asked an aide to call the governor, but somehow he was not reached. We never did get by this point and I had a justly indignant governor to deal with between two and three A. M. in a close restaurant, where he had finally gone, as an escape from the locked and darkened Senate Office Building. He was lenient with me when I explained what had happened, but I fear I have never been completely forgiven.

On July 12, I was able to announce:

"Word has reached me that codes covering substantially all of the bituminous coal industry are nearing completion and will be submitted to the Administration early next week.

"In spite of reports to the contrary, the leaders of this great industry have been working night and day for weeks to effect a compromise of their differences and I am particularly pleased with the progress which had been made in the last few days."

The hearing was set for August 28. Shortly afterward, I was able to say:

"Committees of the United Mine Workers and of the operators in the Appalachian bituminous field have reached the basis of an agreement covering the principal point at issue and which this Administration is willing to recommend to the President."

The intervening time had been practically one continuous and unrelieved series of conferences, sometimes bitter, sometimes calm, but it is preferable to settle such vast affairs across a table, with no matter how much acrimony, than at 10,000 pit mouths with riot and bloodshed everywhere. A battle of words across a table is better than a battle of bullets across a barricade, especially when the spoils of victory are no greater in the latter case.

Nobody will ever know what happened behind those closed doors to accomplish this result, but after all my detractors get through (and some of them are now in the very seats of the mighty) I am proud to say that among the very best friends I gained in NRA are in this industry—John Lewis, whom I regard as our greatest labor statesman, Phil Murray, Van Bitner, A. D. Lewis, and Henry Warum,—on the employees side, J. D. A. Morrow, Charlie O'Neill, Jim Francis, and Ralph Taggart, on the side of employers. They are chieftains in what had been for years the fiercest industrial labor battleground in the United States. Although John Lewis was ill when it became clear what was happening in NRA in September, 1934, there came from his bed a grunt of indignation and a roar of defiance which in one short page and a half transcended all the 65,000 other letters and telegrams I received—"If I had been there, this would never have happened," and—believe me—it wouldn't have happened in just the way it did.

Those who have relations with labor leaders and have some measure of understanding of their problems, know that there is necessarily some industrial (not partisan) politics there to play. Lack of experience with the true situation on my part was, in part, why I selected Mr. Richberg as counsel, and left all labor appointments to the nomination of Madam Secretary. I would do it a little differently if I had it to do over. Politics there may be, but with these outstanding leaders, I have found that all they ask is a square deal and that they dislike politics as much as anybody. In spite of some buffets I have given, I doubt if anybody in this Administration has any better friends in labor than I have with some of these men.

As I shall set forth later in this narrative, I think the final impasse in NRA was due to a strange combination of difference of purpose as to how the *labor* situation should be handled with a design of others to control NRA itself.

As to the first, I never aspired to championship of any conflicting interests. I aspired to impartiality. All that requires is justice and fair play. The Labor Department is by its very nature a "pressure bureau." It is charged by statute with special advocacy of labor. I think that such a department should be confined to such advocacy. That very fact (to my mind) precludes its control of other governmental instrumentalities such as NRA or the labor tribunals. I doubt if there are any strong labor leaders who do not agree with this. I believe that even Francis Gorman, who sped some shafts at me, must know in his heart the equity of this view. You can't help liking this sincere and fiery little zealot. I used to sit and look at his burning eyes across my desk and think; "Boy, you are wrong about some of this but, if I had your job to do, I fear I would probably be ten times worse."

In the autumn of 1933, Mr. Richberg asked me to come into his office. He seemed very much disturbed. He said he feared I was getting an idea that he was trying to interfere in the control or direction of NRA. I was astonished. I had no reason to think any such thing. I trusted him completely and liked him immensely. I told him so. But he had more on his mind. He said that he had friends who believed him to be available for appointment to a very high judicial post.

He said that, of course, it was unethical to electioneer for such an honor, but that it would be advisable for him to be where the lightning might strike if it wanted to. He thought I could help him by taking him with me on visits to the President and referring important speaking dates, which I could not fill, to him. He would become publicly known by the latter expedient and could display his wares by the former. His point, he said, in telling me this was so that I might not mistake the pursuit of this design for any activity on his part to dominate or control NRA.

I was enthusiastic about him then. I promised to do and religiously did just what he asked, I lauded and boosted him on every occasion and especially to the President. I pushed many important speaking dates his way, and never lost an opportunity to advance his cause. He never voiced a disagreement to me while he served on my staff. I recommended his appointment to the Industrial Emergency Committee as its director. I recommended him to take Frank Walker's place in the National Emergency Council. I trusted him implicitly and never suspected him of anything but the utmost devotion to NRA.

But I must keep to my narrative about the codes.

The Bituminous Coal Code was approved on September 18 and that was the third of the Big Six Industries we had striven so hard to capture. It was the hardest fight and the biggest accomplishment of all and it resulted in uniting the Northern and Southern Appalachian and other fields in what I have always regarded as the perfect industrial set-up—a whole industry organized under a code—the whole of labor organized vertically alongside of it—a negotiated agreement between the whole of industry and the whole of labor—a self-contained mechanism for the settlement of disputes without either strikes or lockouts and a growing feeling of partnership and community of interest between management and labor throughout that code. There was almost as much hostility between different coal fields such as Southern and Northern Appalachian as there was between labor and management in certain fields. Putting together the entire mosaic, as just related, was the greatest single accomplishment of NRA and of the men I have mentioned.

There were plenty of hold-over skirmishes of the main battle on the Coal Code relating to captive mines—i. e., mines owned by the steel industry not selling coal to the public but producing it for manufacture of iron and steel. The claim was made that they were not under the Coal Code. Part of that fight I had to conduct from a hospital bed and the President himself had to intervene before it was over. There were a few strikes but the whole thing was settled after some weeks of stubborn resistance. As to that particular claim, the President told the operators "pigs is pigs and coal is coal"—and so they finally went under the code.

But they fought at every step. I had an operation for a painful but not serious ailment and, much to the concern of Colonel Keller, Ward 8 of the Walter Reed Hospital became a hive of activity. He stopped at the door of my room one day when after two hours with the principals of the American Iron and Steel Institute and two or three messages back and forth with the President, I said to Eugene Grace:

"You keep shaking that head of yours from side to side, Gene, and it will twist off and roll on the floor."

Colonel Keller knew neither that Mr. Grace and I had been friends since the war, nor the bantering language sometimes used in that particular group, and I think he expected the heavens to fall and engulf me. He raised his hands in despair and backed out of the room.

A good deal went on behind the scenes in these early encounters. Once in the coal embroglio I called up Andrew Mellon—whom I had never had the honor of meeting and asked his help with the heads of some of his reluctant companies. It came instantly and effectively. Many times in the steel, coal, and petroleum arguments, either through such friends as Gerard Swope and Walter Teagle or directly, if I happened to know the right person, we went back to sources of financial control to bring pressure on heads of companies who were hanging back and we almost always got it. To persuade the reluctance of the shipbuilding industry at one time I had to suggest that we would put the whole naval construction program into the Navy Yards. I didn't have any authority to say that but it was necessary to say, and when I promptly reported it to the President, he laughed and backed it up instantly. There are more ways than one of skinning a cat, and in those early parlous days I think we used them all.

The Lumber Code too came in during this period. I did not conduct these hearings. There was no epic fight in these negotiations, but on the other hand and for the very reason that there was not sufficient controversy to develop the subject, the code has never been as satisfactory as others of the Big Six. We have had to change it more than once, and I fear that it is still not right. The Retail Code came through much faster than we had expected. But the greatest problem of all was presented by the Petroleum Code.

Petroleum is like no other product. It is stored, in great subterranean reservoirs, fully manufactured by natural processes which nobody understands. The adventure in reducing it to possession is the gamble of a hole (usually six inches in diameter at the bottom, thousands of feet down) against nearly all the rest of the earth's surface, that there is one of those elusive reservoirs from 3,000 to 10,000 feet below. If there is, the oil flows up, in a gushing flood, and has somehow to be disposed of. There is petroleum in many states, but the trouble all comes from California, Texas and, in lesser degree, Oklahoma. It can be stated very simply—too many reservoirs have been tapped. A man with a 30,000 barrel gusher in those flush fields regards the flow as absolutely his own, and there is strong common law logic for his thought. But we are very far removed from the simplicity of Saxon England. This natural resource is limited and expendable. The scramble to dissipate it for expedient personal wealth may be good individual husbandry, but it is hardly short of national lunacy. For years attempts have been made to regulate the flow to reasonable current requirements with some regard for other national resources, such as coal and water power. Up until recently the Federal Government had said to those who wanted to do this, "Under the Constitution we *can* not—under the Sherman and Clayton Acts you *must* not."

But NIRA put a new face on this. It offered an opportunity for production control. The Petroleum Industry tried to get together to submit a code. They couldn't. They simply dropped apart in over fifty warring groups. They had a convention in Chicago which resulted only in agreements to disagree, but the largest group did come to Washington with a code. We opened public hearings and, behind the scenes, did a lot of missionary work which finally reduced the factions to about three. In the hearings we let everybody blow off steam. Finally we called for small committees from each group on each of the three great segments of production, manufacture, and distribution. Then we took these groups back to NRA, shut them up in rooms each with an NRA representative and told them to stay there till they *could agree.*

246 THE BLUE EAGLE FROM EGG TO EARTH

Finally we got the issue down to a single major disputed point—arbitrary price fixing or no. I was absolutely opposed to it. I knew that industry pretty well, because I came from Oklahoma and my whole family has been in this business since the first mid-continent field opened. I thought that, if they would control production, price would take care of itself, and we would then need a maximum price to protect the public rather than a minimum price to protect the companies. Finally we worked out an hermaphroditic compromise. I called the town meeting together again, gave them the code that we had thus written and told them "*that was it*"—that within 24 hours I would hear protests but that, essentially, that was it. That was the nearest I ever came to meriting the frequently repeated charge of "cracking down." It wasn't very near because, with the exception of one small group with a highly specialized interest, everybody acceded to that code.

In this sketchy account, it is impossible to convey the strain and time and effort that were expended in the three great battles—Bituminous Coal, Steel, and Petroleum. As far as NRA was concerned, I felt that it was on trial for its life. Everything depended on success in these early major engagements. If, by lack of agreement, we were thrown into a maze of injunctions, mandamuses, and the law's delays, the whole bright hope of abolishing all the ancient iniquities against labor—sweat shops, child labor, employer domination, unstable wages and unlimited hours—would go glimmering. The whole NRA administration would be discredited.

On the other hand, if we moved out to compel codes, the whole of industry would feel that every worth-while thing that has characterized our institutions had gone by the board in a dictatorship far worse than that in any European country, including Russia. We simply *had* to succeed at the very jump-off.

NRA did the job. It did it from one end of this country to the other, and it did it in a few months. I have never heard anybody suggest another formula on which it could have been done. Indeed, it was tried on another formula in several industries in another Department of Government, and with a result of complete impasse. We did not favor industry, and we did not favor labor.

We have been criticized by partisans of both sides. It would be well for some of these people to re-read the President's statement of policy of June 16, 1933 (See Appendix) and the Act which he signed that day. I carried out my oath and those instructions with scrupulous accuracy, and it is my belief that by the policy and administration thus given to the law, NRA did more for working people in this country—organized and unorganized—than all the labor organizations, and all these critics during the entire term of their natural lives.

Perhaps it would have been managed otherwise. It is possible that 7a and the hours and wages provisions could have been rammed down the throat of Industry by statutory or executive decree as some people seem to wish. But I don't believe it. If it had been attempted it would have required the full force of the Federal power, judicial, military, and executive to do it, and I might as well say here that, if it had been attempted in that fashion, I would have been on the other side of the argument.

If I could have consulted my own convenience and wishes, I would have left this job when the Big Codes were in and the President's Reëmployment Agreement had been put into effect in practically the whole United States. I did then attempt to resign. I did not press it because I could not then feel that the organization of NRA was yet in shape for change. I wanted to get away again in March, 1934, but the situation was still obscure.

There is always a pulling and hauling around the desk of any Chief Executive in business or in government. It was so with Woodrow Wilson to an extent which few imagine and especially during the war. But he had a peculiar advantage. By that time his Cabinet had been in four years, and had settled down to fixed relationships. Except for the War and Navy Departments all Emergency Administrations were clear outside the Cabinet. But above all, there were the cohering and compacting effects of war. He could delegate fixed responsibility and back it with plenary authority. When the Allied High Command and certain influences at home tried to undermine Pershing, they were sent packing. When anybody in that Administration tried to bring the President any scurrilous story about an emergency associate, he was ostentatiously ignored. War and the circumstances of an established incumbency made things possible then which are not possible now.

In those circumstances you can get men competent for such

a bitter conflict to espouse public service. But it is not so in peace when at a great crisis you have to try to change customs and viewpoints held for decades. It causes sniping, both in and out of government. Spies swarm. Sometimes an official must subsist on his skill in avoiding (if not promoting) innuendo, or not subsist at all. In the midst of battle with the enemy without he must spend much of his time combating more insidious influences within his own ramparts. That is why it is difficult to get men of sufficient caliber to serve. You can persuade them to start. You can't persuade them to stay. And it is hard to do such a vast job in such an atmosphere or with half-men. I served in official Washington before and during and after the war, but never have I seen it such a whispering gallery and never has it seemed so unkind.

During these autumn days of 1933, NRA organization was new, hastily thrown together, uninstructed, inexperienced, and growing at the rate of 100 a day. For the first time in my life I was trying to operate with a staff and executives all of whom I did not know by their first names and their more or less intimate personal history. Some of these I could not even recognize by sight.

I have been through great physical and mental strain several times, but never more than at this particular period. I was getting about four hours' sleep on an office sofa, and did not go home for days on end. Everybody's nerves were jangled. I remember once Mr. Richberg, who had been working himself to a wraith, came to me at the very heaviest of this load to protest having his department come under some general regulation of the budget about wages and classification of employees. He said legal specialists, even to typists, were different, and that he would resign if he had to be interfered with in that way. I think I answered tartly that every other department had so to comply. I did not intend to be tart, but he went out trembling and in tears and I did not see him again for several days. Nerves were stretched so taut that there were several explosions. Even two-fisted Bill Allen once disappeared for two days in a huff. The Dudley Cates episode was nine-tenths overwork. Most astonishing of all Alvin Brown once went "prima-donna" on me and I had to send two of the younger men away to prevent physical and nervous collapse. One man dropped dead in the Coal negotiations. Earl Howard collapsed in a Garment hearing. Several of my principal assistants had to leave because they simply could not stand the physical strain, and the health of one or two was permanently impaired.

The Cabinet Board to which I had to report required every important action to be submitted and debated. They even proposed at one time to take over the approval or modification of codes upon which we had spent hundreds of hours and study, controversy and compromise, and about which they knew nothing whatever. Some of them started to admonish me because the pronoun "I" appeared in a bulletin until I showed them that it was a direct quotation of a Presidential utterance. Those were the happy days!

# Chapter XXI

# THE BLUE EAGLE

---

"In war, in the gloom of night attack, soldiers wear a bright badge to be sure that comrades do not fire on comrades. On that principle those who coöperate in this program must know each other at a glance."

—*Franklin Roosevelt on the Blue Eagle.*

---

THERE have been both praise and blame of the Blue Eagle and our first "Drive" to get every employer in the country under the Blue Eagle either by a President's Reëmployment Agreement or a Code. In my opinion it was not only right and expedient—it was urgent and so indispensable that I am prepared to risk the prophecy—*when the Blue Eagle goes, NRA will go and the sweat shop, child labor, and unconscionable labor conditions will return except perhaps in a few very large and highly integrated and organized industries.*

No criticism has called more urgently for answer than the one that the Blue Eagle and the so-called Blanket Code (PRA) conception were hasty afterthoughts outside the statute and that the Blue Eagle is unnecessary. I must make the answer to this ignorance because, if future administration goes on any such assumption, it is bound to fail.

There was nothing new about the *idea* of the Blue Eagle. In the official report of the War Industries Board, page 253, *dated March 3, 1921,* referring to *an occurrence of November, 1918,* appears the following:

A system of pledges was required of manufacturers, jobbers, and retailers. *Retailers were required to exhibit a card explaining the particulars of the scheme in a particular place in their stores.*

Thus the Blue Eagle idea was proved necessary in another similar movement in which I had participated fifteen years before.

On May 20, one month earlier than the passage of the Act, before the Brookings Institution, B. M. Baruch spoke in part

of his concept of industrial coöperation, words already quoted,
viz.:

Mobilization of public opinion becomes important. If it is commonly
understood that those who are coöperating are soldiers against the
enemy within and those who omit to act are on the other side, there
will be little hanging back. *The insignia of government approval on
doorways, letterheads, and invoices will become a necessity in business.
This method was a success in 1918. It is a short cut to action and to public
support without which no such plan can succeed. By this method a large
part of the emergency job can be accomplished in short order.* . . .

And as to the Blanket Agreement being an afterthought, let
me repeat a previous quotation from the same address (dated
May 20, 1933) one month before the passage of NIRA.

In certainly a majority of trades the same rule for hours and wages
is applicable. The quickest method is to *bring the uniform cases to swift
action by a blanket rule and then to deal with the exceptions* . . . *a general
rule applicable to 75% of industry could be worked out very promptly by
a conference of leaders in industry and labor* . . . *the idea is to get the
widest possible area of industry under the rule at once and then to provide
for the exception*—and by exception I mean,
  (*a*) Modification
  (*b*) Special cases
  (*c*) Recalcitrants.

That is precisely and exactly what we *did*. I trust that this
documentary evidence will lay forever the repeated assertion
that PRA and the Blue Eagle were afterthoughts.

This essay of Mr. Baruch's is so succinct and cogent and it so
clearly states the whole philosophy of NRA, from which we have
not departed, that I have quoted from it freely. And lest there
be the slightest remaining doubt of the deliberate long study of
the principles of NIRA, I refer to the quotation from his address
before the Boston Chamber of Commerce—three years *earlier*.
As I have tried to make clear, many forward looking men had
long held these opinions and they were the guides of my faltering steps.

It takes at least six weeks to put one of the great major codes
completely through the NRA mill from original negotiation to
final approval. As we announced, before the law was passed, the

avalanche of codes was fore-shadowed by the announced intention of 400 industries to submit codes at once, and our initial
studies showed that there must be several times as many soon
to come. A shorter method was needed at the outset to bridge
the longer process of the codes.

The difference between a code and a President's Reëmploy-

ment Agreement—miscalled the "Blanket Code"—is that the
former is a proposal for self-government by an entire industry
or by a substantial majority. It presupposes an organized industry closely knit in a trade association integrated nationally
or over a wide region. It looks toward industrial self-government
within that industry by a Code Authority which shall act with
a representative of the government who, while attending its
meetings and having access to what it does, observes but does
not participate—with one important exception—he can veto
what the Code Authority does on the ground that it violates the
code or the law or is incompatible with the public interest. A

Reëmployment Agreement (PRA) differs from this as follows:

In a PRA an individual or a firm separately engages with the President to live up to a specified schedule of trade practices. He doesn't agree with others of his craft, although all in that craft may separately agree with the President. There is no Code Authority. The rules are necessarily elementary and usually refer only to wages, hours, and conditions of labor.

A Presidential Agreement can be made in 24 hours with a minimum of argument and of subsequent administration.

There were eight compelling reasons for the Blue Eagle and PRA.

The first was simply that, unless something were done at once to close the gap to code completion, the mere physical limitations on the process of code manufacture would withhold the benefits of NRA indefinitely.

There is this peculiarity about the NRA principle. Not only do companies and localities compete with each other—partially for trade—completely for labor, but whole industries also so compete. For this reason when a change like NRA comes along —raising wages, shortening hours and inevitably increasing costs—one company in an industry cannot accept it unless practically all other companies in that industry accept it. For the same reason, neither can one industry or one locality accept it unless all industries and all localities similarly situated accept it. One of the astonishing disclosures by the NRA hearing is the extent to which degraded labor conditions in one locality reach out through competition to degrade the conditions in another industry or locality. Thus the Birmingham Cast Iron industrial group, especially in companies operating on extremely low labor rates for their negro workmen, even after paying heavy freight, were able to compete in the Detroit and Grand Rapids districts, many hundreds of miles away, leaving no recourse to salvation of the older northern branch of that industry except *to degrade its own labor.*

To illustrate the same principle as between groups of an industry, rather than localities: Somebody starts a sweat shop operation in the metropolitan area—say in the Connecticut Valley. His cheap goods begin to flood into New York. The legitimate manufacturer is confronted with a choice between following same lead or going out of business.

Exactly the same principle preserved child labor. Nearly all manufacturers wanted to see it go, but some, by lowering their labor costs through employment of children, barred the road of others to economic decency.

In fact this (and this almost alone) is the *fundamental* principle of the successful quest for decent labor conditions in this country. To permit such marked inequality in labor costs is to ask the company or the industry or the locality which complies, to accept an unconscionable handicap in the struggle for economic existence. For these reasons it was necessary in inaugurating NRA to find some means to create a norm for labor conditions in all industry and all localities at about the same time. The code process was too slow to do this, and that was the *second* essential reason for PRA and the Blue Eagle.

By no means were all industries organized in trade associations. Only a few were—certainly not more than 20% by industries or 10% by establishments. Many of the 400 applying for codes were not ready to receive them. A code requires some kind of industrial organization. PRA does not. That was the *third* compelling reason.

The first reaction to the proposed New Deal, even before anybody knew exactly what it was going to be, was the vast speculative anticipatory activity already described. The Cotton Textile Industry approximated 1929 rates of production. People who were not even in that business began to buy that product and store it away in warehouses. Prices were soaring far in advance of wages, employment, and purchasing power. It was indispensable to do something to avert a new collapse and crash—a *fourth* inescapable reason for the Blue Eagle.

We talk about interstate and intrastate commerce. As John Marshall once said: "In commerce we are one people," and that was never more forcibly demonstrated than upon passage of the Recovery Act. We were raising costs by increasing payrolls. Intrastate commerce and industry compete with interstate commerce and industry. Unless we could find some rule to put them on the same basis of hours and wages, we would have been scarcely justified in doing anything at all because intrastate operations would simply have ruined interstate enterprise. This was so clear and threatening that no man who lived through those anxious days will ever again be persuaded that there is any important enterprise in this country that is not (in the language of the Act) "*in or affecting interstate commerce.*" We had an astonishing lesson which it is vitally important that the whole country should understand. *State lines are not the significant lines in American commerce.* If there are any clear lines of demarcation they are regional rather than state boundaries. *The areas are economic rather than political.* As has been explained, the general low wage scales in certain whole groups of states, and especially the wages of negroes in some industries, had spread their effect like a great grease stain over large areas of the map of the United States, degrading the wages and living conditions of labor in other regions far removed.

We had to devise a means of insuring some improvement by operators working physically intrastate, to protect interstate commerce from the most sinister and threatening aspect of the depression—predatory wage and price cutting to the imminent threatened destruction of American living standards. It is a constant process of leveling with no other direction than downward. If an individual voluntarily *agrees with the President* to pay standard wages for standard hours, in consideration of being allowed to display the Blue Eagle—statute or no statute—this difficulty has been abated, even though the only remedy for violations in intrastate commerce is removal of the Blue Eagle. This was a *fifth* controlling reason for the PRA and the Blue Eagle.

With a law affecting established practices of nation-wide extent, except in glaring, outstanding, and important cases, you could no more enforce it by relying on court process and criminal prosecution alone than you could enforce prohibition. To enforce it fully we had to have an aroused, militant, and almost unanimous opinion. To make it possible for such a public opinion to support those who were coöperating to create employment and purchasing power and to withhold support from those who were not, there had to be a symbol easily recognizable, striking and effective. We designed the Blue Eagle for this purpose. That was the *sixth* reason for the Blue Eagle.

The bird was at once attacked as being a foreign and cabalistic design. As a matter of fact, except for the lower part of him he is about the oldest old artificial thing in America. He is the Thunder Bird—an Amerindian ideograph of unmeasured antiquity. Some evangelical commentators in the Tennessee Hills said he was the Beast of the Apocalypse and affected to prove it by counting the serrations of his wings. I immediately ran for

Holy Writ, but I could not count that way. He was designed for visibility and uniqueness rather than as a speaking symbol —I sketched the idea on paper after talking with Henry Wallace about Thunder Birds, but the actual design was by *Charles Croiner* and was contributed. Adam Warfel of St. Louis went to

a more aggressive antithesis—the Black Buzzard—but of course we never used it. It just gave us a laugh.

There was an immediate necessity for starting the whole of industry on codification. The President's Reëmployment Agreement provided for wages and hours on a little more drastic scale than was convenient for some reluctant industries. Relief for them lay in submission of codes and an accurate determination after a public hearing of what the exact rates should be. There was a sort of indirect persuasion in this situation. The Blue Eagle and PRA brought in all the codes within a few months— that was the *seventh* reason.

Finally (an *eighth* reason), as a proved rule of administration on a grand scale, it is much easier to lay down a general rule

and then deal with the exceptions than to attempt to deal with each case separately. The President's Agreement laid down and applied the general rule and scared up the exceptions. Then the codes permitted us to deal with the exceptions. We should have failed on any other plan.

These eight reasons for the Blue Eagle campaign are not now stated for the first time. They were echoed like a muezzin over the housetops from the very first. I have never heard any of them refuted in logic. I have heard only slogans, shibboleths, and catch-words pounded out in the good old neolithic fashion like tom-toms on a war drum until thoughtless people began to repeat them as reasoned conclusions.

There have been six similar mass movements of this nation depending for support on almost unanimous popular participation. The Selective Draft, the Liberty Loan Campaign, the Food Administration, the War Industries Board Mobilization of Industry in 1917 and 1918, and the Blue Eagle Drive in 1933. I had been a party to effecting three of them and had been in contact with all. There is no question that, to make any such thing successful, you must have a country united in a common cause and it must be a situation poignant and intense. The five mass movements in 1917 and 1918 had the war for a common cause. In 1933 it seemed to me that we were facing an even greater danger and that all people knew it and were sick of inaction.

I called up Senator McAdoo and asked him about his organization for the Liberty Loan Drive. He gave me the genius of that great *tour de force*, Charles F. Horner of Kansas City. He is an enthusiast, an idealist, a man of intense loyalty and devotion and almost child-like ingenuousness and he threw himself into his work with the ardor of a crusader.

On July 21—and this was only five weeks after the law was passed—we issued this press statement:

The National Recovery Administration today inaugurated a nationwide educational campaign designed to speed the return of prosperity through expanding the purchasing power of the consumer.

In a telegram to the Presidents of the Chamber of Commerce in every city of more than 10,000 in the United States, Hugh S. Johnson, Administrator, requested them to take the initiative in forming local campaign committees to carry on the drive. Coöperation of outstanding local citizens and organizations is to be solicited by the Chamber heads. Eventually the campaign will be organized along state lines and carried down to individuals in every community in the country regardless of size. The message of the administration will be carried by varied channels, including speakers both in public meetings and by radio, newspapers, display advertisements, posters, and others used in previous government campaigns of information.

The telegram which launched the drive follows:

"Will you take the initiative immediately in organizing a campaign committee in your community to be composed of the Mayor, the

official heads of the Chamber of Commerce, Clearing House Association, Rotary, Kiwanis, Lions, Retail Merchants, Federation of Labor,
Advertising Club, Federation of Women's Clubs, Welfare societies,
Ministerial Association, Real Estate Association, and any other civic
organization which in your judgment is representative of an important
element in the economic life of your community. The function of
this committee is to direct a campaign of education and organization which is to be a part of a national movement to speed the return
of prosperity through the expansion of consumer purchasing power in
accordance with the principles set forth in the National Recovery
Act. I will communicate with you covering the further steps in this
campaign upon receipt of your reply."

In the meantime, Charlie Horner had done everything. There
was scarcely a national organization with local representation
that had not been enlisted and responded enthusiastically. The
whole radio system of the country was donated and the most in-
fluential leaders and spokesmen of nearly every party, creed,
and segment of our national life had been enlisted. Of course,
the most important message equaling all our other efforts put
together was the President's. He said in part:

The proposition is simply this: If all employers will act together to
shorten hours and raise wages we can put people back to work. No
employer will suffer because the relative level of competitive cost will
advance by the same amount for all. But if any considerable group
should lag or shirk, this great opportunity will pass us by and we will
go into another desperate winter. This must not happen.

We have sent out to all employers an agreement which is the result
of weeks of consultation. This agreement is in accord with the voluntary codes of nearly all the large industries which have already
been submitted. This Blanket Agreement carries the unanimous approval of the three Boards which I have appointed to advise in this,
Boards representing the great leaders in labor, in industry, and in
social service. The agreement has already brought a flood of approval
from every state, and from so wide a cross-section of the common
calling of industry that I know it is fair for all. It is a plan—deliberate,
reasonable, and just—intended to put into effect at once the most
important of the broad principles which are being established, industry
by industry, through codes. Naturally, it takes a good deal of organizing and a great many hearings and many months, to get these codes
perfected and signed, and we cannot wait for all of them to go through.
The Blanket Agreements, however, which I am sending to every employer will start the wheels turning now, and not six months from now.

There are, of course, men, a few of them, who might thwart this great common purpose by seeking selfish advantage. There are adequate penalties in the law, but I am asking the coöperation that comes from opinion and from conscience. These are the only instruments we shall use in this great summer offensive against unemployment. But we shall use them to the limit to protect the willing from the laggard and to make the plan succeed.

In war, in the gloom of night attack, soldiers wear a bright badge on their shoulders to be sure that comrades do not fire on comrades. On that principle, those who coöperate in this program must know each other at a glance. That is why we have provided a badge of honor for this purpose, a simple design with a legend, "We do our part," and I ask that all those who join with me shall display that badge prominently. It is essential to our purpose.

Already all the great basic industries have come forward willingly with proposed codes, and in these codes they accept the principles leading to mass reëmployment. But, important as is this heartening demonstration, the richest field for results is among the small employers, those whose contribution will give new work for from one to ten people. These smaller employers are indeed a vital part of the backbone of the country, and the success of our plans lies largely in their hands.

Already the telegrams and letters are pouring into the White House—messages from employers who ask that their names be placed on this special Roll of Honor. They represent great corporations and companies, and partnerships and individuals. I ask that even before the dates set in the agreements which we have sent out, the employers of the country who have not already done so—the big fellows and the little fellows—shall at once write or telegraph to me. And it is my purpose to keep posted in the postoffice of every town, a Roll of Honor of all those who join with me.

The response to that was immediate and perfectly overwhelming. Telegrams and letters by the tens of thousands poured into Washington for days. No such volume of mail had ever been received by the government and I doubt whether, even during the war, any such unanimous response ensued.

The Blue Eagle Campaign—as soon as political and nonconformist opponents began to dare—was criticized on two principal grounds: that it was ballyhoo; that it was a boycott, and later, that it promised more than it delivered.

I want to answer the latter first because that is simply a question of fact. I have already quoted verbatim from public records every statement I made in prophecy—that I refused to prophesy, that my hope was to put 3,000,000 men to work under Title I. As soon as the Blue Eagle Campaign was in effect we took an actual questionnaire census of reëmployment under the Blue Eagle and it showed roughly 2,785,000 which happened to be within 2 or 3% of Mr. Lubin's reëmployment figures independently arrived at in the Department of Labor. The third criticism is simply a misstatement of fact.

But as to "boycott" and "ballyhoo"; of course these are just epithets and not reasons or arguments—like calling religion a "fake."

A boycott is a consumers' strike—sometimes political like Chinese refusal to buy Japanese goods—sometimes economic like the "Buy British" movement in England and many hundreds of "Patronize Home Products" campaigns in this country. It is a perfectly legitimate economic weapon recognized and applied in the United States since and before we were a nation—what were the Boston Tea Party and Colonial resistance to British importation, but a boycott?

No—"Boycott" was an epithet. What these critics wanted to do was to paralyze NRA, for the sole reason that they didn't want to pay higher wages, grant shorter hours and abolish sweat shops and child labor. But they did not dare to say that, so they resorted to chanting "boycott—boycott—boycott," like savage witch-doctors around a fire in a war dance where, having no argument, they incite murderous emotions by continuously repeating "*Hoo*-i-yea—*Hoo*-i-yea, *Hoo*-i-yea" and beating voodoo tambours. Our people are getting too far away from the primitive beginnings of the race to heed the rumblings of such distant drums.

There was a political reason far deeper and more subtle than this. The Blue Eagle put the enforcement of this law into the hands of the *whole* people just as did the Selective Draft Plan, which Secretary Baker adopted as against military enforcement and said that his reason was that if the people didn't support a war, a Democracy could not wage a war.

It was the exact antithesis, for example, of prohibition enforcement where an army of Federal snoopers tried to impose on the people through pains and penalties a statute which most of them did not approve. The President hit the nail squarely on the head when he said, "*There are adequate penalties in the law, but I am asking the coöperation that comes from opinion and from conscience. These are the only instruments we shall use in the great summer offensive against unemployment. But we shall use them to the limit to protect the willing from the laggard and to make the plan succeed.*"

Recalcitrant employers did not like this, the old guard and the Old Dealers did not like this. There are many ways to control or avoid Federal enforcement by prosecution but there is no way to avoid public opinion implemented by even so mild a right as to buy where you choose and to decline to buy where you do not choose. All any seller had to do to get the President's "shining badge" was to pay his employees a minimum of $12 or $13 a week for forty hours of labor and, as I had occasion to say at that time, "Men have died and worms have eaten them but not from paying human labor thirty cents an hour."

From the crustacean political standpoint it was simply too close to letting our people have some hand in their own affairs to suit their dear old predatory precedents and that was and is all there was to the Hottentot howl of "Boycott."

Recently a report by W. H. Davis to the new NRA "Board" condemns any method of enforcement except conventional criminal prosecution and inferentially refers to the Blue Eagle as "Boycott." Mr. Davis was apparently called by the Board as an authority because I once tried to use him to help me get compliance. While I have the greatest respect for him, his high purpose, and his unusual attainment in *ex parte* argument, his efforts on compliance were not fruitful.

"Ballyhoo" is what a circus barker does to get people to spend their money for tickets to a side-show which isn't worth the money. It is the constant repetition of lies, incitements, or exaggerations and I was accused by nearly all of them of being the "biggest and most blatant ballyhoo artist in the whole New Deal."

It is true that I believed zealously and earnestly in what I was doing. When I had decided to take my job, I said to Bernie Baruch, "Chief, I wish I had your faculty for getting things done through charm and astuteness and polish and your genius for saying things very positively but so gently that nobody ever takes offense." Then he told me the story of Paul

Berlenbach who was a slugger of the Dempsey type before whom nobody could stand. "But then," he said, "*somebody came along to teach him to box. He didn't last six months.* Somebody with a wallop got in the ring with him and, when he began dancing around and delivering fairy taps, they carried him through the ropes feet first. Go in there and be yourself and not Bernie Baruch, nor Jim Ham Lewis, nor Lord Chesterfield, nor anybody else but just yourself."

This I tried to do and if sometimes the verbal result savored of a cavalry barrack, my only excuse is that I spent the formative period of my life in that environment. I talked as I had always talked and in carefully re-reading all of it, I still can't see the "Ballyhoo." Out of the whole lot I have picked what is generally said to have been the worst example and while this is not a book of speeches, I have no apology to make and I include a few paragraphs—unedited and unexpurgated, not only to let the reader judge for himself but also because they express the philosophy which then informed us.

It was delivered at St. Louis to a visible audience of 26,000 and over both radio chains.

There is one reason to expect success. This is a move to bring happiness back to homes, and homes are the peculiar province of wives and mothers. It is they who have borne the brunt of the four years' blight on decency in living. They are the purchasing agents of America. Women do 80% of our buying. It is more accurate to say that they, in some measure, control 100% of our buying. It is they who can put the Blue Eagle on everything that moves in trade or commerce. The cause could not be in surer hands. Men might argue about how many business angels could stand for the point of an economic needle—and let the chance go by, but a woman in support of her home is about as safe for triflers as a Royal Bengal Tigress at the door of a den full of cubs. When every American housewife understands that the Blue Eagle on everything that she permits to come into her home is a symbol of its restoration to security, may God have mercy on the man or group of men who attempt to trifle with this bird.

The only thing to make the President's plan effective is to *understand* the President's plan. And all that is necessary to understand the President's plan is to know that every employer who can show the Blue Eagle *has already raised wages and made new jobs and that he cannot keep it up unless everybody acts right now to support him and buy his goods.*

That simple but necessary program depends on just one thing

for its success—the instant and intensive activity and support of the mothers and wives and sisters and sweethearts of this country and on nobody else in the world.

Our men had the leading part in the Revolution which *made* the nation—and in the Civil War which *united* it, and in the World War which *glorified* it. But, this time, it is the women who must carry the whole fight of President Roosevelt's war against depression, perhaps the most dangerous war of all. It is women in homes—and not soldiers in uniform—who will this time save our country from misery and discord and unhappiness. They will go over the top to as great a victory as the Argonne. It is zero hour for housewives. Their battle cry is "Buy now under the Blue Eagle!" and the bird is blazoned on the banners in their van.

Those who are not with us are against us, and the way to show that you are a part of this great army of the New Deal is to insist on this symbol of solidarity exactly as Peter of the Keys drew a fish on the sand as a countersign and Peter the Hermit exacted the cross on the baldric of every good man and true. This campaign is a frank dependence on the power and the willingness of the American people to act together as one person in an hour of great danger. And that brings us to the critical point of the program which I must make with all the emphasis at my command.

This thing won't last three months unless all men who now have employment and all who are now to be put back on the payroll—or to have their part-time work increased—*turn right around and pour the entire benefit back into the channels of trade.*

Our people have smiled their way through this hell—there is not one who has not made his sacrifice. If he kept his job he gave something to somebody. He helped some friend or some member of his family—too proud to ask for public help—too much up against it to refuse what we kindly call a loan. No use harping on that. . . . It is the most sublime chapter in our story . . . the secret of every decent person, which, to every decent person—is no secret at all. The blundering silent sentiment of this self-styled, hard boiled people of ours is enough to bring tears to the brazen eyes of a squatting Buddha.

To preserve a hostage to future fortune, people who have a little left have adopted a non-buying policy that is fatal to recovery. It is an unemployment psychology that sends us shabby to our work. Unpainted houses—cracked shoes, many times half-soled—shiny pants—rattling automobiles—dyed dresses—refurbished wardrobes —all these badges of unselfish husbandry must now be replaced if this plan is to have a fair chance to do what we hope for it. We must shake ourselves out of this four-year-old idea of doing without against a rainy day and we must do that overnight. . . . Buy! Buy now! Buy within prudence everything you need and have so long denied yourselves. It is the key to the whole situation.

The President said in his inaugural that he believed in putting first things first and the first thing in this great program is to get *Blue Eagles in every window*. The time for dealing with the chiseling fringe will come as soon as that is done.

We all know the possibility of an Iscariot in every Twelve. Even Judas survived for a season—and then hanged himself for shame. As soon as this great modern legion is marshaled, it will be time enough to look about us for Judas. . . . At this time, we ask only, that you visualize the rare case of a man who has betrayed the confidence of the President and the people of this nation and, behind the outspread wings of the Blue Eagle, has inveigled the women of this community to support his business, and then imagine that, after just complaint and fair and patient hearing, he is at last found out as one who would prong pennies in violation of a spontaneous confidence of his government and his neighbors.

*Guilty as Charged*. Guilty of trifling with this great chance to lift this country out of economic hell. Guilty of a practice as cheap as stealing pennies out of the cup of a blind beggar. What should be done with such a man? . . . As happened to Danny Deever, NRA will have to remove from him his badge of public faith and business honor and "takin of his buttons off an' cut his stripes away" break the bright sword of his commercial honor in the eyes of his neighbors—and throw the fragments—in scorn—in the dust at his feet. It is a sentence of economic death. It will never happen. The threat of it transcends any puny penal provision in this law.

The Blue Eagle is a symbol of industrial solidarity and self-government. If people who are willing to coöperate for a great national purpose are not permitted to wear a badge to distinguish friend from foe, then soldiers ought not to be permitted to wear a uniform or carry a flag. Warfare should decline to guerilla sniping. The chivalry of men in battle ought to give place to well-poisoning and assassination and it was well that Richard of the Lion Heart, unvanquished in every field from Palestine to the English Channel, should die, as legend has it, from an arrow poisoned in the Caucasus by the Old Man of the Mountain to be discharged in Normandy.

I made many such speeches but this one marks the nadir of all my sinning. I can't think it was sinning. I believed these things. I still believe them. I believe them so hard that I feel that unless they are kept alive NRA will fail. I think it is failing now because people who do not understand the fundamentals of NRA are neglecting them.

Of course, the country had to be told about NRA. Some districts lagged and some forged ahead. Enemy propaganda was stronger in some places than in others. These were perilous moments. In spite of the work in Washington which was so great that sometimes for days at a time—6 hours out of 24 was all I could spare from work—it was absolutely necessary to go all over the United States to confer with local leaders and to make speeches—sometimes three a day. Fortunately, we had the army air service to help us—a big fast Condor plane, with a desk in it. The speeches were written on hops from city to city. We visited every important town in the country except New Orleans, and flew a distance considerably greater than the earth's circumference.

Within a few weeks doubt about the first great step was over. This country was astir from coast to coast. Along the line of march were such men as stood on the banks of the Hudson while Fulton's steamboat got up steam and cried, "She'll never run—she'll never run!" We also heard a similar complaint in Washington for a month. We liked to remember that when the *Clermont* began chunking up the Hudson River, men ran alongside crying: "She'll never stop—She'll never stop." We soon heard that also. "Beware—What is the government going to do with this dangerous weapon?"

Of course a lot of people signed the Blue Eagle Agreement not knowing what it meant. A negro bootblack in St. Louis signed it, cut his own work to 40 hours and then appealed to NRA for the rest of his $12.00. The general idea that NRA was expected to put 3,000,000 people to work got around, and a good many thousand thought it meant three million new jobs in the NRA department in Washington. They inundated the Commerce Building, and it took weeks to correct that impression. A little tailor named Maged was prosecuted *not under NRA but under a New Jersey statute* in a kind of racket that was going on there —and actually sent to jail by a New Jersey Court. NRA had nothing to do with that. Yet some papers still carry that as a black mark against the Blue Eagle, although Maged at once telegraphed me not to take his Blue Eagle away or disturb the code because it had been his salvation—*and those newspapers knew that.*

The Blue Eagle drive was one of the greatest of demonstrations of unselfish patriotism but it brought out a good deal of pure cussedness besides. Fake associations sprang up all over the country to collect "dues." All kinds of fake eagles and misuse of consumers' eagles were shortly discovered. 95% of cases considered were settled by explanation and argument and yet chiseling never ceased.

The climax was a Blue Eagle parade in New York, in the early part of September, 1933, arranged by Grover Whalen who had been doing the job there. I think it was one of the greatest parades ever held in the country. It proceeded in columns of masses all one day and most of the next night. It was just a jammed river of humanity flowing up Fifth Avenue and its distinctive feature was color and cheer—cheer such as I had not observed in my four years' previous residence there. These people were convinced that they had seen the worst. Hope and confidence had returned.

I stood in the reviewing stand in that parade and there were hundreds of people I knew who waved as they went past. Down below were massed batteries of cameras and I knew if I raised my hand higher than my shoulders, it would seem and be publicized as a "Fascist salute." So I never did raise it higher, I just stuck my arm out straight and wiggled my hand around. But that didn't help me—*Time* came out saying I had constantly saluted *au Mussolini* and even had a photograph to prove it, *but it wasn't my arm* on that photograph. It wore the taped cuff sleeve of a cut-away coat and a stiff round cuff with an old fashioned cuff button and I never wore either in my whole life. I think it was the arm of Mayor O'Brien who stood beside me which had been faked onto my body.

That was a high point in NRA history. Within four months PRA and the Blue Eagle had:

(a) Brought 96% of Commerce and Industry voluntarily under NIRA.

(b) Abolished sweatshops and child labor.

(c) Obtained an agreement from 96% of employers under it to recognize the rights of labor under 7a.

(d) Put 2,785,000 bread-winners back on pay-rolls and increased annual purchasing power by $3,000,000,000, and that is several times the aggregate result accomplished by all the other Recovery Administrations put together.

(e) Established 40 hours as the maximum work week and

$12.00 as the minimum weekly pay for the lowest paid type of common labor in the United States, and practically took the wages of labor out of the field of industrial competition.

(f) Changed desperation into hopefulness not only among employees but among employers throughout the country.

(g) Acted as the greatest single educational force in homely economics in our history.

(h) Created, for the first time, an economic government throughout the United States imposed upon the political government and nearly as wide in extent.

(i) Awakened the conscience of the country to its best interest and its duty to erase these old iniquities.

Now no labor organization on the earth and no conflict between labor and management could have done these things. None of the critics of the Blue Eagle has anything of accomplishment to measure against these results. This was the first effective step that had ever been taken to benefit the white collar class, and that class, for some reason or other, had never seemed prone to organize nor have I ever seen until very recently any outward move on the part of the A. F. of L. to organize them. They ought to be organized. In my opinion it is only in organization of all the workers in this country that we can hope for balance in our economic structure.

I must hasten to add that I claim no personal credit for these things, even though in stating them it may seem so. Somebody has to speak for the devoted workers of NRA and I don't know who else should.

The real leader was the President. All credit for inception, inspiration, organization, and execution goes to him. To prove this it is only necessary to ask "What would have been the reaction to the Blue Eagle, the request for PRA's, the intense enthusiasm that followed, if he had not spoken?" It would have fallen flat.

The people who did the real work were the unpaid volunteers —tens of thousands of them—in the field and the relatively small and partially unpaid staff in Washington—men, whose unselfish work I can only sketchily and incompletely describe or accredit here. I was only a kind of top sergeant acting for the Captain in the White House. To prove this, I need only refer to his initial order given on June 16, which I have attached as an Appendix, which is so clear and eloquent and which has been followed so faithfully as to leave no doubt of where true credit lies.

It is impossible to tell the story of NRA in strict chronological sequence of events and carry forward the story of that sequence. Thus it happens that completion of the Blue Eagle Campaign, the establishment of the routine of code-making and the approval of the Big Six Codes came at about the same time. That marked a distinct turning point in whatever was to be the program of NRA. I had intended to stay only six months when I came in April. That was all I could afford. So at that time, I tried to resign. It has been said that I did so because of the constant sniping of government subordinates in other Departments, and the prima-donna antics of two men of my staff, or because of the absence of cohesion, coördination, and teamwork between various elements of the Recovery Program. But that is not so. That was part of the job which I anticipated and expected. It was an added sap on my strength, but it was no cause for my action. This time the President called me on the telephone and gave me one of his good-natured scoldings which I probably richly deserved. I made up my mind then to go on until about March, when, as I computed the bulk of code-making would be finished, we could have a round-up of criticism and complaint and thus determine any necessary changes in action, policy, and organization and then I thought I could turn readjustment over to others.

Nobody knows better than I that the 1933 autumn enthusiasm for the Blue Eagle lapsed for two reasons—first: because compliance was not enforced vigorously enough; second: because no Blue Eagle drives were instituted. When I decided to decentralize some of NRA powers to State Directors, I received instructions from the Executive Director of the National Emergency Council to do nothing until the National Emergency Council should set up its State Directors. *This held up the creation of a territorial compliance organization for months.* Similarly, just as Charles Horner had drawn up a new plan for a rather less spectacular but much more effective Blue Eagle drive, I received instructions from the same source to postpone it until the new "Housing" drive was ready—but that is not ready yet.

About this time also Mr. Richberg reported to me (what I already knew) that there was some serious lack of common understanding between what NRA thought and was doing and what the Department of Justice thought and was doing and that the prospect of prosecution in important cases was not as bright as it might have been. I had too much to do to attend to that. I asked him to try to compose any difference which he saw between us and the Attorney General and the Federal Trade Commission, saying that I would rely on him for that.

These things dampened ardor and postponed action when action was most needed. They dragged action out until the latter part of July and from that time on the full and vigorous functioning of NRA was seriously impaired by many inventions.

That Blue Eagle was an effective fowl, and he can be made effective again to the tune of reëmployment of about a million people but not by any "deliberative" administration of NRA which sits in purple silence—like Buddha on a lotus flower in serene and effortless contemplation of its composite navel.

# Chapter XXII

# THE LITTLE FELLOW

---

"To these crockodile tears they will add sobs, fiery sighs and sorrowful countenance."
—*Anatomy of Melancholy—Burton.*

---

PRETTY early in this story two or three young politicians discovered the Little Fellow. Just what they meant by the Little Fellow they are coy about saying—but it is a juicy political mouthful and if they were a little hazy on economics and on the law they voted for and I swore to execute, they were certainly letter perfect and full to the lips on this kind of politics.

Of course we know all about the real Little Fellow. B. M. Baruch said at Boston in 1930:

Consider our machine-tool industry alone—since its figures are a direct measure of the progress of mechanization of industry at large:

In 1914, 13,500 establishments used 1,256,000 primary horsepower to produce one billion six hundred thousand dollars' worth of product. In 1925, 11,800 establishments used 2,714,000 horsepower and produced five billion dollars' worth.

Turning from this barometer of mechanization to the actual growth of manufactures: The 1914 figure is not available but, in the sixteen year period 1909–1925, we practically doubled our use of horsepower and nearly trebled our quantitative output of manufactures.

Such figures of increase are so vast that the mere recitation of them conveys no adequate idea of their tremendous meaning.

It is a marvelous industrial system we are creating, but it exacts a dangerous price. It requires larger and larger units in every business and *it wipes out the little fellow.* Industry continues to combine in ever greater groupings until the trend seems to be toward an almost unitary national producing engine. Everybody has to specialize and almost nobody is wholly independent. We are all, in some measure, parts of our great economic machine.

To cure this condition he recommended an NRA.

I recognized, as NRA progressed, the necessity for a court of industrial appeal from the codes to look into particular cases, grant exceptions, and make recommendations for code changes. When this talk about the Little Fellow began, I suggested this. I was told that it would avoid a Senatorial investigation. I replied that I expected that anyway and would welcome it. I suggested first that Senators Nye, Borah, and Norris form a committee with complete access to all that we had done or were doing and this was considered for awhile but finally rejected—I think properly. We then worked out an idea of an independent Court and, in what now seems a moment of total aberration, *I myself suggested Clarence Darrow!* Samuel Seabury was asked to head the Board and declined. That put dear old Clarence up for Chairman. I did not know him personally although I had always admired his consistent intransigence and his barnyard philosophy. But Mr. Richberg knew him—had indeed been an old friend and associate. He recommended the Board and Mr. Darrow and all thereunto pertaining.

When Clarence came I think he meant to do everything he could to help. He told me that his idea was to hear every complaint, come to a conclusion, and then bring it over to NRA to see what we could do to right any wrong and relieve any hardship that he might discover. He volunteered the suggestion that he was not there to start any newspaper trial of cases or to put boulders in our stony path but only to be helpful.

But Clarence is not so young as once he was. He brought in a younger man named Mason and another named Thomson and they had political ideas. They took a room in the New Willard for offices. Right next to it this hotel had fitted up a dining room where the NRA staff could meet at luncheon and by some quirk in acoustics the door between was a sounding board rather than a barrier. Booming voices coming through informed my staff what was going on at all times and that a newspaper campaign to knock NRA into a cocked hat was to be started at once, based on any dirt the Darrow Board could dig up—and lots and lots of other things.

For some reason the press did not come up to these expectations. But Bloody old Jeffries at the Assizes never conducted any hearings to equal those for cavalier disposal of cases. They condemned codes in a half-hour "hearing" upon which the men who had made the code and the NRA officials who had

approved it had spent weeks of investigation, agreement and
compromise, and they refused to allow any explanation and appearance from these men. It was a Cave of Adullam to which
every man who had a grievance, real or fancied, could come to
the wailing wall and have his complaint avidly encouraged
and promptly underwritten without the slightest inquiry into
its merits. Little was called for from the files by NRA and
it was only too apparent that many of the codes passed upon
and condemned had not even been read by the Board. No
codes were sent back to NRA for correction. Instead a "Report
to the President" was made and given to the press. The emi-
nent socialist Charles Edward Russell had been called in to
write it and its principal recommendation was that the government forthwith adopt Communism as the only solution of its
difficulties.

We promptly announced that, as far as NRA was concerned,
we would pay no more attention to the Board and its reports
than if neither existed. I felt sorry for Clarence Darrow. He
stated that he had not even read the communistic recommendation when he signed it and did not know it was in there. Mr.
Darrow came over to see me at the height of the ensuing
hullabaloo. I had no resentment against him—I did not know
why he had come to see me. I treated him as courteously as I
knew how and with all the deference due his age and great
attainments. We went out riding in an automobile to Arlington
in the evening and we talked about anthropology, comparative
religion, and whether man has a soul.

There is a wax dummy in the window of an ancient factory in
Alexandria—the effigy of a murdered watchman carrying a
lighted lantern—put there I think before the Civil War on the
idea that the murderer, like Eugene Aram, would revisit the
scene, reveal his horror at this seeming ghastly reincarnation
and go away "with gyves on his wrists." We talked about that
and the stories which that suggested and we didn't talk about
NRA or the Darrow Board—until we were getting back to
Washington and then he said that he wanted to discuss just
that. He wanted to go back to his and my original formula.
I told him that I feared it was too late with the Board as it
then existed, but that I would speak to the President about
it.

We tried to dodge the reporters, but with no success. All I could say was "Well we talked about the Trinil Man, the Neanderthal Man, the Piltdown Man *and the Little Man.*"

But the Darrow Board expired with its $50,000 appropriation and I set up an Industrial Appeals Board which is really doing some good. The Little Man Issue, as such, is political buncombe but in the controversy here there is an issue on which all that has been done under the Recovery Act may be completely annihilated.

Political critics of NRA and even some sincere doctrinaries of the old school are still convinced that the codes hurt the Little Fellow in business. Before going into this let me emphasize that the only *"Little Fellow"* complaint of wide application of which I have any knowledge—and I have scanned them all with care, is that the *Little Fellow does not want to pay code wages for code hours.* But code wages for code hours are of the very essence of NRA. For example, a sweat shop simply could not exist if it paid code wages for code hours or, if it paid them, it would not be a sweat shop.

So far as NRA is concerned, it had no choice in the matter. It was following language laid down by the President of which the part pertinent and already quoted is:

In my inaugural I laid down the simple proposition that nobody is going to starve in this country. *It seems to me to be equally plain that no business which depends for existence on paying less than living wages to workers has any right to continue in this country.* By "business" I mean the whole of commerce as well as the whole of industry; by workers I mean all workers—the white collar class as well as the man in overalls; and by living wages I mean more than a bare subsistence level—I mean the wages of decent living.

Throughout industry, the change from starvation wages and starvation employment to living wages and sustained employment can, in large part, be made by an industrial covenant to which all employers shall subscribe. It is greatly to their interest to do this because decent living, widely spread among our 125,000,000 people eventually means the opening up to industry of the richest market which the world has known. It is the only way to utilize the so-called excess capacity of our industrial plants. This is the principle that makes this one of the most important laws that ever came from Congress because, before the passage of this Act, no such industrial covenant was possible.

NRA carried out that policy as a sort of religion. If paying a minimum wage of $12.00 is the oppression of small enterprise, of which these men complain, I accept all blame. But, the complainants never say that this is the protested oppression. They do not dare to say so. They advance a vague and tenuous generality—that the Little Man is being oppressed by "monopolistic tendencies"—a subject fully covered by Chapter XVII. They don't dare say that decent wages is the oppression because to say that and act upon it would be to abolish the whole benefit to labor from NRA and labor controls votes.

The question raised by these complaints concerning the small employer is neither difficult nor obscure. It is simply as to the place of the greater amount of human suffering and oppression —an employer who chisels on the rule of minimum wages—or his workers. It is whether the small employer of five to thirty employees who complains now to these champions (and among these—not many but blatant—will be found the greatest chiselers under NRA), or his *workers* are the most to be pitied. The answer is that—in view of all that he can and sometimes has put in increased charges to the consumer (usually about double what NRA has really cost him), he is not in distress.

We know that he used to say of his high prices, in 1918, "it is the war." He now says, "it is NRA." We have heard of all the stingy, sleazy and sweat-shop products he sells as genuine. We know of the leisure and laughter he has coined into greasy nickels. We know that, in spite of all this, he is not satisfied with his profits. Who is the more oppressed because he is now asked to pay wages high enough to allow his people to raise their heads in human decency? . . . If the answer is he, then these critics are correct and this law ought to be amended. But if the answer is that it is his workers who are to be considered, then these politicians should not prevail.

To plumb the depths of feeling with which I approach this subject, one must consider the frightful results of depression on human labor that the great NRA goldfish bowl revealed —black men working in a steaming lumber swamp for seven and five cents an hour—ten and even twelve hours a day. Children toiling in factories for very little more—ten hours a day—55 hours a week—and sometimes on night-shifts. Women in sweat shops and garret slums bending night and day over garments and pieces of garments and not earning more than enough to buy food on a bare subsistence basis. From these right up to factories or stores on a ten to twelve hour day, six days a week, with wages equivalent to twenty cents an hour—it was this sort of thing that NRA set out to correct by an average 40 hour week with an average minimum $12.00 to $13.00 per week. Even that is not the wage of decent living in by far the bulk of this country. But the cold truth is that the obligation to pay these minimum wages is 95% of the "Little Fellow" Complaint.

Who is the real Little Fellow—the black man in the swamp —the child in the factory—the women in the sweat shop—or is it the small enterprise that says it cannot exist in competition unless it practices those barbarisms? Is the President right when he says that "No business which depends for existence on paying less than living wages has any right to exist in this country" or is my good friend Mark Sullivan right in predicting the disappearance of NRA because he thinks that it would give more production at lower costs to let small factories pay the lowest wage at which they can get help and that to do so would also take men off relief rolls at $7.00 a week?

I have never had the slightest doubt that the President was tight and, besides, Mark is wrong on another score—the Little Fellows hiring men at $7.00 a week would not bring in any *added* production or create any *new* employment. They would simply force Big Fellows to press down their wage scales. Purchasing power would be depressed accordingly. Production and employment would not be increased. They would be decreased because the price of foods, other products not affected by NRA, and all such fixed charges as rents, rates, and taxes would remain the same, but wages would be lower.

As is said in another chapter, this is all a question of balance and degree but I am very sure that the majority of decent people in this country do not want their balance and degree set at any initial figure as low as Mark would have it—which just means "no bottom" at all and I doubt if there are many who would quarrel very much with the figure which was set by the President in PRA and which was agreed to by more than 95% of the employers who are subject to NRA.

But apart from all this, it is a pity that we can't throw this Little Fellow bunk out of the window and address the real question here squarely on its merits. There are two such questions.

1. Shall we lower minimum wages and raise maximum hours under NRA in favor of Small Enterprise as such? We have just talked about that, and I have had my say. My answer is no. I do not mean that there should not be greater flexibility in differentials, exceptions, and modifications, but I do mean that nobody, big or little, has any right to engage in competitive business if his only method of doing so is to pay less than $12.00 a week for 40 hours of human labor. This is the vital question of whether we are ready to take labor out of the field of industrial competition. I am convinced that industry as a whole is ready to do that.

2. Shall we abolish NRA and go back to hours and wages left to the vagaries of every economic wind that blows under unlimited competition?

This second question reveals the deadliest danger of NRA —the theory that NRA and the Anti-Trust Acts under the Federal Trade Commission can exist side-by-side without composition of the philosophy of either. Mr. Richberg seems to say they can. I say they can no more mix than oil and water. It can no more be done than you can put two quarts of fluid into a one quart cup at the same time. This subject is fully discussed in another chapter. But I must say here with all earnestness that unless this issue is bravely and unequivocally and finally resolved, we might as well abandon hope and scrap NRA outright.

Mr. Richberg as general counsel agreed with me as I understood him in all these principles of policy. Indeed, as I have said, I recommended to the President, before he went to Hawaii, the creation of the Industrial Council, of which he is the head and his appointment to that position. In this capacity it was agreed between him and me that he would make it his chief duty during the President's absence to try to work out with the Federal Trade Commission and the Department of Justice some reconciliation of conflicting aspects of policy of their and our views.

He had been representing NRA on the Steel Code Authority, and had reported to me that we were rapidly approaching an ugly impasse. We had approved a code for the iron and steel industry. Yet the Federal Trade Commission was busily engaged in preparation to go after them for doing things which, with Mr. Richberg's legal approval and on my recommendation, the President had authorized in their Code of Fair Competition.

Unless I misread newspaper accounts of his recent utterances, Mr. Richberg has recently changed his mind. I think he says that he wants to return to the "competitive system," and eliminate price stabilization—at least some of his words can be so construed. Whether they were qualified when spoken or have been qualified since, I do not know, but I do know that he worked out no composition with the Federal Trade Commission. I believe that he never even tried to do so. The main purpose for which I suggested the Council and him on it seems not to have been achieved.

No Little Fellow needs to fear the amendment of the Anti-Trust Acts contained in NRA. As Senator Wagner said in debate on NIRA referring to the codes: "*It will be the first time that small business will have a voice in the government of Industry. It has none today.*"

In this connection, I quote a letter—one of many thousands received. It expresses sentiments of independent retail druggists.

GENERAL HUGH S. JOHNSON
Washington, D. C.

*My dear General Johnson:*

At the last regular meeting of the National Retail Drug Code Authority, I was unanimously requested to write you a letter expressing the sincere appreciation of the members of the Code Authority for the spirit of fairness to them during your term as Administrator of the NIRA.

The members of our Code Authority were particularly gratified at the many editorial expressions, complimentary of your service, in the leading papers in the country. We are sorry that they did not appreciate your fine worth prior to your retirement. The vote on November 6th was surely of great comfort and satisfaction to you, for no man played a bigger part in the program that was so wonderfully endorsed than did you. Millions who are working today owe their jobs to your steadfast determination to create employment, and thousands of small independent merchants are in business today solely because you insisted on a fair deal to the little fellow as well as to the big one. You have laid the foundation of fair business methods for generations to come. As the plan develops improvements will be made. *But for you and your program the little man would have been crushed out of existence.* . . .

[*Signed*] J. A. GOODE,
*Chairman.*

Industry has been given a right to act in unison, but only in close partnership with government, and under governmental sanctions and supervisions with Federal powers of control so direct, instantaneous, and almost brutal as to make the ineffectual anti-trust laws (which had so signally failed to protect against monopoly) seem mild by comparison.

I admire the Federal Trade Commission, but at this crisis we must look facts in the teeth and by moving in to take over NRA it can only kill NIRA. That Commission was set up to do something of what NRA was set up to do—to improve our industrial condition by letting industry act in unison under the supervision of the Commission. But it was created against the background of a law saying to Industry: "If you *do* act in unison you will be hung, drawn, and quartered." Industry naturally asked: "What *can* we do?" and the reply to that was in effect: "That is a secret. Go ahead and act. *After* you act we will tell you whether you can do it or not and if you have guessed wrong the *auto-da-fé* will commence."

Even the actual practice of asking what industry has done is an inquisitorial process, sometimes lasting a year, at great expense and continuous uncertainty. The net result is failure of original purpose, and, in my opinion at least, a negative cause of the depression of 1929. There was—and there is— about as much coöperation between the Federal Trade Commission and Industry as there is between a Lion Tamer with a black-snake whip, a revolver, and a strong-backed chair, standing in a cage with six great jungle cats snapping and snarling on six star-spangled hassocks. You can't escape the issue—coöperation or competition.

Far from oppressing the Little Fellow, our records show that NRA has not only halted in its tracks a ten year Sicilian Vespers which nearly wiped him out, but has squarely reversed it. When the Bituminous Coal Code went into effect, 4,500 small coal mines that we know of came back into operation, and we know that thousands more of which we have no record have been restored. The Lumber Code brought back 1,500 small saw-mills and 2,000 more have applied for allocation. The Retail and Wholesale Codes, by limiting the use of loss leaders and other devices of mass power of great corporations, saved literally tens of thousands of small merchants. The Rubber Tire truce and Code arrested the impending destruction of the whole retail tire business—60,000 to 70,000 small merchants. The Motion Picture Code gives the small independent producer the first reasonable chance of survival and fair play that he has had in the past ten years.

We might go through the whole list of codes with a similar conclusion. Indeed most of the code provisions are written for the protection of small enterprise. Far from impairing the chance of the Little Fellow, NRA is the greatest charter of economic salvation that small business ever had. Just as automatic machinery and labor saving devices, and great industrial combinations tend to wipe out individual enterprise, it may be that, in the end, new mass methods of distribution will prevail to the practical elimination of small enterprise in merchandising. It may be that it is well to have mail-order houses and filling stations run all tire dealers out—that chain stores should eliminate independents in every line. But this is no time to encourage or accelerate such disruptive change.

The only way I have seen to deter this process is NRA. With ten million people unemployed and general commerce and industry barely recovered from the worst mortality in history, this is no time to withdraw the actual and moral support of NRA from our convalescent structure. To the full extent of the powers of NRA we should maintain the status quo of small enterprise, at least until real recovery sets in. If existing tendencies are not checked and balanced, the time will come when we will have vast pauperism because there is nothing for a great group to do to earn a living.

There are a few slight pegs (more apparent than real) on which the contrary argument may be hung; that the Code Authorities which administer the codes are chosen from Industry and that the Big Fellow may dominate them to the detriment of the Little Fellow; that there are *some* Little Fellows who, for some particular reason, can actually pay code wages and still undersell the Big Fellow; that in causing everybody to report figures to Code Authorities the Little Fellow has to reveal facts which enable the Big Fellow to get him.

But when it comes to citing actual instances of all these things the argument usually halts and fails. They are apprehensions rather than events. In the first place the Federal Government sits in the deliberations of the Code Authorities through a government member who is charged specifically with the duty of seeing that monopolistic abuses or oppressions of Little Fellows *do not happen*. If they do happen it is a failure of NRA administration, not a failure of NIRA or NRA policy. And there is an Industrial Appeals Board to which any prejudiced man may go and get a hearing wholly independent of the Code Authority or of NRA itself. There are very few Little Fellows who can pay code wages and manufacture more cheaply than the Big Fellow. Where such is the case and no unfair method of competition is disclosed, that is a case for exception. There is machinery for such an exception and it should be promptly granted. But the fact is that there is almost no actual price fixing in NRA codes and in any code where there is none, the argument falls to the ground because its premise of price fixing does not exist. Of course, the objection that Big Fellows see Little Fellows' figures is superficial. There are no codes without Little Fellow representation, and hence Little Fellows see Big Fellows' figures too.

There is another chance of abuse especially in retail trade where the local Code Authority in some town gets into the hands of unscrupulous competitors who use their position to exploit their fellows. This is an abuse. There is a local NRA director in every state and it is his business to see that such abuses are corrected.

It is true that there are regional differences in wages long established, and these regional differences should be recognized. They *have* been recognized (although not perfectly composed), but where, as in some districts these old differentials were so great as to amount to exploitation of labor and invasion of the living standards of other areas they ought not to be permitted to continue and we did deliberately attempt to root them out.

My conception of NRA is perfectly illustrated by the Marquis of Queensberry rules in boxing. When this country was young, we used to have fights without weapons. It was a perfectly legitimate *riposte* in the manly art, as then conceived, to insert one's thumb into the eye socket of an opponent, and by a quick movement, deftly gouge his eyeball out—or, if the occasion presented, you could put the point of your knee into his groin and rupture him, or by taking his ear firmly between your upper and lower incisors, neatly or otherwise, tear it off. Of course, by pickling your bare hands in brine or alum (there being no gloves) you could mar him for life almost any time you could connect with his countenance. There you have rugged individualism to the ultimate. I can think of no better instance of it.

But the mortality was heavy and there were too many human wrecks. Therefore the Marquis of Queensberry and other boxing rules were established. I saw Max Baer not long ago bouncing Primo Carnera around the ring. It did not appear that his rugged individualism was much impaired because he could not do any of those old and half-forgotten things. I doubt if anybody ever thought Jack Dempsey's rugged individualism was hurt much when the Wild Bull of the Pampas knocked him into the typewriters and he crawled back to slam the Bull to the canvas four times in as many seconds—and he couldn't even hit below the belt or indulge in the rabbit punch on the medulla oblongata of the Wild One.

That is all there is to the codes. They eliminate eye-gouging and knee-groining and ear-chewing in business. Above the belt any man can be just as rugged and just as individual as he pleases. All he has to do is to start from an even taw line and then all the damage he can do his competitor, by ability, aggressiveness, experience, wisdom, and organization is perfectly legitimate. There is more chance for progress, more latitude for ability, more chance for profit and stability than ever before in our business history.

There is undoubtedly an exhilarating sense of primitive freedom in having absolute license to range through the economic forest and plain, like a war-party of the Iroquois—burning, killing, scalping, and marauding—there is your true ruggedness —but we could not build the great industrial civilization along the Great Lakes until we forced that into the limbo of forgotten romance. Both progress and recovery depend on a similar extermination in commerce.

# Chapter XXIII

# DEAD CATS AND TOM-TOMS

---

"I smelt sickly eggs by the barrel, and rotten cabbages and such things; and if I know the signs of dead cats being around, and I bet I do, there were sixty-four of them went in."

— *Huckleberry Finn—Mark Twain.*

---

SINCE the beginning of time there has been a device of witch-doctors. As Mr. Richberg once said, before what he now calls his dignity got him down, it is to set up a hobgoblin and then dance around the fire, beating the tom-tom and screaming at it. It awes the trusting natives and nine times out of ten it does the trick of misleading people into prejudices against their own interests. There is no limit to which this trick may not go. The priests of Moloch even had the people sacrificing their babies on the red-hot hands of an idol. It is too late in the life of civilization to bring back the abominations of Assyria— but exactly the same sort of witch-doctoring is going on about NRA.

Some say that no such action as NRA was ever necessary —that improvement would have come anyway—that we should now abandon all codes and go back to the old rule of hands off and let the best—or worst—man win.

This comes from some of the very voices that in March, 1933, were most eager for an outright dictatorship.

> *The devil was sick—the devil a monk would be:*
> *The devil was well—the devil a monk was he.*

The memories of these men are short. They were the very leaders of the 1922–1929 boom and bust and it is this same dis-credited leadership that is now saying—"We are on our way out. The Recovery Program had nothing to do with it. Let's abandon the whole thing and go back to the good old days."

This country does not want that—the sale of shady foreign and domestic securities under the appearance of stability of some of our greatest financial houses—million dollar bonuses in industry—unchecked use of depositors' money to support such Florida booms on the Stock Exchange as the 1929 fiasco —a system of banking practices which can wreck the life-time savings of practically a whole people—abuses in our industrial system which can create the practical destitution of half of our population—the unemployment of no less than 13,000,000 breadwinners—an economic and political system which for twelve years can witness the progressive degradation of agriculture to the point of absolute ruin and refuse even to consider an effective stop to the process—a philosophy about extreme depression that the thing to do is nothing at all but just to sit and take it while our economic structure rattles down about our ears and the beams of our political structure are already cracking. This country doesn't want to go down to Endor and call up the black and hideous phantoms of March, 1933, to come back and make their bed with us again—Starvation, Collapse, and Ruin.

What is all this fantastic whirling against our own best interests? *It is the inability of a few people to make sacrifices at a desperate time and for the common good and that is all it is.* Military history has shown that battle is not the most effective test of chivalry and manhood—a siege is. There is little excitement and less glory. Rations are slowly cut down so that men may share and live. Then petty, mean, and cheating hoarding shows up—nerves that cannot take it—hidden selfishness in figures hitherto covered with medals and shining repute, supplications for surrender—treachery, desertion, and treason.

Well this is a siege and in these few instances it is running true to form. But these few instances are not even straws to show which way the wind blows with the brave mass of our people who know that Franklin Roosevelt proposed a plan designed to help every depressed element of our population— industrial, agricultural, financial. . . . They know that, while it creates mutual benefits, it also imposes mutual sacrifice, that it cannot act with equal speed in every part of this country or on every social segment, that it averted disaster and chaos, that it has brought hope, created confidence, lifted despair, and improved the morale of the whole population.

I never had any protest against criticism and it is curious to me that I should have been accused of being sensitive about it —I suppose it was because I answered it. But that, in my concept of how to do the job, I had to do. Nobody likes criticism but any public institution is a peril if it is shielded from criticism, but there is no justification for a silent hauteur when the criticism is wrong. Controversy is the way to truth.

There are some things in a great experimental program like this which are necessarily based on conjecture as to their effect, and the only possible way to gauge that effect is to watch its results in public reaction. Only if government remains fluid and flexible, and invites and acts instantly on criticism, is it possible to carry forward such a plan. We needed it, asked for it, could not have proceeded without it. A free and unrestricted press is an absolute necessity. It is a powerful, if independent, part of the machinery of government.

The first big criticism about NRA was that *there was controversy there.* For crying out loud! That is exactly like criticizing a boxing ring or a court room because there is controversy there. The very Act was conceived in controversy—controversy as old as civilization—controversy among labor, management, and consumers. For reasons recited earlier we organized to make that controversy vocal, public, and intense. We preferred to write the rules for a new economic government of the United States by hearing every side which might have an interest in the result and arriving by compromise at the greatest good to the greatest number and the least possible harm to anybody. I don't know any other way to do it except to have an academic pundit go into some purple silence and emerge with directions to all business which he thinks will be good for it—like Moses from the Mountain of the Law—only Moses had the Lord God Almighty to tell him what to say and I know of no human being with a brain capable of writing even ten inflexible rules for any business in this country.

Of *course* there was controversy. The Advisory Boards were put there to dispute with each other. The public hearings were conducted to bring out every shade of opinion. The negotiations between management and labor were controversial. There was difference of opinion among my own staff which also was set up to thresh conflicting views on the government's part and policy in all this. The town rang with these arguments. But a

new economic structure was being built and people were thinking of these problems as never before. The hammers rang,
the riveters rattled, the saws screeched—but we built something
that will in part, at least, endure. And we did it without any
furtive scheming but in the full gaze of the whole country. I
can't take this criticism seriously.

Then it was said that we had no organization and what we
had was torn with bitterness and jealousy—that I was a one-
man operator and knew neither how to build an organization
nor to act through one. Well, in the war this whole country was
organized for the draft—every state, country, city, and village
in it and that organization was administered. I never heard
either its organizational form or function criticized and it
turned out a fairly good job. I helped to reorganize the War
Industries Board, the Division of Purchase, Storage, and
Traffic during the war, and several industrial companies after
the war.

But let us stick to NRA. All *it* did was to organize 96% of
American commerce and industry subject to NIRA under codes
in about a year. It organized the whole country for the PRA
and Blue Eagle in four months—using a corps of tens of
thousands of people to do it. It settled seven major labor
disputes and sold the plan to the country in the meantime.
If anybody thinks that could have been done other than *or-
ganizationally* or by any one man that ever lived it is because
he does not know this country, or the complexities of its business structure. As a matter of fact very little of the accomplishment of NRA came on my desk. We started with nobody
in the Washington organization and at one time had nearly
3,000 people there. A more devoted, loyal, and efficient group
I never saw—and I have seen a good many organizations. A
Board of seven has been working for weeks and I have yet to
hear of any improvements or change in organization or even of
method in NRA that was not proposed before I left—although
I must disclaim responsibility for anything that has happened in
NRA since I left it.

I do not say the NRA organization was perfect but I do say
that it did its job in an organic method and achieved the end
assigned to it. As to jealousy and bitterness, it is true we had
one or two *primæ donnæ*—by which I mean men who were

*there not primarily for the sake of the job but primarily for the sake of themselves.*

Most of the complaints of one-man operation came from one or two of these men in our own staff who wanted delegation of authority or an extension of confidence beyond the measure of their responsibility, ability, or trustworthiness. When I now learn of all that was done by them in the period from about May to October, 1934, it is just like a story my father used to tell about an occurrence in the Oklahoma Senate. In the earlier days some of the legislators of that rough country were a little weak on classical allusion—but *all* were not. Some mincing dandy was defending a notoriously grafting governor and said that, like Curtius, he had thrown himself into the breach to save the state.

One rough old colleague leaned over to his neighbor and whispered:

"Who was this galoot *Curtis*—what about him?" and was duly enlightened about the chasm opening in the Capitoline hill and—the oracle intoning that Rome's dearest treasure must be thrown in—Curtius, observing that Rome's Dearest treasure was her brave men, casting himself into the abyss.

The old "Sooner" rose, threw his battered Stetson in the aisle, carefully removed his chaw of tobacco and placed it on his neighbor's desk and asked if the gent would yield. It seemed that the gent would.

"He's got it all snarled up about the guv'ner. The guv'ner didn't th'ow hisself into no crack to save the state like Mr. Curtis done. The guv'ner th'owed the state into the breach to save hisself."

It was also said that there was confusion and delay and people milling around the halls of the Commerce Building in haste, and that I did not know what was going on, and comparisons were made between NRA and other departments of government where calm religious peace characterized the unhurried tenor of their way. Tombs are like that.

It is true that business descended on NRA faster than we could man the organization to handle it. It is true that I could not get space to house the people I had and that made congestion. It is true that many people came to Washington with ready-made code provisions written in their own interest and expected to rush out with an NRA signature on the dotted line without waiting for the other fellow to be heard from. These things made for delay but it should not have been otherwise. There were also cases of culpable delay—cases of cockiness by young assistant deputies—not many, but some.

But we then had a rule that every written communication must be answered, or at least acknowledged, within 24 hours. (It is no longer true in the new period of deliberation.) Every time I learned of unjustified delay I corrected it—looking back on the sum total of accomplishment I think it is a speed record —not a record of delays. As to my not knowing what was going on—perhaps some people thought so—perhaps some still think so but I had a succinct digest every day of every bit of NRA correspondence and wherever I saw in that digest something that I thought I needed to see in full I sent for it. Perhaps that may not give too much comfort to one or two Richelieus in and about NRA today—but it is a fact.

As to congestion, I had foreseen that at the outset and arranged for one building large enough to accommodate NRA at its maximum size and had even plotted the flow of work there. But some unseen hand reached out and frustrated that.

From one month to another the allegation was published that we had gone over to Labor and then that we had gone over to Industry—in about equal doses symmetrically spaced. That is inevitable to an umpire. It was urged at first that we were going too slow but toward the end that we were going much too fast and especially that nobody could render sane judgments who was whirling so rapidly as I in *my* own personal squirrel cage—that I was overwrought—"nerves a-twitter."

It is true that there were weeks on end when I averaged four hours' sleep and eighteen hours' work at night and more weeks when I averaged six hours of sleep. But I then had the faculty of lying down and going instantly to sleep anywhere at any time for ten or fifteen minutes and I did this frequently. Colonel Keller at the Walter Reed Hospital, one of the world's greatest surgeons, is also one of my best friends and I went out there for a thorough going over every three months and until toward the very end—there was not the slightest impairment of any function.

The reasons I felt that I had to maintain the pace of work I practiced were (during the early months) first, that if I could not demonstrate NRA by almost unanimous acceptance at the outset, the whole thing would fail and, second, that we were keeping hundreds of business managers away from their work at great expense and just at the exact time when, above all else, business needed resident management and instant activation. The latter reason always remained. Some people felt that they could not possibly take the last word from anybody else and while I deprecated this and avoided it as much as possible it was sometimes necessary to see as many as 120 people in a day. Mr. Richberg is recently quoted as saying that too much was attempted. He never voiced this hindsight criticism while the work was in process. My reasons for what I did are stated in Chapter XXI.

The myth about my not being able to make good judgments on account of exhaustion is just not true. They may not have been good judgments and I am clearly convinced that many of them were not. But they were the kind of judgments I always make and here is a point that well meaning friends (from whom God save us) who insisted that I knock off work at five and also go on a long vacation leaving my functions to a "deliberative" committee always forget—I had been studying and planning and working on the fundamentals of NRA for nearly four years. I had been through two very similar experiences during the war—the draft and the War Industries Board. My work with Mr. Baruch had taken me into the essentials of nearly every principal industry. I was a lawyer with an engineering education and an intense business experience. I knew many if not most of the principal industrial leaders. I had helped put the pieces of the Recovery Act together and knew every line in it. I had personally planned the organization, method, and regulations of NRA. And, as this record demonstrates, the fundamentals of what we were doing had been planned and studied with B. M. for many years—all of which was new to them. If such a word can be applied I was a professional and they were—and apparently are—very far from that.

Then came the assertions that I was dictatorial, hard-boiled, ruthless, and opinionated. These, of course, are personal characteristics of which I am not qualified to speak. I only rejoice in the fact that, so far as I know, nobody has yet said that I was a liar, or a cheat, or a crook, or a grafter, or a political trimmer, or unfair, or disloyal (either to those working with me or above me) or a quitter, or a traitor to my Chief. As to the shorter, more robust and vulgar Saxon monosyllabic epithets, I am aware that I have garnered perhaps the world's choicest collection of these dead cats, but since I confess to hurling quite a few myself, I feel even with the world on that.

But all these were small-arms fire compared with the really heavy artillery—*that we had bulldozed and domineered and regimented big business*—that we had "sold out" to big business and promoted big business monopoly; *that we had rooked the consumer by permitting high prices*—that we had repressed the free upward movement of prices; *that we had withheld from Labor the full benefits of section 7a and favored company unions* —that we had sold out to the American Federation of Labor —*that we had raised wages too high*—that we had kept wages too low—that we had robbed the press of the constitutional guarantee of freedom and—*worst of all*—that we had operated to rob and prejudice the farmer.

Some of these have been the subjects of particular chapters of this book or have been otherwise discussed herein. Here I want to touch lightly on others and to take up the last one first.

Right at the very outset somebody in the Department of Agriculture (including AAA) began to spread through the Mississippi Valley the dogmatic assertion that NRA, by raising prices for things that farmers buy faster than farm prices were raised—principally on overalls and cotton gloves—was prejudicial to agriculture. This propaganda produced, at first, a distinct resistance to NRA in that area. I don't know who did it, and I don't want to know, but I know who didn't do it. It wasn't George Peek who is an intimate friend of many years' standing and who, if he wanted to have a fight with me, would come right over to my office and have it—we've had plenty. And it wasn't Henry Wallace for whom I have formed a warm attachment and who just doesn't do things that way. And it wasn't Rex Tugwell.

Now it was literally not true that NRA had lifted prices of the things farmers buy faster or farther than the prices of farmers' sales had been lifted. In the first place, farm prices had been lifted farther than those of any other group and the improvement in them (while by no means sufficient) is still greater than the improvement in the other group. In the second place, the lift of other prices—especially cotton textiles—was caused in part by influences in the Recovery Program other than NRA. It will be recalled that the administration was extending all powers of government to lift *all* prices to the 1926 level and the principal device at that time was the debasement of the currency. This worked pretty well on export farm products where its effect is purely arithmetical. In the Cotton Textile Industry the price of raw cotton doubled—a pure Farm Relief measure—the processing tax was another net addition to the cost of goods—and NRA increases in labor costs (which were disgracefully low before) all combined to increase the *cost* of manufactured goods 100%. In short the bulk of the increased cost of overalls and cotton gloves was due to Farm Relief measures and not to NRA. But the propaganda in the Farm Belt was that it was *all* NRA.

As to my own interest in Agriculture and study of its problems, the following is an excerpt quotation of Henry Wallace's *New Frontiers*, p. 145:

The idea of fair exchange value had been described in a pamphlet published under the title *Equality for Agriculture* . . . the names of the authors appeared as George N. Peek and Hugh S. Johnson. *Eleven years later* George Peek as administrator of AAA was to help launch the first attempt to obtain fair exchange value for farmers *while his associate of 1922*, General Johnson, was directing another great recovery effort, the NRA . . . the idea of fair exchange value was finally approved even if all the Peek-Johnson plan was not. . . .

When it is said that NRA and the Blue Eagle have not done for the farmer all that he hoped the answer is that NRA had no such protean duty. It was set up to do for city workers what AAA was charged with doing for farmers.

But the wholly unjust propaganda against NRA going out to farmers from sources I have never clearly identified still continues. Even though NRA was designed particularly for urban workers it had a great beneficial effect for farmers. Their greatest market is the domestic market. We can search all over the world for backward and crippled countries to whom to loan millions in the hope that they will buy the products of our farms and factories, but we will never find a country with power to consume as much as 125,000,000 Americans within one tariff wall. If NRA has enriched that market it has done well by farmers and deserves their best wishes and most enthusiastic support.

By actual count, it put 2,785,000 city workers back on payrolls and added $3,000,000,000 to the purchasing power of the American domestic market in the year ended May 31, when propaganda was at its height, employment in this country had increased by 32%—all payrolls had increased by 28% and payrolls in manufacture (where NRA had the most direct effect) had increased by 57%. During this same period, the cost of living increased only 11%.

Cold percentages don't mean very much to one not accustomed to deal with them, but these figures simply say that—as to any group of three men who were employed a year before, one extra man has been added. They mean that, to every dollar of industrial workers' power to buy farm products a year ago, more than fifty cents has been added. These increases are very great. They are among the most hopeful signs in the economic sky. NRA is not entitled to credit for all of this. But the President's program as a whole is.

What the President started out to do was to restore to agriculture its pre-war purchasing power. In March, 1933, the purchasing power of what farmers produce was just about 50% of what it was in the pre-war period 1910–1914. In other words, it took just twice as much farm produce to buy a plow or a binder or a peg-tooth harrow as it did before the war. Now, considering the seven basic crops as defined in the Adjustment Act—prices in June, 1934, were four per cent higher than pre-war prices and the purchasing power of this group had advanced from about 50% of pre-war in March, 1933, to about 85% of pre-war purchasing power in June. In other words, the New Deal had *achieved about 70% of the gain necessary to restore pre-war purchasing power to these crops.*

We can't have a ruined agriculture and a prosperous industry any more than we can have a prosperous agriculture and a ruined industry. The President's measures for industry have been effective to the extent just stated. His measures for farmers have been equally effective—but the industrial plans have done as much to help farmers as the Farm Plan, and the Farm Plan has done as much to help industry as has NRA. It is for this reason that enlightened self-interest should make farmers as stalwart for NRA as for any titular farm measure under consideration.

I want to make it clear that I do not minimize the value of the effect of check and balance of this sort of criticism. It is easily conceivable in any planned economy that one effort will outstrip the other. The farm criticism when its basis is right will be a wholesome check.

We did not regiment or domineer business. *There is not a code or a code provision in the whole category that was not agreed to by business.* I proposed to let the licensing section of the law lapse because I did not want to maintain even that threat. All codes were submitted voluntarily. I sometimes used every persuasion I could bring and I am, unfortunately, tactless and vehement in argument but while I have heard *ex parte* critics accuse me of bulldozing business I never have heard of any code committee saying this—*not one single one.*

Of course the charge that we sold out to big business or unduly favored it is the precise reverse of the charge of bulldozing it and is equally untrue. There is no doubt that some deputies and assistants could never reconcile themselves to the labor provisions of the law and were not carrying them out in the spirit that animated them—not consciously but because of long habits of thought in a contrary direction. Whenever I found that this was true I let such men resign.

On the other hand we did not favor labor. Believing implicitly in their cause as defined in the Act, I nevertheless rapped them so hard when I thought they were wrong that it gave the enemies of NRA within the government the opportunity they sought to stultify it. I rapped industry just as hard and I conceived both rappings as duties. I would do the same thing over again.

Mr. Richberg ruled and I approved the ruling *pro tanto* that, under the law, while an employer might legally make a closed shop contract yet when he came to enforce it by requiring a man to join this or that particular union not of his own choosing, the employer would be violating 7a. This meant that majority representation could not be contracted for and executed as exclusive representation. I went further and said that I did not regard a majority and a minority union in the same shop as practicable but I still insisted that such was the law I had sworn to execute. But I went much further and said that I did not believe that a contract to do an illegal thing is a good contract and therefore that the closed shop contract on a majority vote was not a good contract.

This was all very unpopular with labor but it was the law. Mr. Garrison of the National Labor Board made it more unpopular by ruling to the contrary. In my opinion, under Executive Orders of the President he had no power to overrule an NRA pronouncement on NIRA and the President's own administrative interpretation of this act and, whether he did or not, I have read his reasoning and it offers nothing of legal logic or statutory interpretation. It is not reasoning at all—it is an opinion that such a ruling is expedient. It refers to precedents which have no bearing because they ante-date the statute and it flies squarely into the teeth of the plain words of NRA.

I also agree that it was expedient and that the law should be amended but I do not conceive that having sworn to execute a statute I have any right to change it. I am informed that Mr. Richberg has been able recently to make his own interpretation comport with the Garrison ruling but I have not, as yet, been able to perform this extraordinary feat. Such is not the law, although I think with Mr. Garrison that as a practical matter there cannot be two parallel unions in one plant. I am very sure I know the answer to this serious impasse and that it is not the forcing of any academic view down any throat. This subject will be fully discussed in Chapter XXX. The situation has been further complicated by a court ruling in the Houde case and a further Richberg pronouncement which the conservative press reported as crystal clear. To me it merely confused the labyrinth which I cannot solve—and if one did get to the center of it, he would find just what Theseus found in the original labyrinth—the great Cretan Bull.

Other criticisms which I have collected for convenience earlier in this chapter could not be discussed here without repetition. But, if this book is to be of any value, justified criticism and acknowledged blunders should be just as freely confessed as unjustified criticism is answered here. I have really tried my best to do that. When people say that I resent criticism, they forget that I invited a perfect round-up of criticisms last April and convened critics from all over the country to make them. They forget that every public hearing was a forum for criticism and that there were many of them every day.

They forget that I held press conferences as often as necessary and never dodged a question, lied in an answer, or failed to encourage reporters not to pull their punches. Of course, this gave opportunity for criticism by everybody and I had to take it as best I could. I never had any fun at all myself. But now I am going to. I am going to criticize myself.

In the April open forum I pointed out faults, or indicated improvements in NRA, viz.:

1. A more uniform and equitable rule of national price stabilization in those cases where it is necessary to maintain wages at a decent standard against the certain results of predatory and cut-throat competition, and further insurance against increase of price faster and further than increase of purchasing power.

2. A more effective rule on costs for the purpose of maintaining rules against sales below costs of production.

3. Uniformity of wages and hourly rates in competitive industries.

4. Uniform classification of areas for the purpose of the North-South differentials.

5. Further reductions in hours per week and further increase in hourly wages.

6. Certainty of protection against monopoly control and oppression of small enterprise and, especially, the inclusion in codes of adequate buying (as well as selling) provisions to guard against oppression of small business.

7. A much improved method for securing prompt and effective compliance.

8. A safe method of financing code administration without racketeering and abuse.

9. Elimination of inconsistent or conflicting provisions among various codes.

10. Adequate labor and consumer representation in an advisory capacity of Code Authorities.

11. Uniformity of governmental representation on Code Authorities.

12. Wider use of mechanism for settling labor disputes in connection with code administration.

In addition to this, as I see my principal blunders, they were:

1. To have taken the job at all after I knew that NRA and PWA were not to move forward under a common coördination.

2. I should not have had three Advisory Boards. I should have had an Advisory Council with three departments—one each for labor, industry, and consumers. I corrected this before I left, but once a bureau, a board, or a commission digs in, it is not easy to root out.

3. I should have insisted that the NRA Consumers' Board be a department of a Consumers' Council outside of NRA with liaison to all administrations.

4. I should have been less vehement in going after some small-fry critics—I only dignified them by answering at all.

5. I should have insisted on my intended resignation in June and October, 1933, and in April, June, and August, 1934.

6. I should have declined to postpone the organization of a Compliance system and the new Blue Eagle drive which I projected in April of 1934 and which I delayed at the request of the Director of the Emergency Council.

7. I should not have temporized, for fear of hurt feelings, in securing the resignation of a few men whom I knew eventually to be disloyal or out of sympathy with the Recovery Act.

8. I should never have acceded to the appointment of the Darrow Board.

9. The Blue Eagle should never have been withdrawn in cases where the Department of Justice found no sufficient grounds for prosecution.

10. Service industries (i.e., industries which sell service rather than commodities) should not have been brought under codes. They should have been given President's agreements in local groupings when a large majority agreed.

11. Small town employers and small employers should never have been exempted from the codes. Some system granting wider differentials should have been worked out, but nobody should have been totally exempt.

12. NRA had a vital interest in proper mechanism for the settlement of labor disputes. I should have insisted on a National Labor Board impartial throughout in personnel and wholly independent of any department of government.

13. The plan of rotating members of the Industrial Advisory Board was wrong.

14. A full time and aggressive government member with an assistant each for Labor and Consumers should have been ap-

pointed to each major Code Authority the moment the code was approved and he should have vigorously pressed its organization and administration in strict accordance with NRA policy.

15. A clear-cut agreement on policy as between NRA, the Federal Trade Commission and the Department of Justice, should have been insisted upon at the very outset.

16. I made the mistake of thinking that you can be frank and forthright in this kind of a job. My office door was always open to my own organization, and I had a rule that any member of my staff could sit in on any conversation. I couldn't see everybody who wanted to see me, but I was willing to make appointments for anyone who had a real right to see me at any time I could, at any hour between 10 A.M. one morning and 2 A.M the next morning.

The present system of the New Board seems much better adapted to Washington today. They meet for the greater part of every working day to deliberate. During this period of silence there can be no interruptions—either by note or telephone except from Mr. Richberg or the White House. They talk not at all. The Dalai Lama—the Living Buddha is not more closely sealed. They have profited from my errors and from what I went through; they are right—only I couldn't do the job that way if I had it to do again and neither could they if they had the task of putting 96% of industry under NIRA in four months and under codes in a year. But the phase of code-making is past. This is a new phase of Code Administration—correction of all my errors and completing the unfinished window in Aladdin's palace. It *should* be done with deliberation to the end that there shall be no more mistakes.

It is unfortunately impossible to think that we have found in this new Board the High Court of Commerce described in this book, a tribunal of elder economic statesmen with the prestige and dignity in business which the Supreme Court of the United States has in law—a place where, as a last resort, disconsolate Industry, Consumers, or Labor—where'er they languish —can bring their wounded hearts as to the Mercy Seat—

"Earth has no sorrow that Heaven cannot heal."

. . . . . . . . . . .

There has just been brought to my attention the report of a President's Committee on Economic Planning, which criticizes NRA and asserts:

(1) That its leader was inept and opposed to economic planning;

(2) that the codes were hurried and inconsistent and thus lacked perfection and had actually deterred economic planning;

(3) that NRA has made no progress in working out wage differentials;

(4) that NRA has left the wage and hour pattern in worse condition than it found them;

(5) that there is no proper coördination among Federal Administrations which affect the economic pattern.

All but one of the names attached to this broadside are unfamiliar to me—as authorities or otherwise—and that one is not known to me as that of one qualified to speak on this subject. Yet the report is at least semi-official and so entitled to more consideration than such a proclamation as that of the Seven Tailors of Tooley Street, which began—"We the People of England."

It is true that I was inept.

It is not true that NRA opposed economic planning in the sense in which we understood it. On the contrary, NRA invented the only economic planning ever put to actual test.

It is true, in general, that the vexed question of wage differentials was not completely solved by the codes but they are so much further along than they were when we began that there is no just comparison. Many other questions were not satisfactorily resolved by the codes. But I doubt if anything in this "report" is more critical of particular NRA shortcomings than is this book. But when this so-called "report" proceeds through these specific statements to such general conclusions as that NRA obstructed economic planning and left the wages-and-hours pattern more confused than it found that pattern, it makes itself worthless.

Before NRA you could *plan* until you were blue in the face, but it was like planning a collision between Donati's comet and the planet Uranus—there was no mechanism to make your plan effective. Faulty as the code structure may be—feeble as it is rapidly becoming—it is still a keyboard upon which may be played such harmonies as a qualified performer may invent.

There is, at last, a pattern in American industry which did not exist before and the difference between the pre-NRA situation and the present one is about that between the cosmos "without form and void; and darkness was upon the face of the deep" and—let us say—the Second Day of the Creation when there was at least light and a firmament dividing the waters from the waters.

As to there being no improvement in the wages-and-hours structure, these critics have permitted their epithets to run away with their facts. The average work week before NRA was about 52 hours. But the extremes ran all the way from 72 to 36. Under the codes both the average and the almost universal rule is a little less than 40 hours. With few exceptions, the upper extreme is 48. But the fact is that under NRA, industry has gone from chaos of work weeks to an almost uniform 40 hours. Generally speaking, the minimum wage is also standardized.

If by "wage differentials" the Committee means the pattern of wages above the minimum in any plant or industry, then the answer is that the law prescribed for NRA a *fixation of minima only*. If it means *regional* differences in wages, the answer is, as I have pointed out in this book, that this subject is still far from a satisfactory solution, but as compared with the previous condition, the improvement has been very great.

As to the codes having been arrived at by bargaining and with considerable variety of pattern, the implication apparently is that NRA should have created a rule of "planned economics" and then rammed it down the throat of each industry in turn. Such was not the law and any attempt to have done that would have failed from the beginning. This subject is fully discussed elsewhere in this book. AAA did try to do that—but it got no codes.

As to lack of coördination among Administrations I agree heartily with everything except the remedy proposed—another pale pink Committee. I have said so much on this subject in this book that repetition would just be regurgitation.

Perhaps I should not attempt to answer these academic musings, but when they come embalmed in the amber of such a title as "Report of the President's Committee on Economic Plan-

ALL QUIET ON THE WESTERN FRONT.

ning," the title page compels attention even if all the other pages might better be ignored.

. . . . . . . . . .

On this whole subject of dead cats, however, I want to risk another short quotation from a speech I made at Chicago on August 3, 1934.

Naturally there has been some confusion and uncertainty. Some of this comes from careless reading of codes and bulletins. Some of it comes from faulty codes. But with these troubles freely admitted, whoever heard of a new system of government—industrial or otherwise, moving off into perfect action from the moment it was announced. Why, Moses had to traipse the children of Israel all around the Sinai Desert through three months of desperate suffering before he even dared to suggest the decalogue and then—39 years and nine months more before they understood it well enough for him to let them go into the Promised Land to try it out. And think what happened to him as an administrator because he had made a few slips in running his show and in making speeches. He just got buried on Mount Nebo and never saw that early NRA pass into full fruition. I often think of Moses.

His NRA was a code of only ten short articles and according to latest reports it isn't working perfectly even yet—after some 4,000 years of trial and error and even after the great reorganization of the years 30 to 34 A. D. But some of our critics now complain that in 450 brand-new codes there is some non-compliance and some backsliding. They are howling calamity because, from the very start, every article of every code did not swing into perfectly ordered motion like the stars and systems of a Universe ordered by the Almighty on a mathematical formula. Why even on that Cosmic Plan, every once in an astronomical while, a star explodes, a comet collides with some other astral body, and a shower of meteorites hits the earth. All that is no reason for saying that the Solar System is going to hell and the shortcomings of NRA are no justification for the continued carping of political critics or the oily tactics of a few self-seeking chiselers.

On the other hand, if early last summer somebody had told you that within a year 96% of Industry would be operating under self-governing codes, voluntarily assumed, you would have turned away in utter disbelief. I think we have done pretty well. Furthermore, I think that every word of specific criticism showing up any bad point in any code or in the administration of any code is all to the good. It is the most potent corrective there is. It keeps people on their toes. It wipes out abuses and—much as it may sting at the moment of its utterance—we all ought to welcome and encourage it. I *do* want it. I am not kicking about it. What I am kicking about is the sort of criticism that points to one spot in this slight economic acne of NRA, and starts out shrieking "kill that thing, it has a pimple."

Well, nobody is going to kill the good in NRA. During the next few months it should learn what is bad and rub that out, what should be strengthened and strengthen it. And this greatest economic experiment in the history of the world will leave its legacy of proved benefit in the happier future of our business life for many years to come.

To those in Government who may have been alarmed by criticism of NRA and the apparent bulk of it I commend once more the thought that here you have millions of people affected by NRA but the kicks are *from less than one per cent of the potential kickers*. Remember Burke's aside in commenting on the French Revolution:

Because half a dozen grasshoppers under a fern make the field ring with their importunate chink, whilst thousands of great cattle repose beneath the shadow of the British oak, chew the cud and are silent, pray do not imagine that those who make the noise are the only inhabitants of the field; that of course they are many in number; or that, after all, they are other than the little shriveled, meagre, hopping, though loud and troublesome insects of the hour.

And also to my belabored ex-associates let me quote the great T. R.:

It is not the critic that counts; not the man who points out how the strong man stumbles or where the doer of deeds could have done them better. The credit belongs to the man who is actually in the Arena whose face is marred by dust and sweat and blood; who strives valiantly; who errs and comes short again and again because there is no effort without error and short-coming; but who does actually strive to do the deed; who knows the great enthusiasm, the great devotion; who spends himself in a worthy cause, who at the best knows in the end the triumph of high achievement, and who at the worst, if he fails while daring greatly, knows that his place shall never be with those cold and timid souls who know neither victory nor defeat.

And anyway, as the doughty Dawes observed, when the bear-baiting Graham Committee tried ineffectively to draw him into political criticism of the conduct of the war:
"*Hell'n Maria—we did the job, didn't we?*"

# Chapter XXIV

# FREEDOM OF THE PRESS

---

"A mountain was in labor putting forth dreadful groans and there was in the region the highest expectation. After all, it brought forth a mouse."

—*Phaedrus's Fables.*

---

I DON'T know who first set up the straw-man about NRA interfering or attempting to interfere with the Freedom of the Press. The first time I ever heard about it was in connection with the President's Reëmployment Agreement and the Blue Eagle. We had set up a Board to modify any unexpectedly harsh applications of that agreement in particular cases. The American Newspaper Publishers Association sent their representatives down to negotiate certain changes. They mentioned some such clause but in the agreement, as finally drafted, it was not included through some error and the document was signed without it. Next day, however, they returned and requested the inclusion of something to the effect that nothing in the agreement should be construed as waiver of the Constitutional guaranty of a free press.

I remarked that, while there might be ground for saying that a man could waive a Constitutional guaranty put there for his individual benefit, such as a right to trial by jury, he certainly could not waive a provision put there, not for his benefit but for the benefit of the whole public. If he could, then a few individuals could in many cases simply amend whole clauses of the Constitution and do what even Congress could not consider. But I said that, since the reservation, in my opinion, would have no more legal or practical effect than if it had not been written at all, I certainly had no objection to its inclusion. That was done and I thought the matter was at an end.

But immediately in certain sections of the Press great apprehension began to be expressed about *some move on the part of the Administration to violate both the Constitution and the Code.* That charge affronted the President and he insisted that the Executive Order approving the code should state exactly his comprehension of what constitutes Freedom of the Press. The language was as follows:

Of course, also, nobody waives any Constitutional rights by assenting to a code. The recitation of the Freedom of the Press clause in the code has no more place here than would the recitation of the whole Constitution or of the Ten Commandments. The freedom guaranteed by the Constitution is freedom of expression and that will be scrupulously respected—but it is not freedom to work children, or do business in a fire trap (or violate the Laws against obscenity, libel and lewdness).

That section of the Press which had been making the most of these charges scattered their indignation over many issues, and especially about the language in the last three lines. The language was not well chosen. For that I alone am to blame. I drafted it. I did this in accordance with the President's principles as he had expressed them to me but, I confess, ineptly. The last three lines from the dash to the end would have been less objectionable if the words in parentheses had been omitted. Also, the rest of it would have been practically in his language. It must be obvious to any fair-minded person that the idea sought to be expressed is that Freedom of the Press does not grant license to the press to do things that would be prohibited to the whole public by the police powers and particular examples were given to clarify the general rule stated in the last sentence before the dash. For the harsher irritants in those expressions the fault was mine.

But after all that is very far from the point. There is no danger to Freedom of the Press. No Administration in my lifetime has encouraged it so much. Far from attempting to still criticism the President in press conferences expressed the opinion that there was not enough of it to be healthy. And, as far as NRA was concerned, no arm of any government anywhere at any time ever went so far out of its way to invite criticism. The very form of organization was a mechanism for criticism. NRA policy was *the truth through controversy rather than conjecture.*

It is fair to refer to the great spring round-up of criticism for the purpose of improving NRA policies and practices.

From the moment I took control of NRA, I did everything in my power to encourage full and instant disclosure of whatever happened—favorable or unfavorable.

When you do this I think you have correlative right to answer criticism. This is part of the public debate on which such an experiment as this must survive or perish.

With such power as resides in the press, there always rides responsibility. The press has a responsibility to be fair. It owes that responsibility, not to government, but to the people who rely on government for their salvation, at a desperate time like this. Public criticism deserves public discussion. NRA had a responsibility to the public—a course of action to defend in the public eye. The public relied much on NRA. For example, it was not fair to say of every act of government which is misunderstood or proves unpopular—"*That* is NRA."

The newspapers knew that NRA had nothing whatever to do with farm relief or public works—or monetary policy—or Home or Farm loans. Branding NRA as a cause of every dissatisfaction was, as Mr. Richberg said, setting up a hobgoblin and screaming at it. Such is not the discharge of the public responsibility that goes with the great public power of the press.

Most of the prominent newspapers that assailed NRA are severely Republican in their sympathy. We could hardly expect that such journals as New York *Herald Tribune*, the Chicago *Tribune*, or the Chicago *Daily News*, whose affiliations and political allegiance have never wavered, could be very enthusiastic about a Democratic policy. I have little quarrel with them. You always know where to find them and if I were on the other side of any such argument, I would be punching just as hard and just as continuously.

There has been a constant reiteration that the Administration tried to institute a press censorship, a radio censorship and a control of editorial utterance and news columns. Just how any executive department of the government could effect this depredation was not indicated. With the Congress making the laws and the Supreme Court, in session, to prevent anything unconstitutional being done, the NRA might as well be accused of attempting to prevent the tides from ebbing and flowing or to repeal the law of gravitation. Finally, however little the press may have liked the language of the Executive Order—the clause they asked for in their code *they got*.

And if the censorship was supposed to have been one of criticism—the result is a joke. I am quite sure that both NRA and myself hold the all-time record for newspaper panning in the short space of time considered. Except for a few punches a little below the belt, I did not mind it. In fact I rather enjoyed it. Some of the best cartoons I've known were included. The artists have been kind enough to send me many of the originals and some of them are priceless.

Most of the pummeling was really constructive and helped guide administration but in a few cases it was not—it was designed for some other purpose than just stating a point of view on a public question. I fear that a little of it may have come from the look-out men for the Old Deal, the rugged ones of the great Delusion. Like the Three Little Pigs we had to look through the keyhole at them to see whether they were really the sick sheep in need of a stable or the Fuller Brush man bringing "a semple" or whether, in very truth, they were the Big Bad Wolf who was trying to get us to open the door that he might make a toothsome morsel out of us.

All NRA asked of the public was that it correctly appraise the source and private interest of this sort of publicity and discount it to the precise extent that a special interest was disclosed. These stories were nearly all one-sided. They never gave NRA a chance to state its case and the only way it could do so was by radio speeches.

There is another cause for this sort of thing—the necessary inaccuracy in the appraisals of men who have to produce a column of news *every day*. It makes for half-baked and ill-founded stories. It is the curse of modern practice. Controversy is always news, and this results in whole pages of fake controversy. Considering it all, the most encouraging thing about NRA criticism was that half of the reports said we had done one thing and about an equal number that we had done the precise reverse. At least that shows that even if we were no good, we were at least impartial.

Latterly, lacking little of substance—at least little that could be demonstrated—professional criticism degenerated into personal appraisements of, and assaults on some of my associates who were principal NRA officials. By this time I had acquired a sort of pachydermatous indifference and I did not mind being a human pin-cushion, but some divisional administrators and others did not have so much tough scar tissue and attacks on them affected their work. A conspicuous instance was a syndication by a writer who dared not sign his name to his personal strictures and blandly advanced as a reason the astonishing statement *that these men were his friends and that if they knew that it was he who was assailing their reputations he might lose their regard.*

With a little less than libel, a trifle more than backstairs gossip—this writer, in whose veins there must flow something more than a trace of rodent blood, exalted some chiefs of departments in NRA who were weak and threw mud at some who were strong, for no other apparent reason than to provide salable copy. They were produced by some mercenary character-assassin—firing, masked, from ambush, without the courage common to 90% of men to step out into the open and meet his adversary eye to eye.

It was a frequent statement that recovery in other countries has been more rapid than here. But an international study by the wholly impartial London *Economist* disproved that. It concerned *real* wages, that is the purchasing power of workers' wages. It covered France, England, Germany, and Italy. The showing was astonishing. It proved that from the very day of the passage of the Recovery Act that curve started sharply upward in the United States and that it has never declined. Any fair study of every economic aspect showed exactly the same thing. Business had then advanced some 44% from its extreme lows. It is a greater advance from a deeper depression than has occurred anywhere and its beginning happened to coincide with the advent of Roosevelt. Its forward impulses trace to his acts.

It is bad enough to say that the President's program has not been responsible for Recovery, but some go a step further and say it actually has *retarded* recovery; that it has nullified its benefit to production and employment by raising the cost of living faster than it has raised purchasing power. To the average wage earner this charge means that, while there is more money in his pay envelope, he has to pay out more than this wage increase for the things he buys. This subject is discussed in another chapter. The charge was simply not true.

While we welcomed criticism we wanted it to be true. I think that this particular sort of criticism is intellectual immorality.

When we get into the realm of business statistics, we are treading a field where the average person in a Pullman car or in a golf club locker room, or in an Elks Lodge, or around the stove in a cross-roads general store, has to take somebody's word for it. He has to put in most of his time earning money to buy gasoline for the car and shoes for the baby, and even if he had more leisure, unless he devoted most of his time to it, he would not get very satisfactory results. He has to rely on some analyst. He has to trust somebody. It certainly is not a discharge of the public responsibility of the press to tell the great body of the American people the thing that is not—in a matter which affects their very means of life.

In the face of NRA's accomplishment for working people from one end of this country to the other, we were rather impatient of the few cases of institutions under public trust which set out to convince people that real wages have been reduced by NRA, and thus that both employment and production had decreased. Commentators on economic theory do not add much to actual administration either in or out of government but academic mercenaries who write this kind of thing for publication are more dangerous than a professor or two in a departmental ante-room.

Around the end of my administration it seemed as impossible for NRA to get its story told correctly by some of these as it is for a camel to pass through a needle's eye. Notwithstanding denials of some of my friends, I have been told of orders to a reporter to send in no news favorable to NRA but to play up everything that might be construed against it. In some instances disturbing news stories were published which had not even a faint color of factual foundation. And some of these were papers which asserted that NRA sought to interfere with the "Freedom" of the Press!

I think it is not *freedom* of the Press to suppress or garble important news of public affairs which happens not to be in accord with some personal policy or opinion. That is *domination* of the Press and as sometimes practiced, it is domination for a private interest contrary to the public interest—a far more dangerous thing than domination by government. But I know of no remedy except radio refutation. For, bad and vicious as all this is, the guaranty of a free press is so precious that the cure of such abuses cannot be censorship or control of either editorial or news expression.

The only recourse I knew was to appeal to the Press itself to discipline these few cases. I did ask that they submit a code containing provisions which would leave elimination of unfair practices to their own self-governing bodies. I hoped they would straighten out the reporter and newsboy controversy. Such a code cannot be imposed. It must come spontaneously from their ideas of self-government and NRA could do nothing about it. In my opinion, at the time I left NRA the vast majority of both business and labor would not give up the codes and I believe that NRA retained the bulk of public support. In such a situation why we did not have a better press was beyond me. I grew weary of protesting.

In some of its aspects, however, I had no more pleasant relations than I had with the people of the Press. Among the Washington newshawks, one of my best friends was Paul Anderson, who, I think, filters faster and gets the gist of a situation more quickly than any one I know. Little Bobby Allen annoyed me a lot, but I liked him. His wife, Ruth Finney, is considerably the better man. Turner Cattledge has a baby face that masks a keen intelligence. He can ask the deadliest of questions with an expression like the Age of Innocence. Francis Stevenson was very close in my affection. Frederick Storm is as good and dependable a newsman as you can find.

Among the commentators, Mark Sullivan used to pan me unmercifully but our friendship goes back to my early twenties when, although I had never met him, he wrote me letters when he was Editor of *Collier's*, letting me know how I could improve what I was submitting and he was rejecting. Our friendship has suffered nothing because we didn't think alike and I hope and believe I can say the same for Frank Kent although he used to burn me up. Walter Lippmann was always considerate of my troubles and Arthur Krock usually treated me with kindly care. Ralph Robey who, as I think, is our ablest financial commentator, didn't like NRA either but I don't think he carried it over to me. Will Rogers is kind to nearly everybody—especially to old Oklahomans. His father and mine were buddies, so I can't claim any special kudos because he was always kind to me.

I foresaw by intuition the trouble with the publishers. The

Code Committee was composed of as fine a lot of men as I met in NRA and my first preliminary interview with them, before any controversy had really arisen, ended with my remark that I wished I might never see them again except socially.

A real friendship grew up between myself and Howard Davis of the New York *Herald Tribune*. I think everybody loves Amon Carter—anyway I do. I had one or two real militant champions like C. J. P. Lucas of Louisville and Emory Thomason of the Chicago *Daily Times*.

But to me the dean of the whole fraternity—the wise Ulysses who kept my erring feet on the path whenever he could reach me—was Charlie Michelson. As long as I could be where Charlie could edit my speeches or manage NRA publicity, I never made any very bad blunders. He is the only man that ever wrote any part of a speech for me, and the part he wrote was the best part. There is not a sweeter, brighter, or more lovable man in the Administration than Charlie Michelson.

In spite of all the panning, the whole press treated me more than fairly—some of it even affectionately—when I got out. I assume it was overwhelming relief.

After all, to paraphrase my favorite poetess,

> "*But oh my foes and ah my friends,*
> *It was a lovely fight.*"

# Chapter XXV

# THE SETTLEMENT OF MAJOR STRIKES

---

"All government—indeed every human benefit and enjoyment, every virtue and every prudent act—is founded on compromise and barter."

*—Edmund Burke.*

"Force is no remedy."

*—John Bright.*

---

AFTER creation of the National Labor Board, NRA never had any duty—or even any business—to intervene in strikes. Before that it did and after that, the very logic of circumstances forced it in on several occasions—indeed, it was sucked in against my will on *every* occasion of a strike or threatened national bearing, up to the time of the second threatened Textile Strike. In that case, I was delicately invited to abstain both by the Labor Department and the National Labor Relations Board. Madam Secretary said to me several times that a strike is not an unmixed evil and to a friend of mine she observed "The trouble with Hugh is that he thinks a strike is something to settle."

Now I do not say this in criticism of Secretary Perkins. She is one of the ablest of the Cabinet. For a good many months she was my most trusted friend. I used to go to her with my principal troubles. She is building up the Department of Labor, and as a zealous official she naturally seeks to strengthen it. It will be amply demonstrated in this book that I think she was building it into a field where it should not go when she sought to have it guide the labor tribunals. I thought they should be wholly impartial. That is an honest difference of opinion. I think I am right. She thinks she is right. My only complaint is that she did not make a clear-cut issue and let it be resolved. But the Secretary is a woman, and I don't know anything at all about how to handle that kind of a disagreement. Perhaps if I had had the adroitness of my dear friend Senator Lewis in his campaign against Ruth Hanna

McCormick, all might yet have been well. I still think that Miss Perkins is my friend personally. But I fear we are far apart on fundamental policy as to the function and status of the Department of Labor.

NRA ought not to have anything to do with labor troubles when they reach the stage of strike. As I have pointed out earlier, my first proposed organization, before the act was passed, included an independent tribunal to handle such troubles, to which proposition apparently some one in the Cabinet objected. It became early apparent (as it had been proved beyond peradventure during the war) that such a tribunal would be an absolute necessity, so I later suggested the Wagner Board and this time it was approved.

But, even with the Wagner Board functioning—and later—there arose occasions when the very integrity of certain codes demanded action by NRA which no purely judicial tribunal could possibly address.

There is a point here of overwhelming importance which seems to have been completely overlooked. There comes a stage in every dispute where the intervention of an impartial tribunal is an absolute necessity if we are to preserve peace. And before that time comes it is necessary to see to it that such tribunal actually *is* impartial in appearance as well as in fact. It must be possessed of no dogma favoring one side or the other. It must make no expedient decision or interpretation of law. It must be under no shadow of influence, either political or from any administrator or head of any governmental body having any statutory duty to conserve the position of one side or the other.

But, even with all these qualities, in this new art of industrial self-government under Federal supervision, it does not follow (any more than it does in litigation) that the first or even the last recourse upon the appearance of trouble is for such a tribunal to hale contestants into the spotlight, to begin a trial in the newspapers, and put both sides on the defensive—all shields advanced, all swords raised.

Such a course frequently is the worst thing that could happen because it hampers peaceful composition and the induction and maintenance of "united action in labor and management" which is the stated purpose of the law. It does not look to such united action. It looks to imposed action, and, as I shall try to demonstrate in particular examples, it often makes united action impossible and leads straight to the edge of the bloody issue of industrial or even, as at San Francisco, *public* war.

I am speaking of strikes of national or wide regional bearing. For isolated labor disputes I think the present system is as good as it could be. But when great labor leaders, representing thousands of men in a whole industry and responsible for their peace and wages, have occupied or are moving toward the trenches of an advanced position on one side; and great leaders of an industry responsible to tens of thousands of stockholders for the successful operation of their plants are also moving to dig in—there is always a short breathing space where frequently a quiet conference between leaders on both sides, in the presence of some one with power and authority to help (so far as government can help), but who is sitting there not as an arbiter—not to impose anything—but solely to tender his good offices and what aid he can bring—where such a conference can bring not only composition and peace but a new feeling of helpful coöperation. The outstanding example of this is the situation of the Bituminous Coal which starting from the bloodiest and most inhospitable history in all of industry, turned out to be the model for labor-management relationship.

Through all this troubled period, the man who has done this more than once, and so ably and effectively that he developed a technique and set a precedent which is actually a new thing in industrial relationship—is the President himself—and, watching him, I also learned the great possibilities of his method. But the President can't give the required time to this sort of thing. It sometimes takes hours and even days and anyway, considering his great office, it is unfair to inject him into these tense controversies.

I know that the best chance for peace lies in the President's kind of action, because I have seen it practiced to the salvation of tens of millions of wages, the avoidance of much bloodshed and of the possible wreckage of Recovery. But that kind of thing can't be done by a quasi-judicial tribunal, especially when it is colored with partiality, and it can't be done by some minor official or moderator or conciliator of the Department of Labor. It can only be done by somebody with sufficient prestige, confidence from both sides, qualities of leadership and knowledge of both the industry and the labor in it, to assure both sides of common sense and even-handed fairness.

Under NRA, the first of these very dangerous situations was the Bituminous Coal strike on that dark and bloody ground which has been the scene of more conflict and bitterness than any other industrial area. I *had* to get into that because there was no Labor Board, because it grew out of negotiations for the code, which were not all concluded, and further because it threatened at a time when any spread of it would have simply paralyzed industrial production in many industries just as we were getting our first real stirrings of recovery. It was settled as are all such disputes—by interminably patient negotiation sprinkled with appeals to every angle of persuasion or interest that could be reached such as financial backing behind reluctant management, personal solicitation and similar approaches— which a quasi-judicial body could not even consider using.

Another vast national threat was in the automobile industry and exactly the same kind of problem was presented. The Wagner Board was functioning then but agreements and provisions for settlement which should have been included in the code itself were missing and I felt a responsibility for arriving at a solution which would provide them. All that was done by me was done in the closest kind of coöperation with Senator Wagner. Indeed he and I worked like a glove and a hand, and it was only after he left that I encountered what seemed to be a feeling in the Department of Labor of an exclusive proprietary interest in labor disputes which seems now to make it appropriate for me to apologize for having helped to settle seven strikes of national bearing. In both the coal and the automobile settlements the President intervened and as I have said, established the technique for this kind of settlement by negotiation.

A third menace was again in the Bituminous field, growing out of the Captive Mine situation, this time threatening to involve the whole steel industry and that, too, was settled by the same methods. I am quite sure that it never could have been settled by a quasi-judicial proceeding. We were too near litigation on a major scale, and general principles were not as firmly established then as now. It sounds simple to say that these strikes were settled "by the same methods." But it was not simple. It was one of the most difficult and dangerous negotiations we had and it dragged out for weeks.

A third Bituminous Coal strike on a national scale threatened upon the occasion of renewal of the first wage agreements. This one was a thriller because we were within a few hours of a general walkout from every Bituminous mine in the country—some 350,000 men, and when John Lewis says there is going to be a walk-out you can be sure that there will be one. The dispute there was over regional differentials in wage scales which by the terms of the previous settlement had been left to me to decide. I had not been able to get all districts to agree that the differentials I proposed were fair or even that they had been left with me to decide. That time I *had* to act in diverting the strike because I held the key to its cause. I fixed the differentials arbitrarily to avert the strike and then straightened inequalities out later by negotiation. I was severely criticized for doing this and there is no doubt that it was not in accordance with our general policy of hearing first and acting afterward—but necessity knows no law. No harm was done and a vast strike was averted. No Labor Board could have done that because it depended on a special function left with me and involved an intimate knowledge of the whole economic complex of a tortured industry, which we had gained through months of intense application.

I intervened in the first threatened Textile strike which happened a couple of months before the one that was later actually called. I had the best reason of all for injecting myself into the second situation because what was proposed there was not a strike at all in any proper sense. It was not a strike against employers. It was *a strike against the code, which is a strike against the government.* No strike was necessary to amend that code. All that was necessary was to apply for an open hearing and amend the code (if amendment was warranted), as the code was made—in the Goldfish Bowl.

The Textile Code was dear to my heart. It was Code No. 1. It came at a time when the whole of industry was wavering as to whether it would submit codes at all—even including those who had told me before I took my job that they intended to come forward at once and do so.

Labor had no rights under 7a or the Recovery Act except in an industry which had subscribed to a code and I doubt if it has any now in spite of two unobtrusive words which Mr. Richberg included in the only amendment of that act.

But when that code came in, the whole NRA project seemed to balance on a needle's point. Until I was absolutely sure that the Big Industries were coming forward with codes, I did not dare to launch the PRA and the Blue Eagle because they carried all industry and the little ones would have been justified in declining to bind themselves if all the big ones were free to do as they pleased. It was one of the most critical periods in the entire life of NRA.

But, as related earlier, George Sloan never failed. Under his leadership the whole cotton textile industry joined and by the code alone raised the hourly wage rates of labor 76%, and at one stroke and in the face of an 8% decline in production employed 140,000 new workers! It was they who showed the way to abolition of child labor. For every other abuse or charged abuse in the industry the machinery to eradicate it was set up in—or in connection with—the Code. To all of these provisions Labor agreed. Tom McMahon made *one* agreement before the hearing on that code and repudiated it in the hearing without any previous notice.

Committees, investigating bodies, and a mechanism for settlement of disputes were set up in the code and Labor went away from that hearing and approved of that code *with the greatest single advance it has ever made in its history*. Labor in that industry was then not organized. It got what it got through NRA. On such instances, I have based my assertion that we did more for labor through NRA, in a few months, than all the strikes and all the unions in this country from the beginning. The Cotton Code was an industrial revolution at least 90% of which was in terms favorable to Labor.

I agree that, before the code, wages were far too low; the 55 hour week far too long and that some other conditions were indefensible. I also agree that even after that notable advance in wages they were still lower than in several other industries. But it is the job of NRA to act with regard to the whole economic structure. It is a delicate pattern and you can't fix it with a sledge hammer. This vast advance in labor costs, coupled with other causes already considered, *advanced the cost of cotton textiles 100% and prices even more*. As already related that caused a practical revolt against NRA in the Middle West and the figures leave no question whatever that it impaired the market for cotton textiles *with a marked decrease in production*.

The demands on which the threatened strike was based were simply out of the question so far as maintaining any balance or cohesion in the fundamentals on which NRA was moving. And from the side of labor strategy the strike was woefully ill-timed. The drying-up of markets and the effort to maintain employment had piled up inventory until it was folly to continue manufacture with a crumbling price structure and an unmanageable surplus. The whole industry would probably have willingly closed down for weeks if it had consulted its own interests.

In these circumstances I pleaded with little Francis Gorman for whom I have not only affection and admiration but a distinct fellow feeling. I couldn't give him what he asked for but *I did get for him what he accepted as enough and he called off his strike.* But I say with reluctance and regret that he did not keep the faith with me. That was a strike threatened not to attain its ostensible objects—they could have been obtained in orderly process by a rehearing on the code. It was a strike to unionize that industry and it was a strike against the code.

It will be recalled by those who have followed NRA that *from the very outset* I expressed the opinion that the ideal form of labor organization is a vertical union on the model of the United Mine Workers with mechanism for the settlement of labor disputes set up as the law intends by "united action of labor and management"; but while the law specifically requires NRA to *promote the organization of industry* it does not direct it to promote the organization of labor but, on the other hand, looks to the absolute freedom of labor in selecting its own form of organization.

For this reason, I felt that I had no right to try to influence the form of labor organization by using any powers under NIRA. This was not just theoretical speculation. The A. F. of L. is composed of both craft unions and vertical unions and the contest wages hot there over this very policy of vertical unions. I could not try to foist my views on labor.

But I did have some earnest and very serious discussions with both management and labor in industries where I thought that labor itself in those industries favored a vertical form. And while I neither got a single commitment nor sought one, *I did go so far as to convince myself that in at least three of the greatest industries in the country such vertical unions on the Bituminous Coal pattern could be set up (in the words of NIRA)* "by united action of labor and management under adequate governmental sanction and supervision." I am sure that this could have been

done, without strife, without loss of time, wages and business
and to the satisfaction of both sides. The only regret that I had
about leaving NRA was that I could not have stayed to carry
that plan through. Other industries would have followed and
it would have been the greatest single economic advance in this
country, since the enactment of NIRA.

To carry the story of the cotton textile trouble to its conclusion—much to my surprise and while I was on a tour of inspection, I began to read accounts of an actual strike along exactly
the same lines as the threatened one and in palpable violation
of the agreements made. Mr. Gorman took occasion publicly to
castigate me and said that nobody but the President could settle
this one. As a matter of fact, according to the press, Mr. Garrison settled it and, I am told, was enthusiastically praised by
the Secretary of Labor for having "developed a new technique"
in that he quietly went between the two parties and obtained
an agreement! That may have been new but it looked rather
familiar to me. Examination of that agreement will show that
it was *exactly the agreement I had made two months earlier* with
Mr. Gorman with the single exception that the *persons and instrumentalities called upon to make findings of facts and opinion
were different persons and different instrumentalities than had been
named in Mr. Gorman's agreements with me*—a change which
Mr. Gorman never even suggested to me while we were nego-
tiating—*and for this, millions in wages and immeasurable losses
of good will were squandered.* It was absurd money-business.

While the strike was still unsettled I had to make a speech to
Code Authorities at Carnegie Hall on September 14th. Since
that speech was severely criticized inside the government and
has been cited as a cause for my resignation, I must quote
what I said:

The Textile Code was the first one to be presented under NRA. I
had been working on it as early as March, 1932—long before Mr.
Roosevelt became President. After exhaustive studies, it was determined that a 40-hour week would re-employ all the people normally
attached to the textile industry (the practice in the industry was 55
hours a week).

These studies were conducted in connection with the labor in that
industry. Tom McMahon sat in as a party to the negotiations and
agreed with their result. Of all the codes, the Textile Code was the
subject of the most exhaustive analysis. It became a precedent for all

others. But the moment the hearing opened and without any notice to me of a change of heart, he appeared on the platform in our first great goldfish-bowl proceeding and repudiated the agreement that he had made with me in the preliminary discussions. It was my first experience with organized labor leadership in the textile industry, and it was not encouraging.

Last June a strike was threatened. It was, as I remember, the fifth great strike of national importance with which I have had to deal. We reached an agreement and on that agreement the strike was called off. *The present strike is an absolute violation of that understanding,* and I must say here, with all the solemnity which should characterize such an announcement, that if such agreements of organized labor are worth no more than this one, then that institution is not such a responsible instrumentality as can make contracts on which this country can rely.

But I would not condemn these men cavalierly. I know young Gorman—there are few more conscientious and sincere men in the country than he.

The trouble is that when you unleash the forces of riot and rebellion you never know when you can control them. I know now how this strike was pulled in contravention of the solemn engagements of the Union.

Men circulated among the delegates and told them that the *government would feed the strikers.* Norman Thomas appeared and urged the strike. He is a *politico.* Whatever there is of economic doctrine in the Socialist party, it is political first and economic afterward, and Norman Thomas—as much as I respect and admire him—had no business there. When a strike becomes political, it has no place in the lexicon of the NRA.

The cotton textile industry is the very last place in this country where a strike should be ordered. It was the first industry to come forward with a code. The code increased employment by 140,000 or nearly 33 per cent. According to our studies, it increased hourly wage rates at least by 70 per cent.

When I think of George Sloan my heart weeps. I knew what kind of opposition he went up against [in his own industry]. He overcame it all and got these concessions for labor which were at first opposed by practically the whole industry. It is a pity that he now has to take the rap in the dissension between labor and management on this proposition.

Now that statement was the literal truth. Nobody can deny that it was the truth. It was a public situation. It had to do with a code for which I was responsible. It went very deep into the integrity of NRA. I have never been able to see why there need be such a thing as concealment in such a case. I had belabored management in the coal strikes much harder than this. Before I made that speech I called and asked for suggestions. I was advised to call Governor Winant of the Cotton Board and ask if I could be of any assistance. The Governor replied that I could be of none. He was quoted in the press as saying that I had promised not to mention the strike in my speech. But there was a witness to that telephone conversation and no such statement was made.

With the threatened steel strike I had nothing to do after the creation of continuing machinery for disputes was set up. In that situation I became angry and made a fool of myself. The established labor leaders in the steel industry had been pushed aside by several zealous young boys who came to Washington and began giving out all sorts of intemperate statements about the President and one of them took some awful wallops at me. I allowed myself to be baited by a clever newspaper man into saying that I had worn more skin off on my saddle riding along the Mexican border than would make half a dozen men like them or something of that kind not exactly conducive to sweet harmony.

I admit that I was not very dignified in many of these incidents. On this occasion I took a big committee of strikers to the White House in the official NRA limousine. There were so many that they were sitting on the fenders, hanging on the running board and one or two standing on the trunk rack. When somebody suggested dignity I said, "Dignity, hell— we've got to get these men back to work," but in retrospect it might have been better otherwise.

After that I determined that I was never going to get into another strike settlement. It involves the rôle of umpire and nobody loves an umpire. It gets you nothing but the enmity of both sides and, every time you do it, you take the lethal risk of failure. One single failure in the volunteer position in which I was latterly placing myself, especially in view of the disapproval that I later learned I was harvesting from Madam Secretary of Labor and, as I have heard, Mr. Richberg, would have been fatal. Nay, more—as it turned out, *success* was fatal for through sheer good luck we made no failures in seven starts.

Although I had made many engagements to inspect the NRA

organization on the Pacific Coast I had broken them all and caused a good deal of hard feeling. Early in May, I pledged myself to a definite itinerary which would put me in San Francisco on July 17. Several weeks before that the longshoremen's strike became acute out there, and the Secretary of Labor sent my Assistant for Labor, Eddie McGrady (who was also Assistant Secretary of Labor) out there. I am not criticizing that, although as events turned out it was bad judgment. There was not a better man in the country to send, except that he was a professional labor man and hardly to be regarded as wholly unbiased and that she had agreed that he would remain with me where he was badly needed until we should concur to the contrary.

He ran into a mare's nest, seeming almost to reach agreement on one day only to find himself frustrated the next. I knew what he was doing only in a casual way because if there was one thing I had promised myself it was that I would not stick my neck out on that one and he also urged me very strongly to the same effect.

The point I want to make here is that my arrival in San Francisco on the 15th had nothing whatever to do with that strike. That itinerary was a swing clear round the country in an airplane. It included ten cities and the San Francisco date was fixed by the award to me of a Phi Beta Kappa key from that chapter at my Alma Mater, the University of California.

When I got to Portland I saw the first results of a general strike. In my speech there I declared I would have nothing to do with it and commended both sides to the President's Special Board sitting in San Francisco and especially to my own Assistant, Eddie McGrady, who was a member of that Board and who, by this time, had been out there several weeks. It would never occur to me that a man of McGrady's viewpoint would not be valuable, but I knew at the time that his official connection with the Department of Labor was not conducive to agreement because employers were bound to think him prejudiced.

I did not know what a general strike looked like and I hope that you may never know. I soon learned and it gave me cold shivers. We were flying a big army plane which could not land at Presidio on the San Francisco side so we landed on the Oakland side of the Bay expecting to take an automobile to San

Francisco. There just weren't any automobiles. The general strike had closed the filling stations and paralyzed the transportation of the city. I took a small plane to the Presidio where General Craig—my captain for many years in the old army—let me use his car to get to town. I had lived several years in San Francisco and what I saw shocked me—physically. The food supply of the population was practically shut off, except by the individual grace and permit of a general strike committee run by an alien Communist. Even hotel dining rooms were closed and street cars were held up. A barber at the Palace Hotel sneaked in and offered to "bootleg" me a haircut! The economic life of the city was being strangled. There was fear that the power, light and water supply would be shut off. A foreign enemy could scarcely threaten more than that. Eddie McGrady met me and told me that he saw no hope for a settlement. On their own motion, several responsible union labor leaders came to see me. Though they were reticent, it was perfectly apparent, in talking to them, that they had no sympathy with the general strike and that they were being controlled by the influence on some of the men of one Bridges, an avowed Communist and a citizen of Australia, and that what they most wanted was to break that influence.

About this time I learned that the University of California had canceled my speech in the Greek Theater for fear I might be injured by Communists and there was no police protection because the whole force was needed to watch the situation in Berkeley.

Of course, I could not stand for that. It would have been an acknowledgment that there actually was a Communist domination and that an officer of the government was afraid of it. It would have had a serious effect along the Coast and perhaps throughout the country. I insisted on making the speech and while that did not move the Dean, Jack Nyland, whom I shall later introduce, got on the telephone and finally persuaded him. Although transportation was practically paralyzed in the Bay cities and although notices of cancellation of my speech had been published widely and notice of its reinstatement had not—the Greek Theater was almost full. Late on the night before its delivery, I sat down and wrote that speech. This is the pertinent part of it:

I think that labor is inherently entitled to bargain collectively through representatives of its own choosing. I think that the employer who denies or even obstructs that right is anti-social and I am very sure that, in the present trend of human opinion throughout the world, he is bound to go down. In this stage of specialization he can no more stop the rush of economic trend than the Dane, Canute, could sit on the seashore and stop the incoming tide.

I will go a step further and say that in the American shipping industry including the loading and unloading of ships, the right has not been justly accorded. These things cannot be avoided by legal cavil. They are necessary to humanity in this age and they will prevail. The whole force of American opinion is behind them and that means the whole force of the Federal Government and—let there be no doubt about it—that government will use every power at its disposal to assure them. If the shipping industry does not fully and freely accord these rights, then on its head will lie every ounce of responsibility for whatever may happen here. I think that their present position is extreme and unreasonable and must be tempered if we are to have peace.

But there is another and a worse side to this story. You are living out here under the stress of a general strike. Now the right of dissatisfied men to strike against an employer recalcitrant to his obligations under the law is inviolate. This government has supported it and will support it to the limit. It is a weapon in a two-sided conflict. But the *general* strike is quite another matter. It is a threat to the community. It is a menace to government. It is civil war.

We learned during the war that there are worse weapons than great guns and that economic strangulation is the most potent of them. One side of a warring business element can no more use it than it could go into the street and shoot innocent bystanders down in cold blood with machine guns.

You just can't do it in this free country. It won't work. If the responsible elements of organized labor do not purge themselves of this blight immediately, they will set the clock of labor organization back ten years. I am for organized labor and collective bargaining with all my heart and soul and I will support it with all the power at my command, but this ugly thing is a blow at the flag of our common country and it has got to stop.

I lived in this community for many years and I know it. If the Federal Government did not act, this people would act, and it would act to wipe out this subversive element as you clean off a chalk mark on a blackboard with a wet sponge.

But this is not primarily a duty of the community, much less a duty of the National Government. It is a duty of responsible labor organizations. It is their duty of patriotism. It is their duty of self-preservation. They must erase this sinister bar from their escutcheons. They must run these subversive influences out from their ranks like rats if they are to retain the respect and support of the American people and of the National Government, which otherwise is theirs to command.

Why this situation is made-to-order for a just settlement. Both sides are taking extreme positions. That makes a trader's paradise. But insurrection against the common interest of the community is not a proper weapon and will not for one moment be tolerated by the American people who are one—whether they live in California, Oregon, the Mississippi Valley or the South, East, or North. It would be safer for a cotton-tail rabbit to slap a wildcat in the face than for this half of one per cent of our population to try to strangle the rest of us into submission by any such means as this. Let's settle this thing and do it now.

Before I got back to San Francisco responsible union men had ousted several Communist leaders and within a few hours the general strike was broken. In all these negotiations John P. Nyland, one of the ablest lawyers on the Coast, gave the responsible union leaders to understand that (while neither he nor I would talk composition of the longshoremen's strike till the general strike was called off) when it should be called off, he would not only urge submission by employers to the President's Board, *but would represent the interests of the labor unions* before it. He is one of the most powerful advocates on the coast, and these men trusted him.

The general strike broke off but my connection with it did unalloyed harm to me. Obscure influences which I do not yet know did everything possible to forestall me. Nyland himself came to me and asked if I had any authority—and intimated that somebody had suggested that I had not. The President was in Hawaii, but I called the White House late at night and, with the consent of the President's Board, was authorized by Marvin McIntyre to speak for that Board. I called the Secretary of Labor and explained the situation to her. She said she was glad I was out there and I did not understand her even to intimate the slightest objection. Although, during my entire time in San Francisco, I was either in continuous session for from fourteen to sixteen hours a day with representatives of labor or others, or was writing my Berkeley speech, or delivering it, somebody called Washington and even the President in Hawaiian waters, attacking both myself and Senator Wagner, who was in Portland, and suggesting that we be withdrawn.

As soon as I heard this from friends in San Francisco I made the calls to the White House and the Secretary, which I have already mentioned. Although I thus obtained permission from the President's Board to speak for them at their request and confirmed this authority at the White House and with the Secretary of Labor, the mere fact that the *general* strike had been thus settled and not by the Board seemed to arouse animosities in Washington that have never subsided. The President's Board had authority only in the Longshoremen's Strike and not in the much more serious general strike. I knew nothing at all about this Washington backfire until I returned and found myself confronted with a situation which I shall presently describe.

As a matter of fact the contestants in the *general* strike did not seem to want to deal with the President's Board, and the employers would not have dealt with it at all. I called the governor and he told me that he was going to declare martial law next day (the day the general strike was broken). I pleaded with him not to do that. In the tension that existed it would have resulted inevitably in bloodshed on a very broad scale. When you put a loaded rifle into the hands of an amateur soldier he is naturally pretty apt to think that it is there for some purpose and when you suspend civil law in a region where a whole community—not just some employer and his employees—are in a state of electrical high tension, something explosive is almost certain to happen. Why, we did not even declare martial law during the Fire in San Francisco, although troops were freely used. After regular troops came in nobody was hurt but in some National Guard zones several people were shot. In my opinion, Jack Nyland was the man who held that situation in hand during twenty-four hours of the most tense period I have ever lived through. He and I had a beautiful fight at our first conference but I left that place with a great respect for that man and we were in perfect agreement.

Nobody 3,000 miles away, especially nobody who has not lived in the atmosphere of the Pacific Coast, can realize to the full the dangerous possibility that existed in that situation. California was once an independent republic. In the days following 1849, its people so far isolated by mountains and desert, learned how to take care of themselves and they take pride in their continuing ability to do so. I think they rather resented any Federal interference at all.

Theirs was somewhat the attitude of the old mountain trapper, who blundered in between an old grizzly and her cubs on a narrow ledge along a cañon wall where there was room neither to turn nor run and who, drawing his long knife, as the bear rose up to charge, sent up a little prayer to heaven, "Don't help me Lawd, I'm a sinner. Jus' stan' aside Lawd and see the mos' gosh-awful ba'ar fight in the Rockies. *All I ask* Lawd is that you just don't help the ba'ar."

But with the commerce of our whole west coast tied up—both interstate and international—and a condition of economic insurrection threatened in three states, the Federal Government while not helping the ba'ar could not indulge any desire just to stand by and see a ba'ar fight.

Of course, I once more swore "never again in strike settlements." But the end was not yet. I had to go to Chicago on a long-planned engagement and I got there at the very climax of the stockyards strike. That had vital importance for two reasons: first, it was interfering with the shipment of starving cattle on Harry Hopkins' salvaging plan—indeed it had paralyzed those shipments—second: negroes were being used as strikebreakers to take the jobs of Back-of-the-Yards Irishmen. I came asserting that I would have nothing whatever to do with that matter which was in the hands of the Regional Board. Both sides came to me to say that there was no hope of settlement through that Board, that the situation was desperate, and that there would be serious race-rioting within forty-eight hours. Harry Hopkins' assistant, Howard O. Hunter, came and backed that up. Hunter, like Hopkins, is one of the real finds of the New Deal.

The Chicago situation grew out of a prior agreement to leave all matters in dispute to Federal Judge Sullivan. He had made a preliminary finding and then a strike had been called without referring the matter back to him. For some reason which I never understood, the Regional Board had not been able to effect a settlement, although a representative sat with me and I thought agreed with all that was done. Negotiations were between two of the fairest-minded representatives of both sides that any one could ask for—John Black—whom I had known for years—for the employers and Redmond Brennan—whom you only had to know for a few minutes—for labor. It seemed to me since both sides kept reiterating their faith in Judge Sullivan that all that was necessary was to get both to agree to submit the whole controversy back to him and to abide by his decision. It was also necessary to get Judge Sullivan to agree to act again after the rather cavalier way in which he had been treated.

This took about forty-eight hours of the usual sort of horse trading which came to an end on a Saturday afternoon with an agreement to submit the case to the Judge. But it was hard to locate Judge Sullivan. It was a half-holiday and he was on some golf course. Mayor Kelley had detailed to me from the Chicago Police Force to protect our negotiations from intrusion Sergeants Edwin Dailey and John Warren. I never saw more efficient, tactful, polite and able John Laws among all those with whom I have come in contact on this job. If I had remained with NRA I would have had Sergeants Dailey and Warren in very important positions in connection with it. It was indispensable to get in touch with the Judge at once, because all kinds of fireworks were scheduled for Monday. In thirty minutes John Warren had located the Judge *and sent a policeman with a side-car for his convenience to get him to a telephone.* In an hour he was on the wire and had unselfishly accepted his difficult assignment.

The amusing thing about that was that, not long before, Sergeant Warren had run a notorious gang leader to the ground on the same golf course and at the same hole, *playing in a tournament and leading.* When arrested he asked if he couldn't be allowed to play through and Warren *had let him do it and then brought him triumphantly in.* I never enjoyed anybody's society more than that of those two cops. The stories they told would make a much better book than this one.

I made a speech at the Fair while in Chicago and laid a wrist watch on the reading desk to check my radio time. In the rush of people after the speech, I was pushed away from that desk and before I got back to it the watch was gone. Dailey and Warren said: "Never mind—you'll get your watch in the morning." Before the day was over it was in my room at the hotel— no questions asked or answered. In the meantime my friend,

Lou Buss, who is in the watch business himself and who had given me the lost watch, *had given me another one.*

Even before I got back to Washington, I began to get the strongest kind of rumors to the effect that the Secretary of Labor was displeased because of my participation in the settlement of the San Francisco and Chicago strikes.

It came as a shock and a disappointment to me because I had regarded her consistently as being (excluding only the President) my most certain and faithful friend in the Administration. She never asked me to do anything that I did not immediately do. I had confided in her all my most serious troubles and I always turned to her when I needed help. I had never had even an important disagreement with her. But I observed a complete change of attitude upon the moment of my return.

In a casual way she called my attention to a clause in the Executive Order setting up the Labor Relations Board which she said was exclusive of my having anything to do with settlements of labor troubles. She remarked that NRA was not equipped to settle strikes.

With all that I agreed, but I had also insisted that the tribunals to settle them ought also to be independent of the Labor Department because they must be impartial. She was the titular representative of labor. I could not refrain from observing also that even though unequipped, we had had fair good fortune in the seven major situations with which we had been confronted. There was nothing acrimonious about any of this. There never will be anything of that kind from me. I regard Secretary Perkins as a great executive and one of the strongest elements of the Administration, in spite of any disagreement I may have with her on policy. I was still too dumb to realize wherein I had offended.

Nobody had ever protested to me about any such action. I had usually called her up when anything which I thought would interest her occurred and especially had I done this at San Francisco. At both San Francisco and Chicago I had acted with representatives of the Labor Boards.

This began to give me serious matter for reflection and especially when I began to observe other straws in the wind—for example that, when the San Francisco negotiations were at their most tense moment, Mr. Richberg was called from his vacation to Washington to confer about it. (It was settled before he got to Washington.) The President was then absent in Hawaii and none of Mr. Richberg's responsibilities or duties brought him into the field of labor controversy. I may add parenthetically that nobody then in Washington could have done anything about that strike.

There are two more incidents in this sequence. One day we got a request from Mr. Garrison to withdraw the Blue Eagle from the Chicago Motor Bus Company for failure to comply with the Labor Relations Board's decree. Mr. Glancy, who was in charge of that, felt that he could get compliance with the Board's decree and I was extremely loath to withdraw the Eagle if we could get such agreement because that is in part a suburban line and the *only means of transportation to the City for hundreds of commuters*. In such circumstances it was too much to suppose that withdrawal of the Eagle would have any effect whatever and the publicity attending its futility would have a very harmful result in Chicago where we had not one single important newspaper that was not actively hostile and where the whole NRA sentiment was weaker than in any other large city.

I sent Glancy over to see Mr. Garrison and ask him if he would not wait and let us take another crack at trying to get compliance. He had no control over our actions in taking away the Blue Eagle but I was trying to move in harmony with him. He sent word back to me that he did not approve and then wrote me a letter which undertook to lecture me on my administration of NRA, saying that he was going to report my action to the Secretary of Labor. I answered that letter hotly and sent one copy to Miss Perkins and one to the President.

In the meantime, there had been pending in his Board the case of a man whom I had discharged at the request of Dr. Gustav Peck, who was acting head of our Labor Advisory Board. This man had a record as an agitator.

There had been a movement to organize NRA employees in a Federal Employees' Union. I took the position that they had a perfect right to do that although, as to wages and hours, I was not an employer. The rules were made and fixed by Congress and by regulations made in the Bureau of the Budget. In other words, there was no room for collective bargaining with me on this score, but if NRA employees wanted a spokesman to present grievances I thought they ought to have one.

This man was head of a small NRA Union. The first case he brought to me was that of an employee who had made herself very disagreeable and insubordinate in the stencil cutting unit of the Mimeograph Division and she had been fired. When he brought this case up I said that to avoid a shadow of doubt about it I would reinstate her. He protested that and said that so much hard feeling had been created there that it would be most unpleasant for her. I then said I would try to place her in some other department of government. But there are not too many stencil cutters' jobs and it was reported to me that a canvass had been made without disclosing any place. I instructed our publicity department to *make* a place for her.

During this time this man began coming into my outer office with large "committees" to make demands to see me at hours specified by him—or right then and there. As everybody in Washington knew, I was working on a day and night schedule and could see people outside my immediate staff only by appointment. These were Chinese puzzles to put together—to sandwich everybody in—and still give me time for administrative work. In proper organization I had no business to engage in squabbles over employment of individuals in an organization employing at one time nearly 3,000 people. There was not the least doubt in the world that this man was engaging in administration-baiting to impair NRA's standing with labor.

Yet right at this moment his own boss, *the head of the Labor Advisory Board*, came to me and complained that he was not doing his work, that he frequently absented himself, was insubordinate, and ought to be discharged. I did not order Dr. Peck to do this, because this man was President of the NRA Union and the situation was not one in which to pass the buck.

I was being driven to a point where failure to take action would have been a showing of administrative cowardice. I could easily have escaped any responsibility by authorizing Dr. Peck to fire him. But no man can dodge responsibility and expect loyalty from his people. I called the President of the Federal Employees' Union, explained the situation to him and he told me that it was not the purpose of the Union to shield insubordination or dereliction of duty. Accordingly, I fired this man.

Of course a perfect fanfare of publicity broke loose and the head of the Government Employees' Union came to see me in a very different frame of mind. I promptly offered to submit the case to the Civil Service Commission (this was Madam Secretary Perkins' suggestion) as the duly established place for it. This was absolutely refused. Then I offered to submit it to the Labor Advisory Board—refused again. He wanted it to go to the National Labor Relations Board—as it turned out, he knew his garden products. It had no business there because that Board had no jurisdiction. A Federal employee is on a little different basis from that of an industrial employee because he has taken an oath, because his administrative boss is in no sense his employer, and has no control of wages or conditions, and in NRA especially, because we were an embattled army and to most of us hours and wages were not the main point. But I felt that any fair-minded person in the circumstances of this case would find that I had not fired the man because of any union affiliation but because he had put himself clear out of the pale of loyal and effective devotion to public duty and was obstructing a great social movement. Also, and more important to me at least, because I *said* I had not fired him for union affiliation.

I knew nothing about this case except by hearsay. No public official in my position could do more than accept the facts as given upon investigation by such officials as Dr. Peck and the Chief Clerk. Therefore I sent these witnesses to the Board and wrote a letter to Mr. Garrison reciting these facts. *He refused to receive the letter* and wrote me a note delicately intimating that if I did not appear in person to be cross-examined the case might be decided against me.

I had told Mr. Garrison that I had not discharged this man for union activity. There is and there must remain some faith and credit as between heads of government departments. I sent word to him that he must decide as he saw fit. He then reluctantly and with obvious scorn decided to receive the letter I had written reciting the facts of the dismissal.

On the morning after he received my hot answer to his letter criticizing the Administration of NRA he informed me that he was going to decide that case against me—all of which I already knew. The decision as written impugned my official integrity, in neglecting my positive statement that union activity was not even mentioned or considered as a cause for discharge. It was absolutely inconsistent with the evidence and was done with the effect, if not the purpose, of discrediting NRA as an institution by suggesting that it was violating a law which it had been created to enforce. It was in effect a lecture from a heatedly partisan standpoint, as to how NRA had been run and ought to be run.

The only admonition I ever received from the President was about the letter I had written to Garrison. I knew that it had been discussed with Miss Perkins. But, after the seventeen months of effort and sacrifice that I had expended on labor, as a whole, and in view of the result I thought I had achieved for labor and for the Administration, I was too weary to state to him, by way of exculpation, the whole sequence of events contained in this chapter. I only state them here for the sake of the record which seems so painstakingly to have been built to a contrary conclusion. As I wrote Mr. Garrison, I had the delicate job of keeping in the air about six Mills grenades with the pins drawn and I had to consider every withdrawal of the Blue Eagle from all its aspects. But all that was done in both of these incidents was highly embarrassing and very harmful to NRA.

I began to be greatly disturbed and my mind went back over the whole history of this particular strand of events to the circumstance of the drafting of the Executive Order setting up the new Labor Relations Board after Senator Wagner resigned.

The President had set up a committee consisting of Madam Secretary Perkins, Senator Wagner, Mr. Richberg, and myself to draft this Order. He had discussed the subject with me alone and jotted down some notes. Shortly afterward—and before the Order was drafted—I went into the hospital for an operation. One day the other three members of the Committee came to see me while I was still in bed. There was some misunderstanding about that appointment, Madam Secretary seeming to think that I had requested it. I would not have had the presumption to ask a lady Cabinet member or even a Senator to wait on me. I knew, however, that the President wanted the draft of that Order promptly so I assumed that the meeting had been arranged by the White House. I asked if the other three members had met and drafted anything that we could talk about and she replied that they had talked it over, but only in a general way, and that they *had drafted nothing*. At that moment Mr. Richberg's face flushed and he got up and left the room. Madam Secretary added that she had a memorandum from the

President as to what he wanted written into the Order and drew out of her brief case some notes in his characteristic handwriting. She read them and asked if I agreed. They seemed to me to be exactly the same notes he had made in his discussion with me alone and I said, of course, that I did. I was coming out of the hospital in a day or two and I naturally supposed that we were to meet again and draft the Order. But before I got back to my office an order was issued which I had never seen. The order seemed to be in the style of Mr. Richberg. It went beyond the President's notes and contained matter on the controverted subject of the influence of the Labor Department on impartial labor tribunals, with which I did not agree, and upon which NRA had a right to be heard. The President's instructions setting up that Committee was notice of an intention that I *should* be heard.

I asked Mr. Richberg to come into my office and inquired of him when that Order had been drafted. He seemed very uncomfortable and finally said—with some emotion—that he had gotten along thus far in his career without dissimulation and he did not purpose to begin now—that the Order had been drafted *before the visit of the other members of the Committee* to me in the hospital and that that was why he had arisen and left the room when I asked whether any draft had been made. Senator Wagner told me later that he also had not been consulted and that he was in substantial agreement with my view. On the merits of this conflict of statement, I have to decide between Mr. Richberg's assertion and the Secretary's. That is not very important, but as to him, I could only remember that, at the time he sat with this conference in the hospital and he got up and left the room when my vital question was asked, he was serving on my personal staff as General Counsel of NRA and as my trusted and confidential personal friend.

"*Father, I cannot tell a lie. I did it with my little hatchet.*"

# Chapter XXVI

# LABOR, MANAGEMENT & CO.

---

"Labor in this country . . . has not to ask the patronage of capital, but capital solicits the aid of labor."

—*Daniel Webster (1824)*.

---

It is not my purpose here to recount the history of the labor movement in this country, but to make clear the labor policy pursued by NRA it is necessary for me to inflict on the reader at least my view of the principles involved in it, and the results developed.

An era of westward expansion of empire in our country ended roughly with the 19th century. The last big "Opening" of Indian lands was the Run into the Cherokee Strip in 1893. Up to that time at least any American had alternatives to despair. It was not merely that there was "free land" in the West. The new mushroom communities were fields of opportunity for individual initiative to men of every trade, calling, or profession or of no vocation at all.

This country was called and was universally regarded as a haven of refuge for the poor, distressed and down-trodden of the whole world and our portals were open to immigrants of every race and creed except Asiatics who were excluded 60 years ago. That is a highly significant exception. The Pacific Coast is still largely agricultural and only fragmentarily industrial. It is peculiarly a region of American individual enterprise, and it did not want Chinamen because they had been trained to subsist on a few cents a day and they could not be admitted without importing the degraded living standards of teeming China and imposing it on the whole West Coast.

On the East Coast an exactly reverse philosophy prevailed. Industrialism in increasingly larger units was the rule. Men were living on the labor of other men, and the less it cost them the larger their living seemed to be. Cheap immigrant labor was thought to be the surest road to profit, and the industrial network of the East caught the westward tide of immigration and strained it through mills and factories, keeping it as long as it *could* keep it at wages a little better than European wages. Sometimes this was not very long—usually only as long as it took for these alien people to taste the higher living standards of this country. They also could always move on west. The obvious remedy of employers was to encourage a constant stream of non-selective immigration which poured through our portals sometimes at the rate of many hundreds of thousands a year.

But not nearly the whole of this stream strained through the Eastern industrial colander. Part of it stuck and began to demand at least a part of the opportunity of the West in the mills and factories of the East. The old industrial philosophy of high profits through low wages was very stubborn, and the old arrogance of the Hamiltonian theory of an aristocracy of wealth was very haughty. Battle was inevitable—and it came—bloody and seemingly interminable. Compared with the present time, the early handicaps to Unionism were so great that I have never been able to see how it survived. In the first place there was always the broad western road to individual independence for the dissatisfied industrial worker. This no longer exists. In the second place there still continued the never failing stream of mass-migration to take the jobs of any who rebelled and, finally, the political power of employers was so great and that of workers so small that, looking back upon it, the battle seems heroic.

And battle it was, bloody, cruel, and implacable—brutal days in the last great stand to exploit labor as a commodity of commerce behind which lay the shadow of slavery itself and the bloodiest civil war in history. Industry became a field of battle and blood and hatred were welded into much that we produced in this country. One of our difficulties today—in an atmosphere as different from that as air on a mountain top from air in a coal pit—is the wounds and scars and hatreds and distrust and the memories of old oppressions and old rebellions left over from those days. Then even some of our very courts of justice threw their judgments against the rights of men by invoking the common law doctrines of feudalism in an industrialized nation of the 19th century. But the onward sweep of human events was stirring in the ranks of labor.

Beginning at about the turn of the century the bright promise of the West began to dim—it was increasingly better for workers to stay and fight it out than to go on to more quiet sectors. Furthermore, the necessity for fighting it out became greater—the age of specialization, mechanization, and huge integrated industrial units was upon us. As has been repeatedly pointed out in this book, an industrial specialist is a cog in a machine—when he loses his job in a depression there is almost no place for him to turn for a living because he knows how to do only one thing which, standing alone, has but little value. There is little opportunity for new work, and there is none at all for bargaining.

The first generation of industrial barons at least ran and largely owned their own shops. Out in Moline, Illinois, Swedish iron workers used to make the whole trip from Stockholm with only three words of English—"Charlie—Deere—Moline"—Charlie Deere being President of the Great John Deere Plow Company. He knew all his men by their first names and all their personal or other troubles, and they called him by *his* first name if they wanted to.

But the greatest modern industrial clusters are owned by millions of stockholders who never saw the plants and have no idea of what labor problems are. The companies are controlled as to policy by financial houses, far removed from personal contact and managed by financiers, now largely of the second generation, some of whom never saw the inside of a factory in their lives, and would not know what it was all about if they did see one. These great industrial institutions are managed by men who are employees themselves and who have so many other responsibilities that hiring and firing have come to be regarded by them as a relatively minor function attended to by an official far down the line of rank, and generally called "the employment manager."

There is no bargaining in any accurate sense. The Board of Directors is usually composed of officials in the particular corporation or in other corporations, a lawyer or two, and a sprinkling of bankers—now usually younger sons. The modern American directorate is in no sense the attentive legislative unit that is found in Britain. It is too frequently a double row of stuffed shirts, facing inward and performing the functions of a rubber stamp. Such a board sets a basic hourly labor rate derived from cost studies and competitive price schedules. These are converted into wage scales and piece rates on the basis of specification and time studies and the result is passed down to labor like a menu in a restaurant—"Take it or leave it. That is the rate. These are the hours. The working conditions are before you."

There is no strictly uniform practice and this method is tempered by all kinds of exceptions and differences—company unions, shop committees, welfare organizations and company housing plans. Some of these industrial presidents *do* know their men, some come from the ranks themselves. I veritably believe that Walter Chrysler or Charlie Nash could go to almost any bench in his factory or Bill Irwin to any open hearth in Big Steel and do the trick almost as well as the regular man on the job. But these are exceptions and what I have described is the rule. It is of the utmost importance to visualize this situation, because it is deep in the hearts of some industrialists that they have a vested right to continue the rule and this is a chief cause of much labor controversy.

I have no brief for either side. Both are extremists. I know there is a wholesome middle ground, and I think that it is of the utmost importance for us to reach it at once.

But we are getting considerably ahead of the story. It was Buckle I believe who in his *History of Civilization in England* said that the effect of war is always to anticipate and accelerate all natural trends, or words to that effect. The World War did that to us with a vengeance. Even before the American declaration, the rush for production to accommodate the belligerents was such that prices and wages in this country surged upward like the tides in the Bay of Fundy. Immigration was cut off and there began an unbridled competition for human labor which trebled and quadrupled wages. The old "dollar-a-day" school of management moaned and wailed but profit-increases were greater than wage-increases—they managed to bear up under it. Before long some of the brightest of them began to discover an astonishing thing. In addition to the tremendous foreign war demand for all that this country could produce, a sudden new and unprecedented domestic demand began to appear and, after a slight lull for a few months after the Armistice, it resurged and began to tax our factories right up to war-time capacity.

Suddenly industry awoke to the reason. I actually saw this

change in the minds of two or three of the ablest of these old fellows. They realized that higher wages and shorter hours had created right under their noses a market for their product so much more active than anything ever known before that (in the period 1921 to 1929) industrial output and consumption per capita in the United States increased at an unprecedented rate—several times faster than population increased.

In the meantime, the end of the war disclosed the probability of a mass migration from shattered and debt-burdened Europe which momentarily threatened to engulf this country. So the immigration bars went up and labor stood at the all-time peak of its prosperity in the United States. Not so, however, for the institutions of *organized* labor. Things seemed to be going so well without organization that the average worker did not see why he should pay dues to a union.

For the first time, too, the working man enjoyed the facilities of credit. Installment sales-plans and salary-loans multiplied and flourished like the green bay tree. Labor activated industry not only by spending its wages, but also by mortgaging its wages. That was at a time when we were just about to "abolish poverty," have a chicken in every pot and two cars in every garage. The course of that pious project and what happened to it have been sufficiently discussed in this book and elsewhere and never better than by the man who said that we had to revise the formula to "two chickens in every garage."

But when the avalanche came, the sapping of the strength of labor organization through the prosperous years left labor deprived of any refuge, and although employers were implored by President Hoover to delay the threatened wage and work cuts of the 1929 disaster there were vast inroads into the pay and employment of labor.

There is not a destructive war of price-cutting below cost— no retrograde movement in industrial production—no vicious downward spiral which does not immediately result in degradation of the economic status of workers. There is only one place from which the sacrifices of a prolonged price war or downward price tendency *can* come and that is out of hours and wages of labor. That is fundamental. It is something that both labor and industry must learn and cherish. The business of industry is the business of labor. The success of labor is the success of industry. Whether they think so or not, labor and management are partners and until they think and act as partners we can never have peace, nor can we stabilize prosperity. There is never a proper question of what is *the most labor can get out of management*. The real question is what is fairly necessary to the success of the joint adventure. There is never either a proper question of what is the *least that management can pay labor*. The real question is what is the most it can pay to support its own markets and to live against competition?

From what I have seen in NRA I am as sure of these deductions as I am of any physical fact such as that I have a foot, but I am equally sure that the remarks on this industrial partnership amount to little more than a pious generality in respect of any particular industry without four indispensable conditions:

(1) Code organization of the whole of that industry.

(2) Vertical organization of the whole of labor in that industry.

(3) A complete and conclusive system within the industry for settlement of labor disputes, local, regional, and national.

(4) Labor representation on the Code Authority of that Industry.

I think that I can prove this. Consider a company in an industry with either a company union or an outside union which does not cover the whole industry. Let us suppose for the sake of illustration that the management is liberal and wants to cooperate with the union to the uttermost. How far can it go in— let us say—raising wages and shortening hours, or in granting any other improvements in labor conditions, which will increase its cost of production? No matter how degraded the condition of labor in that industry may be that one company can go exactly as far as other companies in that industry with which it competes and *not one step further*. All the strikes and lockouts which attempt to make it go further can have only a single effect—to throw it into bankruptcy and kill for its employees the goose that lays the golden egg.

Or take a company in an industry with locals of a particular craft in—let us say—some bottle-neck department of its production, like pattern-making. This craft is dissatisfied and strikes the plant or even all plants in that industry without consulting the rest of labor in that industry. Against whom are they striking? Against management? Certainly, but far more effectively against all their fellow-workers in that plant or, if it be a strike against the industry, then against all workers in that industry and all workers who make goods for that industry. It is a power that should never reside in the hands of any such minority. If it is exercised against a single company, it can bankrupt that company and destroy the employment of the whole plant crew.

But there are no such limits as this on what can be done for labor in a codified industry with a vertical union. The Code Authority and the heads of the union can sit down together like partners in a business and plan what working conditions and wages they can permit throughout the whole industry without impairment of consumption and hence of production of the product of that industry which is to say of *employment in that industry.*

That is always a business question of the first magnitude and that is why I was so disappointed by the action of the union in the second textile strike. They wrote demands which, if granted, were as sure to decimate production and employment as the sun is sure to rise tomorrow.

The picture in Bituminous Coal is an entirely different story. That industry has serious and threatening competition *as an industry.* It has to compete with crude oil, gas, electricity and —even more significant—with constantly increasing efficiency in the combustion of coal. Does anybody suppose that John Lewis doesn't know that? He has just as much interest in it as the Code Authority. He fights for that industry just as hard as do its managers. There is your real partnership. It is getting stronger every day and the most interesting thing about it is that it was compounded of a wide variety of more bitterly warring elements on both the industrial and the labor side of the table than existed in any other industry in this country. That industry was in a hotter spot than any other in the country. It is far from being out of the woods but it is so much better off than it was in March, 1933, that there are no words in which quickly and adequately to make the comparison. All of which leads to one very definite statement about NRA which is of profound and far-reaching importance. *NRA, to the extent that it has been honestly and effectively applied, has removed the wages and hours of labor from the lowering effects of industrial competition.*

It is of interest to note that several important British Economists recently remarked to a friend of mine that if there had
been done in England for coal, oil and textiles alone what
NRA has done here, instead of an inferiority complex on the
accomplishment, the British Government would hail it as an
epochal achievement. Both France and England are taking
leaves out of the NRA book. The trouble with us is that while
we win the 100 yard dash with a spectacular sprint we just
aren't there on the 440 and the Marathon.

It was just a meaningless generality for Congress to say in
the Anti-Trust Acts that "human labor is not a commodity of
commerce." Of *course* it is a commodity of commerce. The
moment it develops a surplus the price goes down. When there
is a shortage the price goes up. It is imported, exported, and
shipped from spot to spot. It is the first to suffer the effects
of recessions in the price of what it produced and the last to
enjoy the effects of increases in that price.

When PRA—President's Reëmployment Agreement—went
into effect the result was to say to every signer: "Compete as
you will, but *not* by cutting wages below the minimum." The
codes say the same thing: *Why, it is the greatest single contribution of the New Deal to economic stability in the United States!*

I am well aware that its execution is far from perfect. I am
even more acutely aware that its existence is being threatened
by the sophistry that lower wages will employ more people to
produce more goods but the principle has been established and
its operation proved and both management and labor should go
forward from that good beginning to the formula of complete
partnership.

The Recovery Act establishes only minimum base wages and
not wage scales. These are to be negotiated in collective bargaining. I have never been sure whether this is right or not. If
you try to establish scales in a code, you have undertaken an
interminable and probably impossible task and you have left
nothing to the mutual relationship of employers and employees.
On the other hand, if you do not do so, you expose all wages
above the minima to the effects of cut-throat inter-company
competition. When you have a codified industry and a vertical
union the problem solves itself as it did in the Coal Code. The
Code Authority and the union officials negotiate the scale, have
it approved as their collective bargain, and it becomes the

law merchant for that industry until, in collective bargaining, they change it.

But all of this reasoning is entirely predicated on complete organization in both industry and labor. Without *that*, to my mind, the whole thing falls apart in a ruin of uncertain conjecture. For almost every reason stated in this book, such complete organization seems to me inevitable—which brings up unavoidably the troubled question of the company union.

If a labor unit confined to a single company is absolutely free of suggestion, influence, favor, or domination by the management as to form, method, or membership, and in such freedom has been set up or selected by a group of employees, I believe not only that it is authorized by the Recovery Act, but also that any attempt by any government board or official to interfere with it is wholly unlawful. But I also must in frankness say that I have grave doubt that there are very many of such unions in existence. Even if there were, for the reasons I have stated here (which seem to me conclusive) they will not give to either management or labor the full benefits of the Recovery Act, because they relieve neither the management of a particular company nor the labor of a particular company from the competition of cut prices of any other company (with or without a company union) which decides to enter the competitive lists on the basis of reduced wages and increased hours.

The relationship and the atmosphere in respect to 7a is *not right*—it is far from right and it ought to be cleared up. I feel so earnestly about this great opportunity to do an unprecedented work for economic peace in this country, that I am going to say why I think it is not right.

The most potent cause for the seething unrest in the field of industrial labor is hopeless confusion over the welter of contradictory "interpretations" of Section 7a. Mr. Richberg and I jointly made one. The President confirmed that in the Automobile settlement. Mr. Garrison reversed the President and NRA. Then Mr. Richberg reconciled the NRA and Garrison interpretations by inventing the term "voting unit" which in my opinion reconciled nothing but greatly increased the confusion. Then a court reversed Garrison in the Houde case. Then Mr. Richberg reconciled that in still another interpretation which has been hailed by the highly conservative press as "clear" but which, to my mind, is a "yes-and-no" conclusion which adds nothing but perplexity.

It is highly important to decide the question beyond peradventure because it is causing more bitterness and loss of time, money, and production and bad administration than any single force. The only authority that can now clear it is Congress.

I think that the right of free organization should be made unequivocal—that the right of compulsion should be denied—that two parallel unions cannot function in the same shop.

If a new statute provided for a code agreement to the effect that where a substantial majority of workers belong to a particular freely chosen union, the employer should recognize no other parallel union, half the problems would be solved.

Then if the statute provided for a code agreement to the effect that no employer could require membership in *any* union as a condition of employment the distasteful idea of compulsion would be eliminated.

I strongly favor such a change immediately.

For the present highly unsatisfactory situation, management, labor and government are all to blame. I am going to criticize management first.

Time after time in all the long and painful sessions looking toward industrial peace, I saw mature men get up and walk out of a room because they would not sit at the same table with labor men even though it was in the presence of the Secretary of Labor, who was doing her conscientious best to restore peace. Why, as I had occasion to say in a similar situation, "I would sit down with the Devil himself, if I thought it would make hell any cooler."

There must be a beginning somewhere. I may be mistaken but, for many reasons stated in this book, I do not believe that industry is going to be able to avoid collective bargaining with unions. Managers must manage but there is no reason why they should expect any less give-and-take trading in purchasing human effort than they expend in buying steel to make plows or cat-gut for fiddle-strings. So to trade it is not to "let employees run business" any more than I would be running Henry Ford's business if I dickered to sell him tons of carpet for his cars.

I think that organization of both Industry and Labor to the

ultimate is the only way to meet the serious economic problems with which we are faced. Therefore, I think industry should confer—not as to how to combat the inevitable, but as to a way that would be most acceptable to industry, and still meet the economic requirements of the country. Having arrived at this conclusion, I think that Industry should take the initiative to foster and aid that result in the shortest possible space of time, with the maximum of good feeling and the most conclusive effect.

Next I am going to criticize labor. When the President laid down the basic policy of NRA, he said:

This law is also a challenge to labor. Workers too, are here given a new charter of rights long sought and hitherto denied. But they know that the first move expected by the Nation is a great coöperation of all employers by one single mass action, to improve the case of workers on a scale never attempted in any nation. Industries can do this only if they have the support of the whole public and especially of their own workers. *This is not a law to foment discord and it will not be executed as such. This is a time for mutual confidence and help and we can safely rely on the sense of fair play among all Americans to assure every industry which now moves forward promptly in this united drive against depression that its workers will be with it to a man.*

This request has not been altogether respected. I know of strike after strike that has been pulled without even stating a grievance to management. I knew of agreements for industrial peace made and broken with as little regard for the pledged word as though it had not been spoken. I know of demands made and held as sacrosanct from discussion without regard to the economic possibility of meeting them. I know of strikes against the general public, strikes against a code and NRA and strikes against one perfectly satisfactory employer to coerce another. I know that action by management cited in the preceding paragraph are incitations to acts recited here, but so are these acts of labor incitations to the acts and attitude of management.

On another point *both* labor and management are to be criticized for "jumping the gun" and misleading employees about the meaning of the Recovery Act. So thoroughly did they both do this that it is difficult to place the balance of blame.

Some labor organizers went out and unconscionably oversold

the provisions of Section 7a. They told their men (who have not time to study the statutory facts and decide for themselves and who trusted their leaders) that the *President wanted them* to join this, that, or the other particular union, and some of these are still doing it. It was not true. It is not the function of government to organize labor. The whole intent of the Act was to leave organization and representation to the men themselves, unhampered and uninfluenced by any outside source. Repeatedly the President made this clear and (following his lead) also so did every spokesman for NRA. But, for some reason, this did not seem to reach the men.

On the other hand some employers, who never before had given the slightest consideration to representation of their men in the conduct of business, rushed to initiate company unions in which every right of labor they did themselves "*contrive, enact, behold.*" They also told the men that this was what *the President wanted.* Some of them also are still doing it. This also was untrue, and it was an equal abuse of the confidence of the people for whose benefit NRA was intended. In view of the President's high ideal in providing these benefits, it was bad business on both sides.

The most vocal complaint about the other side "over-selling" comes from some companies whose pots are just as black as Labor's kettle. It always seemed to me that this was not very sporting. Industry had just as great an opportunity in a propaganda contest as did Labor, and while I deprecate both attempts, it doesn't seem to me to lie in the mouth of Industry to admit that Labor won in this selling contest. NRA repeatedly and officially repudiated inaccurate statements by both sides.

In spite of all bickering, great demonstrations of coöperation are going on every day all over the country. The President's recent request for truce has largely been respected. In that kind of calm the few fierce quarrels that spring up will seem to most Americans like somebody turning a fire siren in the midst of a symphony.

George James of the Federal Reserve once told this story in a labor dispute:

Once there was a very poor farmer, plowing a field with an ox and a mule. In the midst of the furrow, the ox had a brainstorm. He said to himself, "I don't *need* to go on pulling together with this mule," so he lay down and chewed his cud—he wouldn't get up and he wouldn't pull. The field *had* to be plowed, so the farmer got into the yoke with the mule. The ox ambled home and ate his hay. At sundown the mule came home tired, but the ox was rested and talkative. He asked the mule:

"What did the farmer say?"

"Nothing—he just pulled on together with me."

"Didn't he even mention my name?"

"Nope"—and then the mule remembered—"Oh, yes. A man drove along in a buckboard and the farmer went out to the fence to borrow a chaw of tobacco. 'Remember now that he *did* mention your name."

"Who was the man?" asked the ox. The mule said:

"It was the butcher."

There is fault enough on both sides to make it hard to say which is the mule and which is the ox. But the field is not being properly plowed. The farmer is the long suffering people and the butcher is public opinion, which is the really effective driving force in NIRA.

The third criticism is coming to government itself, and I will take my own case first. I was far too slow in getting adequate compliance mechanism started. As a matter of fact it isn't started yet. I have a whole pile of alibis, but I am not going to use them here. There isn't any proper excuse for it because nothing short of a result was required and the fact remains that I didn't get that result. I was afraid of too much territorial delegation of power at first, because, of course, the greatest danger in NRA is that several aspects of it can easily be turned into a racket—for example, code-assessments by Code Authorities.

I was afraid that if we let the actual "snatching" of Blue Eagles get out of our own control it might turn out to be the biggest racket of all. I should have taken the risk and then watched it and made examples of abuses. Trifling with, or flouting, the engagements of Codes and Presidential Agreements flourished and the effect was to weaken the prestige of the Blue Eagle. I will never forgive myself for this. It was the worst of many mistakes of judgment that I made.

Also our legal department did not work closely enough with the Department of Justice or in some other way I failed to get prompt prosecutions in outstanding cases. For this also I take full blame, as I do for any justified criticism of any department of NRA—the men in direct charge were chosen by me. At last analysis I was responsible for delivering a result and here also a proper result was not delivered.

But quite as disconcerting as these faults of mine and a thing which in my opinion contributed more and is still contributing more to prevent a cleansing of the atmosphere around labor-management relations, is the fact already thoroughly discussed, that the National Industrial Relations Board is not absolutely independent of any department of government and especially of the Labor Department. However impartial that department intends to be, no amount of argument can change the opinion of most industrialists and of the public, that it cannot be wholly impartial, unless it is completely divorced from any Administration as is a court.

When the second cotton textile strike was on, Major George Berry, who was on the Cotton Textile Labor Relations Committee, tells me, and backs his story with copies of correspondence, that he proposed a quick way out which was acceptable to Labor, acceptable to the Industry, and when presented to Mr. Garrison seemed to be acceptable to him, but he added that he would *"have to see the Secretary of Labor about it."* The suggestion died.

During the A. & P. negotiations the Assistant Secretary of Labor, Mr. McGrady, is reported by the press as "sitting with the Board," where, although I know that *he as a person* did a great work, yet in his official position he should not have appeared at all. In the San Francisco longshoremen's strike he was a member of the Board, although at that very time he was my assistant *for* labor and Assistant Secretary *of* Labor. His duties in NRA were opposite those of my assistant for industry, and it was his job constantly and zealously to advocate the labor point of view. He is one of the best and most loyal friends I have, and he is perfectly aware of the views expressed here. He is a Union man and as effective as they come. But these very facts caused resentment among employers along the whole Pacific so burning and so deep against his sitting on an *impartial* board, that it delayed submission of all the issues in the longshoremen's strike for a long time, and was in part responsible for the crisis so narrowly averted there. A vast improvement in sentiment and action would result from an absolute divorce of labor tribunals from any contact whatever with any other government department.

It is so vitally important to get rid of the bitterness and resentment and hostility that exist on both sides of the Labor-Management argument that there is nothing that I would hesitate to say or do to accomplish that end.

It is my firm conviction that it can be done. I think that when the First Industrial Advisory Board led by Swope, Teagle, and Kirstein were working in Washington it was rapidly in process of being done. They and the Labor Advisory Board were meeting and spending evenings together frequently and the good will and mutual understanding that was being developed lulled me to sleep to the fact that, after they were "rotated out," the good work did not go on.

It must go on. We can't go to any peace or settlement or real conclusion in the present atmosphere of recrimination and sniping.

The cold hard fact is that this government *has no labor policy*. It has deliberately dodged this issue. It cannot be dodged. It is not only political cowardice to dodge it—it is inexcusable folly.

Expanding what I said in an earlier chapter, I believe that I could pick a team made up of men of proved high caliber, who have on their own shoulders the heaviest of responsibilities for their side of the argument, and yet who, through the fire of long service, see this thing in its broader bearing and so have become economic statesmen—I believe that such a team concentrated on this problem could solve it, *and I know of no greater need in this country today. I could name them off-hand*: Here they are: Gerard Swope, John Lewis, Walter Teagle, Edw. McGrady, Louis Kirstein, Sidney Hillman, Walter Chrysler, George Berry, Wm. Irwin, and Mike McDonough.

There are plenty of other men—dozens of them on both sides —but some of them will be needed where they are. I just happen to have seen these men work. I did not leave Bill Green off this list because of any doubt of equality of his ability as an economic statesman, but only because of his position as President of the Federation and his duty to represent craft unionism and vertical unionism alike.

I don't for one moment want to suggest any lack of faith in Bill Green. His duty is advocacy, and he does it hotly and well, but I never saw him in a spot where the national interest was involved when he did not come forward with complete courage and in language that left no possible doubt of where he stood. He went into the center of what promised to be a disastrous steel strike and to a convention that threatened to get badly out of hand and he composed all differences. He repudiated the General Strike on the Pacific Coast with even more emphatic words than mine. He has smashed at Communism whenever it raised its head. He presents the full of his constituents' case on the platform as he should do. In council he is wise and courteous and fair.

I do not mean either (now that I am free vigorously to advocate vertical unionism) to condemn craft unionism. Quite the contrary. Both must survive because it is only in the larger and more highly integrated industries that vertical unionism is practicable. Furthermore, in finding leadership and staff for new vertical units, I think it highly necessary to make heavy drafts on the experienced leaders of the craft unions. One principal cause of extremes in recent incidents is the inexperience of zealous and untrained leaders. Unionism is an art. Leadership therein is a profession, and the people and industries of this country should not be exposed to the administration of this tremendous and dangerous force at the hands of acolytes.

The full possibilities here are never in this world going to be obtained by dragging industries into the spotlight as defendants before Boards composed of men where training in these deadly serious problems is political or theoretical—nor, by the passage of legislation, attempting either to curb the movement of labor toward complete organization on the one hand, or to cram some particular form or unit of labor organization down the throat of industry on the other hand.

I firmly believe that if a council composed of such men as I have suggested—extra statutory and unofficial—were convened and *sent clear away from Washington*, or any other city, for a period to confer among themselves, to get acquainted and to reach agreement, they would return with a community of policy and a practicable plan of action—a labor policy for the United States. Then, if they would proceed to carry it out as diligently as they perform their other daily duties and responsibilities, in a very short space of time we could have the necessary partnership of Labor, Management & Co. formed and far upon its way to function. And I am ever more certain that, if we could do that, we would have accomplished more for this country in both the short and the long run than anything since enactment of NIRA.

# Chapter XXVII

## BENEFITS WITHOUT BURDENS

---

"But ne'er the rose without the thorn."
                                    —*Herrick.*

---

THERE is a single fundamental principle at the basis of all that the President has done. It is to place the governance of affairs and the benefits thereof—both political and economic—more directly in the hands of the people themselves. That is of the essence of Democracy. It is exactly what Democracy means and has meant since centuries before Thomas Jefferson. Of course some people are afraid of democracy, but we are living in a new age.

Given any such principle, its application depends and varies with the circumstances in which it has to act. In Jefferson's day, when it took weeks for even a single representative in an outlying district to come to the capital and months for important news of men and events to infiltrate through the whole population, Democracy in actual government had to act through representation. Men, families, and communities lived and died without even having journeyed 100 miles from the place of their births. It was impossible for people to act more directly. They had to rely on representatives not only for individual judgment and action but for news and interpretation of every great and disputed policy. Furthermore the country was far from uniformity in thought, race, aspiration, or background. There was as much difference in codes, manners, customs, and beliefs between people in Virginia and people in Massachusetts as there now is between people in England and people in France. The thirteen colonies were precariously held together by the most tenuous of ties. Yet Jefferson stood for exactly the same principles of Democracy as Roosevelt holds, to the extent that the condition of the country permitted their application.

Consider the incredible change. Events of even the slightest importance are broadcast today through millions of loud speakers to the most remote crannies of this country within a few seconds of their occurrence. Our people change styles in food, clothing, furniture, cosmetics, and habits of thought, clear across the whole country in almost perfect unison and at the same moment of time. A flapper in Carrizozo, New Mexico, is scarcely to be distinguished from a flapper in Syracuse, New York. Our towns now look alike. Within the space of my lifetime you could almost look out of a car window and tell what state, or at least what region, you were in. Now our architecture is pretty much standardized and when it is not, you are in some show-place of affectation. The movies do the trick in all that the radio and newspapers leave untouched, and so far as manners and customs go we all would be no more alike if we lived like the Iroquois in the Long House. In such circumstance, the idea of Democracy by pure representation pales. There is such a thing now as a composite mind of the American people, and it is no longer nearly so much of a mob mind as it used to be. It is no longer a sort of solar plexus responding to emotions only or to nervous impulse. It is also an informed and considering mind. The depression and the New Deal, and especially NRA, have gone further by way of education in homely economics than anything that ever happened here. I used to marvel at the content of French newspapers and the sight of chauffeurs in taxi ranks reading them. There were columns and pages of economic essays.

Ours have not gone that far, but they have greatly changed and what they lack, the radio supplies daily. That mass mind is yearly more able to control its own destiny, less amenable to intending leaders who strive to mold, guide and use it to serve their own ends. It is constantly better implemented to act for itself and it is momentarily more determined that there is to be a more widely spread receipt of benefits and use of our resources and opportunities and less powerful control of them at their source. No matter what happens to the New Deal in the end, that lesson will not be soon forgotten.

"Give back to the people their pristine liberties," says Herbert Hoover. Yes—but to *what* people? If he means the people that had what they had before 1932, he means the handful who had theretofore taken care of themselves so well. The New

Deal seeks to give more liberty and security to 125,000,000 people and not to concentrate these blessings in too small a group. That is the essence of the New Deal and the aim of all Liberal Government.

And this is triply necessary because of the astonishing economic and mechanical development of the past 20 years. The very form and power and strength of great economic units— billion dollar corporations mechanized to the reduced use of human labor and powerful beyond the ability of any individual to compete—chain systems in distribution blotting out any possibility of individual competition—great medical centers— department store law firms—the entire trend away from individual enterprise and restriction of human reward to wage or salary from some impersonal employer—if these things cannot be checked or at least controlled by the people who serve them for pay, then the few human beings who really do control these powerful and massive organisms will not only conduct them with no more reference to the common good than they elect, but they will also control the government to such purpose as they choose.

This is a vital, critical matter of overwhelming importance. This trend is due to an astonishing scientific and economic development and an even more astonishing political and administrative apathy. Even if there be faults and errors in the President's attempt to whip our governmental system up abreast of the economic and technological advance, the remedy is surely not to go back to the political lapse and lethargy that preceded it any more than it is to attempt to halt the progress of science and invention and economic coalescence. The remedy is to perfect a control system which shall make invention and progress and efficiency the servants and not the masters of the people.

The problem of how to do this had never before even been recognized as a problem by any American government, much less attempted to be solved—never until this administration. No reasonable man could have expected on a March 4, 1933, a solution to spring armed cap-a-pie like Minerva from the brain of Zeus. But the problem had been fairly stated during the campaign and at least the principles of action had been laid down. The people expected (and they had a right to expect) action and they got it. But, as they got it, the President frankly told them that he was announcing no royal road to riches. Of the AAA he said: "It is an experiment." Of his policy in general he said that he was a quarterback and that his policy was to reach the goal but he would have to suit action unto occasion and could not possibly write the game chart in advance—and how he did get panned for that! It was just simple honesty and good horse sense.

Trial-and-error—it is the only possible formula for such a situation—unprecedented in any history. Yet for his brave frankness in saying what he would do, he was said to be like Columbus, who when he sailed didn't know where he was going, and when he arrived didn't know where he was, and when he got home didn't know where he had been. That was a good story, but nevertheless he *was* Columbus and he had *discovered a new world*. Without suffering grievous trial and many errors he never could have done so. When his mutinous crew of critics insisted that he had no course and his mate asked what to say, the poet thinks he said: "Why say, 'Sail on—sail on and on!'"

I know nothing of partisan politics, but—whatever may be the fate of the New Deal—I am sure of one thing: Franklin Roosevelt has taught our people that this country does belong to them! Never again will powerful groups control it. The pendulum may swing back and forth, but it will never again seem to come to a dead stop at an angle 45% away from straight up and down. The Liberty League was hatched in the wrong nest. The political as well as the geographical center of the United States is moving westward. America is on its way to pure democracy with a small "d."

If the people are to progress with a wider participation in benefits and a more intelligent functioning of the improved mass mind there must be unity and powerful purpose and these are infrequent in democracies. They are possible only when two essentials are present—a pretty unanimous popular conviction, and a leadership toward which it can turn. That happened once in the war, when the aspiration was to quench a conflagration which was consuming the youth of all nations and the leader was Woodrow Wilson, an apostle of peace, and yet, when occasion came, the greatest lord of war who ever trod the earth.

The conviction now is that it is time to take a nation half

destitute—out of what the President once called—*four years of economic hell.* The leader is as well fitted for this task as Wilson was for war—a cheerful, kindly, intensely human man, who has descended into the shadows and fought with beasts at Ephesus, and come forth smiling, soul unscathed—an inspiration to every man who has wondered why—blameless—the modest fruit of all his efforts should be swept away—and he, wholly helpless to prevent it, must sit and suffer hopelessly. The appearance of the right man at the right time has happened before in our history so often as to give point to a favorite theme of high-school oratory, *"The eternal stars shine out when it is dark enough."*

Once it was Washington. Once it was Jefferson. Once it was Andrew Jackson. Once it was Lincoln. Once it was Woodrow Wilson—and now it is Franklin Roosevelt.

There is no use trying to trace the silver thread that ties these great men together. Times change and necessities differ. What was good for the agrarian America of older days is probably entirely inappropriate to this mad age of whirring machinery, but this single thing seems clear—that we are effecting the purpose and judgment of a great champion of the mass of men —that where he leads in this crisis in the world's affairs, we ought to support him, for thus—and not otherwise—are human ends attained.

What we are trying to do is to bring this country out of an economic hypochondria, into its proper heritage of material health and it could be done easily if every man would do his part. We will have to do it desperately, if any considerable number hold back either through lack of faith or in the selfish hope that they can evade taking the burdens that are their legitimate portions and so profit by the patriotism of others. There is no group strong enough to block the effort of the nation as long as it remains a national effort. That at least was my opinion and that was why I extended myself to make the Blue Eagle a universal symbol.

The doctrine was, first of all, a doctrine of action. The plan was based on the proposition that American people can do anything, if they are only provided with the means to do it. It was something of the idea of the man who when asked whether he thought Andrew Jackson would go to heaven answered: "He will if he wants to."

The greatest service NRA could do was to restore hope and confidence. Through the Blue Eagle it tried to give people something definite that they could do and hope for, and instead of leaving them helpless under the bludgeoning of a great disaster, to show them how they could act together to fight it. That is a human value which cannot be drawn on any chart but it ought to be the very greatest element of Recovery. Napoleon said, speaking of the efficiency of armies: "The moral is to the physical as three is to one." When he took the tattered and dispirited Revolutionary troops up into the Alps they were a starving rabble. But he showed them Italy. Within ten days after his first Italian campaign opened they began destroying one splendid Austrian army after another until they had beaten six times their own numbers with never a defeat. That is what we could do if somebody could just convincingly show us Italy. I thought we had done that in the autumn of 1933—I still believe it would have worked if we could have enjoyed any continued unity of action. It is far from being too late yet.

All the pieces in the jig-saw puzzle of prosperity are certainly here now except two or three. Here are warehouses bursting with all good things. Here are the finest factories in the world. Here is a solvent country with abundant credit and an almost perfect mechanical system for communication, transportation, and the exchange of goods and services. Here is a fine, couragcous, willing, and unselfish people, in a land teeming with resource, and we have seen the assembled picture of which these jig-saw pieces are parts. We could have put them together long ago but for the missing pieces of—faith in ourselves, confidence in our future, belief in our institutions and the leadership at the head of them. What we need above all is to develop an unfailing willingness to accept the burdens necessary to attain the benefits received.

A study of the alleged faults of NRA will reveal one single human frailty in each complaint—a wish to retain its benefits and a plea to avoid its burdens. Almost every class is in some manner benefited. Very few say: "Away with the whole thing." But there is hardly a group which for the benefit they receive are wholly willing to accept the accompanying burden.

I must here confess my faith in a principle not yet too clear in the New Deal—a principle without which I think all the rest is sounding brass and tinkling cymbals.

I think the profit motive is the basis of all human incentive. I think a squirrel and an ant hoard and that if you destroy safety against an evil day and the American homilies of thrift, hard work, and self-dependence, you destroy everything for which we have fought in this country.

But I agree that these fundamentals were intended for all men and that we cannot permit them to be prostituted for the benefit of the few. Prosperity here only awaits the assurance that frugality and hard work are the lot of every man and that their benefits will not be dissipated by any invention. That is the essence of the American system and, if I thought it were in danger, I would defend it with all my heart.

The friends of the New Deal outnumber its enemies by many thousands to one. But the few enemies have advantages. They are powerful and they do not scatter their shot. They want just one thing, and they know exactly what they want—to scuttle the Recovery Program, make the Blue Eagle walk the plank, hoist the Jolly Roger on the Ship of State, and sail back to the good old piracy that brought the crash of 1929 and all that has happened since—and I must say with regret that just now they are making excellent progress.

With the numerical odds so hopelessly against them—with the wreckage created by their leadership still smoking, there is a temptation to ignore them. But there *is* one way in which they can succeed—the old Napoleonic strategy of "Divide and Conquer"—split the friends of Recovery into small quarreling groups and then absorb each one in detail.

NRA can succeed only if a very great majority of the people and of business not only want it, but actively support it. Therefore it is necessary for it to be understood. You have to have some such symbol as the Blue Eagle, through which its friends can act vigilantly in their own interest. The government refuses to buy except under the Blue Eagle. Most of our people at first refused to buy except under the Blue Eagle and one Blue Eagle industry can refuse to buy from any industry which is not also under the Blue Eagle. That device was effective enough to secure the benefits of the plan to business, labor, and the people. I fear it has begun to lag and I must say if that fails, NRA is finished.

The designing leaders of the opposition know this. It forms the basis of their strategy to "divide and conquer." They don't like the Blue Eagle principally because it does give the

THERE'S LOTS OF MISSIONARY WORK YET TO BE DONE.

people wider control of economic forces. The essence of their political faith has always been that the people must take what these leaders choose to give them. The essence of the Recovery Program is the exact reverse of that and there is not enough room in the whole country for these two policies to live side by side. The methods of these leaders almost wrecked our economic structure and the issue now comes to this: Either they will take back their ancient privilege of doling out what they please of our resources and opportunities or our people will keep control. They will succeed if these leaders find a way to force the vast mass of beneficiaries of NRA apart by playing upon the discontent of separate groups.

That is the great danger. If we are to rely upon a whole people to support a law, that law must please nearly all of them. No law can do that completely. With every benefit there come burdens and therein lies the chance to "divide and conquer." Unless the friends and beneficiaries of NRA are willing to take the bitter with the sweet, they are risking all that they have gained under the Recovery Program.

When I left NRA there was not one of the industries under codes which would willingly give up its code. Labor would not like to surrender its position under the law.

Except at the very heart of the opposition leadership, not even enemy spokesmen ever suggested abolition of NRA and the codes. But (alas!) here the great national concert of purpose falters. Codified industry, organized labor, farmers and consumers, all sing the same song in varying words: "Keep NRA but cut out its objectionable features"; "Keep the codes but cut out their restrictions"; "Keep Section 7a of the Act, but impose no responsibility on labor." These complaints do not mean the same thing when spoken by any two particular groups. In nearly every case "objectionable features," "restrictions," et cetera, all simply mean "burdens" and the slogans all reduce to the same thing. "Roses without thorns" and "Something for nothing."

Of course that is impossible. The best we can do is to balance burdens and benefits equally so that the net result is good. That was the job of NRA. But, however fair the result may be, if these groups are not content with fair burdens, then the defense of NRA is wide open to every one of these assaults.

NRA has been the first to insist on continuous improvement in its first tentative steps. Any man who for a moment could expect within a few months practically to reorganize the greatest industrial unit in time or space and not make mistakes expects a miracle. But the way to cure faults in the codes is not by statute. Not by strikes against codes—not through the courts—but through NRA itself. This is because, under the law, if NRA makes a mistake, the President can and will change it within 24 hours. The other methods either take months and years or end in bloodshed and riot.

Very early in NRA a partisan leader of the Old Deal—a professional friend of the farmer whose political record on farm legislation shows that he can "crook the pregnant hinges of the knee where thrift may follow fawning" began to rage through the farm-lands with the charge that NRA would hurt the farmer. It is just not true of the final result. It did increase the price of some things the farmer bought, but by nowhere near the amount of the benefit he received both from the enrichment of his domestic market and from other aspects of the Recovery Program. Yet, at a very critical period in the life of NRA this wedge was thrust in between NRA and a large part of the Mississippi Valley. The burden the farmer was asked to bear was infinitesimal compared with the benefit which was being given to him to help bear it. Yet farmers were asked (and some were persuaded) by refusing the slight burden of NRA to align themselves on the side of the enemies of the Recovery Program and to range against all that has been done for them by taking the part of men who for twelve years have coldly refused them the slightest relief from old political policies which have almost destroyed them.

Another example is the attack on NRA, by saying that it "oppresses the Little Fellow." That too has been discussed in this book. It has been proved that in so far as there is Little Fellow trouble due to higher wages, both Little Fellows and Big Fellows have been burdened, but this country has got to continue employment and maintain wages or sink back into a worse depression. The benefit of living wages comes to the whole country and the Little Fellow has been literally snatched from destruction by other fair-trade provisions of the codes. He should be the last to complain of the slight burden of living wages.

At the beginning of NRA, a deputation of presidents of certain great chain variety stores, one of which at least depended on sweating of both suppliers and employees, sat at my desk, imploring relief from the $12-40-hour week. In a quavering voice one multi-millionaire said: "But don't you realize that you are driving us Little Fellows out of business?" They were "Little Fellows" because they run little stores—thousands of little stores. It was too much for me. It was even too much for them and the windows rattled with everybody's laughter. But it is not too much for these enemies of NRA.

Yet this charlatan Little Fellow propaganda has fooled some people, aroused some opposition to NRA and again justified the strategy of "Divide and Conquer"—benefits without burdens.

It is arrant buncombe based on partisan desire to wreck NRA. The only attraction I find in it is the awe we all have for supreme achievement. Even Dr. Cook carved his niche in the Hall of Fame when Admiral Peary came back and proved Cook's discovery of the Pole a fraud. Dr. Cook had not reached the Pole but he was not without distinction. He had told the biggest whopper in history. He had displaced Ananias, Baron Munchausen, and all romancers in sacred or profane writ. Our political Little Fellows also achieve merit. They have dramatized the greatest nonsense in the world.

Absurd as is all this—the perversion of the Consumer situation really caps the fantastic structure of the "Benefits without Burdens"—"Division and Conquest." The argument runs this way: NRA spreads work by shortening hours, and it raises the cost of living and therefore NRA is bad for the consumer.

But we are *all* consumers. The great majority of consumers are wage earners. If 14,000,000 potential wage earners are unemployed and many more are on half wages, they can consume little or nothing. As consumers, they should not complain of a plan that restores their jobs and raises their wages. Yet the claim here is that, in doing this, NRA is *hurting* consumers. In other words a man (in his rôle as a consumer) should oppose a plan which (in his rôle as a wage earner) is enabling him to consume at all. This carries the enemy strategy of "Divide and Conquer" to heights that make the senses stagger. It divides a man against himself. He is to be a New Dealer when he produces but an Old Dealer when he consumes—he is to have all of the benefits but nothing at all of the burdens.

It can't be done. You can't have your cake and eat it. Of course the Recovery Program must not be permitted to increase the cost of living as fast as it increases the people's power to purchase and consume. That has not happened yet, and there is not one word of truth in statements that it has happened.

The epidemic of strikes is not without this aspect of benefits without burdens. Quite apart from organization, bargaining, and strikes, more has been done for labor, simply by the Administration of NRA and the formation of codes and agreements, than has been done in any similar period of time. Too little attention has been paid to the benefits of unorganized labor. This Administration is charged to keep open the path to complete organization of labor, but it is charged equally, by the law, with the welfare of unorganized labor, which is by far the majority of workers. NRA did more in six months for both organized and unorganized labor than all the labor organizations ever did in all the previous history of this country. In the record of this critical time, history will never forget what Franklin Roosevelt did. In every important early labor dispute, while the technique was being developed, he set aside all other affairs of the nation and, in his most crowded days, sat patiently, hour after hour, with labor and industrial leaders, personally familiarizing himself with the problem to insure that the rights of both sides under the law were fully assured. These were all benefits from NRA—the only burden imposed by that Act is a modicum of patience and forbearance. Workers ought seriously to consider this, when advised to rush recklessly into the waste and wreckage of a wide-spread strike—especially when there is a peaceful way to the redress of grievances.

Industries fight for every ounce of benefit included in the codes. But I know of some which have used every device from tricky evasion to forthright resistance to escape the burdens of Section 7a. And I know of many who attack NRA because Section 7a is there at all or not treated as a dead letter. They regard 7a as a burden. But if they take the benefits, they should accept the burden. If Section 7a is a burden, it is part of the bargain they made in their extremity to save themselves a year and a half ago.

Non-compliance! Dereliction of statutory duties—it is not just a misdemeanor—it is failure to *play the game in a great national crisis.*

It is the same old story: "Take the benefits but avoid the burdens." It permits the enemies of Recovery to "divide and conquer"—it threatens the whole program. Needless, unwarranted, if not lawless, resistance to the statutory rights of labor by management—needless, unwarranted use of extreme weapons by labor when there are so many effective alternatives at hand—it is just another aspect of the same thing—the kind of thing that constitutes the greatest danger to the recovery program and the whole New Deal. Like farmers, like "little fellows," like consumers—both management and workers also must give something when they take something. They also must play the game.

We have the group already discussed who favor NRA, but who say: "Oh, NRA is a wonderful social advance but it promoted monopoly. The Anti-Trust Laws should remain in full effect right alongside of NRA. Industry cannot be permitted self-regulation under codes.

If the government itself is to have the benefits, during the emergency, of an almost complete supervision of a planned economy, it cannot, at the same time, avoid the burden—if burden it be—of a considerable latitude of industrial self-government and self-regulation under strict federal supervision.

I have tried to cover in this chapter what experience has shown to be the chief danger to NRA—the reluctance of benefited groups to assume burdens with benefits, the possible loss of necessary solidarity, through the aid thus given enemies through group discontents to destroy in detail what they would not even dare to attack on a solid front.

They have gone far with such slogans as: "The whole Recovery program is actually retarding recovery." "Take off the brakes," etc. "Take off the brakes" means "Back to 1928."

This country simply cannot do that. 1928 was pregnant with the disaster of 1929. Mr. Hoover announced a theory. It was obviously wrong when he announced it and it was proved wrong within the year. There was no employment for many millions of people then except work paid for by expanded credit that was of no more substance than the outer air. He, himself, stated and proved that our only hope to continue to employ millions and maintain industry was to lend bankrupt countries the money to pay for our unmanageable surplus production of everything from wheat to automobiles. That was no reliance at all. The real substantial underlying facts were almost as menacing then as now. The New Deal may be wrong in some important particulars but it is surely right in some others. We should learn by experience which is the only way such things can be learned. We should discard what is bad and retain what is good and eventually know how to master and control this over-capacitated under-consuming economic machine of ours. Before we follow old leaders back to the methods practiced in 1928, let us recall exactly what those methods were:

1. They permitted child labor and resisted change.
2. They had a system which exploited agriculture to the verge of ruin for the benefit of certain industries or industrial areas and they refused relief—even food—to farmers *but they did feed hogs.*
3. They successfully prevented labor organization and collective bargaining on any but a limited front, and they almost succeeded in destroying that.
4. They permitted the operations of banking to become a racket and omitted to do anything to make the people's savings safe from the rapacity of the trustees of these funds.
5. They permitted operations of the Stock and other Exchanges to proceed like gaming tables and never turned a hand to warn our people that investments there were like bets against the turn of loaded dice.
6. They permitted operations of the bond market (which should have been a very "holy of holies" of investment security) to become a sort of glorified casino with all percentages in favor of the dealer, and in loans to bankrupt countries, they actually invited economic innocents to the slaughter as a means of sustaining prosperity.
7. They made never a move to maintain wages, to preserve the purchasing power of wages, or to adjust employment to available work by shortening hours to the end of preserving jobs.
8. They flatly denied any direct responsibility of government to relieve human suffering in the day of economic disaster.
9. They discouraged every move toward old age, or unemployment, or disability relief.
10. They permitted corporations—especially in the utility fields—to turn words into capital stock and to sell it to people at values which could earn only at rates and charges out of all proportion to the service rendered.

11. They omitted to interfere in competitive practices which could only result in eventual monopoly, present starvation wages, unconscionable hours of labor, and constantly increasing unemployment. And they preserved without change the archaic Anti-Trust Laws under which these destructive practices were actually fostered.

12. They insisted on a monetary and debtor system which made dollars so dear and relief so difficult that the mountains of debts incurred under that system threatened to enslave the whole people.

That is what they want to go back to and that is what the beneficiaries of the present program will aid them to get, if we do not bear the minor burdens imposed, for the sake of the greater benefits received.

Let us live up scrupulously to the obligations of the law, the codes and the agreements. If they are wrong—and some of them are wrong—let us speed their change promptly and justly. Let us aggressively and faithfully support the Blue Eagle. Let us accept our rights moderately and our burdens fairly. Let us play the game. Let us do our part. And above all, let us not go back.

# Chapter XXVIII

# NRA WARS AND RUMORS OF WARS

---

"What the government of Athens needs is a good delousing station."
—*Unknown Greek author of very ancient but indeterminate date.*

---

I was fairly well acquainted with the whole corps of Washington correspondents during the war and much better acquainted with the present group. I don't know whether it was the war atmosphere, and the strong cohesion of government itself under war conditions, or whether it is a most astonishing improvement in technique—but, as between the trying for anything that would make news by that old crowd, and the literal *excavation of it* by the new, there is about the comparison that exists between a gimlet or a brad-awl and a dynamite gang with a battery of five-ton steam shovels. I honestly believe that nothing of importance goes on in the Capital that they do not know it as soon as it starts—and usually as soon as somebody begins thinking about it.

A favorite method is for one man to come to you and say: "There is some pretty bad stuff coming out of AAA about you and NRA"; and so—"bzz-bzz-bzz"—never anything definite —never any names. And if in comment or discussion you let anything pass your teeth of either a controversial or even argumentative nature—the trick has been done. Back hot-foot to AAA etc. "You really ought to hear Johnson on such-and-such"—something definite now and a name to use and thereafter—back and forth like a shuttle. Pretty soon a fabric has been woven which, with at least some faint color, can be headlined "*Wallace and Johnson in Big Rift.*"

Multiply the possibilities of that by several scores of subordinate officials in both administrations. Combine and permutate it as between officials in the *same* administration (which leads to such headlines as: "NRA torn with strife") and some idea can be gathered of the source of most of the unsettling

366

and disturbing news stories and the labyrinthine whispering gallery which Washington is today.

During the first year of NRA I was unequivocally alleged to have had hot controversies with:

The President,
Attorney-General Cummings,
Secretary Morgenthau,
Secretary Ickes,
Secretary Wallace,
Secretary Roper,
Madam Secretary Perkins,
Budget Director Douglas,
Administrator Hopkins,
Administrator Peek,
Assistant Secretary Roosevelt,
Assistant Secretary Tugwell,
And dozens of other officials.

As a matter of fact, and during the period stated, the only one of these officials with whom I had even had so much as a few tart words was George Peek and he and I had been having them for seventeen years—whenever we wanted to. It has come to a pretty pass if you have to give up such a time-mellowed habit of soul-satisfying shindies with your best and oldest friends. As to the rest, right up to the very end no unkind word was ever passed. With Secretaries Cummings, Morgenthau, Roper, Tugwell, and Henry Roosevelt and Lew Douglas there was never a spoken difference of opinion. Harry Hopkins and I had a little tiff in the hall one day that was my fault and although Henry Wallace and Rex Tugwell probably did not agree with me on some questions of policy, it never was the subject of quarrel or controversy.

I say this to remove the false idea that NRA was a sort of stormy petrel of the New Deal so far as wars or even saber-rattling are concerned. But I do not say this to create an equally false idea that NRA lay in a nest of eiderdown within the New Deal, or indeed within the Administration itself. It didn't and, so far as I am concerned, it would have been far better to have had a few robust rows than to try to carry the load beset by phantom and nameless opposition such as I had outside, and—in the last few months—inside NRA.

I never had to cope with that before in my life. I couldn't do it if I had to. It doesn't exist in the Army. It did not exist in the Administration of the Draft, or the Mobilization of Industry under the War Industries Board, or in any industrial company with which I ever had dealings. To the extent that aptitude or training for playing that game is necessary to whoever heads NRA, I was utterly unqualified for the job.

We began to plan NRA and to sketch out its organization in two ante-rooms to Ray Moley's office in the State Department. Even before the Act was passed this became impossible. Visitors waiting for interviews had to sit in rows around the walls of the same room in which important and sometimes confidential conferences were taking place. It was Bedlam and all thinking and writing had to be done at night.

I asked for temporary quarters and got several bays or stalls in the Commerce Building which, I veritably believe, is the worst-planned and least efficient modern office building in the world. These were small steel alcoves opening on a common corridor like nothing so much as the pay toilet in the Union station. A vast press of work was upon us and it was becoming very clear what the organization would eventually look like, what space and arrangement it would need, and how its various Departments would be grouped.

There was an ideal building for this purpose in the Old Post Office Building at 7th and F streets. I was familiar with that building because it was there that I had done the biggest job of my life—the Selective Draft—and I knew just how NRA would fit in there. I got a promise from the Committee that was then allocating space that we could have it. Whiteside donated his lay-out experts from Dun & Bradstreet. I took the principal members of our staff down to look it over and we were getting ready to move when, without any consultation with or advice to me, I got orders to stay where I was. Why, I do not know. It may seem a very little thing, but in my opinion it was one of the greatest handicaps we had to bear. From that day to this NRA has never been housed in a manner that encouraged efficiency—people crowded into rooms so closely that business could be carried on neither in privacy nor health nor comfort—cognate departments housed in different parts of town and in no less than seven buildings—constant shifts of rooms, equipment, and personnel until the search for a department you may have visited last week in one place

would take you to three or four places. It was this that gave
NRA a constant appearance of haste and confusion.

I have mentioned the Cabinet Board under which NRA
at first tried to function and have tried to make it clear that
I am not criticizing a single member of that Board. They were
appointed to that duty and they did it. But I am very sure
that Cabinet officers, each with his own Department to run,
cannot sit in judgment, singly or jointly, on the acts of another
absolutely new department, working furiously on a thing of
such new intendments and such wide and all-inclusive operation as NRA. They felt that they had to edit all the orders and
regulations that NRA might publish and they actually proposed to pass on the validity and substance of all codes. Of
course that came from unfamiliarity with the nature and extent
of our work but I was put in the peculiarly unpleasant position
of "wanting to be a dictator," or "a prima donna," or "not
coöperating" if I pointed out that we could not possibly do the
work assigned to us on any such formula. I resisted that. I
had to resist.

This did not make for unity of action. The head of PWA
and AAA sat in the NRA Board but the head of the NRA
Board had nothing to do with the PWA or the AAA Board.
Integration was impossible on this formula, the effect if not
the purpose of which was repression.

I laid claim to no place in the official hierarchy. I was perfectly willing to be less than the dust beneath anybody's
chariot wheels. I repeatedly said that I had neither political
nor personal ambition and I certainly conducted myself as
though I meant it. I pride myself that during my entire administration of NRA I never made one concession to expediency for political or personal reasons. But I did want to be
given an opportunity to do the job. I did not want to interfere
with anybody else and I did not want anybody else to interfere
with me. I do not mean that I objected to coördination—I was
the constant exponent of it. I recommended and insisted on it
over and over again to the very end. I urged the formation of
Frank Walker's Council, pledged him my willingness as far as
NRA was concerned to abide by any decision he might make
and to support him to the limit and then, in our intimate
friendly conferences, chided him for not making more use of
his authority.

No other Administration or Department ever asked me to do anything that I did not do or to refrain from doing anything that I did not cease—nor did any other Department or official of any other Department ever ask me to sail on any other course than the one NRA took or protest or admonish or seek to counsel with me about varying views that they might have. It would have been far better if there had been more of that.

I realized that I was hitting pretty hard in frequent speeches and I asked more than once if I was doing anything that I ought not to do, or omitting anything that I ought to do, or talking too much or too vehemently, but I was always encouraged to go on as I was going.

The NRA Board went out when the National Emergency Council came in. That was the first attempt to get something in the direction of coördination among the various sprawling massive administrative efforts but it did not do it. It was a large meeting held in the Cabinet Room. The meetings consisted of reading the minutes of the last meeting and then the mimeographed weekly reports to all the government agencies. Some were long—three or four thousand words—and some were not. I have been severely criticized because mine merely recited the status of code making and any outstanding events on a half sheet of foolscap. I could have written much longer ones, indeed I could have composed a weekly thriller on the serial system, for things were certainly moving in NRA those days. But all these reports had been circulated to everybody the day before. I suppose everybody had done as I had and read them all. Whether or not this is so they, or summaries of them, were read again by Mr. Walker. Then such as desired to do so talked. I never saw a real question of major importance arise until toward the end of each of these meetings when the President came in, usually for about fifteen minutes. From that moment, things would begin to happen. He asked searching questions, gave brief but clear instructions about anything he had in his mind and generally displayed himself as the leader he is.

The Executive Council was a little different. The President himself nearly always attended that. It was smaller and, being vitalized by his presence, more was brought out and more accomplished. But it did not ring the bell of coördination. It too was too large. It never had a pre-arranged agenda that would have brought fundamental conflicts and policies to the surface and it left the situation about where it was before.

As related before, Mr. Richberg had asked me to do all that I could to bring him in contact with the President, saying that he did not intend to interfere with NRA but had high aspirations for a great appointive office, and I suggested Mr. Richberg to the President to serve during Frank Walker's absence. Frank Walker had to take a long leave of absence to attend to his own affairs. Still feeling the crying need of coördination especially among AAA, NRA, PWA, FERA, FTC, and the Department of Labor, I suggested the Industrial Emergency Committee composed of the heads of these administrations, and that Mr. Richberg be also made Executive Secretary of that. This was done and here, I believe, we shall either see some real action, or else it will break up in a riot of *primæ donnæ*— which, of course, is a possibility.

But I am getting away ahead of the story of wars and rumors of wars on the NRA front.

After the merger of the Recovery Board with the Emergency Council, I expected a period of comparative calm on the NRA front.

Mr. Richberg was very restless, telling me from time to time that his private affairs were going to make it necessary for him to resign and, once again becoming quite disturbed over some complaint that messages and orders had been sent directly by me to people in the organization not "through channels." I found that there were little flots of complaint about this stirred up by somebody.

As to not "going through channels" there were emergencies wherein I had to act and act at once. "*Through channels*" is a military expression connoting the old War Department red tape system, which before it was cleaned up was a fearful and wonderful thing. I tried to avoid such terms and methods in NRA because people were too apt to say that I was a Top Sergeant anyway. But here it came back to haunt me with reverse English. Yet if criticism of NRA method were to be put on that ground, I think I knew more about how the old Army game worked than anybody around NRA. And, with all I know of it, this was the first time I ever heard that a Commanding Officer (if so it must be put) could not give an order on the spot, on his own responsibility, and without consulting half a dozen staff officers and passing it through half a dozen hands. The present paralysis of NRA is due in part to the adoption of a system that, before its abolition, cursed the army for a century—no decision, no responsibility and a continuous passing of the buck from Dan to Beersheba.

The instances of this were few, of no importance and far between but they were used by some Absalom at the gates as a constant irritant to create dissatisfaction within and complaint outside the organization and to put weapons in the hands of enemies. I did not know that then, but I know it beyond peradventure now.

Some of these incidents seem so petty that I am ashamed to write them. But the fact is that these small things were constantly churned to a harassing froth which kept the organization in uneasiness and some turmoil and gave rise to almost daily newspaper stories about dissension and confusion.

There was a constant story that my ante-office had too much authority in dealing with visitors and requests for action, rulings, and decision. We had in our outer office one of the most courteous and able receptionists in Washington—Mr. Reiman. He remained in that job for the love of it and of me. He had been an important industrialist himself—the full peer of several of our divisional administrators. I offered him the office of deputy several times, but he declined the larger dignity and salary and the higher-sounding title because he knew, as I knew, that his position was of great importance even if it carried no title, and that he would be difficult to replace.

We tried to rid the Administrators' Staff of the insolence of office, and to see that people got taken care of promptly and courteously, and I have heard of very few instances where such was not the case.

Miss Robinson, my Administrative Assistant, often disposed of calls where she could do so to the satisfaction of the applicant—never otherwise. And she never did anything without my specific consent or, if it were an emergency, without reporting it to me at once. I had tried half a dozen people in these general outside contact places with such unfortunate results and so much complaint that when Mr. Reiman and Miss Robinson gradually absorbed this work, I backed them up. There was some complaint about this but it was not from the public whom we were charged to serve.

There is not room here to tell of the thousands of attempts to put something over on NRA that were caught in the outer office. Here's one that wasn't: At one time I was told that a man (not in NRA but with whom I frequently chatted) actually collected a fee in this fashion. A case was up in NRA for change in a Reëmployment Agreement which the client had signed. "Why that's a cinch," said this slicker. "Hugh and I are just like this (and he crossed his fingers). I'll fix that for you this very morning. He'll be coming through this hotel lobby on his way to the office in a few minutes." According to this story, I did come through almost at once with my two dogs on a leash to give them an airing. I was accosted by my first name and accompanied to the door, and even out on the sidewalk—laughing and talking about nothing at all. The PRA change went through in ordinary course and without a hitch, being one of a class in which such changes were allowed as a matter of policy—a process very ably and swiftly handled by Bob Stevens—*and the fee was collected.*

I can't vouch for the truth of this second-hand story, but I have been told very circumstantially of people who came to NRA to serve close to me—who told other officials just to "leave it to them" to get something that had been turned down by me. But little of that kind of thing got past my Administrative Assistant. I often had to sign papers without reading them—merely asking the proponent what was in them. In nine cases out of ten she caught this stuff, when it was wrong, before it went to mail or record. Instances of blunders in the terrific weight of correspondence from my office were almost non-existent. Miss Robinson is the best person I have ever seen in that sort of work. She was so nearly indispensable to me that I could not have done the work I did without her.

Away back in September, 1933, I left NRA in the hands of a small committee when I went to Detroit to get the Automobile Code. When I returned what I found convinced me of what I already knew, that committees are fine for counsel, but not worth a continental for action—the old Army aphorism that a Board is something long, narrow, wooden, and full of splinters. I made up my mind that I would never do that again.

Along about May, 1933, some protesting friends who have been since disclosed as something less than loving began coming to me saying with singular and pertinacious persistency and *co-*

*hesion:* "Hugh, you need a rest. Just put NRA in the hands of a committee and go away and hide yourself for a month. We'll see that it rocks along." Rumors began to come to me of casual meetings *outside of NRA* to discuss the same project which I was finally to hear at the White House after months of this persistent effort.

Some of these people even went to Bernie Baruch with the same suggestion. He warned me against the committee idea as an executive factor in NRA, although we had both talked of a Board something like a Board of Directors to determine policy —not to execute it—and I thereafter formally recommended something of that kind. Bernie also constantly warned me against leaving NRA in the hands of the "committee" protagonists when I was absent.

Late in the spring of 1934, Mr. Richberg came to me again and said he thought I still harbored some thought that he was scheming to get control of NRA. He said he thought so because when he had made the last of many statements that he *must* resign about June 30, and could not possibly consider staying longer, that I had received the suggestion complacently instead of protesting as I always had before.

Why he should have felt that I thought he was so scheming is beyond me. In the first place, there was nothing that I hid from that man of either my personal or my official troubles. I had a genuine affection for him before we had worked together a month. While he had never been charged with any responsibility except giving advice I let him act for me in a more confidential relation than anybody else. I had no secrets from him and I trusted him as I would have trusted my own brother. I liked his society in the very few chances we had to sit down and talk about things far removed from NRA—of people we had known years before or of incidents that we knew about in common. I had even talked about practising law with him after our work should be done.

I never lost an opportunity to praise him or to advance his interests. I had never suspected him of any such things as a desire to change NRA or control it, and being in my full confidence, he had known, for a long time, that I could remain with NRA for only a little while longer. My resources were being rapidly exhausted. There was illness in my family and as I confirmed in the let-down after my resignation, my own clock was running down. I had confided all this to him with the utmost freedom—I again reassured him that I suspected him of no attempt to control NRA and again it passed from my mind.

On June 26th, I submitted to the President my thoughts on reorganization of NRA in order that he might have it on his trip to Hawaii. Shortly after this, on June 30th, the Industrial Emergency Committee was formed at my suggestion. This consisted of Secretaries Perkins and Ickes, Administrators Hopkins and Johnson and Mr. Richberg as Executive Secretary. It was intended to work out at last some real coördination among emergency efforts. About that time the President had a talk with me—a very affectionate conversation in which he said he wished I would go away for a vacation while he was gone to Hawaii, and leave NRA to any temporary set-up I desired. (No committee was proposed.) I told him about my engagement in San Francisco and several other places and said that I would take my mother to the Colorado Mountains after that trip and try my best to get a rest. Mr. Richberg was going away too. I was looking forward to some real relaxation. The President said that he thought very well of my suggestions about reorganization of NRA but to my suggested resignation, waved his hands and said: "Later perhaps, but not now."

On July 2nd, the President wrote me one of the kindest notes a man could receive from another one, telling me that he and I and some others had been too close to the forest to see the trees and making it quite specific that I should go away for a month and not come back unless it should prove absolutely necessary. He said that he wanted me to get in racing trim to carry on with him to the close. I was very much affected by that truly genuine token of friendship and made up my mind that, in spite of all my apprehensions about staying away too long from NRA, I would stay for a month as he wished, regardless of anything else—and because so evidently he did wish it.

I left Washington on July 11th, intending a leisurely trip with only a few speaking engagements. It was fearfully hot. We did not fly high enough, got our engine over-heated and had to go back from a point half-way between Laramie and Omaha. It was at the height of the great drought. I had often flown over the Mississippi Basin but I had never seen it like this. The seared checkerboard of ruined fields and the yellow and white sandy ribbons of such parched streams as the North Platte with dense dust clouds rolling across them left no doubt of the distress of the whole shriveled Valley. After three days we picked up the snow-top of Mount Hood—*150 miles away*, and finally came down at Portland.

That is where I got my first sight of the general strike on the Pacific Coast, but I still was determined to have no more to do with strikes. I made a speech at Portland commending settlement to the President's Longshoremen's Board and left there hoping to renew acquaintance with many old friends in San Francisco and not to do anything else. Though I did not then suspect it, events at San Francisco, all of which have been previously related, were really the beginning of the end of NRA.

# Chapter XXIX

# THE LAST ROUND-UP

---

"Gonna saddle ol' Paint for the las' time an' ride."
—*The Last Round-up.*

---

I HAVE just reread (November 15) a complete file of two great Metropolitan dailies and of the Washington papers from June to October, 1934. That was the period in which the reorganization of NRA and my departure therefrom occurred. During the latter part of August and the first part of September, I did not read the newspapers as they came out, because at the President's suggestion I was taking a vacation in as near complete seclusion as I could get and trying to erase NRA from my mind completely. It was then that the first part of this book was written. The other day a friend advised me to look at this publicity.

This rereading of the whole file shocked me for reasons which I shall state later on. Critical events which I considered so confidential that I would not even repeat them to my intimates found their way into the press in great detail—always colored by truth—never accurate in truth. Conversations, letters, and memoranda were reported in approximate accuracy but in versions seemingly designed to a single purpose which this narrative will make apparent.

I shall quote these conversations and memoranda only to the extent that accounts of them—not quite accurate—have been given by the press and published from one end of the country to the other—and then only to the extent necessary to correct departures from accuracy. No other course is compatible with my public responsibility.

My memorandum of June 26, 1934, in which I recommended a form of reorganization of NRA, including my own immediate elimination therefrom was excerpted in colorable exactness in the press. In precise form it was as follows:

1. *Code Making* is almost at an end. This required concentration of effort by a large and devoted organization. Something of a similar function on a reduced scale which we can call "Code Revision" will continue to be necessary and a permanent unit of organization will be required for that. It should be a small body of present employees who have shown themselves to be experienced and adept at Code Making.

2. *Code Administration* which is the supervision of organization of industries for self-government (Code Authority) and the participation and administration by government in all that they do, will require about the same form of organization as we now have for Code Making—that is, a grouping with subdivisions according to the grand divisions of industry, with further subdivisions of clusters of particular industries. This will involve simply a switching of function and not of organization.

All of the above is short and simple to state but it is of profound importance. The trouble with NRA was the hiatus between Code Making and Code Administration which after a good deal of study I had deliberately invoked but which incurred the danger of impairing the early working of the vast new machine. That has become a deadly serious matter but the suggestion in the preceding paragraph would have cured it. It has not been cured yet.

3. *Staff Functions* which are the technical services required for the old as well as the new phase should be served about as they are today, that is, with Divisions for Planning and Research, Law, Publicity, Office Administration, Review and Policy.

4. *The Three Separate Advisory Boards* should be merged into one Advisory Council, composed of nine members—three each for Management, Labor, and Consumers. Each of these groups of three may have such advisers and office staff as prove necessary.

5. *Labor Disputes* should be handled
   (a) (Initially) by Industrial Relations Boards in each of the great industries, with appeal to:
   (b) A National Labor Board which should also
   (c) Have jurisdiction over disputes in industries too small to have separate Industrial Relations Boards.

I cannot too strongly urge that all these Boards should be entirely impartial throughout their personnel and in all their circumstance. If they are not, nobody is going to submit their disputes without reservation. We shall simply have a continuation of existing unsatisfactory conditions. Also the idea of equal representation for management and labor, with one impartial member for government, is proved error. It simply puts every critical decision to the vote of one person. Finally, every appointment should be by the President.

This labor disputes organization should not be in NRA, but neither should it be under any control of the Department of Labor—that would be fatal because of the immediate and unanswerable charge—*Not Impartial*. It should be attached to the Department of Labor for use of facilities and administrative direction of "mechanical" personnel, but it must not be controlled, directed, or manned thereby. If it is it is sure to fail for the same reason that the Wagner Board was not altogether satisfactory.

I feel sure that my position on this point was right.

6. *Administrator. The permanent supervision of industry is not a one-man job.* There should be something comparable to a "Board of Directors" with a Chairman and a President, the latter to act as the executive for the Board—the Board to be selected from:

(*a*) The professions; Economics, Education, Law, Engineering.

(*b*) Industry; Outstanding and impartial leadership.

(*c*) Labor; Outstanding and impartial leadership.

These should be all of first rank and should all give full time. They should be appointed by the President and no one else. They should act as a High Court of Economic Relations and, subject to the President, pass finally on or create all NRA policy and be responsible to the President for all NRA policy and administration. A Board composed of persons with other direct government responsibilities outside of NRA will be worse than useless—a handicap and not a help—because the problems here are too complex and fundamental to expect their solution by less than intense concentration. It is very disheartening as well as ineffective to spend vital and extended effort on these vast problems and then have to submit the result to the judgment of people who have only a superficial knowledge of them.

Of course these remarks derived from experience with the old Cabinet Board.

7. *Present Conflicts.* This government must take a clean-cut decision between the theory of the Recovery Act—regulated com-

petition to support and stabilize wage rates—or the theory of the Federal Trade Commission Acts—absolutely uncontrolled competition in spite of wage rates. The two ideas cannot exist side-by-side without composition of some inherent conflicts. This is not as hard as it seems but it must be done at the earliest possible moment. At present NRA has not the support of the F.T.C. and neither has it the full support of the Department of Justice.

Mr. Richberg had undertaken to try to work out a *modus vivendi* on this absolutely vital point. It is not worked out. It is a stark conflict of essential principle. It must be composed in one way or another.

8. *Personnel. Application of the foregoing recommendations would shortly make superfluous the present Administrator, who will always be at your disposal in any capacity,* important or otherwise, as long as this emergency lasts, but who feels that the task of pioneering this great experiment is about over and that a different form of organization and method is more appropriate for the future problem.

9. *Time Limits.* Code making should be completed by September 1st and, in the meantime, the organization for Code Revision should be carved out of the present code-making units and what is left there should be shifted to Code Administration. Also during this period the "Board of Directors" or "Court of Economic Relations" should be determined upon and their executive selected so that, at about that time, the new method and form may start to act.

10. *What should not be done.* The foregoing supposes a unit (Code Authority) chosen by each major industry by a method approved by the President, for self-government of that industry, in accordance with its code. With each such control unit sits a government representative (with veto power but no vote) and, where necessary, with him, an adviser for each labor and consumers. This should be the dead-line beyond which control by industry should *not* go. In other words, it is recommended that there never be any over-head industrial council, composed of or selected by Code Authorities, or otherwise, which shall have any administrative or executive powers derived from NRA. That function must be jealously guarded by government.

This letter was not shown to Mr. Richberg until several days after it had been submitted. That was not intentional on my part. I just did not happen to have seen him for two or three days and I believe that I thought I had shown it to him until he told me in a chat in my office that it had been mentioned as having good stuff in it, but had not been shown to him.

I then got a copy for him and asked some of the younger men in the organization to give some study and thought during my absence to the principles therein expressed so that we could have something to work on upon my return about the middle of August.

At Waterloo, Iowa, I made a speech and adverted to the Hitler Massacre with horror. I had seen the results of Villa's summary executions in Mexico and I linked the two together. This, I understood, caused two diplomatic protests.

I have already related the circumstances of the settlement of the San Francisco general strike. I thought I was serving the interests of the whole administration and, as I have related, did nothing at all until I had communicated with both the White House and Madam Secretary Perkins. After settlement was under way, I was shown a newspaper clipping of several days before indicating that the Secretary had declined to comment on the strike except to say that the general strikers were just "bad boys." I have been told since that she expressed an opinion that employers themselves were responsible for it and that my settlement of it was "*undesirable.*" William Green of the A.F. of L. had condemned the strike vigorously. So, of course, had I. But even this little crossing of wires had not indicated to me then that I was doing anything objectionable to Madam Secretary because I thought she and I were such good friends that she would have told me in that case.

I made a speech at Los Angeles and I put my neck out again there because (while making it very clear that I was speaking for myself alone, and had no connection whatever with the political end of the Administration) I said that George Creel was a friend of mine, that he and I served in coördinate positions of responsibility during the war and that he had been State Director for NRA during my Administration. I said I knew him for an able and faithful public servant and that, if I had a vote, I would prefer him as governor to an unknown quantity in high public office such as Mr. Sinclair.

I had to fly immediately back to San Francisco to see about final reference of the Longshoremen's dispute to the President's

Board. The whole incident had taken up so much time and an engagement to speak at Chicago was now so near that the plan to rendezvous my scattered family in the Colorado Rockies did not seem very promising.

I went to San Diego and Tia Juana and Ensenada where I spent the time fishing and getting some real rest and exercise. From there I went to Okmulgee, Oklahoma, to visit my mother and, on August 2nd, arrived at Chicago to make a speech. The settlement of the stockyards strike was literally forced on me as has been earlier related. But that too apparently stirred up and kept the home fires burning as I was later to learn.

I had had only about ten days' vacation in my month's absence from Washington, and I made up my mind to rent a cottage on the Delaware Beach at Bethany where almost absolute seclusion is possible. There was serious illness in my family, and this time I could let nothing interfere with a real vacation.

While I was planning it I began to get some idea of what had happened. I found that the morale of the NRA organization had practically been destroyed during my absence. Everybody was uncertain. The rumor was rife that the whole policy of NRA was going to be changed and its entire personnel recast. Just at that time the press began to be filled with the disturbing kind of rumors and comment already mentioned. In the usual anonymous and impalpable fashion it was intimated to me that the sources of all this would be found somewhere in government itself—trial balloons. I could not put my finger on the center of infection, but the symptoms were unmistakable—the morale of NRA was literally shattered. Action slowed, died down, and almost ceased.

Mr. Richberg came to me just before I went away and practically demanded that I set up the Board I had mentioned in my memorandum of June 26, 1934, immediately, and before I left for Bethany. I told him that I had not yet selected the Board and would not recommend one until I had. He still insisted that I constitute a Board out of some of my staff, and when I said rather abruptly that I would not, he replied almost threateningly:

"You will get a lot of resignations of your principal officials at once if you don't."

I laughed and left him, but it gave me something to think about. Of course, it was not true and was proved *not* to be true, because I did not appoint that Board and there were no resignations. But the inescapable significance was *that he had been discussing these matters with somebody of my staff.* At this point it is appropriate to say that he knew next to nothing about administrative problems in NRA outside of its legal aspect and the Steel Code. He is responsible for neither the mistakes nor the accomplishments of NRA.

Now I have seen my work kicked over and been licked lots of times in my life in lusty combat in the light of day, and I think the record will show that I never winced or cried aloud. But no issue was ever made here on any policy or action. No one ever came to grips on any point except such things as whether a particular Department should be classified by the Budget Bureau as all others were, whether I should give instructions through one channel or another, and where this or that official should sit on the platform at the April round-up for criticism, when the President was to speak.

In this other field I am not even competent to fight. I think an official should give loyalty to those who work at his direction and I assume it in everybody close to me—to the extent that I couldn't even allow my own people to talk to me confidentially against one of their associates. Some of them began to try that in this very case late in 1933, but I would not entertain or credit it. Because of these activities NRA was frustrated and stalled during my absence—indeed from early August. It was stalled and it is still stalled. I shall not try to learn this sort of war. One of my first recollection is an old gospel hymn which fascinated me when I was a little boy. It has always haunted me. It has been out of print for a long time. I looked for it in old book shops for three or four years, and finally found it in *Gospel Hymnal No. 1.* It has as good a lift and tempo as any of Sousa's martial 4-4's. It ought to be revived and a copy of it pasted on the browband of the hat of every official who is charged with the duty of playing any part in a united effort. Quoting from tricky memory, the first verse runs:

### ONLY AN ARMOR-BEARER

Only an armor-bearer, proudly I stand;
Waiting to follow at the king's command.
Marching if "onward" shall the order be,
Standing by my Captain, serving faithfully.

Hear ye the battle cry,
Forward the call,
See, see the faltering ones,
Backward they fall.

Surely the Captain may depend on me,
Though but an armor-bearer I may be.

You can't get results in a great war like this without team work, and the philosophy of the armor-bearer is necessary to any team work in any aspect of human life.

The burden of the press conjectures, repeated day after day, during the period of my absence and which I have just read for the first time, was that Madam Secretary and Mr. Richberg were bombarding the President with plans of reorganization of NRA drawn up by them, which would put NRA under controls unsympathetic with what had been done and would face the policy of NRA squarely about. In other words, my plan of reorganization was intended to make NRA effective in its new *phase*. Their plan, according to these press rumors, seemed to intend to wreck the old NRA and start a new one.

Now not one word of this was said to me—by anybody. No plan of this kind was ever brought up for discussion. Mr. Richberg was even directly quoted later as saying that he had *never been* in disagreement with me on policy and I repeatedly said that I knew of no disagreement. Madam Secretary had never suggested any change of policy or method to me. I know from the President's frank talks with me that *he* had no such plans.

Of course that kind of publicity was more than enough not only to demoralize the NRA organization itself, but to kill the coöperation of business with NRA and the confidence of the public in NRA—all of which it duly and effectively did.

If, after a year of such effort and accomplishment as NRA had shown, I needed any justification for making these developments clear in this book, these facts and circumstances are ample and "if that be treason make the most of it."

The public is not interested in these personal squabbles, but it has a vital stake in NRA. As I have said in my preface, I regard NRA as a holy thing. I think it did more for millions of desperate people than all other emergency administrations combined. More important still, it was such a social and economic experiment as—once failing—can never be revived. I gave it everything a man can give without hope of reward or fear of consequence and with accurate and announced prevision of exactly what it would do to me.

I have not a single complaint of the fulfillment of that prophecy. I have been amply rewarded by a glorious adventure. But if I were willing to defend NRA in the open, I had a right to have it attacked in the open. Whether its policy under me was right or wrong I do not know. I only know that whereas it lived and was indeed vibrant with life—*now look at it.*

It was on August 18th, several days after his return from Hawaii, that I saw the President, although I had talked to him over the telephone. When I did see him I told him that, due to all the constant sniping, I thought it would be far better for him if we should complete the reorganization at once and let me resign. I had become a shining target for attack—which did not concern me but which was having a murderous effect on NRA and in part on the whole Recovery Program. I had become a sort of Arnold von Winkelried. I had expected that and it had its advantages. I was the person in the Administration best fitted to take it because I had no political possibilities, but now that I was convinced that this and other things had practically stopped NRA, it seemed clear that further continuation would do more harm than good. Also my own personal situation had reached a point where it seemed impossible to continue.

The President did not agree. He said very flatteringly: "I need you and the country needs you." He insisted that I stay until NRA organization was complete. I told him that the uncertainty that had been created in NRA during my absence required some kind of decision to be made at once to preserve a shattered morale, that the newspaper men were waiting for me, and that I would have to tell them something. As I understood him, he said to tell them I was to stay right where I was. The press reported that he had said practically the same thing to newsmen. But he added something that rather puzzled me and indicated to me powerful cross-currents working on NRA—that he would have to quiet Mr. Richberg and Madam Secretary down.

I went out to be swarmed over by newspaper men who seemed to know more about what was going on than I did. Indeed, before I was fully aware of what was up, my friend Charlie Berryman published in the Washington *Star* the cartoon on the following page.

The reporters had but one question—"Are you going out?"
I said:

"I guess my feet are nailed to the floor for the present. I am
not going to resign now."

That news reached NRA before I did. If there were any

BOARDERS, BE GOSH!

principal officials who were ready to resign if I did not at once
abdicate to a Board to be set up presumably by Mr. Richberg,
I do not know who they were. When I got back to my office
after the press announcement that I was to remain for the
present and until we could complete reorganization, I found it
full of NRA officials. The whole organization seemed to return
to life. Before that, it was so dead you could smell the faint
scent of Lilies of the Valley—I confirmed that feeling by a large
number of short interviews with principal Divisional administrators, who told me of the shocking condition of uncertainty
that had been created in my absence. I began vigorously to
plan a series of important moves to restore the morale which
had so obviously been shattered.

I went to the White House again on Monday as I had been requested. To my surprise I found Mr. Richberg and Madam Secretary there ahead of me and, while they responded to my greeting, *neither of them looked up.*

I feel justified in relating the details of that conference also because somebody leaked that too, and the principal points were recited—however inaccurately in news stories at the time.

I knew intuitively what was coming. I knew it because one of those absurd, inconsequential quirks of memory that seem to come at critical times flashed across my mental vision—the two peons who were skinning a cow at the barred gates of Santa Rosalita Rancho during Pershing's punitive expedition in Mexico when Georgie Patton, in search of that great killer, Candelario Cervantes, and his gang, appeared suddenly "out of nowhere" with his patrol. Georgie knew instantly that he had cornered his quarry because neither peon raised his eyes. Without rhyme or reason that incident flashed back to me when Mr. Richberg and Madam Secretary did not look up. They too had been skinning a cow.

The President spoke to me pleasantly and then, using the exact words of June 16, 1933, said: "I am going to explode a bomb-shell." He proposed that I go abroad with a commission, "B. M. Baruch, Gerard Swope"—anybody I wanted to take, to study recovery in European countries, retaining salary and title as Administrator. I asked what would happen to NRA and he said that was a detail. I replied: "Mr. President, of course there is nothing for me to do but resign immediately." I did not protest. I did not argue for any other conclusion. I did not complain.

Madam Secretary instantly protested my resignation and added that I must be given full credit for the work I had done. I said: "You can neither give nor take credit from me." I had set up a small committee to act temporarily on policy while I was at Bethany, among them Alvin Brown. Mr. Richberg immediately attacked it. He had never gotten along with Mr. Brown. I replied rather hotly, to which he said: "You don't understand me." I answered: "You mean I *did* not understand you. I understand you now—*perfectly*." The President said that I did not realize the importance of what he wanted me to do and referred rather wearily, I thought, to "all this pulling and hauling" and to the constant publicity about it. They and not I were responsible for the "pulling and hauling" and the attendant publicity. But no more apt words were ever spoken. I instantly concluded that the only possible removal from him of this bickering burden was for me to resign and do it quickly. It was the only thought I had just then. It was conspicuously apparent that NRA had become such a bone of contention, such a center of attack, such a source of official cacophony that both it and I had been made by these things a burden rather than a benefit. There was no tenable consideration for me but to remove myself as I had repeatedly publicly promised to do whenever I thought that any such situation had arrived. Beyond peradventure of doubt it had arrived now.

"*Pulling and hauling*"—Nobody will ever know how much of it goes on around that devoted desk. I had scrupulously avoided it. I had endeavored to avoid making issues because it seemed to me to be a cruel dis-service to bring there one single thing that could possibly be diverted. It is clear to me now that I did not make issues enough. It was my fault and not the President's that the true picture was not presented to him.

There were insurmountable personal reasons why I could not go abroad—reasons which I had confided both to Mr. Richberg and the President. There seemed to me absolutely no alternative course. I had to resign. Yet the whole incident had happened so suddenly and with so little warning—no warning at all —that I realized the need to be alone for a little while and asked for that consideration.

I told the President that I would have to think the situation over and perhaps consult some friends. Everybody stood up. I left the room supposing the interview to be at an end. Mr. Richberg and Madam Secretary remained. That was reported by the press as my "stamping out" of the President's office. With my military training I simply *could not* do such a thing. It did not occur to me at any moment of that interview and it has not occurred to me since to blame the President and I have never criticized or said or done a disrespectful thing toward him. I will go a step further and say I have never even had a disloyal or disrespectful thought for him, much less taken that kind of action.

It is not unusual for a few people in a conference to remain for post-mortems with the Chairman or Chief—and it has always seemed to me to be wrong. I don't like to have it done in my own conferences and I have never done it myself. If there is anything to say affecting other conferees it should be said in their presence. If not, the time of a busy executive should not be consumed by taking advantage of such an occasion. Furthermore, it will be remembered that these two were in conference before I arrived and, considering the nature of the talk after I came, it did not seem proper for me, at least, to hang around after it was over.

I have never suffered more than I did in the next few hours before I wrote my letter of resignation and in writing it. I consulted nobody and confided in nobody. I tried to call Bernie Baruch in Prague but could not reach him. Suddenly it seemed to me there was nothing in the situation to consult *anybody* about. *It was open and shut.* I would have done anything within reason rather than to add to the President's burdens but to stay on and let these two, under my own name, wreck the work of my hands, was not within reason or possibility.

How could I ever again expect to protect NRA organization, policy, or morale under the *title* of Administrator but with Mr. Richberg in opposition in a position of real control for which I had suggested him and to which I had done everything in my power to make him available. Madam Secretary and I had apparently never agreed on my view that labor tribunals should not be influenced by the Labor Department, and, with stronger reason, I could not agree that the Labor Department should control NRA also. Both of these officials had just demonstrated an ability to change the situation of NRA without according me a hearing, or even raising with me a single point for discussion or even according me the courtesy of a word.

Somebody else might be able to pull the tangled threads together again, but it had passed beyond my power. NRA was very dear to me, but after all it was not my property. It was just one element in a Federal mosaic for which the President and not I was responsible. It was better for him and better for the whole enterprise for me to erase myself. It must be very clear that the only other conceivable alternative would have been for me to raise a great issue that might and probably would have created nothing but further dissension and a greater impasse.

I sat down and wrote a resignation and a letter explaining. A purported account of that letter reached the press through some channel which I have vainly tried to identify. It was published in an Associated Press dispatch, and, while incomplete and incorrect in part, was so circumstantial as to indicate that some one had seen a copy. Only a few people in whom I repose confidence have ever seen my carbon which I did not send to the files; that letter contained some purely personal matter growing out of close and affectionate relations.

Relating to this subject it recited the circumstances of my taking my job, of the organization of NRA, of its divorce from PWA, of the facts exactly as related in this book which had compelled me to the conclusion that I must go at once, and especially a narrative of the afternoon's conversation precisely as stated here.

Several people have been accused of advising my course of action. It is not true. I cleared my office of even my confidential secretary and locked the door. I was alone for several hours until that letter was written.

My letter went over to the White House at about ten o'clock on the night of the day of the events related. An answer came back within an hour—an answer so affectionate, kind, considerate, understanding, and long-suffering, that I felt lower and more ashamed of myself than ever. Abraham Lincoln never wrote a more human or beautiful letter. If I had been the President I would probably have boxed my ears and written "finis" to the tale. But the result would have been the same. The letter asked me to see him again.

I left G. A. Lynch—a classmate at West Point—in charge of NRA and went to Bethany Beach. Friday morning I flew back to Washington where I stayed only long enough to see the President who was shortly going to Hyde Park. Then I flew back to Bethany. In this interview the President asked me to work on a plan for NRA reorganization in more detail, bring it up to Hyde Park when it should be ready and, in the meantime, to let him run NRA so that he could see at first hand what its problems were. I went off and tried faithfully to do this.

Of course there were things in my own office that I wanted and also the question of the extension of the Automobile Code came up—which I knew neither Pat Lynch nor anybody but myself could handle on account of its history and background. I found that Lynch wouldn't talk to me over the telephone. I learned later that Blackwell Smith (Mr. Richberg's NRA

Assistant) and Lynch had been instructed *not to talk to me*. If it had ever been doubtful, it was then perfectly clear that the policy and form of NRA were out of my hands.

From that time on I was practically hermetically barred from action toward reorganization in NRA—although I was still nominally Administrator. That was wrong. I was wholly and personally responsible for NRA. Whatever happened was my fault up to the time when I finally insisted on leaving. I had tried my best to go. I had a right and the public had a right either to my responsibility or my elimination. Except for a few days after my return from Bethany and, because of Lynch's peculiarly difficult situation, NRA was practically paralyzed again and from that time forth for weeks which, in addition to the paralysis of morale which occurred during my earlier absence, meant that for nearly three months NRA had been comatose—and it is comatose still.

About the tenth of September, I went to Hyde Park with the NRA reorganization plan which I had been requested to submit. I spent the whole evening with the President, and saw him next morning again. It was a meeting altogether affectionate and pleasant. I think that we were never closer in heart and mind in all our association than we were that last night that we spent together.

There is no more question in my mind about the President's personal feeling about me than there is of my feeling about him. Neither is there any question of our substantial agreement about NRA. It is just that it does not lie among human possibilities to pierce so much intrigue and to keep intimate contact with so many snarls as confront that job. I had been remiss in not going oftener to see him. But others camped on his doorstep and doubtless painted for him a picture of NRA which by this time it seemed hopeless to refute.

The plan of reorganization of NRA which I submitted to him at Hyde Park has been stated with partial accuracy and discussed at length in public prints. The actual document is given verbatim below. We talked it over for hours.

*Subject:* Reorganization of NRA.                    *September 9, 1934.*

1. As I wrote you June 26, NRA is too big for one-man control now that it passes from code making to administration. But I fear this remark has made misunderstandings. I recommended a Board analogous

to a Board of Directors—that is, a Board to *create* policy—but not a Board to *execute* policy. No Board can be executive. The trouble with NRA is that one man is charged with *making* policy, *executing* policy and *judging* both policy and execution. NRA is a new form of government—an economic government superimposed upon a political government. Since it now covers more than 95% of industry and commerce it is nearly as wide in extent as political government—a thing so vast that very few critics and commentators comprehend what has been done. For exactly the same reason that political government is divided into legislative, judicial, and executive branches, so also should NRA now be similarly divided. Judicial (settlement of adversary proceedings) and legislative (making broad policies) should be completely divorced from executive (administering codes) and the two former functions reposed in Boards wholly separated from NRA proper. But these Boards should neither supervise nor undertake *execution*—which in every American experience—governmental or economic—is a job for single responsibility and authority. There is no exception to this rule that I ever heard of.

2. I am not sure that NRA is not too big a job for any personnel that we can reasonably expect to assemble, but I doubt if it would be proper or expedient so to conclude without more complete experience. If this is wrong and it is desired now to make a *drastic* change, then there *is* a simple formula.

I. Set up a National Industrial Commission empowered to license acts which otherwise would be violative of the Anti-Trust Acts, and to revoke licenses in any case of abuse, and with no other function.

II. Write 7a into substantive law and do not leave it to code agreement.

III. Write child labor, maximum hours and minimum wages, and other conditions of labor into substantive law and do not leave them to code agreement.

IV. Set up a National Industrial Tribunal to hear complaints, settle disputes, and refer decisions to the Department of Justice or Federal Trade Commission for punitive action.

V. Let the Labor Department investigate and present cases of labor violation and Commerce Department and Federal Trade Commission investigate and present cases of violation or abuse of Trade Licenses.

This would completely demobilize NRA and provide a far simpler form and method, but query:

(*a*) Have we given the codes a fair trial?
(*b*) Would not such a sudden change be ruinous?

(c) Can we successfully write 7a and wages and hours into a statute and enforce it or even maintain its constitutionality?

(d) Would not the whole thing be regarded as a new "Prohibition" attempt and meet the same fate?

I think the answers to all these questions negative this change for the present and my recommendations are:

1. *Create a National Industrial Commission* (legislative) which should have, subject to the President, the duty of deciding questions of policy not only for NRA, but *for the whole recovery program*. This is vital because, if we cannot get parallel and correlated policies, especially as among NRA, AAA, FTC, FERA, and the Department of Justice, NRA might as well cease. For example, we cannot get prosecutions by the latter and we are rapidly approaching a condition where we may be prosecuting a company for violating a code at the very moment when FTC is prosecuting the same company for complying with it. For example, also, CWA has paid double code wages for common labor with a result that people have absorbed relief funds when there were industrial jobs for them. It is an impossible stultification.

As I stated in my letter of June 26, people with other governmental duties should not sit on such a Board. Ideally, it ought to be composed of people like B. M. Baruch, Leo Wolman, George Peek, Louis Kirstein, Dr. Bruere, Ray Moley, Adolph Berle—i.e., men with no partisan interest and a strong sense of public service. But if, for reasons of expediency or precedence, they must be Cabinet officers, you might use the Attorney General, the Secretaries of Agriculture, Commerce, and Labor, and the Chairman of the Federal Trade Commission, with perhaps two other members such as Leo Wolman or Ray Moley, and an Executive Secretary such as Adolph Berle. By these means we might bring the Department of Justice and the Federal Trade Commission more nearly in line on unified policy if they had this definite responsibility for successful policies for the whole program. Certainly the people who are *executing* the emergency program ought not to sit on this policy board.

The Board would hear those in charge of execution of policy and representatives of labor, industry, and consumers, and it would make decision on policy in the light of all this. Its decision should be final and binding on all. They should not attempt to supervise execution and they should confine their action to broad policy such as wage rates under all agencies, price fixing, coördination of AAA agreements with NRA codes, minority labor representation, correlation of industrial with agricultural prices, punitive action, adjustment of FTC action to NRA action, or vice versa, etc. There will be a field of regulation on minor matters that must be left to administration.

This suggestion was made on the broad plan to divide NRA into three parts—*legislative* (policy forming); *executive* (administrative) and *judicial* (settlement of all controversy). But these functions were to be clearly separated. The legislative or policy-forming board was not intended as such an Aulic Council as paralyzed the Austrian armies in Italy by trying to perform executive functions. The suggestion was not followed in the following principal particulars:

(1) Heads of NRA Departments *were* appointed.

(2) The Board attempts to *be* executive.

(3) The Board was not sufficiently familiar with the economic philosophy of NRA to act without a great deal of preliminary study.

(4) The Board was an NRA Board not a general Board.

2. *Create a National Industrial Tribunal* (Judicial). Give it jurisdiction, not only over 7a, but also over *all* questions under NIRA and the codes which reach a robust stage of adversary proceeding such as maximum hours and minimum wages, sanitary and other working conditions, and also *all fair trade practice disputes* or other disputes *under codes*, so that there would be left in NRA nothing whatever of judicial function on important disputes. You could either expand the NLRB to include men fitted to pass on judicial questions under the codes, or you could have one Board for labor disputes and one for other code disputes, or you could have a super-board with divisions for these two types of questions. I favor the latter. Also our new "Little Fellow" Board (Industrial Appeals Board) should be transferred as a division to this Tribunal. This Board should be above suspicion of bias which I fear the present NLRB is not—industry fearing that it is dominated by the Labor Department, which is a statutory advocate for labor. The decisions of this Tribunal should be final (subject to the Courts) and should be passed to an NIRA section in the Department of Justice for appropriate action (see III below). Cases would come before this Tribunal:

(I) As now by complaint of an aggrieved party.

(II) By reference.

(III) By complaint arising in the Departments of Labor or Commerce.

The Department of Labor should constantly investigate labor conditions under the codes and should refer violations in the first instance to the government representative of the Code Authority and, if prompt remedy is not forthcoming, to this Tribunal where it should prosecute them to a conclusion. The Department of Commerce and the Federal Trade Commission should act similarly as to unfair trade practices.

This recommendation touches the same old sore spot of Labor Tribunals on which enough has been said. Perhaps I am wrong but I believe the Department of Labor is properly an advocate and that any court to pass on controversy should be wholly impartial.

3. *Create an NIRA section in the Department of Justice* charged with all punitive action under NIRA including removal of the Blue Eagle. At present, NRA cases are in the Anti-Trust section of the Department of Justice where the whole training and viewpoint are not in accord with the principles of NIRA. We cannot get prosecution on the very strongest cases. We now have a Litigation Division in NRA whose efforts are largely thus frustrated. *This has done more to rob the Blue Eagle of effect than any one thing.* Furthermore, removal of the Eagle has heretofore been in NRA. In the Harriman case we removed the Eagle and the Department of Justice reported no indictable offense. There are many other similar instances. If that Department has complete responsibility for and control of the whole subject of punitive action, we should at least have uniformity and no cross purposes. My suggestion is that the Attorney General appoint a special NRA Assistant and that he take over our Litigation Division.

4. NRA becomes then a purely administrative body with neither legislative nor judicial functions, charged solely with carrying out decided policy and *making the codes work.* Immediately, all part-time government representatives should be taken off Code Authorities. Veteran deputies (there are about 60) should be appointed government representatives on as many codes as they can conveniently handle. To each should be assigned, to sit with him constantly, a legal assistant, a labor representative, and an economic adviser representing the public and consumer interest. A vigorous drive should be put on in the next sixty days to get ever single Code Authority into active operation, consistent with basic policy and free of abuse. This is absolutely vital if we are to succeed.

This has never been done. The Code Authorities are languishing and breaking up.

5. The most baffling problem in NRA is the fact that, while industrial self-government exists in *economic* areas (i.e., the several

industries), surveillance and actual administration in the field resides in *geographic* areas. For the latter reason, we have State NRA Officers supervising *all* codes in *a* state, but we must also have government representatives on Code Authorities supervising *particular* codes in *all* states. It makes criss-cross administration. There is only one answer and that is for the State Director to act, within his state, as the agent for all government representatives on all codes. To do this well, it is necessary that all Department of Labor (national and state) representatives, investigators, and conciliators, all F.T.C. representatives, and all Department of Commerce field officers be requested to keep in contact with the State Director and assist him within the fields of their authority at all times.

Some attempt in this direction is apparently being made by Mr. Richberg for the National Emergency Council. It should not go to the extent of leaving nobody in such state who is solely responsible for NRA in that state.

6. There are many problems within the NRA Washington office itself, but these are being rapidly cleared and simplified. If NRA is thus relieved of all policy decision and of all judicial and punitive administration by these Boards then its problem becomes single and relatively simple and the work of internal organization can be promptly completed.

When I got back to Washington from Bethany about September 15th, and saw the new and far more serious disorganization and demoralization into which the whole personnel had again been plunged by the events which I have related, it became overwhelmingly evident to me either that I must now make an outright issue that would be embarrassing to the whole Administration—and to nothing more than to NRA itself— or else I must remove myself entirely. The latter seemed to me to be the only manly course. I accordingly wrote the President on September 24th as follows:

*New York City,*
*September 24, 1934.*

The President
    Hyde Park, N. Y.

*Dear Mr. President:*
    The reorganization of NRA which has been the subject of so many conferences and memoranda between us, is becoming momentarily more urgent. We are in agreement upon the general form of reorgani-

zation and I do hope you will now also see eye-to-eye with me on the subject of my resigning from a job which as reorganized seems altogether superfluous. Added to this are private considerations which are becoming more and more poignant. I therefore urge again your acceptance of my resignation.

Our cordial and warm relations over so long a time make it unnecessary to say that you will continue to have my loyalty and, when circumstances permit, my services in the new duties you have in mind.

While I feel that my executive responsibility should cease at once, may I suggest that this resignation be effective October 15, in order to give me time to make such study of records as will enable me to make my final report.

Sincerely,

Since this correspondence has been made public I feel justified in including the text of the President's reply:

*Hyde Park, N. Y.*<br>*September 25, 1934.*

*Dear Hugh:*

It is because you and I have felt for some time that NRA has fulfilled its first phase and calls for revision of its organization, that I am accepting your resignation, to take effect October fifteenth, as you suggest, in order that you may study the records preliminary to the making of your final report.

I repeat what I have so often said to you—that I am happy not only in our friendship and your loyalty, but that in a time of great stress and fear your courage, enthusiasm, and energy were a very potent factor in restarting a stalled machine. More than that it will always be remembered that under you the NRA, in only a little over a year, accomplished long overdue reforms in our social and business structures. The elimination of child labor, the recognition of the principles of a fair wage and of collective bargaining, and the first efforts to eliminate unfair practices within business—these among many others are chalked up to your credit.

I hope much that during these next few months you will get a thoroughly deserved rest, and that then you will be able to help me further in new duties and new tasks of public service.

I shall see you in Washington very soon,

Faithfully yours,<br>/s/ FRANKLIN D. ROOSEVELT.

Hon. Hugh S. Johnson
National Recovery Administration
Washington, D. C.

There is the whole record. There have been many deliberate if insidious attempts to make it appear that I was "let out" on account of some personal shortcoming, some open breach of policy, some clear cut issue, some failure to do my job.

To take the last one first, I think I can stand on the record. On June 16, 1933, the whole of commercial and industrial pattern of the United States was unorganized. It was just a congeries of millions of separate units—like a quart of sea sand. On that the Congress gave NRA a mandate to assemble and compact them into a cohesive and interrelated system—like a brick. But the plan for doing this, the organization or machine to accomplish it, the leadership to secure voluntary action and public support were *without form and void*—not a scratch of a pen on paper, except our own anticipatory effort and the President's general directive of June 16, 1933.

One year later, on June 16, 1934—that part of the task assigned to NRA was practically done. I have tried to narrate here the record of the doing of it, but all these scores of pages cannot tell it half so well as the President's gracious half page, just quoted.

As to the general policy of NRA, that was laid down in the President's directive of June 16, 1933. I stand on that. I never departed from it. I am a soldier and those were my marching orders. Not only were they never changed—they were never even debated by anybody.

As to personal shortcomings and ineptitude, I cannot speak, except to say that I know I have them by the score. I do not approve of me at all. I am a sort of jack-of-all-trades and master of none—impulsive, and full of sins and bad habits—to all of which "*peccavi! peccavi!*"

But so long as among them are not charged crookedness, disloyalty, self-seeking, inaction, incompetence, or peculation, I don't just know what they have to do with the construction and accomplishment of NRA.

Perhaps the answer to all this may be found in what has happened since control of NRA passed into other hands. I was told that a certain very competent official could not be utilized in an important position because "they will say—*he is a Johnson man.*" It has also been circumstantially stated to me that the Blue Eagle must die because as long as it flies "It stands for

Johnson." I fail to see any justification for just that kind of personality in such a task as this.

This is a most revealing circumstance. It is one thing—and a thing very necessary to concerted action—for a newly elected or even appointed official to "turn the rascals out" and to replace strangers by sympathizers. But this is not that case. There is hardly one of the present NRA Administration that I did not bring there—many of them thus lifted from obscurity to this prominence. There is not one of them that did not serve side by side with me professing loyalty and agreement. They made no issue with me. It was never intimated to me that they were not all "Johnson men."

Johnson was nothing but a figure representing the collection of policies laid down by the President which were NRA, and if any there were not Johnson men, how could they in conscience serve at all? If any served merely to form a clique of conspiracy to proscribe the rest (which I do not for a moment believe) it was an affront to Americanism in such a high emprise. It is a formula that puts a premium on disloyalty and rewards treason with a civic crown.

NRA advanced its officials and supported them. If any did not agree with what was done *after* a decision had been made, there was always a clear course. Repeatedly at staff meetings I urged and demanded robust adherence by every man to his own point of view, whether I agreed or not. Time after time I brought men into NRA *not because they agreed with me, but because they didn't*. I put such men in the foremost ranks. Outstanding examples are Leon Henderson and Tom Hammond. Both proved to be as loyal and true as men can be and both stood manfully to their contrary opinions. I hardly think that anybody could have attended our NRA farewell meeting and believed there were many there who were not loyal. I know there were not many.

Men whose mental processes are otherwise cannot prevail. This is not the Italy of Machiavelli—it is the United States of Franklin Roosevelt. A man may—and many do—lift himself by such means but without loyalty and frankness, faith, and a sure intent, nobody can last long in the atmosphere of the New Deal in America.

It may be that the whole NRA idea was wrong. If it was it

ought to be discarded. But if it was not it ought to be supported. If it is to be retained I fear for the future. It would be an act of cowardice and dereliction of a public duty if I suppressed that observation. I fear it because little is being done to support the Blue Eagle and without the Eagle NRA cannot survive. I fear it because code administration is not vigorous and the Code Authorities have to have action and decision to continue. I fear it because I think NRA depends wholly on public support and NRA must continue its Goldfish Bowl policy or die. I fear it because control has been unbalanced and NRA must remain impartial or perish. Finally, I fear it because every one of the few indications of policy evidence compliance with the opinions of groups who have opposed NRA from the beginning.

Take from NRA public support and confidence, control against cut-throat competition, enforcement of code provisions —especially of unfair trade practices and labor safeguards—and it will not last six months. That, I fear, is exactly what is happening and it does not lie within my repressive powers to suffer this in silence.

Upon the publication of my resignation about 65,000 letters and telegrams came to me from all parts of the country and, I am told, a large number were received at the White House. Some of the principal members of the organization and employees came to me to say that they were going to resign. George Buckley, George Berry, and Ed McGrady did resign in spite of all I could do or say to dissuade them. All kinds of threats and rumors of defection in Code Authorities and immediate withdrawal of codes came to me. Some labor leaders had said they were through with NRA and were going to see to it that in the A. F. of L. Convention Mr. Richberg and Mr. Clay Williams should both be condemned by resolution.

I had intended to go away from Washington without saying anything to influence any there about NRA. But these threatening circumstances required something of me. I thought highly of the whole Board. They had all served with me. I think all but one of them are my friends. Upon whatever has happened to NRA and in respect of all I fear for it, I am sure that they have little choice. They have been uniformly kind and courteous to me. At that critical time for them, the important thing (as it seemed to me) was to keep the NRA organization together and efficient and to retain the support of it by both Labor and

Industry so I did all I could to sidetrack the condemnatory resolutions, to prevent withdrawal of codes, and resignations of officials. It was for this reason that on October 1st I an-

nounced that I wanted to say good-by to the people who had worked with me so devotedly.

They crowded the large auditorium of the Department of Commerce and all the corridors. The National and Columbia Broadcasting systems had coupled their national hook-ups. It was pretty hard to stand there and look down at hundreds of people who had worked with me more zealously than any departmental organization ever worked before. To most employees NRA was not a government bureau—it was a crusade. There were people there—just clerks and messengers—who to my knowledge had worked as hard as I had—who, regardless of our night shifts, had to be driven away from their desks because they thought as I did that they were doing something not only to relieve present distress but to improve the lot of working people in this country forever. It just tore at my vitals to think of being separated from them and to have to give up a place in the ranks of such an army. I thought of them all as my own kind of people and it was hard even to begin to speak. The speech is short enough to quote and, as written, was as follows:

*My friends of the NRA:*
This occasion is at once one of the saddest and one of the happiest moments of my life. Happy because we are looking back at a job well done and because for the first time in over sixteen months I am free from tremendous responsibilities and killing duties. Nevertheless it is sad because it is probably the last time we all shall meet together. When I see so many people who for months have fought with me in this great cause, and it is borne in upon me that I am leaving the army which fought so well together, I cannot help but be sad. A more devoted, loyal, unselfish and hard-working group than you are, I have never known.

So this is one of the most poignant periods of my life. It is hard for me to talk to you at all. I expose myself to this moment which cannot be less than emotional because of a loving devotion which you have given me as a man, apart from any official connection—although on the official side if there was ever a better, harder-hitting crowd than this one, I have not heard of it. Without the close personal affinity that has existed among us all, this community of devoted workers could never have done that which legislatures, courts, industrial and political pundits have always said could not be done. You can treasure in your hearts your part in as great a social advance as has occurred on this earth since a gaunt and dusty Jew in Palestine declared, as a new principle in human relationship, "The Kingdom of Heaven is within you," the Sermon on the Mount, and the Golden Rule.

Our work is but a distant echo of those ancient precious precepts which have changed the face of the whole world. "Echo" is not the word. "Effect" is the word. In one short year, under the leadership of our inspired President, you have done more for those who are weary and heavy laden than all the militant organizations for social conflict that have existed in this or any other country since the beginning of time.

If NRA were to be regarded as nothing more than a practical school of economic and philosophical theory, it has been the greatest edu-

WHAT IS "HAMLET" WITHOUT HAMLET?—BY JERRY DOYLE

cational force that has ever existed. Nothing that is being done in labor relationships—nothing that it is proposed to do but has its inception here with you. It is not so much what we could produce in dollars and cents, by a feat of industrial magic, that counts, as it is what we could put into the conscience of a country. And while I resent bitterly any libel that we have not created employment and increased wages to the full of our promise, I say to you again that a new philosophy of the rights of men with which we have impregnated this whole nation is the important and the vital thing about our work.

It is improper to use the personal pronoun "I." Nothing could have been done here without you. This is your work rather than mine.

It is not necessary for me to say that my departure from leadership of you in this holy thing has been to me an agony of spirit which has racked me, physically and mentally, far more than all those days of 18 and 20 hours with which we used to carry on to the edge of exhaustion.

Be it ever remembered that I entered this task with the expressed prediction that in my concept of how it must be done it would destroy the man who tried it. I said I was as a man mounting the guillotine on the hair-breadth risk that the axe would not work. I said it would be red fire in the beginning and dead cats and oblivion in the end. I undertook it with that understanding and, therefore, I have no complaint and am entitled to no sympathy on the result—Why?

Because I had determined to act on two new principles:

(1) I would be an absolutely impartial umpire as among the inherently inconsistent claims of labor, management, consumers, and agriculture, and never favor one against the other. I deliberately invoked that controversy by our very form of organization, and I know of no other form and have heard of no other form that would have done the job.

(2) I believed that it would be a new and grateful experience in American political economy for a man to tell the truth—never try diplomacy at the expense of truth—to state his mistakes as he made them, and to say exactly what was his just judgment on every question before him regardless of any criticism that it was neither good diplomacy nor good politics.

I think you, who know, will all agree that to those two principles I have been faithful, but it has once again proved tragically true that you cannot do those things in political life.

I cannot let two circumstances pass without comment. The first is the great goldfish bowl idea upon which we set out—the idea that everything must be done in the open, that every single conflicting interest must be adequately represented on every economic question and that NRA was never to be more than an umpire. That was not in the law. Nothing of our organization or procedure was in the law. The law created principles but prescribed neither policy nor method. Together we created that. It is our baby and nobody can ever take it away from us. We brought the whole of American industry and commerce within the principles of NIRA under the Blue Eagle within six months, and that is ours—to us—black and white on the record. There it stands, written and irrefutable, and—as to our detractors who have opposed all these things—"not all their piety nor wit can call it back to cancel half a line nor all their tears wash out one word of it." There is nothing in the reorganization of NRA that alters one single principle of the things you and I worked out together and, I venture to say, there will be nothing. Those principles are right and either they will prevail or NRA will not prevail.

We can stand on that, you and I. It is an accomplishment of which all the worthies could be proud. I am writing to each of you a letter stating your part in this great work and expressing my undying gratitude for what we together against powerful and insidious opposition have, by the grace of God, thus far accomplished.

Some of the most important and able and dutiful and faithful among you have, by one means or another, sent word to me to know whether you should continue to serve under the new régime or whether, in a devotion to me which has brought tears to my eyes, you should go out like Pertinax after the defense of the wall in *Puck of Pook's Hill.*

It is beautiful and touching and quixotic, but please bear with me while I say that it is sentimental foolishness. Why this NRA is our creation—yours and mine. This great accomplishment belongs to you far more than it does to me. If from failing hands I "throw the torch, be yours to hold it high, if ye break faith with us who die, we shall not sleep, though poppies blow in Flanders Field."

Let me tell you a little secret: In the latter part of May, I began to feel that, in view of the criticism addressed to me alone—and never to you—I could no longer be effective as Administrator of NRA without creating and winning a bitter issue, which I did not care to invoke because I thought that making such an issue could only hurt the cause. So at that time I began to urge my own retirement. I proposed a form of reorganization—roughly on June 26th and very specifically on September 9th, and that form is, with some exceptions, what you are getting today. Each and all of these proposals included my own elimination for the simple reason that if NRA was to be retarded and paralyzed by attacks on me as a person, I ought not to be here. This devoted cause is greater than one man or any group of men. It is a myth that any man on earth is indispensable to any cause or thing. Very often the crucifixion of a man means more to the thing he is trying to do than all his living efforts. And even if that were not true, the last words of Madame Butterfly engraved on the haft of her Samurai dagger express my philosophy about this whole business:

> "*Con onor muori*
> *Chi non puo serbar vita con onore*"

which to those who know Mussolini only as a shining name means roughly, "To die with honor when you can no longer live with honor."

To all of you who have faith and loyalty to me there is nothing to apprehend in the reorganization of NRA. If you will examine it closely you will find that, from stem to gudgeon, it is composed of men brought here by me and who are my friends, faithful and just to me. I will never raise so much as a little finger to influence them or anything about NRA—when you are out you are out. But I say to you in all earnestness that if I had had full choice of them, I would not have known how to select better people. They are your own kind. They have borne the heat and burden of our long fight together. They have, with all of you, that sense of comradeship that comes from shared rations in a siege or deadly perils born shoulder-to-shoulder in a shell hole. I hope and believe that they can get far better coöperation and far fewer dead cats than I ever could and for that reason I believe that you are surer of success and security with them than you could ever have been with me.

Therefore, I have just one parting request to make of you, and if you love me as much as some of you have protested, I ask you to give to these seven men who have been selected to take my post, the full measure of loyalty and devotion that you have given to me. And may I add this, that if you following only one weak vessel could accomplish so much in our first year, you following seven stronger men should be able to accomplish more than seven times as much in your second year. Please do it—not for me—but for the President and the principles of NRA which he has so clearly laid down and which have done so much for our country, mentally, morally, spiritually, and materially over the past fifteen months.

You and I have known from the beginning that the time would come when I would have to go and you would have to carry on. That time has now come.

The present form of organization is best suited to the new task before you. You have been given an Administrative Board of the highest caliber. This reorganization was a necessary step and a good step.

From the beginning it has always been one of the favorite tactics of our enemies to create a picture of internal bickering and strife. These have been used especially against NRA because by its very nature it demanded that every point of view be heard and encouraged. In such a task there must inevitably be conflict of opinion, but when the time came to resolve those conflicts and to act NRA never hesitated and will not hesitate in the future.

But honest differences of opinion are one thing and malicious gossip and intramural politics are an entirely different thing. As far as I am concerned there has been none of the latter. I earnestly hope that there will be none.

## JOHNSON'S "SUCCESSOR" GOES TO WORK

During the past few weeks I know there has been some uncertainty in the minds of many of you as to your future and the future of NRA. You should be glad that these questions have now been resolved for you and you should go back to your desks and attack the new phase of your work with increased vigor and zeal now that you see the course clear before you. As you know, I am no longer in a position to speak with authority, but I feel sure that there will be no drastic and sudden changes of organization or personnel to cause you any apprehension.

When I first took this job, I predicted an ever increasing volley of dead cats directed at me. Just before I resigned there seemed to have been a regular "last call for dead cats." I imagine that some of my friends of the press wanted to concentrate their shots at the last minute, because in the future they will have to scatter them over thirteen or fourteen different people instead of just one target which they had before.

And yet, since the news of my leaving was out, the whole tenor of public comment has changed. My desk is piled with editorials, telegrams, and letters, any one of which would bring tears to the eyes of a brass Buddha, but I'd rather not talk about them.

There remains only to say good-by to you and this, in my present state of emotion and effection, I cannot do. I shall be here for a few days. I shall devote most of my time to seeing those of you who care to see me and sit down for a few minutes' chat. If you will state your wishes to Miss Robinson, she will arrange the time when this can be done, so none of you will have to wait.

And now that it is time to go: "The Lord bless thee and keep thee. The Lord make his face to shine upon thee, and be gracious unto thee. The Lord lift up his countenance upon thee and give thee peace."

That speech was delivered as written up to the last three lines. Then my attention was diverted by some sound that I did not at first identify but—in the little pause that I made to look around —was unmistakable. People were sobbing audibly and when I looked down at the first four rows which I could see clearly, they *all* seemed to be weeping.

I hadn't counted on that. The papers said *I* wept. I didn't— but I couldn't go on with the beautiful Mosaic benediction— my voice just choked and all I could say was:

"God bless you."

# Chapter XXX

# THE FUTURE

---

"The objective in the mind of every thoughtful man is to restore to distressed humanity the opportunity to earn its daily bread—to get people back to work again. . . . Men can not go back to work until money goes back to work."

—*B. M. Baruch—Senate Testimony—February 13, 1933.*

"What is good in NRA will live—and it ought to live. What is bad will die—and it ought to die."

—*NRA Press Conference, December, 1933.*

---

In this chapter I am expressing my personal opinions. Wherever they may be found not to be in accord with existing policy or action this cannot properly be construed as criticism of what is being done. It is merely honest difference in point of view. The President does not need to be told that whatever my own judgment may be I would as an executive bow to his and fight for it with all that I can give.

Removed from official life, I feel free to think independently and to say what I think openly. After all it is only one man's thought.

In my opinion the question of the future of American Recovery resides in ten problems:

1. Debt—public and private
2. Taxes—Federal, State and local
3. Money and public credit
4. Labor and management
5. Industry and employment
6. Relief
7. Agriculture
8. Foreign Trade
9. Coördinated and Cohesive government
10. The Future of the Recovery Program

These problems may be thus separated for the purpose of discussion but they are not separate. They are co-relative and they merge into each other with indistinguishable demarcations. It is almost impossible to talk about one without finding yourself all mixed up with another. It is not the purpose here to write an essay on economics or lift the curtain on a new crateful of white rabbits, but only to express a faith in a few fundamental principles.

Before proceeding to discuss these questions, it should be urged, as has been stated earlier, that every element for prosperity is here—money, vast pools of credit, great resources, starved demand, fine facilities for manufacture, sale and distribution, and a brave, active, alert and patriotic people. It is trite to say that the single missing element is confidence.

But confidence felt by whom? By workers? By farmers? No; farmers are producing as much as ever and will so continue. They have to. But workers can't work unless somebody will pay them wages. The answer as to whose confidence must be restored is so obvious that it hardly seems debatable.

"Men can't go back to work until money goes back to work," and money *won't* go back to work unless those who have or are responsible for money to invest in creating work know that, once it is out of their hands, no magic is going to frisk it away like fairy gold turning into crisp and colored autumn leaves.

It is perfectly clear that recovery in a big and quick and powerful wave awaits only an impeccable assurance in deeds and not words that no such thing will happen. That is all there is to it. It could be done immediately. And unless it is done promptly, there is no end in sight.

There is now current a lot of impassioned appeals to banks and industries to get busy and start recovery. Some business associations have even talked as though they could do this. To me that seems nonsense. If any businessman held the key to recovery all this time and did not use it he ought to be lynched.

No business held that key. Banks and business corporations are trustees of O. P. M.—other people's money. They are there to do business when they can do so safely and in proper discharge of their trust. They are avid to do it when they can do it that way—i. e., profitably. But there are penitentiaries and bankruptcy courts and public condemnation for people who play recklessly with their obligations. No amount of belaboring business and talking about timidity by men who never conducted a business in their lives is going to change these essential responsibilities.

To demand that industry at once give employment to 10,000,000 men is a demand that it produce far more goods than it can sell or increase its plant capacity when there is no market for its product. No responsible management can do this, and surely no such thing can be done in the threat and uncertainty that beclouds the present economic horizon. To make this demand and couple it as Mr. Richberg recently did with a threat that, unless industry does so employ these millions, the government will, smacks something of the modern caveman who wooed the object of his affection with the statement "Love me ———— you, or I'll beat you to death."

Furthermore the threat itself of the government employing 10,000,000 men is absurd. When these idle had work, the American business turn-over was about 90 billions of dollars. It is now about 40 billion. At the most that government could do, it might employ 3,000,000 by spending 3 billions, but it is not a gap of 3 billions that is to be bridged. *It is a gap of fifty billions.* And that gap must be bridged if we are to have recovery. That can happen only by creating justified confidence in the political economy of the United States, and such superficial bulldozing will not create that confidence.

## 1—THE PROBLEM OF DEBT

The paralyzing and persistent force which has prolonged this depression is the terrific debt burden contracted on high market values of real estate, securities, and commodities which remained after these values and the markets in which they might be sold had shrunk to a fraction, leaving the debt in full effect at its original figure. That placed upon commerce and industry and upon the consuming power of every debtor, a burden many times heavier than the debt burden before the collapse. It was this more than any other single cause that ruined business.

Now there were two ways, or a combination of two ways to meet this situation—one by a surgical operation and the other by a pulmotor and continuous artificial respiration. The first was to recognize that the values on which the debts were made were mere phantoms—never truly existing and gone forever—and on that recognition fearlessly to cut down the debts themselves. The latter was to try to blow value back into the deflated assets and incomes upon which the debts were erected.

By one of these methods, or a combination of both of them, or by just simply sitting in the steam like a savage with smallpox and grimly sweating it out to the death, was recovery possible.

We did not choose to sweat it out and we did not choose to cut it down. We chose to try to restore value to the assets on which the debt was based by various devices. Now nobody in the world had ever done this by design without creating a cataclysm such as the complete destruction of the German mark, the Russian ruble, the French assignats and the Confederate currency. But we thought we could do it and there was reason for thinking so. We tried it through reduction of the gold content of the dollar. We tried it earnestly and thoroughly and sincerely, but the reason wasn't good enough and the method did not work. Prices refused to rise in inverse ratio to the gold content as promised by the plan.

Now I think it was wise and right to have made this attempt— it was a laboratory demonstration of the fallacy of an old illusion. (I cherished it myself.) But I believe it would have been wiser either to have coupled with it, or to have tried separately, a deliberate scaling down of debts and I am sure it would still be wise and that it is urgently necessary.

It could have been done and it still can be done in a combination of two ways.

1. We can amend the bankruptcy laws to provide, in the shortest and most direct and effective manner possible, for a realistic scaling down of debt by composition and discharge, with the consent of a majority of the creditor interests, under the widest discretion of the Federal Courts to prevent abuse.

2. Instead of having the government take over home and farm and other mortgages *on valuations that no longer exist* (a policy adopted on the assumption that value could be blown back into them), let a government agency offer to take up any of these securities (that have value) at an appraised figure —but not to exceed say 75% of face value—pool them—offer to the mortgagee debentures at the scaled-down rate with principal and interest guaranteed by the government and to the mortgagor a new mortgage for the scaled-down debt. If this operation were completely carried out, the government would have only a contingent liability on a narrow margin of widely disseminated risk; the mortgagee would have a gilt-edged

security in place of his shaky mortgage, albeit on a reduced basis, the mortgagor would have a chance for his life and the country would be relieved of one of the chief causes of continued depression.

It is of the utmost importance to apply *this principle also to public obligations of all political units*—States, counties, cities and municipalities.

There is some opinion that it is too late to do this now but I feel sure that is wrong. Nobody ever goes in to replace an old tumble-down or ruinous brick structure with a white marble palace without first sending in the wrecking-crew. This we have failed to do. It should have been the first step and the most vigorous of all steps. It is never too late to do the right and the wise thing. It is not too late now to do this.

## 2.—The Burden of Taxes

Everybody pays taxes. It makes little difference who gets the receipt, the consumer pays it all. The assertion that you can take it all out of the corporate income or of individual income in the higher brackets is blatant demagogy.

Take the "processing" tax of the AAA by which the manufacturer pays into a fund to give to the farmer a fixed levy on every unit of production. What happened? That and other governmental emergency measures *doubled the price of cotton overalls to the farmer*. It is the farmer and the worker who wear overalls. It is they who pay the tax even if the original assessment lies against a big corporation. It is so of every tax. They are drags on consumption—and hence on production, and hence on employment and hence on the poor—the wealthy will always be comfortable but the poor must fret under the daily care of keeping out hunger, thirst, and cold. You can't distribute wealth by grotesque and demagogic taxation—you can only distribute poverty. If you tax a corporation it will only peg up its price to the consumer and whether it be levied against canned beans, or blue overalls, or anything that moves in commerce, the person who consumes pays it. It cuts down his power to consume and makes directly against production and employment.

Our great lag in employment is in the heavy or capital goods industries—that is to say, those which make locomotives, and big machines, and factories, and hotels and houses. Nearly half the unemployment in the country—perhaps 5,000,000 bread-winners who ought to be working there—have been out of jobs for three or four years. Now people without very much money do not buy any of these things. Most of them are bought by big corporations. But corporations can't buy them unless they can sell stocks and bonds to get the money to buy them. And no man is going to buy their stocks and bonds unless they can show that they are going to make enough money to pay dividends on the stock and interest and amortization on the bonds. Until the capital goods industry and other industries using their products can show how they can make money, nobody is going to see rëemployment in this great pool of idleness. All the berating of banks for not lending money to start these industries will not change that situation or give the workers in those industries back their jobs. And no public works program alone can initiate the activity necessary here to employ the labor normally appurtenant to these industries.

Now the people who have much or little idle money or mort-gagable future income to buy stocks and bonds are the people who have above a bare subsistence basis and there is where the government has tried to pile on nearly all the taxes.

I know a man—and he is not one of the country's wealthiest men either—but if he made a dollar the various tax burdens of city, state, and nation would take 83 cents of it. It is going to be pretty hard to convince him that he ought to take *any kind of a risk at all* to make a dollar. If he risks it and loses it, he loses it all. If he risks it and makes anything he gets only 17% of what he makes. He would be a fool to put it into anything that did not have about a 6-to-1 chance of profit and almost nothing now has such a chance. Nothing less than a great fear of marked inflation will move that man.

This is an extreme case, but it illustrates a point. You can get taxes so high on particular sources that you won't get revenue but you will paralyze the production of anything in this coun-try except only things like food (which people have to have or starve) or tobacco (which is a habit and won't be denied) or clothing and coal (which people have to have or freeze) and that is pretty nearly the state we are in today. You don't get revenue because you stifle trade and adventure. You could get

far more another way. And you don't relieve the poor because
they pay the taxes anyway. But you *do* oppress the poor because
you destroy employment.

Yet, as everybody knows, we will have to have more revenue
from taxes in this country than we have ever had to have before
in our history. The point is: let's look facts in the teeth and
put those taxes where we can get the most revenue with the
least harm to consumption which means production which
means jobs which means recovery and prosperity.

Our present revenue schedules are the result of pure political
baloney and are not designed for maximum revenue. To that
extent they are dishonest and one of the greatest obstacles to
recovery and reëmployment in this country.

I am not going to discuss that here because the principles of a
proper schedule of emergency revenue were discussed by "Muscleinny" before the 1932 conventions and will be found earlier
in this book. It is just as pertinent now as on the day it was
written. We *must* have revenue. We *must* have recovery. Let's
figure out a tax schedule to replace the thing we now have
which is a stark barrier to both.

In this emergency everybody who has anything coming in
ought to pay *some* tax—even if it is only one dollar a year—to
support the brave efforts of the President to see that everybody
who has nothing survives without physical suffering or loss of
pride and self-respect. That would not provide much revenue
but it would give everybody a personal interest in the credit
of the United States.

The whole revenue schedule should be revised with courage
and honesty to the end that it shall encourage recovery,
maintain the credit of the government beyond peradventure of
doubt, and keep us amply supplied with money to insure at all
events against any impairment whatever of the health, pride,
comfort, and welfare of all our people.

We are doing that after a fashion, but we are risking the
wreck of our ability to continue to do it at all by the manner
in which we are proceeding. Taxes on every conceivable source
should be just as high as we can make them and still keep the
machine that manufactures revenue at maximum efficiency.

What is true of the Federal Government is true of all government in this country—state, county and municipal. What is
needed more than any single thing is not just a conference of

governors but a convocation of delegates on a specific agenda worked out by experts for tax reform and coördination throughout this country. That requires no statute but could be done by the executive on the strength of the confidence of the public in what he plans or does.

The capital gains tax should be cut in half. England has none. It is a direct threat to business enterprise and so to employment —the most direct threat that could be devised.

The inheritance taxes should be levied against inheritors and not against estates. Take the case of an aging man with an estate appraised at 15 millions of dollars. He knows that inheritance taxes will require 7.5 millions in cash. In today's sterile market appraised values are worthless. In so large an estate its prompt liquidation would cut it in two.

The combined result of these facts is constant forced liquidation—constant caving in of the whole capital structure. Properties carried on books at vast sums simply have no realizable value. Who would buy a great metropolitan hotel or office building? Under their tax burdens and in existing conditions they are liabilities—worth less than zero—you can't get recovery of business activity in such an atmosphere and we must have business activity or perish. Practically every governmental policy retards it.

Monetary policy is one of the principal barriers to recovery— a barrier that could be broken down with a result of greatly increased revenue and it will stand to bar recovery and employment until it is broken down.

### 3—The Problem of Money and Public Credit

I have yet to meet the man (and diligently have I sought him) who really knows, with even passable certainty, anything worth while about money. It has been the principal and the hottest incentive of the human race since the beginning of history. It is the goal of the fiercest and often the most ignoble appetite of man. If there is one subject about which knowledge should have been attained in the literal thousands of years since its appearance, it is money. But it did not work that way and this book certainly is not going to attempt a discourse on that subject.

A few things we *do* know empirically through the history of thousands of incidents.

Whenever people think, for any reason, that tangible things are going to be worth more than the dollars in their pockets they scramble to turn dollars into tangibles. And conversely, when they think values are going the other way they scramble to trade things for dollars. The first kind of scramble makes prices go up—the second makes prices go down. It is all a question of what people *think* whether prices go up or down. When they cease to think, or think very fast and furiously we have what we call a runaway market or a panic. We either pay silly prices for Florida land lots or, as in 1929, for a share of stock. Or, on the other tack, we sell our perfectly good securities for a song as many of us did in February, 1933.

In such times, it is not a question of what people *think* but a question of what people *fear* and of how they will act in a panic of fear—as a man will run from his burning house carrying a pillow and leave his watch and pocketbook to be burnt, in the place where the pillow rested. In other words, the value of money is a matter of mental process—deliberate and based on facts most of the time, but confused and even lunatic when *enough has happened to cause panic fear.*

In a general way, the value or rather the stability of a nation's money is based on four pillars: (1) The amount of gold it has in its Treasury to back up the amount of paper money outstanding; (2) Whether it is a creditor or a debtor nation; (3) Whether it has a favorable or unfavorable balance of trade; (4) The safety of its fiscal policy.

Just what the whole effect of a gold reserve may be is not certain. Gold may be necessary in settling unfavorable balances of trade—that is, paying for what the nation buys (imports) in excess of its sales (exports), but when it exports more than it imports this may not be important. Or, if it is a debtor nation, gold may be necessary in squaring interest and maturities. But, if it is a creditor nation, this also may not be so important.

If a nation spends on government more than it receives in taxes it is like an individual who lays out more than he takes in —he has to borrow. If the chances are that he will surely be able to pay interest and principal when due, he can borrow in prudent amount and for a reasonable time. If the chances are otherwise, he can't borrow—not until he snaps out of it and cuts down his spending or increases his income or both. It is somewhat the same with a nation—except that a nation can do something an individual can't do. It can print pieces of paper, or metal, or use wampum or even hokum and say to all its citizens —"here, this is money, take it and like it." Whether it can get away with that for long is another question. It can't get away with it at all when all four pillars mentioned in the preceding paragraph are gone or rotten. We know that. But can it get away with it when only one is bad and all his rest are good? Nobody knows—it was never tried in those circumstances.

And just what bearing each of those four pillars has on the value of money or which of them is the most important, nobody knows. When a nation starts to print money or issue funny money with all four pillars rotten or absent that money gets to be utterly worthless very promptly and by the process of making it worthless, all debt is wiped out. And some other very terrible things happen. It doesn't get worthless over night. Prices begin to go up. Everybody rushes to trade their money for things and that makes prices go up faster. Finally they go up so fast and so far that a million dollars today won't buy what a ten dollar bill would buy a year ago. This is fine for people who have *things* to sell. But it is ruin and starvation and loss of savings and everything of value *to every man who works for a salary or wages and depends on them for a living—to widows and orphans living on insurance, to people who rely on incomes from bond or mortgages or pensions, or savings in the banks.* For all these people—the great working and middle class of our population, probably 80% of *all* our people—it is just confiscation of everything they have and of the purchasing power of what they can hope to earn.

This has happened several times in history. It happened in France at the time of the assignats. It happened here during the Revolution, with the Continental currency, and that is why we still say "not worth a continental." It happened here also with the Confederate currency. It happened in Germany and it happened in Russia.

But there was this circumstance which makes all of those incidents entirely different from what exists in the United States now—in every one of those instances, there was no gold reserve, the nation was deep in debt to other nations, the nation bought and imported more than it sold and exported, and its fiscal policy was terrible.

This country has more than 100 cents in gold for every dollar of its paper money. It is a creditor rather than a debtor to the world and it sells more than it buys in world markets so that on neither score does it have to export net money balances. (When a country has to pay such balances to other countries, its money goes under an arithmetical formula and if it isn't very good that fact is demonstrated to the world. Its value goes to nothing promptly.) Our favorable position on all these tests tends to make and keep the dollar valuable and to maintain the credit of the United States in spite of all the manhandling it has suffered at home.

Only in *one* of these four pillars of value is the money and credit of this country in danger. Its fiscal system and policy is bad. This Administration did not start that. It was started in 1930. It is bad not so much because of immense and necessary spending beyond income but because we have not frankly borrowed the money to pay the excess of our expenses over income. We have used obscure devices to get that money. There has not been much real borrowing from the people of the United States for a long time—there has been mostly a forcing of government bonds on banks and a series of bookkeeping entries whereby the government took the depositor's money from the banks and put government obligations there in its place. We have coined not our credit but our debts. With that kind of operation nobody knows the real status of the credit of the United States in a free market for its obligation. This kind of thing has been going on for at least four years. How long can we keep up that magic without destroying confidence in the public credit? Nobody knows, but it is all on the *bad* side of the ledger. That is the only question—and there is no historical precedent for the answer because there is none for the condition of a nation standing on three perfectly sound financial legs and only one rickety one—the question is: "How long can we go on playing with the broken leg and not produce the state of panic fear that might impair the confidence of people in the money and credit of the nation and produce a cataclysm worse than anything we have known?"

Nobody can tell us. But our excursions into unknown fiscal fields are very delicate and dangerous things for, once the credit of the United States slides, all credit in the country slides with it.

Recently, we have been knowingly playing with the value of

our money with the deliberate and announced purpose of creating *just enough fear* of its future to make people want to change it into goods in the hope that we could thus increase prices to— say the 1926 level—as a way to blow value back into assets so that we can pay off debts. That overlooks the terrific burden that would be thus placed on wage and salary earners and consumers generally—but let that pass. All that we have done so far has largely failed to work that way and the Roosevelt dollar is still as sound as any money in the world.

There are those who believe that if we could get the fear motive to work, the situation can be controlled. In other words, they think that *just enough fear of the value of money* can be created, by monkeying with it, to cause a national mental state where people will want to change their money to things to start prices upward and at some point—say the 1926 price level—that we can *turn off the fear motive and stabilize prices*. We actually tried that, but never got enough fear turned *on*, much less ever had a chance to see if we could turn it *off*, and stop the rise in prices.

Fear and panic about other things rarely are subject to this kind of precise control and even if they were it certainly would take a master hand and mind to push them just far enough and not one thread's breadth further—like some great surgeon chiseling delicately away at the skull of a mastoid sufferer, until only a pink skein of bone as thin as gossamer remains between the last film of disease and the brain against which one touch means death. The great surgeon whose fingers, long trained and directed by a specialized mind, have the touch of a butterfly wing—the essence of his genius is *"to know when to stop."* Any butcher could cut out the disease. But who can do it and yet save the life which the disease threatens?

If there be any such specialist in this country I don't know who he is, or where he is, or from whence he got his training. I think we cannot afford to fool much further with the Federal credit. I never thought you could regulate panic or secure prosperity through fear.

Yet, we must still have billions to spend to relieve distress. It does not seem too difficult a problem. Two roads are open— one to degrade the Federal credit—the other to maintain it and use it.

One is to try to *scare* money out of people by *threats* to its value—the other is to try to *persuade* money out of people by *creating confidence* in its value. The fear plan seems harum-scarum on any analysis. There is no instance of its working in the world's history except to a result of collapse and ruin. On the other hand, the only sound recovery that ever came proceeded through confidence and not through fear.

I think it is about time to try the certain route. Everything is ripe for it. We have suffered long enough.

For the latter purpose one simple rule will serve. To balance the ordinary expenditures of government with certain revenue. To borrow frankly in the orthodox manner for every necessary cent of extraordinary spending. This can be done if only interest and a prudent charge for amortization be provided by new revenue properly distributed on the law of diminishing returns, and then segregated to the debt account.

A suggestion for this, by way of example, was also proposed by "Muscleinny" in June, 1932, and need not be repeated here.

On such a basis this country can and should borrow and spend every dollar that is necessary for emergency spending and to provide relief. We probably would have spent $30,000,000,000 more than we did in 1917, '18 and '19 if the war had run on into 1919—and nobody turned so much as a hair. The credit of the country is ample for this new war, if only it is preserved.

The whole structure of private credit rests on the public credit, and as long as the latter is threatened—either by rash action or the *fear* of rash action—private credit will remain where it now is—hibernating in a hole. Not all the threats, entreaties, and blandishments in the whole world can cajole it out to activate business, as long as this shadow hangs over it.

The other road—scaring money into tangibles, by turning fear of values on and off—is a bar not only to production and employment, but it is a threat to the whole working and white collar element of this people. They have borne the brunt of this depression and they stand on the spot for any further practice of any fiscal policy which may prolong it—some 80% of the population—they are the forgotten men—the actual forgotten men whom old Sumner had in mind and most accurately described.

I firmly believe that if steps were taken tomorrow to put the monetary and borrowing policy of the Federal Government beyond the shadow of doubt that this depression would be relegated to the limbo of forgotten things in three months' time.

## 4—The Labor-Management Problem

This problem was discussed in an earlier chapter. After as acute an experience with it as any man has had, I am very sure that it is much further from any composition than it has ever been since I had anything to do with it. The battle lines are drawing nearer and the tension is higher with every month that passes. It is another of the principal factors retarding recovery. Something must be done about it and be done quickly. For reasons fully developed in this book, I am convinced beyond question:

(a) That, while there should be no compulsion to join any union on any man—either from government, management, or labor —we should favor organization on a vertical pattern quite to the extent of England.

(b) That we should favor voluntary industrial organization of industry under codes.

(c) That the natural partnership which should exist between labor and management must be approached at once on a basis of mutual confidence and concession and that any attempt to do it by compulsion is abortive.

I never yet heard of a shot-gun wedding that lasted beyond the doorstep of the Justice of the Peace. I think the whole system in which the so-called impartial boards is set up is wrong, because I know that one side does not regard them as impartial. I think it is futile to marry these two natural spouses by haling them into the limelight as defendants before the public. It simply raises every hackle of defense and acquires at best but a sullen acquiescence. I think the suggestion of a conference of principal labor and industrial leaders made earlier in this book is a practicable suggestion. At least I know that an unhurried and undisturbed deliberative counsel of such practical leaders on both sides, who already have learned to respect and admire each other in NRA, would come forth with some far better suggestion than any we yet have tried.

My specific suggestions have already been stated in the chapter on Labor and Management. Briefly they are:

*By Statutory Revision*

1. To put Section 7a beyond the question of doubt as to its meaning and specifically to provide

    (*a*) that when a substantial majority of employees select a certain form of organization, no other parallel organization shall be recognized.

    (*b*) that no employee should be required as a condition of employment to join that or any other organization.

2. That a national labor policy be worked out in conference between principal labor and industrial leaders, submitted to the President for amendment in the public interest if necessary and then adopted for administration and be vigorously supported. We have no labor party now.

## 5—INDUSTRY AND EMPLOYMENT

Before considering the problem of reëmployment at all, there is one drastic suggestion in which I thoroughly believe. There are non-declarant aliens employed, or employable and on relief, in this country, variously estimated at between 2,000,000 and 3,000,000. There is small justification for this. It would create no avoidable hardship to exclude by Codes of Fair Competition, or in rules governing relief or public employment, any person who is not a citizen or a declarant or who being a declarant has not become a citizen of the United States within the minimum legal time limits—and to deport all who can and do not qualify. It would give prompt employment to a good many citizens.

It must be recognized that not over 1,000,000 persons normally employed in the Consumers' Goods Industries (not including sales distribution and auxiliary services) are now without work. About five million unemployed are appurtenant to the heavy goods industries.

There are probably between 9,000,000 and 10,000,000 unemployed altogether. It would be possible to reëmploy 1,000,000 men by vigorous administration of NRA. Nothing yet in sight by Public Works will reëmploy 1,000,000 men in the heavy goods industries. I believe that a vigorous attack on the Public Works Program could double this figure—I mean reëmploy 2,000,000 more men in capital goods this year. I do not expect any such result and, even if it came, it would leave a vast pool of unemployment which nothing within the power of government can reach. Nothing can reach it except to persuade private investment back into capital goods and that raises every one of the questions discussed in this chapter—especially *debt*, taxes, fiscal policy and the relationship of labor and management. It raises also the question of restoring a little more of practical realism to the legislation governing securities and the exchanges—not a great deal, for in spite of all the cries against it, that legislation was proved necessary by all that happened up to 1929, and should never be relaxed except in those features where theory has crowded too closely on common sense.

If these problems were worked out, we would not have to worry about capital goods and the construction trades. A flood of private capital, long held in leash and avid for work, would rush out of a thousand hibernating holes and much of it would head straight for these long slowed uses.

After nearly a year and a half of intense concentration on this problem, and an opportunity to see all aspects of it pass in review, I feel confident in saying that not much more can be done at this time by the formula of shortening the work-week at the same pay. I say this because I am sure that the increased cost (as matters stand today) would reduce consumption and hence the available number of jobs. This subject is discussed in an earlier chapter. But I do not mean to say, by this, that the possibilities of this formula are nearly exhausted. I say quite the contrary thing. If, by other means herein suggested, we can at last get the upward spiral started, I feel very sure not only that we can then give it an added spurt by shortening the work-week at the same pay, but also that we never are going to have complete reëmployment in this country without shorter hours and higher wages as a permanent policy. There is no such thing as over-production considered apart from under-consumption but there is such a thing as *over-capacity to produce*, and let the man who doubts it say for example how, without an export market, we can dispose of 800,000,000 bushels of wheat per annum when our digestive apparatus will not take more than 600,000,000. For all reasons stated in an earlier chapter, we will have to maintain balance and control throughout our economic mechanism for a long time to come.

This can be had only by organization, codification and self-government of industry under governmental sanction and supervision and based upon at least the *general principles* of the Recovery Act. That will require an issue to be resolved between the principles of NRA and the anti-trust principles. If it turns out that the former must go down there is nothing before us but blind-staggers for another indefinite period. We should be back exactly where we started. "As the dog returneth to his vomit, so doth the fool to his folly."

Many of these subjects have been discussed at length in preceding chapters. Specifically I believe that we can create a great improvement if we synchronize and approach with real vigor under a single administrative control, the following projects:

(1) Reinvigorate NRA to get universal acceptance and compliance with existing provisions of maximum hours and minimum wages—we could reëmploy 1,000,000 men.

(2) Completely mechanize and motorize the Army. Start at once construction of semi-suburban rural colonies coupled with industrial centers by cheap and effective rapid transit; provide by bearable loans and shared expense for railroad reëquipment, electrification, and elimination of grade-crossings; break all bottlenecks and speed to completion all existing projects; give additional support to the constructions, renovizing, reconstruction, and repair of homes by private means—we could reëmploy 2,500,000.

These are emergency measures, the real steps to enduring recovery are the others mentioned in this chapter.

## 6—Relief of Human Suffering

No other consideration of all the ten Recovery problems stated and discussed in this chapter can by any sophistry be twisted, or by any genuine philosophy be used, to avoid the absolute obligation of national, state, and city governments to see to it, not merely that the bodies and souls of people who want to work and can't are kept together—but that their self-respecting and even haughty (if it must be said) Americanism is preserved. It is utterly unjustified in a case like this to say—as is often said—"they are the victims of their own folly," or "we can't penalize the rugged old quality of thrift to save the shiftless" with a side dish of reference to the fable of the ant and the butterfly. We can't do that for three reasons.

No individual or group is responsible for the crash and depression and least of all the majority of those who now suffer most. But a certain conduct in leadership and government (and a certain sheep-like followership by all of us) *is* responsible for much of it. In such a result the duty is on leadership and conduct of government, and, indeed, on all of us, to retrieve disaster and to bind up the wounds our mass madness has caused.

Government has just simply failed in its sole purpose and justification when people cannot live under it and earn their bread in the sweat of their labor. We must see to it that some 40% of our people do not sink to beggary—if not for human sympathy—then for the sake of our own jolly old skins and the maintenance of our political institutions.

Finally, if none of these *compulsions* existed, we would have to acquit ourselves of this obligation because we are one people under stress of terrific forces of dissolution and like soldiers in a siege, we must share our rations, if we are worth the name of Americans. Of course, there are rats in our ranks—big ones and little ones—as I have cause enough to know, but they are so far in the minority as to be negligible. The chief reason why this country must acquit itself of this obligation is moral rather than economic or political. It is because it could not look itself in its shaving mirror every morning without nausea, if it failed to do so.

You could have sifted the country with a fine-meshed sieve and not have found a better Relief Administrator than Harry Hopkins. He is a go-getter. He is obsessed with no such "uplift" slush as might require as a condition precedent to filling a hungry stomach that the recipient submit to a snooping about his home surroundings by a social service worker and sit out a free ticket to a Mendelssohn concert. He moves across straight lines to his objectives and if he has a tongue like a scalpel, the skinned usually deserve what they get and more. I think he has done the cleanest-cut job in the whole Recovery Show.

I do think, however, that throughout the whole make-work program, not in FERA especially, but everywhere, too much money is spent on making the relief dollar do the work assigned —in other words, that relief dollars could be made to go further. If this is so, it needs attention, because relief dollars are not easy to get, and they are going to be progressively harder to get as time proceeds.

I think that there is a field in relief for personal loans to heads of self-respecting families who in normal times would be rated by any lending agency as good moral risks. A big reserve for loss could be written off against these and composition could be made from time to time to keep any such borrower from being weighed down to hopelessness by the constant accumulation of an overwhelming debt burden.

The Army is skeletonized. The training of officers and non-coms with these two-squad companies is a joke. Here lies absolutely idle a vast provision of barracks, quarters, mess equipment and bedding. Without making full provision of uniform and other items of expense, without providing more pay than pocket-money—without taking enlistment obligations more than for say a six months' period—without transporting men for long distances—and using an existing overhead and not creating a costly new one, there are hundreds of thousands of single men without dependents who could be absorbed here with great advantage to their own physical and mental welfare, with a very considerable release of jobs for men with dependents, with dividends to the nation in training of men to citizenship and the bearing of arms, and to the officer and non-commissioned officer personnel of the Army in handling full strength tactical units. These men could even be educated in night schools—and all this at very slight expense. I do not know about the applicability of this to the Navy, the Marine Corps, and the National Guard, because I am not so familiar with their training and mechanism, but I imagine that there is some leeway there.

The same point of saving expensive overhead is pertinent to activation of heavy industries by mechanization of the Army.

It seems to me that the proper contribution of cities, states, and counties should not be left so much to persuasion, and where Hopkins' organization finds that they are laggard beyond peradventure, that *all* Federal activity should be suspended there until they do their part.

This is a matter of vital importance. If for every Federal dollar coming to a state as little as 30 state cents were required as an inevitable condition, there would be a very great increase in care of economy in distributing it.

I suspect that the network of salaried Federal employees on emergency and other jobs throughout the country receiving more than is necessary for relief (in many cases much more) absorbs too much of relief ammunition, which, if passed on to the objects of their solicitude, would make the relief appropriations go much further to reach the result which all are seeking. I think it is urgently necessary to make an immediate survey of this system. I would not dare hazard a guess of what it would show but I think it would lead to beneficial action.

Finally, I think that the entire pattern of relief and emergency work should be systematized. In the first place, the whole administration of recovery is moving in a fog of obscured facts. How many people *are* unemployed and where are they? What is the part-time employment situation? What actual changes occur from month to month? You can't get this by questionnaires. You can't get it by any orthodox census method without such delay and cost as to make it impracticable. But, in the draft we once took a census of 10,000,000 men between the ages of 21 and 30, and at another time took one of 30,000,000 more (40,000,000 altogether) between 18 and 45. We did it in 24 hours and had the essence of the returns in Washington next day at negligible expense. We did it by using the nation-wide state systems for election registrations and manning it with such volunteer workers as school teachers, accountants, trained clerks, etc. It was proved to be almost absolutely accurate by the later calls of men and their examination. The method is wholly applicable now. The difference between this and the census method is that, instead of having enumerators do the leg-work, the registrants call at the registration places and have their cards filled out by instructed people familiar with the work of filling out forms. The registrant is given a registration card and this is a condition precedent to relief or emergency work of any kind. The census would be complete. We would certainly vastly improve the whole Recovery Program if we had this data from month to month.

Finally, effort should be made to allocate jobs by families rather than by individuals. This is especially true under NRA. I do not know what the situation is elsewhere, but I am convinced that the amount of money we are spending and the activity under NRA could be made very much more effective by systemization. This is intended as criticism of nobody. It is a suggestion that after so much furious effort we take stock, rally, and reform our lines, and move forward to a new objective.

## 7—AGRICULTURE

This is another question of obvious over-capacity to produce. One would think that the way to solve that problem would be to check that over-capacity, the chief basis of which is acreage. The way to do that is to rent or buy the surplus acres and return them to the public domain. Almost no price is too much to pay if we can thus achieve balance between industry and agriculture—a subject already discussed in this book. There is also no question that a tremendous saving to the farmer could be made by consolidation in the existing channels of distribution for his product, all the way from his fields to the consumers' table. It should be saved and returned to the farmer. It is true that such consolidation would make new unemployment in the field of distribution but that would be a far simpler problem to address than the steady degradation of the agrarian segment of our population which is and for years has been the blackest economic crime of American administration.

Just as I believe that, by the establishment of minima, industry is willing to aid in taking wages out of the field of competition, so do I believe that it is willing to sustain agriculture by paying a living price for farm raw materials. This was done in tobacco and I believe it could be done at least in animal products and wheat. It cannot be done by bulldozing and belaboring these industries but I think it can be done by aiding and supporting them.

Of course, the quest for new foreign markets is important, but when we recall that *we import more animal and vegetable products than we export*, it is pretty hard to see why some method to give the American market to the American farmer first or at least to increase his preference therein would not be a counsel of prudence and justice.

The truth is that a combination of all means should be sought but no glittering generality should be permitted to stand athwart a solution.

## 8—FOREIGN TRADE

A little more ruthlessness in its own interest would not be a bad thing for this country. If we can produce vegetable oils

and fats, even at a little higher cost than we can import them
and if our agriculture has no sufficient home markets for its
present products and cannot sell them abroad, we could give
it those home markets and kill two birds with one stone—
improve agriculture and give industry a new home market far
better than its present market. It would increase the speed of
our turnover if we gave to our own industry, agriculture and
husbandry, everything that we could reasonably take away
from similar foreign enterprise.

Furthermore, if we must take, for example, tons of coffee
and fruit and nuts from Brazil, we should have our *quid pro
quo*, if not in full preference for our farm implements, railroad
and construction equipment or anything she uses, then at
least in some three-cornered or even multilateral deal to include
nations which *do* supply her needs. We should see to it that,
for every trade-favor we give, we get at least an equal favor
in return. The day is past for flat scaling of our tariff barriers.
We look out on a world walled into hermetical trade compartments. We ought to give nothing without getting something.
What our State Department needs is a corps of Yankee traders.
They've got a pretty good one in George Peek but they ought
to take the wraps off of him, clothe him with ample authority
and let him bring home a little bacon. That is what the world
will continue to do to us and, what it has already done com-
pares with this slightly hard-boiled suggestion as murder to
swearing profane oaths on the Sabbath day.

## 9—Cohesive and Coördinated Government

In the whirl and rush of the early recovery program the right
hand hardly knew what the left hand did, but that metaphor
is weak and sickly. It was more than a centipede; and of the
seventy legs on one side, one did not know all of what the
other sixty-nine on its side were doing, and nothing at all of
what seventy on the other side were about. The result was un-
questionably a partial failure of purpose of the charted result
and a very distinct cancellation of one effort by another running
counter to it.

On November 1st the papers carried an Executive Order
dated October 29, the preamble of which recited a purpose of
coördination, and the body of which created a new National

Emergency Council composed of all the Cabinet, the Director of the Budget, Secretary Howe, the Executive Director, and 20 others who are heads of twenty out of some 140 independent Administrations—33 persons in all. This Council (including the Cabinet) is to advise the Executive Director, to present business to the President, to coördinate and coöperate with the activity of Federal agencies. It is to do so under rules and regulations prescribed by the Executive Director.

The Executive Director in addition to prescribing rules and regulations is to execute the functions and perform the duties of the Council; i.e., to coördinate and coöperate with the activities of all Federal agencies under regulations by the Director and he can do this through any person he may designate. He can appoint, fix the compensation, and prescribe the duties of anybody he thinks he needs to do these things. With the consent of a state he can use its whole machinery for any Federal purpose and, with the consent of any Federal agency, its whole machinery.

Tucked away in the bosom of this new Council is a "subcommittee"—the Industrial Emergency Committee which controls the operation of NRA, FERA, PWA, and AAA. The only Cabinet member without an emergency job who is serving on that Committee is Madam Secretary Perkins. She and the Executive Director are the only ones who have no direct responsibility for what the others do.

I have seen a memorandum by a distinguished authority in the British Cabinet. During the war it had expanded to some score and a half or more of members and was unwieldy. The Prime Minister selected a small sub-committee and they became the steering committee of the top-heavy structure. The analogy here is almost perfect. We have a President, who under our form of government has far more power than the British King and now we have an Executive Director who has all the power of a Prime Minister—the broad grants of this order *could* mean anything, and will be interpreted to mean anything from all to nothing, as turns out to be best.

This is a start in the right direction. It is the lack of coördination that has frustrated effort to this moment—one department canceling the effort of another sometimes to a standstill. If I were charged with the selection of a coördinator, I would try to find somebody who at some time in his life had organized or managed or led, or even coördinated *something*—but, as between no coördination and a group of geniuses and real co-ordination and even the Executive Director, I would take the latter every time.

Army organization *principles* are the oldest in the world. Change has been tried and failed. The trials have been the sternest possible in human experience and by one channel or another it had been proved again and again in loss of blood, treasure, and the existence of nations, that the direction of about five and not more than six great heads of executive effort is the limit of human capacity and that an army or even a division takes an enormous staff. The present administrative organization of our government is as big as several field armies. The New Executive Council set-up is, in my opinion, and for this reason, impracticable.

One hundred and forty separate and independent units report to the Executive, who simply found it impossible to co-relate them. To say that one Executive Director can now do what the President could not do is just to say that the former is a better coördinator than the latter which you can be assured is not within telescopic vision of the truth. The President can make the lion lie down with the lamb and both be happy, and can charm a canary out of a tree to sit on an eagle's beak. I know because figuratively I have seen him do it—not once but many times. Indeed I never saw him fail to do it. He is the greatest conciliator and coördinator the world has ever seen. You don't solve a problem just by shifting it from one pocket to another pocket. The Emergency Council was not fully effective because there were too many units and the meetings were futile. The new Emergency Council, on this score, is worse because it is larger.

In order to solve any problem you must break its big pieces up into little pieces, each not larger than one man can handle. Take the present Emergency Council as an example. It might be divided into any one of several groupings, for example, the following:

1. Permanent departments of government.
2. The Treasury plus 8 fiscal or financial or financing agencies represented in this Council.
3. Six agencies dealing with construction.
4. Three agencies dealing with power, transportation, and communications.

5. Three emergency agencies dealing with agriculture, industry, and relief, plus the Federal Trade Commission.

Perhaps a better grouping, even though it might even recast some of the present Administrations, would be:

1. Fiscal and financial.
2. Defense.
3. Industry (including labor, commerce, agriculture, and relief.)
4. Public Works and property including communications.
5. Legal.
6. Foreign Relations.

Either one of these groupings is as many as any one man can properly coördinate or administer.

Now if there were an Executive Director or Assistant President corresponding to each group and "coördinating" no more than six Administrations or Departments within that group, the High Executive Director or Premier or Grand Vizier might have a Chinaman's chance (as a sort of Chief of Staff to the President) really to coördinate, and really to prepare business in an orderly way for presentation to the President, but no living man without a staff constituting a sort of composite brain for him could do even that job intelligently.

But beautiful charts and organization plans and pious hopes, like the Michigan formula of "a punt, a pass, and a prayer" will not do the job. The crux of the whole problem is to enlist brains, experience, and ability. I could not do it in the atmosphere that surrounded NRA. The President could for these higher functions, if he made the stark demand, but the combination of practical experience (rather than theoretical conviction) with intelligence and ability plus the rare and peculiar mind without bias and attuned to unselfish public service as an end of itself and not as a means to personal or institutional aggrandizement, is almost an unknown quantity in this country.

There were such men in the beginning. England deliberately trains such men. We don't seem to have them. Of course, if we have them not, we must do the best that we can with such men as we have. I think I could name perhaps ten out of all my broad circle of acquaintance among leaders in the United States.

However inadequate, what has been done is a good begin-

ning. I have an idea that it is a single step in an evolutionary
process. It is a good step and a necessary step, but it is not
nearly enough.

## 10—The Future of the Recovery Program

As far as NRA is concerned, I have said from the beginning
that what is good in it will live—and ought to live—and what is
bad will die—and ought to die. I believe that we have gone far
enough to know what is good and what is bad and, since getting completely away from it, I think I see much more clearly
what ought to be done.

In the first place, nothing whatever should or can be done
until certain legal conflicts are completely cleared.

1. Does NIRA so surely amend the Anti-Trust Acts that nothing
   done under the plain authority of a Code of Fair Competition or
   an agreement with the President can be construed as a violation
   of Anti-Trust.
2. Has the President any authority to impose a code not proposed
   and agreed to by a substantial majority of an Industry?
3. May penalties such as withdrawal of the Blue Eagle and fines
   agreed to by code members be enforced or may only statutory
   penalties be enforced?
4. Can a majority labor representation maintain a closed shop contract?
5. Is there authority under NIRA to write complete wage scales
   into a code?
6. Can the decisions of NRA tribunals be enforced?

There is only one way to clear this ground and that is by
amending the statute.

Unless the conflict between NIRA and Anti-Trust is clarified
NRA should be abolished. It does not mean a thing. Unless the
other five uncertainties are clarified there is nothing ahead but
controversy and confusion.

NIRA ought to be completely rewritten to provide for purely
voluntary associations of industries or parts of industries or
groups of employers or groups of employees in either codes approved by the President or individual or group agreements
with the President. When such codes are subscribed to by substantial majorities (both by number and volume of business)
their provisions should become standards of fair practice for

all individuals in such groups and violation of such practices should subject the offenders either to statutory or code penalties or both. But determination that such violation has occurred should be made by special NIRA tribunals, which determinations should be enforceable in the courts or by withdrawal of the Blue Eagle.

The present NIRA does not permit employees to have a code even if they want to and there are many groups that badly need codes—for example, nurses and salesmen. Also if all labor unions had approved codes the public would be better protected and the union would be far stronger. I think unions should be codified and made responsible for their contracts.

The Blue Eagle should be specifically authorized by statute and required to be displayed by members of codes or agreements and on invoices and goods of such members. All public purchasers should require the Blue Eagle. Each code or agreement should contain a stipulation that all its members will require the Blue Eagle on all its purchases.

You can't make NRA effective without the Blue Eagle and you can't keep the Blue Eagle if his legal authorization is in doubt.

The statute should (as does the present law) require inclusion of its labor provisions in every code or agreement and it should not attempt to make those provisions substantive law, because to do so risks the constitutional validity of the Act.

The labor provisions of codes should make it a violation of any code agreement for any employer to institute, advocate, support, maintain, or encourage any particular labor union or in any way to suggest, require, or influence by term of employment or otherwise, any particular union; *except that*, where, under a code or agreement representatives of a substantial majority of all employers in an industry or part thereof have subscribed to a code or agreement, and have agreed with representatives of a substantial majority of employees in that industry or part thereof; then any such agreement, when approved by the President, may become part of that code even though it excludes any other form of labor representation thereunder—but this should not be construed to close any part of the industry to non-union men.

The effect of these provisions would be to encourage vertical industrial unions and codified industries. They would ban any company union influenced in any way by employers. They would not permit the "closed industry." I do believe that, as a matter of expediency, two unions cannot exist in the same shop. I do not believe it is fair by any invention to *force* any man to join a union. Therefore, I think that there should never be a shop "closed" to non-union men any more than there should be a shop closed to union men. My suggestion would be that, when a substantial majority of men in a shop choose representatives, no other union should be recognized in that shop.

The reasons for these views on labor have been fully developed in this book. In my opinion, they would constitute a revolutionary improvement. I think there is nothing more urgent than to get the labor-management atmosphere cleared and the suggestion of the joint committee is, I think, of vital and emergent importance.

In my opinion, no authority should have a right to impose a code or an agreement—all should be voluntary, but on the other hand reënforcement of the Blue Eagle would mobilize and concentrate public opinion to the support of codes and agreements.

There is a crying need for immediate administrative reform in NRA which could be had very promptly under a revised statute and which I am convinced cannot be had in existing circumstances.

I would put a commission immediately to work on the question of wage differentials as between north and south, big cities and small towns, large employers and small employers, and I would hold a public hearing on their findings and make it a condition of continuation of any code that these differentials be adopted.

I would cut out price fixing in all but a few codes, such as Bituminous Coal, and substitute therefor a system of price posting and publicity and a system of effective public tribunals where any complaint of cut-throat competition could be promptly heard, resolved, and relieved.

Most of the talk about production control is moonshine. It is practiced in only a few industries but when it is practiced it is a stark necessity. If some legalistic and theoretical commentators knew a little something about the codes they criticize, their advice would be worth something more than zero.

Unregulated excess productive capacity *was the prime cause of the depression.* That does not mean nation-wide restriction of production or even any restriction beyond curbing gross excess but there *is* need and there will continue to be need of the right to restrict where that becomes necessary to avoid ruin from unmanageable surplus. This subject is fully discussed in an earlier chapter.

I would immediately man and organize every Code Authority and abolish all codes where prompt organization and effective administration could not be had. I would put experienced deputy administrators on Code Authorities as government members.

I would set up a system of code tribunals, make their decisions effective by implementing the Blue Eagle and by providing for court enforcement of their orders where necessary.

I would get an executive leader for NRA and abandon reliance on any committee or board for any administrative or executive action.

So much for NRA. There are many other needed reforms but this much would do the trick—this much is necessary for any continuing operation of NRA.

As to the rest of the Recovery Program, I would put into prompt effect the principles developed in this chapter as a foundation for any hope of prompt success. I would assemble the heads of AAA, NRA, PWA, FERA, RFC into a committee under an Administrator of a Recovery Program. I would require the prompt submission of a coördinated six months' schedule of action for all five agencies. After that was approved by the President, I would return it to the Recovery Administrator and make him responsible that it moved in unison.

What argument is there for *not* doing this? Only individual sensibilities. They have absolutely no place in this emergency pattern. What argument is there for doing it? Only that it is indispensable to prompt success.

The Future of the Recovery Program is certain. Time works for it. All economic influences tend back toward normality. We can aid or retard them by political artifice. After a vivid experience and many mistakes, I believe they can be aided by the suggestion in this chapter and elsewhere in this book. I think the adoption of some of these suggestions (such as the restoration of confidence in fiscal policy) is necessary to avoid retarding them. But in spite of all we can do to hurt and whether we do or omit all we can do to help—recovery will come sooner or later because the natural forces impelling it are stronger than any artifice.

Nothing can stop a country of boundless resource and 125,000,000 unified and able and vigorous people within one tariff wall. It is just a question of whether we shall have to sit helplessly or act unwisely and so wait for months or years or decades or whether we can move with vigor and good economic engineering and cut the waiting time to half or a third or even a smaller fraction.

# APPENDIX

## NATIONAL RECOVERY ADMINISTRATION
### Bulletin No. 1.

## STATEMENT BY THE PRESIDENT OF THE UNITED STATES OF AMERICA OUTLINING POLICIES OF THE NATIONAL RECOVERY ADMINISTRATION.

### *June 16, 1933.*

---

THE law I have just signed was passed *to put people back to work—* to let them buy more of the products of farms and factories and start our business at a living rate again. This task is in two stages—first, to get many hundreds of thousands of the unemployed back on the pay roll by snowfall and second, to plan for a better future for the longer pull. While we shall not neglect the second, the first stage is an emergency job. It has the right of way.

The second part of the act gives employment by a vast program of public works. Our studies show that we should be able to hire many men at once and to step up to about a million new jobs by October 1, and a much greater number later. We must put at the head of our list those works which are fully ready to start now. Our first purpose is to create employment as fast as we can, but we should not pour money into unproved projects.

We have worked out our plans for action. Some of it will start tomorrow. I am making available $400,000,000 for State roads under regulations which I have just signed, and I am told that the States will get this work under way at once. I have also just released over $200,000,000 for the Navy to start building ships under the London treaty.

In my inaugural I laid down the simple proposition that nobody is going to starve in this country. It seems to me to be equally plain that no business which depends for existence on paying less than living wages to its workers has any right to continue in this country. By "business" I mean the whole of commerce as well as the whole of industry; by workers I mean all workers—the white-collar class as well as the men in overalls; and by *living* wages I mean more than a bare subsistence level—I mean the wages of *decent* living.

439

Throughout industry, the change from starvation wages and starvation employment to living wages and sustained employment can, in large part, be made by an industrial covenant to which all employers shall subscribe. It is greatly to their interest to do this because decent living, widely spread among our 125,000,000 people, eventually means the opening up to industry of the richest market which the world has known. It is the only way to utilize the so-called excess capacity of our industrial plants. This is the principle that makes this one of the most important laws that ever came from Congress because, before the passage of this act, no such industrial covenant was possible.

On this idea, the first part of the act proposes to our industry a great spontaneous coöperation to put millions of men back in their regular jobs this summer. The idea is simply for employers to hire more men to do the existing work by reducing the work-hours of each man's week and at the same time paying a living wage for the shorter week.

No employer and no group of less than all employers in a single trade could do this alone and continue to live in business competition. But if *all* employers in each trade now band themselves faithfully in these modern guilds—without exception—and agree to act together and at once, none will be hurt and millions of workers, so long deprived of the right to earn their bread in the sweat of their labor, can raise their heads again. The challenge of this law is whether we can sink selfish interest and present a solid front against a common peril.

It is a challenge to industry which has long insisted that, given the right to act in unison, it could do much for the general good which has hitherto been unlawful. From today it has that right.

Many good men voted this new charter with misgivings. I do not share these doubts. I had part in the great coöperation of 1917 and 1918 and it is my faith that we can count on our industry once more to join in our general purpose to lift this new threat and to do it without taking any advantage of the public trust which has this day been reposed without stint in the good faith and high purpose of American business.

But industry is challenged in another way. It is not only the slackers within trade groups who may stand in the path of our common purpose. In a sense these groups compete with each other, and no single industry, and no separate cluster of industries, can do this job alone, for exactly the same reason that no single employer can do it alone. In other words, we can imagine such a thing as a *slacker industry*.

This law is also a challenge to labor. Workers, too, are here given a new charter of rights long sought and hitherto denied. But they know that the first move expected by the Nation is a great coöperation of all employers, by one single mass action, to improve the case of workers on a scale never attempted in any nation. Industries can do this only if they have the support of the whole public and especially of their own workers. This is not a law to foment discord and it will not be executed as such. This is a time for mutual confidence and help and we can safely rely on the sense of fair play among all Americans to assure every industry which now moves forward promptly in this united drive against depression that its workers will be with it to a man.

It is, further, a challenge to administration. We are relaxing some of the safeguards of the antitrust laws. The public must be protected against the abuses that led to their enactment, and to this end we are putting in place of old principles of unchecked competition some new Government controls. They must above all be impartial and just. Their purpose is to free business—not to shackle it—and no man who stands on the constructive forward-looking side of his industry has anything to fear from them. To such men the opportunities for individual initiative will open more amply than ever. Let me make it clear, however, that the antitrust laws still stand firmly against monopolies that restrain trade and price fixing which allows inordinate profits or unfairly high prices.

If we ask our trade groups to do that which exposes their business, as never before, to undermining by members who are unwilling to do their parts, we must guard those who play the game for the general good against those who may seek selfish gains from the unselfishness of others. We must protect them from the racketeers who invade organizations of both employers and workers. We are spending billions of dollars and if that spending is really to serve our ends it must be done quickly. We must see that our haste does not permit favoritism and graft. All this is a heavy load for any government and one that can be borne only if we have the patience, coöperation, and support of people everywhere.

Finally, this law is a challenge to our whole people. There is no power in America that can force against the public will such action as we require. But there is no group in America that can withstand the force of an aroused public opinion. This great coöperation can succeed only if those who bravely go forward to restore jobs have aggressive public support and those who lag are made to feel the full weight of public disapproval.

As to the machinery—the practical way of accomplishing what we are setting out to do, when a trade association has a code ready to submit and the association has qualified as truly representative, and after reasonable notice has been issued to all concerned, a public hearing will be held by the Administrator or a deputy. A Labor Advisory Board appointed by the Secretary of Labor will be responsible that every affected labor group, whether organized or unorganized, is fully and adequately represented in an advisory capacity and any interested labor group will be entitled to be heard through representatives of its own choosing. An Industrial Advisory Board appointed by the Secretary of Commerce will be responsible that every affected industrial group is fully and adequately represented in an advisory capacity and any interested industrial group will be entitled to be heard through representatives of its own choosing. A Consumers' Advisory Board will be responsible that the interests of the consuming public will be represented and every reasonable opportunity will be given to any group or class who may be affected directly or indirectly to present their views.

At the conclusion of these hearings and after the most careful scrutiny by a competent economic staff the Administrator will present the subject to me for my action under the law.

I am fully aware that wage increases will eventually raise costs, but I ask that managements give first consideration to the improvement of operating figures by greatly increased sales to be expected from the rising purchasing power of the public. That is good economics and good business. The aim of this whole effort is to restore our rich domestic market by raising its vast consuming capacity. If we now inflate prices as fast and as far as we increase wages, the whole project will be set at naught. We cannot hope for the full effect of this plan unless, in these first critical months, and, even at the expense of full initial profits, we defer price increases as long as possible. If we can thus start a strong sound upward spiral of business activity our industries will have little doubt of black-ink operations in the last quarter of this year. The pent-up demand of this people is very great and if we can release it on so broad a front, we need not fear a lagging recovery. There is greater danger of too much feverish speed.

In a few industries, there has been some forward buying at unduly depressed prices in recent weeks. Increased costs resulting from this Government-inspired movement may make it very hard for some manufacturers and jobbers to fulfill some of their present contracts without loss. It will be a part of this wide industrial coöperation for those having the benefit of these forward bargains (contracted before the law was passed) to take the initiative in revising them to absorb some share of the increase in their suppliers' costs, thus raised in the public interest. It is only in such a willing and considerate spirit, throughout the whole of industry, that we can hope to succeed.

Under title I of this act, I have appointed Hugh Johnson as Admin-

istrator and a special Industrial Recovery Board under the chairmanship of the Secretary of Commerce. This organization is now prepared to receive proposed codes and to conduct prompt hearings looking toward their submission to me for approval. While acceptable proposals of no trade group will be delayed, it is my hope that the 10
major industries which control the bulk of industrial employment can
submit their simple basic codes at once and that the country can look
forward to the month of July as the beginning of our great national
movement back to work.

During the coming 3 weeks title II relating to public works and
construction projects will be temporarily conducted by Col. Donald
H. Sawyer as Administrator and a special temporary board consisting
of the Secretary of the Interior as chairman, the Secretary of Commerce, the Secretary of Agriculture, the Secretary of War, the Attorney General, the Secretary of Labor, and the Director of the Budget.

During the next 2 weeks the Administrator and this board will
make a study of all projects already submitted or to be submitted
and, as previously stated, certain allotments under the new law will
be made immediately.

Between these twin efforts—public works and industrial reëmployment, it is not too much to expect that a great many men and women
can be taken from the ranks of the unemployed before winter comes.
It is the most important attempt of this kind in history. As in the
great crisis of the World War, it puts a whole people to the simple but
vital test: *"Must we go on in many groping, disorganized, separate
units to defeat or shall we move as one great team to victory?"*

# INDEX

Unemployment, relief plan drawn up by Johnson and Baruch, 36; relief plan adopted by Moline Company, 107; summary of events leading to the depression, 138; NRA attacked on issue, 164; effect of labor-saving machinery on, 166; beginnings of Recovery Program, 191–219; bulk of, in heavy or capital goods industries, 196, 423; figures, 284, 423.

Unionism, in the U. S., 335 ff.

Unions, vertical, 317, 339–49; company, 342; craft, 349; provisions for the encouragement of, 435–6.

United Mine Workers, 226, 241, 317.

Van Bitner, 226, 241.

Vertical unions, 317, 339–49.

Villa, Pancho, raids Columbus, N. M., 62, 64; Pershing's expedition in pursuit of, 65–6; character, 65; levies on Mormons, 71; reference to executions causes diplomatic protest, 381.

Volmer, top sergeant, 34.

Wages, NRA policy, 163 ff., 196, 220 ff., 268, 274 ff.; lesson of the war years in respect to, 173, 337; scales before NRA, 191; Textile Code, 232–3, 316; suggested increase under NRA, 295; not completely solved by the codes, 298–9; charge that they have been reduced by NRA, 308; conditions prior to 1929, 364; permanent policy advocated by General Johnson, 424.

Wagner, Senator Robert, author and sponsor of Recovery Act, 204, 205; Chairman of the National Labor Board, 205, 209; quoted on codes, 278; relations with General Johnson, 314; attack on, 325; on committee to draft Executive Order setting up new Labor Relations Board, 332–3.

Wagner Board, 312, 314, 379.

Wainwright, Mayhew, 63.

Waite, Col. Henry M., 206.

Walker, Frank, 243; committee, 369–70; leave of absence, 371.

Wallace, Henry, Sr., 105.

Wallace, Henry, Jr., 142; *New Frontiers*, 180–3, 291; estimate of, 182; offers Mr. Baruch job as Administrator of the Agricultural Adjustment Act, 191; discusses design of Blue Eagle, 256;

loyalty to NRA affirmed, 290; relations with General Johnson, 367.

Walter Reed Hospital, 244, 288.

War Department, reorganization following charge by Senator Chamberlain, 86.

War Industries Board, in control of industry, 86–7, 88 ff.; friendships formed, 103; the leadership of Mr. Baruch, 113; methods suggested by Baruch as guide in crisis, 153–4; official report (Mar. 3, 1921), 250; mobilization dependent upon popular participation, 258.

War Policies Commission, 154.

Warfel, Adam, 256.

Warren, Henry, 226.

Warren, Sergeant John, 327.

Warum, Henry, 241.

Washington, George, 355.

Wells, Frederick, 105.

West Point Military Academy, Hugh Johnson first Oklahoman to graduate, 16; Johnson an undergraduate, 20–8; mutiny marking new era, 24; characterized, 33–4.

Wetmore, Frank, 107.

Whistler, undergraduate at West Point, 25.

Whiteside, Arthur D., 214, 368.

Wholesale Trade Code, 235, 279.

Wigmore, Dean, of Northwestern University, 84.

Williams, Major General C. C., 92, 214, 400.

Wills, Mr., of the Ford Company, 235.

Willys, John, 103–4.

Willys Corporation, 104.

Wilson, Woodrow, war and the Selective Draft, 78, 81, 83; incensed by charge that War Department had broken down, 86; letter designating General Johnson as representative of the War Department on the War Industries Board, 89; makes War Industries Board control agency of industrial mobilization, 94; appoints Industrial Board of the Department of Commerce, 101; association with Mr. Baruch, 111, 112, 113; labor-wage policy under, explained in Raskob speech, 120–1; quoted on war volunteers, 156; suggests possibility of High Court of Commerce and Labor for peace, 173; opposition to, 247; quality as a leader, 354–5.

Wilson, Mrs. Woodrow, 134.

Winant, Governor, 320.

Wolman, Leo, 205, 393.

Women, an important factor in the Recovery Act, 213.

Wood, Leonard, 55.

"Work or Fight" order, 84–5.

World War, record of Medical Corps in fields of venereal disease, 40–1; the Selective Draft, 73–85; accomplishments of American Industrial and Manpower Mobilization, 94; comparative strength of Allied and Central Powers, 94; cost to the U. S., 94; U. S. manpower, 94–5; Armistice, 99; effect on industry, 176, 337.

Wright Brothers, 28.

Yaqui Indians, 66.

Yeager, Dick, 13.

Yosemite National Park, First Cavalry detailed to guard, 47.